BLOO

Blood Brothers

The Inside Story
of the Menendez Murders

Ron Soble and John Johnson

HEADLINE

Copyright © 1994 Ronald L. Soble and John M. Johnson

The right of Ronald L. Soble and John M. Johnson to be identified
as the Authors of the Work has been asserted by them in
accordance with the Copyright, Designs and Patents Act 1988.

First published in Great Britain in 1994
by HEADLINE BOOK PUBLISHING

10 9 8 7 6 5 4 3 2 1

ISBN 0 7472 4693 9

Printed and bound in Great Britain by
Cox & Wyman Ltd, Reading, Berks

HEADLINE BOOK PUBLISHING
A division of Hodder Headline PLC
338 Euston Road
London NW1 3BH

Acknowledgments

From John Johnson: For Peggy and Dylan, most of all, and for my parents, who gave me a passion for truth.

From Ron Soble: For Anne, for helping the MAC talk to the PC; and Mark, a top-notch prosecutor; and Robert A. Pugsley, criminal law professor at Southwestern University School of Law in Los Angeles, for helping us through the legal thicket.

I will persist until I succeed.

I was not delivered into this world into defeat, nor does failure course in my veins. I am not a sheep waiting to be prodded by my shepherd. I am a lion and I refuse to talk, to walk, to sleep with the sheep.

The slaughterhouse of failure is not my destiny.

I will persist until I succeed.

—OG MANDINO,
The Greatest Salesman in the World

Prelude

He was fifteen and gangly, with oversized ears and a romantic's appreciation for nature and hatred of the smallest injustice to a dumb animal. He wrote self-revealing poetry to the boys and girls he liked, but he was no awkward adolescent dreamer. He was an athlete and the center of an elite group at his elite high school. His crowd were all privileged and some like him were rich, so the nicknames they gave each other were more grand than the gritty monikers gang members in the valley hung on each other. One friend was King. Another was the Wizard. The poet, Erik, was called Shepherd because he wanted to lead people to a deeper understanding of the mysteries of life.

Erik and a friend whose father was an executive at one of the Hollywood studios went up one weekend to the friend's cabin in the mountains north of Los Angeles to compose a screenplay. They turned out a sixty-two-page thriller called "Friends," a bloodthirsty saga about a wealthy young man who murders everyone close to him before dying with a sardonic smile on his face.

The boys hoped to have the story made into a movie, but the poet's mother was unimpressed with the work. "Boy, this is lousy writing," she joked to a friend as she typed up the manuscript.

But if it was formulaic, the screenplay was nonetheless filled with dramatic imagery far beyond the reach of most high school students. If the language was bombastic, the pictures drawn with words leaped off the page as the author meticulously arranged very grisly detail of his story. He left no doubt that he saw with clarity to the black heart of his antihero, whom he named Hamilton Cromwell.

The pivotal scene occurs when Cromwell discovers his parents' will. "To my beloved son Hamilton, a man I have respected and felt proud to father," he reads, "I bestow the Cromwell estate, and the money in my Swiss account—one hundred and fifty-seven million dollars—and the pride of the family, the portrait of Oliver Cromwell."

Hamilton "smiles sadistically," then murders his parents with a weapon called a razor rope. He inherits their sprawling estate, a groveling butler named Harold, and enough money to continue his chosen lifestyle, consisting mainly of eating in the best restaurants before going off to kill his next victim.

There were several versions of the screenplay. In the first the protagonist murders his parents as coolly and effortlessly as ordering a pizza, and without any apparent motive. In scribbled notes on the screenplay, Cromwell is portrayed as "a character worthy of Jekyll and Hyde," a reference to the fictional physician whose rapacious side was let loose by a potion. Hyde needed no reason to harm others. He was purely evil and enjoyed it, and that was explanation enough. The message was that man is a barely civilized animal whose hatreds are barely kept in check by social conditioning and threats of punishment. The only thing unusual about Hamilton Cromwell's soulless evil was that he had no Jekyll.

In the second version the authors supplied a more contemporary explanation for Hamilton's blood lust, one more satisfying to an audience taught to believe there is a psychological explanation for every act of aggression. When Hamilton delivers the eulogy for the father he has just slaughtered, he reveals his motive to be revenge.

"I can only hope he loved me as much as he loved all of you," he complains, addressing a gathering of mourners as his father's coffin is about to be lowered into the ground. "Sometimes he would tell me that I was not worthy to be his son. When he did that, it made me strive harder to go further, to prove to him that I was worthy just so I could hear the words 'I love you, son.'"

Hamilton begins to cry. "Nothing I have ever done was good enough for this man, and I never heard those words."

Which was the truer telling? The story of a predatory man-beast who killed for sport? Or the tale of a boy who became unworthy because, in his father's eyes, he had always been that way?

Hamilton Cromwell would not answer. He would have smiled that twisted smile, content to let the viewer decide for himself.

"Friends" would never become a movie, but two years later, millions would meet Hamilton Cromwell.

Nightmare on Elm Drive

The evening of August 20, 1989, was warm, and the residents along Elm Drive had their windows open to the soft nighttime breezes. Beverly Hills often seems to have a fairy tale quality to it, a sense that nothing bad can intrude, but never more so than when nature consents to add its gloved touch.

The big white Mediterranean-style villa that Jose Menendez had purchased the year before for $3.5 million was near the end of the 700 block, just a short walk from the Rodeo Drive shopping district and the new city hall and police complex. In the family room at the rear of the house, Jose, dressed in a light shirt and blue shorts, sank into the sofa to watch a James Bond thriller, *The Spy Who Loved Me*.

It was Sunday and the maid was off, so Kitty Menendez, wearing a lavender sweatshirt and white jogging pants, went into the kitchen to fix dessert for herself and Jose. Kitty was not much of a cook; her mind was always going in too many directions to have the patience for it. But she was not planning an elaborate snack, just a couple of cups of blueberries and whipped cream.

The couple's two college-aged sons, Erik and Lyle, were out for the evening. A friend who had been expected for bridge called to say she wouldn't make it because she was spending an extra night vacationing up the coast in Santa Barbara.

That meant Kitty had Jose to herself. Just the way it had been twenty-five years earlier when she had fallen out-of-control in love with the handsome Cuban immigrant whom other students at Southern Illinois University called "Hosee" in mocking homage to his poor English. Then, Keety and Hosee had stayed up all night playing George Shearing records in the dark on a scratchy hi-fi. Kitty's roommate, Jo McCord, was convinced Jose would never amount to much. Later, she would be astonished to find out that the man she had dismissed as a bare-chested ne'er-do-well had gone on to become president of his own video company, with an annual income approaching $1 million.

Older now and heavier, Kitty still had the uncomplicated good looks of the small town beauty queen, with deep green eyes and big sweeping curls of dyed blond hair. Over the years the Menendezes had had their share of marital strife, for Jose had an appreciation for beautiful women that sometimes went beyond the aesthetic. But they had been working on their relationship, and she had told friends recently they had never been happier. After returning to the family room, cups in hand, Kitty snuggled into the sectional sofa next to Jose.

The family room was one of the most used rooms in the house. It was stocked with videos that Jose got through his company, LIVE Entertainment, which distributed movies and children's cartoons to video stores. The large-screen television was the centerpiece of the room and was set directly in front of the tan sofa. Off to the side was a reading table. There was a bar in the corner, and on one wall was a floor-to-ceiling bookcase displaying sixty tennis trophies, all first place, won by Lyle and Erik, who had been ranked among the top one hundred junior players in the nation.

Jose and Kitty nibbled as they watched. Soon, however, Jose put down his bowl. The drink he had earlier—he rarely had more than one unless he was celebrating a successful deal—was having its soporific effect. He crossed his ankles, put his hands across his stomach, and fell asleep. His head, with its thick layers of dark hair, lolled back against the big cushions. Though bedeviled by insomnia, a curse of her nervous disposition, Kitty dropped off too. The one place she could always sleep was in Jose's lap.

Besides, they were exhausted. The whole family had been out deep-sea fishing until almost midnight the night before on the *Motion Picture Marine*, a fishing boat often rented to Hollywood executives. They had caught a couple of sharks, but that was beside the point. The purpose of the trip was to help Jose gain experience so he could impress a potential client who enjoyed shark fishing. His meticulous preparation, even for a social

engagement, was only one of the things that set Jose Menendez
apart from the competition.

The sounds of the movie obliterated any stray night noises
that might have filtered in through the French doors that opened
onto the backyard and the professional-quality tennis court. For
there were night sounds to be heard along the heavily forested
street of brick and brass palaces. At about 10:00 P.M., a teenage
girl waiting for her boyfriend noticed a small white hatchback
pull up near the Menendez mansion. Two men got out and took
something from the trunk and walked toward the house. Then
the girl lost interest and looked away.

Two men with shotguns moved up to the front door. The
mansion had an elaborate security system to repel invaders. It
had been once rented to rock stars such as Prince and Elton
John. There were heavy iron gates in front and a burglar alarm.
Jose could never seem to remember to turn on the system,
even after his black Mercedes 560 SEL was stolen a few weeks
earlier from the semicircular driveway in front of the house.
Kitty was more cautious, advising her sons to "lock the doors,
close the gate, turn on the alarm." Her sense of caution had
escalated in recent weeks, as if she sensed imminent danger.
She locked the door to her bedroom and kept her .22 rifle close
at hand in the closet.

This night the gates were open and the alarm was off. The
attackers came through the French doors that led into a dark
wood-paneled study at the front of the house. Passing a poster
of Martin Luther King, Jr., a hero of Jose's because he had also
climbed up from the bottom, the two men with guns crept into
the hallway of white marble and hesitated. A carpeted stairway
led to the bedrooms on the second floor, and the lavish master
bath with its skylight and stained glass window. Off the foyer on
the ground floor was an immense sunken living room, at least
forty feet long, with high ceilings, two sturdy couches, several
chairs, and a grand piano with the sheet music "American Pie"
on its stand. The house was impressive almost in spite of its
owners, who had declined to purchase for $350,000 the furnish-
ings from the previous occupants. Instead Kitty and Jose had
decorated in bland white.

The attackers could hear the television from the family room
and, surprisingly, as they moved down the hallway there was no
alarm from Rudy, one of the two family dogs, who guarded Kitty
so jealously that a stranger could not easily approach her. Had

there been barking, Kitty, a light sleeper on her best nights, would have awakened immediately.

As the men entered the room, which was dark except for the light of the television screen, they saw Jose sitting at the end of the couch nearest them. Kitty was at the far end, lying under an Indian blanket. A cup with the remains of the berries and cream was on the table in front of them. For just a moment everything was frozen. Then one of the attackers squeezed the trigger on his .12 gauge Mossberg shotgun, and the concussive explosion filled the room, transforming it from a scene of bland tranquility to one of horror. "No, no, no," Jose, awakened too late, yelled in vain. Two shots went wide and buried themselves in the French doors behind Jose, shattering the glass and pockmarking the wooden shutters with shotgun pellets. One pellet went through the doors into a tree next to the pool. One blast slammed into Jose's left elbow, one tore into his right arm, and then another.

As the coup de grace, one of the killers walked around behind Jose, put the barrel of the shotgun to his skull, and blew off the back of his head. The body slumped slightly to the right. His hands still rested on his stomach, as if in contented slumber. His feet reflexively slid off the coffee table to the floor, leaving a scuff mark.

He had been killed so quickly that he had had no time for fear or plead for life. But it would have been hard to imagine him pleading. He was too clever a deal maker for that. Argued, maybe, presenting a case for survival, his eyes searching the killer's for a soft spot he could exploit.

Kitty, on the other hand, was a full participant in her death. Awakened to full alertness by the explosion that splattered her with Jose's blood and viscera, she leaped to her feet.

"My mother had made a run for something," her son Erik would say later.

She only got a step or two away when she was brought down. There is no way to be certain of the order of the shots, but the one that felled her might have been a shot that almost missed her altogether, grazing her right leg on the calf. Or it could have been one that struck her right arm, fracturing it.

She fell between the couch and the heavy wood coffee table, then rolled over in pain and terror and struggled to her feet, stepping in her own blood. She was on her feet again long enough for the blood from her wounds to flow vertically down her leg. She tried to stagger off, but another shot was fired,

stopping her in her tracks. As she fell again, she saw her killer
walk over and take better aim. He blasted her as if he were
following a written procedure, working his way up and down the
body. She was hit in the left thigh from close enough range that
the hard paper wadding that contained the pellets bored deep
into her leg, breaking it. She was shot in the right arm, then in
the left breast, perforating the lung. A quart of blood flooded
into her left pleural cavity.

The dull roar of firing weapons echoed around the big house.
The family room was filled with the acrid smell of gunpowder,
and thick clouds of suffocating smoke turned the air a dismal
yellow.

So many shots were fired, in fact, that the killers ran out of
ammunition and the firing abruptly ceased. Each shotgun held
six rounds.

But Kitty was not dead. Her wounds were so grievous that
she would die, that was certain. For the moment, however, she
was still breathing, moaning stertorously, her body on the
Persian rug covering the parquet floor. Miraculously, horrify-
ingly, she was trying to crawl away, trailing blood and viscera.

The killers paused, uncertain what to do. They wondered if
the mortally wounded woman would live to tell police what had
happened. Deciding they could take no chances, they ran back
outside to the car and reloaded, this time with birdshot, smaller
than the ball-bearing-sized pellets they had been using.

Then one of the killers sprinted back into the house and
leaned over the coffee table to place the shotgun against Kitty's
left cheek and fired. A total of ten blasts had been pumped into
her body, and four had struck her in the head, shattering
the skull.

There was one more thing. Both Jose and Kitty were shot
near the left knee, which at first would seem puzzling, one more
gratuitous signature in blood. But when the police began hunting
for suspects, the kneecap wounds would become more important.

This was the way police and others pieced together the
murder from the available evidence. Years later, an entirely
different account of the slayings would emerge, and people who
had by that time become enthralled by the case would have to
choose which one to believe.

Seemingly indifferent to the fact that they had just filled the
neighborhood with the harsh rattle of shotgun fire, the killers
carefully gathered up the shell casings from among the spreading

pools of dark blood covering the rug. Then they walked out the front door and drove away.

The killers left behind a shocking scene. Bits of brain tissue dribbled down Jose's back. Other tissue had landed in clumps on the sofa. Blood was everywhere. The couch where Jose was killed was swamped with it. Jose's white shirt looked as if it had been dyed red. The killers were themselves marked in blood after so much close-up firing. The force of a shotgun blast against flesh is so powerful that it blows blood and viscera backward toward a gunman.

The most sensational crime in the history of Beverly Hills— the only one even comparable had been the shooting of mobster Bugsy Siegel thirty years before in his girlfriend's house only a few blocks away—had just been committed in one of the most brazenly brutal ways possible. Yet no one along Elm Drive seemed to take much notice.

A man who lived directly behind the mansion heard "popping sounds" in the cool darkness, but was not troubled by them.

"I didn't think anything of it. I didn't even think it could be gunfire, especially around here," he said later on. "It was just pops from quite a distance. These houses are quite solid, you know, and it really didn't sound that impressive."

A small boy in another house anxiously asked his mother if the muffled explosions were gunfire. His mother assured him it was nothing.

It was after eleven when Erik and Lyle Menendez returned home. Though it was late, they had one more appointment. They were scheduled to meet a friend for a snack at the Cheesecake Factory in Beverly Hills, a hip bar and dessert shop that serves dozens of varieties of cheesecake. Eighteen-year-old Erik wanted to get his fake identification so he could have a few drinks.

Erik pulled his maroon Ford Escort to a stop out front, and the two young men climbed out of the car. Both brothers were athletic and darkly handsome, like their father. Lyle was the older and more dominant of the two. Just twenty-one, he had squared shoulders, a firm set to his jaw, and such a powerful presence that even adults his superior in age and experience looked to him for approval when they spoke. Erik was taller, with an angular, almost horsy face that was full of expression.

Entering the house, the brothers saw nothing awry at first. There were no toppled chairs or broken glass. Then they came on the family room.

"As soon as we walked into the room, there was no crying," Erik said later. "There was just silence."

After being transfixed by the horror around them for a time unmeasured, one of them spoke. "Oh, my God."

Each reacted differently to the carnage. Lyle's efficient, taking-care-of-business side took over, and he went to call the police.

Erik stayed in the family room, almost hypnotized by what he saw. He was unable to look away. He bent down to inspect the corpses. He felt curiously removed, analytical. It was hard to connect these bodies with anybody he knew.

"They look fake, like movie dummies," he thought to himself.

Erik had seen only one other dead person. Three years earlier, his grandmother, Kitty's mother, the dour, long-suffering Mae Andersen, had suffered a heart attack and died right in front of him during an airplane flight. But this seemed less real, maybe like a movie scene with dummies playing the parts of the victims. He leaned over and touched one of the bodies. The skin felt like wax. Strange.

And his father's face, he thought as he scrutinized it inch by inch, was weirdly inflated. It didn't look like him at all. The shotgun blast had reinvented the man's features, elongating the face and making it more angular than in life. The skull had been forced outward on the right side, drawing the lips back. The eyelids were half closed, and the whole effect was to give the face a soft wryness.

Or perhaps what was so weird about it was that he had never seen his father look so vulnerable, so unable to take care of himself. He would not be getting up out of the sticky soup of his own blood to assume command of the situation and sort things out. A situation like this would have sorely tested him, but Erik had little doubt Jose could have made sense out of it and restored order. That is, if he weren't slumped over with a hole in his head the size of an orange. He was incapable of doing anything about anything, from now on and forever.

"No," Erik screamed.

Lyle dialed 911 at 11:47 P.M., and by the time the call was picked up he was frantic and sobbing.

"Yes, police, uh," he said.

"What's the problem?" the dispatcher asked.

"We're the sons . . ." The caller broke down.

"What's the problem? What's the problem?" the dispatcher asked again, more irritated.

"They shot and killed my parents," he sobbed.

"Pardon me?"

"Shot and killed my parents."

"What? Who? Are they still there?"

"No, no . . . Erik, man, don't," Lyle shouted while the confused dispatcher held on.

Then, "Erik, shut up."

The first dispatcher leaned over to her co-worker. "I have a hysterical person on the phone."

A second dispatcher took over and asked what had happened.

"I didn't hear anything, I just came home," Lyle replied.

"Are they still in the house, the people who did the shooting?"

"Erik, get away from them," Lyle screamed.

"Who is the person that was shot?"

"My mom and dad," Lyle wailed.

The police promised to send an ambulance, and Lyle hung up to wait. The enormity of the scene in front of them now began sinking in.

"These aren't just two people," Erik thought. "These are our parents."

While they waited for the police, Erik called Mark Heffernan, whom the family paid $60,000 a year to coach Erik, and told him what had happened. Heffernan, a blond, athletic man with a sun-carved face, lived in Santa Monica and left for Beverly Hills as soon as he heard.

Beverly Hills patrol officer Michael Butkus was the first to arrive at the mansion. He and his partner, John Czarnocki, got out of their car and cautiously approached the house. It was very dark and quiet. After a few moments he heard screaming, and two young men ran out the front door, side by side, almost in step. They ran out the front gate and fell to their hands and knees on the grass parkway near the street and began screaming and pounding on the ground. "Oh, my God, I can't believe it," they shouted over and over.

Butkus and Czarnocki ordered the boys to sit down, and they quickly obeyed. For some time police could get nothing out of them. Erik was irrational. At one moment he would ram his head into a tree. The next he leaped to his feet and tried to sprint back to the house, only to be restrained by Lyle.

Police questions brought little information. "Just go see," one of the young men suggested, pointing at the house. "Go in and see."

By this time Sergeant Kirk West arrived to coordinate the

search of the house. His team moved carefully inside, in case there was someone armed in there. Two other officers swept the large living room with flashlights, then signaled West that the room was clear. With his hands he motioned them to stay where they were, that he would check out the room behind him. The lights were on, and the television was blaring. He took one look in the family room and backed out. The scene was so strange he didn't really register it. "Why would you have mannequins on the sofa?" he asked himself.

He looked again, then a third time before he was convinced these were people, covered in blood. He walked over for a closer look, all the time scanning the room for gunmen. He didn't touch them, but he didn't need to. No one could survive after spilling that much blood. West backed out, leaving the crime scene for the detectives, and led a search of the rest of the house. In the master bedroom upstairs, where Kitty kept her treadmill, he found Rudy and two unfired .22-caliber rifles in the closet.

As the search continued inside the house, officer Maurice Angel stood guard over Lyle and Erik. Angel thought Erik was either babbling in grief or knew who had killed his parents. "I'm gonna kill 'em," he shouted. "I'm gonna torture 'em."

Angela Scott, a neighbor on Elm Drive, was getting ready for bed and had just finished brushing her teeth when she heard a "horrible, pathetic scream." She looked out the second-story window of her mansion and saw Erik Menendez curled up in a ball, sobbing hysterically. The sight chilled her, chasing away any thought of sleep.

Emergency vehicles filled the street. Neighbors came out from behind their security systems and stood trembling.

"Please, please tell me he's a drug lord," pleaded one woman, who, like Jose, worked in the entertainment industry.

The Rape of Camelot

At the time of the killings, the most expensive house in Beverly Hills was a forty-thousand-square-foot mansion with two gymnasiums, a disco, a tennis court, and a two-lane bowling alley. It listed for $30 million.

On Rodeo Drive, Japanese industrialists and Arab sheiks browsed along the narrow sidewalks mulling over a $2 million ruby ring at Cartier, or a $3,500 mink-lined denim jacket at Bijan, the appointment-only clothier. The local Rolls Royce dealer sold one hundred and fifty cars a year.

This was the Beverly Hills of legend. And though it too has been scarred by recession, it remains a glittering symbol of American largesse.

Just five square miles in size and populated by 32,000 people, the city operates on a fat $104 million budget. It uses the money to pay the salaries of 650 municipal workers, a work force three times as large as a comparable city.

All these workers are needed to do the extra things the citizens have come to expect. A pothole reported at one o'clock is often fixed by day's end. Each of the thirty thousand trees is carefully manicured by city contract. No leaf blowers are allowed to trespass on the sepulchral quiet.

Even the trash gets special treatment. Inside a plain building behind the courthouse, where Zsa Zsa Gabor went on trial for slapping a Beverly Hills traffic cop, trash trucks dump garbage all day long. City workers sprinkle granulated fragrances of cherry and banana on the mounds until the big semis arrive to pack the garbage off to the landfill.

"If there were a Camelot on earth," a city councilman said a while back, "it's Beverly Hills."

Now, in a single bloody night, Beverly Hills had been transformed into one more battered little community trying to come to grips with mindless violence. A town whose streets and customs would be leeringly examined for six minutes by a tabloid television show.

Sixty miles away, Audrey Zoeller picked up the ringing phone, nudged her husband, Les, awake, and handed over the receiver. The Beverly Hills homicide detective awakened to news that a couple had been murdered in one of the big mansions on Elm Drive. It sounded bad. How soon could he be there?

"I'm on vacation," Zoeller protested, the numbness of sleep fast receding. It was being replaced by a resigned sense of duty.

"You *were* on vacation," came the reply.

Police chief Marvin Iannone was appointing Zoeller to head up a five-man team to track the Menendez killers. It was a huge investment for a small police force, and Iannone expected results quickly. A chief's job could grow very uncomfortable when those Hollywood executives began calling downtown for daily updates on the murder.

It was apparent that this would be the kind of all-consuming case a cop loves because it could make his career, and hates because it can wreck his life.

Zoeller hung up the phone, climbed out of bed, and headed for the shower. He was thirty-eight but looked younger, with the earnest face, close-cropped sandy hair, and rigid self-control of an ROTC recruiter. After cleaning up, he dressed in the walk-in closet so as not to disturb his wife and three young children, asleep in the big stucco house that looked over the cactus-dotted hills and row crops of eastern Ventura County. On dewy nights he could smell the wet sage, and the eerie warbling of the coyotes in the canyons made him feel as though he were on the frontier instead of another brown-scrub suburb of Los Angeles.

Zoeller had none of the case-hardened bitterness of cops who have watched too many autopsies. He always got wrapped up in his cases until they got under his skin. Maybe that was why he was the department's top homicide investigator. Of course, the competition was not great. There were only two regular homicide detectives on the force. A town that averaged two murders a year hardly needed more.

But Zoeller had several characteristics of a good investigator.

He was curious, smart, and extremely dogged. Once he got his teeth into a case, he absolutely refused to let it go.

Until now Zoeller's most challenging case had been the Billionaire Boys Club, an investment fraternity and social club dreamed up by a brilliant young man named Joe Hunt. The BBC was supposed to bring its members, all affluent young men from the best families, riches through stock speculation. The club broke up with $900,000 in losses and freelance journalist and con man Ron Levin dead.

Hunt boasted the police would never make a case against him on Levin, who he is said to have felt had burned him in an investment deal. But Zoeller did. Hunt was convicted and sentenced to life in prison.

A second BBC insider, Reza Eslaminia, was convicted of murdering his father, a wealthy Iranian businessman. Hedayat Eslaminia, fifty-six, was kidnapped in San Francisco, placed in a steamer trunk, and driven to Los Angeles, where he was to be tortured into turning over his assets to the club. Eslaminia died en route.

Ironically, a television movie about the exploits of the BBC had appeared only three weeks before the Menendez killings. Reza Eslaminia's brother attended Beverly Hills High School with Erik Menendez.

When Zoeller arrived at the mansion, he found the investigation well under way. Detectives were on their hands and knees, poking around in the blood for anything the killers might have left behind. They found some wadding, but that was all.

One thing the cops were sure of as they picked through the stomach-churning carnage in the family room was that this wasn't just murder. There was pathological hatred in this. "Somebody was sending a message," growled one policeman.

Coroner's investigator George White arrived to pick up the bodies, and Zoeller briefed him on what he knew, which wasn't much. There were no suspects. No weapons had been found.

The first thing White did when he walked into the house was to stand stock still, watching and listening. "Many times a crime scene will talk to you," he said later. This one talked about wealth and power. Blue suiters, as cops are known to the coroner's men, were everywhere. The tangled mass of cords from their video and lighting equipment covered the floors.

The smell of death was in the family room. This was not the overwhelming odor of decayed bodies, but the less pungent organic smell of blood. There was so much of it that it filled the air like an aerosol, White thought.

The room itself was a mess, cluttered with the Sunday paper, stacks of mail, and clothes hanging over chairs. Paperwork from UCLA, where Erik was registered in the fall, lay near Kitty's body as though she may have been reading it before dropping off to sleep. This messiness was typical of the Menendezes, who lived their lives in a perpetual state of hurry and disorder. Known as a "last-minute" person, Kitty once laughingly told a friend while she was sprinting for a plane that her family had never walked through an airport in their lives.

Despite the clutter, White knew this was not the mess of a house turned upside down in a robbery. He decided the victims were acquainted with their killers. Either that or the killings had been some kind of professional hit. He ignored several policemen who were theorizing that the French doors had been shot out by attackers breaking in, not by wild shooting from inside the room. "Forced entry was not indicated," he wrote in his report.

White turned his attention to Jose. The body was still seated on the couch. He looked relaxed, White thought.

There was confusion about the head wound. Coroner's investigators at first believed that it was an exit wound, created when the killer put the shotgun in Jose's mouth and blew out the back of the head. The press soon picked up this bit of horrifying, and erroneous, information and spread it around the globe.

Kitty's body was almost under the coffee table, with one leg extending onto the bottom platform. Despite the violence done to the bodies, White noticed the faces were recognizable. Kitty's was a mask of horror. The mouth was open in a silent shriek, with only one tooth showing. The right eye was obliterated, and the nose, pushed crazily off to an angle, was filled with blood. Only the left eye, turned slightly in, was left as a recognizably human feature.

To establish the time of death, White made an incision under the rib cage on Jose's body and inserted a small device that looks like a meat thermometer. The body temperature drops about a degree each hour after death. With practiced precision White shoved the device into the liver, which retains heat the longest because it is the largest organ in the body. The temperature read 90 degrees. It was 5:44 A.M.

Jose's body was wrapped in a plastic sheet to be driven to the coroner's office in downtown Los Angeles. As it was being lifted onto the sheet, his brain fell out onto the ground.

Lyle and Erik, meanwhile, were taken to the police station for questioning, but not by Zoeller, who remained at the crime scene. Police did not consider the brothers to be suspects. The cops just wanted to see if they knew anything that might be useful in solving this case. The boys, as they were known to almost everyone despite their ages, were willing to help and patiently answered the questions of Sergeant Thomas Edmonds, the police detective supervisor.

The questioning took place around a table in one of the temporary trailers that housed the police department while the new city hall complex, built in a luxuriant Spanish-inspired Baroque style, was being completed. As they talked, it was apparent the brothers were intelligent. Lyle especially chose his words carefully, and his delivery was thoughtful and deliberate. He didn't seem intimidated by a bunch of cops asking stern questions.

It was also apparent that these two were extremely close. Friends said they never knew two brothers who were closer, though their personalities were very different. Lyle was aloof and witty, while Erik was sensitive and hoped someday to be a writer or actor—that is, if he couldn't make it on the pro tennis tour. Of the two, the older son, Lyle, was by far the stronger personality.

Their reactions to the murders were different. Erik was plainly distraught, frequently sobbing or near tears, unable to sit still. Edmonds had to call off the questioning after only twenty minutes when Erik broke down.

"I don't know where my black dog is, and I need to find my little black dog," he replied irrationally when Edmonds asked if he knew what might have led to the murders.

Then he asked, "Are they dead?"

"Yes," Edmonds replied, provoking loud sobs.

His older brother's mood, on the other hand, was "almost the opposite," according to Edmonds. He never cried. He was under control and answered questions methodically.

Through the questioning, a chronology of the day's events emerged. Erik had practiced tennis on the court behind the house in the morning, located under the guest house at the back of the property, where Lyle was living. The family then went into the family room to watch a tennis match on television in which a friend was competing. The brothers went out shopping at the Beverly Center mall in the afternoon and then, around five, made plans to get together with a friend at a food festival

that night. Called "A Taste of L.A.," the annual event at the
Santa Monica Civic Auditorium featured dishes cooked in some
of the city's best restaurants. They left home about eight, and
drove to Westwood, adjacent to UCLA. They wanted to see the
new James Bond movie *License to Kill* before going to Santa
Monica. The lines were too long, so they headed back to
Century City and saw *Batman*.

Next the brothers went to the food fair to meet their friend,.
an old tennis coach from New Jersey who had recently moved to
California, Perry Berman. They said they got lost on the way
there and missed Perry. They called him from the auditorium
and decided to meet later at the Cheesecake Factory. Then they
drove home for Erik's ID.

Clouds of gunsmoke still hung in the air when they walked in.
Both Erik and Lyle said they saw it.

"I smelled, smelled smoke everywhere and, uh, it was inside
the room," Lyle said.

That would seem odd to Zoeller. The first cops on the scene
didn't see anything like that.

Lyle told Edmonds about his mother's nervous mood of late,
about her fears and her obsession with locking doors. She had
recently armed herself, he said.

"Uh, only my brother and I know this but, uh, uh, she was on
the verge of contemplating suicide," he added. "She was very
edgy and suicidal in the last few years."

He didn't explain his reasons for thinking Kitty might want to
kill herself. He didn't say Kitty had had emotional problems for
years, or that she had made a halfhearted suicide attempt with
prescription drugs just two years earlier.

Finally Lyle was asked, did he have any idea who might hate
their parents enough to kill them?

As it turned out, he did have a suspect: the mob.

"I believe he died because he wouldn't, you know, I believe it
was organized crime," Lyle said later. "I believe he died because
he wouldn't cooperate with such activities."

That fit what a lot of police had seen at the scene. From the
way it was done, it was apparent it was the work of real pros.
There were no clues.

Then there were the shots to the knees.

"It was definitely a message killing," offered one law enforcement source familiar with the underworld. "There's no question
it's organized crime."

It was not clear why the mob would like Jose dead, though

the cops would discover Jose's business dealings had taken him into some dark alleys of American industry. It would not be hard to see how Jose Menendez, a hard-nosed negotiator whose business style made him more enemies than most, might have stomped on the wrong toes.

"His motto is a deal a day," Lyle said, explaining his father's swashbuckling, bottom-line-oriented style in business. "He's squeezed out a lot of weaker people.

"But that's the way, the way, you know. If you're weaker, you lose."

When the interviews finally dragged to an end, the boys were released with thanks for their cooperation and pledges that the police would do everything they could to find their parents' killers. The sun was already beginning to wash the night out of the morning sky off to the east when Lyle went to call relatives and tell them he was an orphan.

"I would give a million dollars not to have seen what I saw that night," Lyle was heard to say.

"Many times a day you go over events that happened that night," Erik said later. "Go over what could possibly have happened if you had gotten there earlier. Lyle and I almost did not go out that night.

"Lyle and I could easily have been in that room."

But before they got their rest, they had an important errand. They went over to the mansion, which was still cordoned off, and asked if they could get their tennis rackets. Top-notch players could not afford to miss a day on the court.

One thing the investigators did not do was give the two brothers a gunshot-residue test, which can determine whether a person has recently fired a weapon.

There are two procedures. In the first the investigator dips Q-tips into a diluted nitric acid solution and swabs the hands. Metal particles such as barium, antimony, and sometimes lead can be extracted from the cotton. Barium and antimony are unique to weapons. In the second procedure, aluminum stubs with double-sided tape are applied to the testing surface, picking up by adhesion the same barium, antimony, and lead. The tape is then analyzed under a scanning electron microscope.

Detectives are trained to perform these tests by the Los Angeles County Sheriff's Department. But it's always the call of the local investigators whether the tests should be administered.

Nobody seriously suspected the boys. No, the failure to do

the test was significant only because it raised doubts in the minds of some outsiders about whether the Beverly Hills cops were up to the challenge of investigating a mob killing, which is considered one of the most difficult crimes to solve. Even with all of modern crime-fighting's arsenal of scientific tools in use, solving a mob killing is chancy at best. Cops who failed to use the weapons they had were just making it easier for the bad guys.

"They're drowning," one organized crime expert sniffed.

Immigrant Son

Thirty-five years earlier, ten-year-old Jose Menendez had gone alone to the heavily guarded airport in Havana to meet his father, a soccer star. Security forces were a nervous bunch at this time. Only two years before, Fulgencio Batista y Zaldivar, a noncommissioned military officer from Cuba's lower class, had seized power to prevent presidential elections he knew he could not win.

This brazen move energized opposition forces, including a passionate young law school graduate named Fidel Castro. In March 1953 Castro had led 160 revolutionaries in a suicidal attack on the Moncada army post in Santiago de Cuba and then went into hiding to prepare for the uprising that would bring him to power six years later.

It was in this atmosphere of domestic turbulence that the young boy with dark eyes stuck out his jaw imperiously, marched up to the customs officers, and demanded admission to the airport security area. With his open, innocent face and large eyes he must have presented a comical sight. Yet there was also something commanding in him.

"My name is Jose Enrique," he announced as haughtily as he could manage. The nonplussed security men let the brash youngster pass. The encounter revealed what his adoring mother, Maria, would call his "king complex." Royalty never used their last names, and neither would he.

"He was very proud of himself," his mother, a slim, striking woman with white hair who was herself a sporting legend in Cuba, said in heavily accented English. "He was he."

In that one incident the boy demonstrated the characteristics that would make the adult Jose Menendez successful in a foreign land: the self-confidence bordering on arrogance, the eye-twinkling charm that caused his betters to indulge and then help him instead of slapping him down, sometimes even as he was trampling on them, and his innate certainty that in a world of sheep, he was born a shepherd.

The proof that he had more than lived up to his early promise was there on the front pages following the murders.

"A Los Angeles video entertainment executive who once headed RCA/Ariola Records as well as U.S. operations for the Hertz Corp. was found shot to death along with his wife in their Beverly Hills mansion," the *Los Angeles Times* began in one of several stories on the crime. Jose's amazing rags-to-riches personal history was analyzed, neighbors were questioned. It was the kind of coverage, complete with a picture of the mansion taken from a rented helicopter, usually reserved for the movements of a major government figure.

Even the *Wall Street Journal*, which rarely takes an interest in violent crime, put the murder on its cover, lamenting the passing of a highly regarded member of the business community. "He was by far the brightest, toughest businessman I have ever worked with," the *Journal* quoted colleague Ralph King as saying. "He was always ahead of his competition. He always would do more homework than whoever he was meeting with. Even if you were prepared, he was going to be two steps ahead of you. And if you were unprepared, you were setting yourself up to be annihilated."

And he was a straight arrow. "In an industry that is prone to excess," King added, "he was prone to the straight line . . . very friendly, very outgoing, very warm and very much a gentleman."

Gentlemanly businessmen had been murdered before, but rarely had their deaths generated this kind of attention. One possible reason for it was the intoxicating mix of Beverly Hills and murder, of opulence and blood. The blend proved irresistible to television, which endlessly ran film of the bodies being wheeled out of the mansion on metal gurneys. Crime shows staged dramatizations featuring anonymous men firing shotgun blasts, over and over, to punctuate the bloody narrative.

But the story was sketched in richer colors than this. Jose Menendez was that favorite American archetype, the poor immigrant who made good. People who read about the case could hardly help but be drawn into a story that so dramatically played through America's favorite themes. Here was a young man who had fled a brutal despot and come to America penniless. He had lost not only his family's wealth but, just as important, the respect and status his family had had in his home country. In America he was worse than nobody, he was a wetback. But with an undiminished spirit, through hard work and cleverness, he had overcome all the barriers in his path to become rich, successful, and powerful.

Though Jose had faced discrimination as a young man, his success was a stamp of approval on the American system. The nation may be in turmoil over rampant violence, drugs, and racial and class hostility. But there must be a lot of good left in a system that allowed Jose Menendez to rise as high as his talent would carry him.

That talent carried him far. The accounts of his murder dutifully traced his professional rise from a struggling student who couldn't afford a three dollar class fee to his first job as a lowly accountant, to his rapid rise through the Hertz rental car giant, where he ran domestic leasing, and on to RCA Records in New York. There he coaxed record deals out of Annie Lennox of the Eurythmics, guided the rebirth of Jefferson Starship, and supervised the company's expansion into Latin music several years before Cuban singing star Gloria Estefan touched off the explosion in salsa music.

His triumph, however, came in his last years, when he resurrected a troubled company in California's San Fernando Valley and turned it into the nation's largest independent distributor of videos. International Video Entertainment lost $20 million in 1986, but within a year after his arrival Jose had driven the company into the black, with an $8 million net income.

When he died, the company's revenues had soared from $40 million when he arrived to $400 million. His achievements were so impressive that he received a $1 million bonus one year. At his death his estate was worth $14 million.

Jose's achievements seemed straight out of some nineteenth-century romance novel. Then it had all come to a bad—and very modern—end.

"It makes you feel sad about the American dream," said one old family friend.

"My sorrow is not really for myself," Erik Menendez said of the loss in an interview. "He was such an incredible man. Few men like that are ever born."

Jose was six feet one inch, but seemed taller because he

stood erect as a chess piece. He weighed two hundred pounds, but there was little fat. His passion for tennis, which he played whenever he found free time, kept him fit. He also watched what he ate, preferring a plain can of tuna with a squirt of lemon juice for lunch at his desk over a martini-soaked businessman's meal. His only unhealthy habit was smoking, which he could never give up, despite numerous tries.

Jose Menendez was an arresting, handsome man. He cut a dashing figure even in a room full of attractive entertainers at a party or at the annual Grammy awards, which he attended as a record industry executive. His broad shoulders filled out his expensive dark suits. His wavy hair was swept up and off his forehead. His sharp jaw was thrust out in a gesture that communicated his complete confidence in himself. People gravitated to him in those situations, and he welcomed them, standing in the center of a room and entertaining listeners with stories, jokes, and observations, all in perfect taste. "Jose was a big talker, he could talk about anything," said Stephen Wax, one of Jose's few close friends. Wax, a consultant during Jose's RCA years is now a personal manager for musical talent in Los Angeles.

But his good looks and effortless manner weren't what people noticed most about him. What they all recalled later was the way that Jose had of giving his complete attention to the subject at hand. If he met an associate in the hall at Mahogany Row, as the wing of executive offices at International Video Entertainment was called, Jose fixed the person with a penetrating look even when just saying good morning. For that moment in time, said one secretary, Joan White, "you had his undivided attention."

That attention was all-consuming, sweeping up everything in its path like an X ray. The recipient of one of those stares might come away feeling slightly singed, as though too many scans like that might be harmful.

This intensity was a result of the way he had trained his mind. He assessed every detail of a situation, from the curl of a person's hair to the flecks of different eye color in the iris. Nothing was missed or forgotten.

"He could tell you the name of the family dog owned by anyone in a position of responsibility," said an employee of LIVE Entertainment in Van Nuys. International Video was absorbed into LIVE after Jose combined the original video company with several others he purchased, a series of deals that sent the company's stock skyrocketing.

The fact that he never relaxed his attention, even during the most casual hallway encounter with a subordinate, is a characteristic of the warrior who feels he can never let down his guard. And Jose Menendez did often behave like a man at war. Friends used martial words to describe him, calling him a drill sergeant or a field general who barked orders to his aides as if in preparation to storm an enemy fortress. Employees once pasted a picture of Jose's head over the body of Sylvester Stallone's Rambo character, who is spraying bullets from a machine gun.

The legend read, "No Man, No Law, No War Can Stop Him."

Nobody knows exactly when he found Og Mandino. What is clear is that the man's writings were as formative for Jose Menendez as the Bible would be for a future priest.

Mandino wrote a book called *The Greatest Salesman in the World*, an almost metaphysical tale about Hafid, a camel boy of two thousand years ago who travels to Bethlehem and obtains ten ancient scrolls containing the wisdom of super-salesmanship.

The 108-page book is not particularly profound. The lessons are ordinary, and the wisdom plows no ground that Norman Vincent Peale had not already over-farmed. The scrolls are basically a series of pep talks for the soul.

"I was not delivered unto this world in defeat, nor does failure course in my veins," says one scroll. "I am not a sheep waiting to be prodded by my shepherd. I am a lion and I refuse to talk, to walk, to sleep with the sheep. I will hear not those who weep and complain, for their disease is contagious. Let them join the sheep. The slaughterhouse of failure is not my destiny."

Simple as these lines were, they were inspiration for Jose. He was convinced that the mind is a straightforward, if powerful, engine. It responds well to direct commands, frequently repeated. He didn't understand some people's need to dig up the past in a shrink's office at a hundred dollars an hour. Not when all the inspiration you needed to get on with the business of life was right there in Scroll III: "I will persist until I succeed."

He read and reread the book, and kept it close to hand throughout his adult life. It was one of only a handful of volumes recovered from his office, along with the pictures of his wife and sons, after his death.

He had meticulously trained his sons in the same philosophy.

Lyle packed the book in his tennis bag when he went on the road. He could recite long passages from memory.

As consumed as Jose was by business—he made three or four business trips a month, checking on distant operations or planning new acquisitions—he was a committed family man who talked incessantly about the tennis accomplishments of his sons. Only two weeks before his death, he took time off work to fly out to Louisville, Kentucky, and Kalamazoo, Michigan, to watch Erik play in a tournament. Kitty was already there. He filmed most of his sons' matches and studied the results as closely as a football coach, searching for ways to help his boys improve their games.

Friends could see the pride he felt in both of his sons when he talked about them. He told Annie Lennox how much his sons enjoyed her music. It was clear he thought he was delivering a lavish compliment.

He also took seriously his role of molding his sons into educated citizens. At dinner, while the maid bustled about serving food, Jose would raise a topic of debate. It could be anything from the California ballot to the war in Afghanistan. Lyle used to study up for these dinners the way he did for a test at Princeton University, trying to guess what subject would grab his father's attention that day. Old Joe Kennedy used to hold similar debates at the dinner table, and Jose tried to pass on to his sons the same Kennedy-esque pride in family and accomplishment. Just as Kennedy did, Jose wanted more than wealth, which could be used up in a single generation. He dreamed of building a dynasty that would give him a kind of immortality.

His Beverly Hills address and the two Mercedes in the driveway might lead an outsider to conclude that Jose was consumed by materialism, especially since he had worked so hard to reach that status in life where he could afford to buy almost any toy that caught his fancy.

Nothing could be further from the truth, said friends and family. He avoided ostentation and artifice, such as the Rolex watches that so many businessmen used to impress their friends.

"You didn't think of him as a high-powered businessman or multimillionaire," said Lyle in an interview. "He was probably one of the more modest men I've ever met, which is really quite extraordinary. He couldn't care less how he was dressed. He wore 1970 shirts on the [tennis] court that didn't match his socks. He really was just your everyday father."

A hardworking family man who had pulled himself up by his boot straps and raised money for poor children with rare diseases, a cause he adopted shortly before his death, seems an unlikely profile for a man whose body would be shredded by shotgun blasts. And, of course, there was a darker, more conflicted, side to the man.

He could be brutal in business, especially with people he felt were not giving the same percentage of their souls to the company each day that he was. His driven, goal-oriented approach to life blunted his understanding of the frailties of the spirit that might distract others. His own past of deprivation and humiliation inured him to empathy.

He had overcome more than any of them, so he didn't care to hear any whining about problems at home.

His temper was legendary, as was the sarcastic, belittling tone of voice he adopted when dealing with someone he was convinced was incompetent. He didn't mind humiliating people in public either, where others could watch the unfortunate victim being disemboweled by a man with a surgeon's touch. Jose had driven many employees to exasperation, tears, and thoughts of revenge.

"Jose didn't like any sign of weakness," agreed Wax.

His personal credo was summed up in a few words to a colleague. After seeing a look of pain on an underling's face after being humiliated, Jose Menendez turned and said, "I've always thought it far better, Roger, to be feared than loved."

But if he was proud and strong-willed, it was in his blood. The Menendez family's roots reach back several generations to Spain, from where their ancestors migrated to Cuba while the country was still a Spanish colony. It had always been a family of professionals and stand-out athletes. Jose's great-great-grandfather was educated at the Massachusetts Institute of Technology, receiving a degree in engineering before returning to his homeland.

Jose's great-grandfather was a lieutenant colonel in the Cuban army in the 1890s. He helped lead the fight during the country's war of independence with Spain, which began in 1895 and did not end until the United States defeated Spain in the Spanish-American War in 1898.

Independent politically and with growing economic ties to the United States, the new Cuba developed a sizable middle class, about eighteen percent of the population. The Menendez family was well within the upper rank of society.

Jose's grandfather was a professor of medicine at the University of Havana and was quite wealthy, according to the family. He founded a bank, then a big recession hit.

"Rather than declare bankruptcy, he paid everyone off by selling his home, selling his property. He lost everything," said Lyle Menendez.

But he rebuilt. His son, Jose's father, also named Jose, was a renowned soccer player who later owned his own accounting business. His marriage to a champion swimmer, Maria Carlotta Llanio, was a cause for national celebration, said Lyle. She had won two first-place gold medals in a Central American Olympic-style athletic competition—her specialties were the 200- and 400-meter freestyle events—and ultimately became the first woman elected to Cuba's sports hall of fame.

Her family, the Llanios, were if anything even more distinguished than the Menendezes. There were university professors, lawyers, and physicians. Family members said one even treated Castro himself.

When Jose's athletic career ended, he and Maria settled into a comfortable life in an upper-middle-class section of Havana. Their condominium was a place for social gatherings, where friends came to debate the changing political conditions.

"We mixed at the top," said Jose's sister, Teresita Baralt, a plump, kindly, smiling woman known to Lyle's friends as Aunt Terry. Though the family was not rich, their accomplishments in the sports world guaranteed them an honored place in society. "It was more important to have the reputation than it was to be very, very wealthy."

The condominium complex had a swimming pool, and in this competitive family it became more than a haven from Havana's hot, humid weather. The pool was another arena in which to prove themselves.

Terry was the eldest and a highly regarded young swimmer who at one time hoped to try out for the Olympic team. Marta, next in line, two years younger, was considered the "beauty queen" of the family. Whereas Terry was sensitive, guided by her feelings, Marta was strong and outgoing, a bit of a rebel, and would grow into an arresting woman.

Last came Jose, five years younger than Terry. The only boy at home, he was pampered and adored by his mother to an even greater extent than is usually the case in Latin households. The relationship between mother and son was extraordinary, and exclusive. Jose was Maria's passion, a perfect child. According to one family member, she was so devoted to her son that Marta and Terry were mostly raised by their father, a sweet, gentle man who would get them up for breakfast and off to school each day. Then he would let them cry on his shoulder when they complained that Jose got all their mother's attention. Jose was so closely tied to his mother, this family member said, that after his father died he complained that he never knew him well.

Maria was the dominant person in the household, according to the family members, and was absolutely fearless.

She swam competitively until the age of forty-three, and one of her favorite activities was to paddle miles out into the shark-infested waters off Cuba, out into the shipping lanes. There she would swim about in the luxuriant stillness of the deep blue ocean before turning around and heading back to shore. Every day she spent three or four hours in the water. She passed this fearlessness and single-minded devotion to sporting excellence on to Jose, who had no patience with anyone else's weakness.

Maria rarely disciplined her son and refused to let anyone else lay a hand on him, according to the family member. There was a feverish quality to their relationship, this person said, that Jose would later repeat and expand upon with Lyle.

"Maria told Jose he didn't have to listen to anybody because he was superior to everybody," said the family member. "When Jose became an adult, she bragged he had no inhibitions because she never gave him any."

"He was a little terror," recalled Terry. "He was not allowed in the living room when we had visitors because he was impossible. If he didn't like the kid in the family, he would make a comment and the child would be embarrassed."

Others said he was more than a terror. He was obnoxious. He had a habit of biting playmates when he was small and bullying them, punching, and hitting them when he got bigger.

The Menendezes belonged to a country club in Havana which threw a holiday party for the Christmas season, complete with live music and rivers of flowing champagne. The proprietors covered the fifty-meter pool with an expensive wood platform to serve as a dance floor. In 1954, young Jose Menendez set the floor on fire.

In penalty Jose's parents paid $10,000 in damages, a huge sum in those days. Still, Maria refused to allow her husband to say a cross word to her son about it.

Like his parents, young Jose excelled in sports. In this

household sports was not necessarily a voluntary activity. A family member said that when Marta decided to quit swimming at sixteen, they almost "threw her out of the house."

But Jose loved sports. Though skilled in track and football, his strongest sport was swimming and his best event was the breast stroke. He also hoped to try out for Cuba's Olympic swimming team in 1960, but those plans would be short-circuited by the rise of Fidel Castro.

Jose Menendez grew into a handsome young man, with a sharp wit and a youngest child's ability to get his way. He "had a way of pouring on the charm," said one family member. Even when he was caught playing mischievous tricks such as hiding pieces of model airplanes from Terry's boyfriend, Carlos Baralt, his big sister would just sigh and tell him to give them back.

Everyone could see he was bright, but he studied just enough to make acceptable grades. And his behavior continued to be a problem. One family member said he was thrown out of two grammar schools, and he was the only boy to be kicked off the swimming team. "Jose was not a person who abided by the rules," said the family member.

Still, he remained confident that if he needed to do well at something, he would.

Terry's relationship with Carlos Baralt was to play a pivotal part in Jose's life by providing him an escape route from Cuba.

Tall, genial, and measured in his emotions, Baralt also came from a highly esteemed family. But his relatives were professionals and intellectuals. His older brother was the Cuban ambassador to Canada, stationed in Ottawa. His father was the dean of humanities at the University of Havana.

Carlos was attending the university as an engineering student when he met and fell in love with Terry Menendez. Like many university-trained intellectuals, Carlos was repelled by the right-wing policies of the Batista regime.

"We were all anti-Batista and we were pro-revolution," said Baralt.

At first Castro was only one of many opposition leaders, but after 1956 he emerged as the preeminent alternative to Batista, and political moderates began negotiating with him to win promises of reform after Batista was overthrown. After Castro's victory on January 2, 1959, and the beginning of war-crimes trials that led to the execution of six hundred people, Carlos Baralt became disillusioned once more. He began speaking out for democratic reforms in informal campus discussions with other university students.

"Castro betrayed our democratic ideals," Baralt reflected.

A fellow student warned him that expressing his political views in public was "counter-revolutionary" and could be grounds for arrest.

Bustling, vibrant Havana, with its gambling dens and perpetual sun, so attractive to American dilettantes, was history.

At first the emergence of Castro did not change the lifestyle of the Menendez family. But as members of the social elite they were used to speaking out on political issues. Now they found themselves muzzled, everyone except Jose, a brash teenager who spoke out in school against Castro and didn't seem to care who heard him.

Disappointed and alienated in the new Cuba, the Menendezes began thinking of leaving their homeland. It was a painful prospect.

"When you've lived in a country all your life, and when you are still comfortable," it's difficult to suddenly pick up and leave, Terry Baralt said.

In 1960, the situation grew dramatically more dangerous for the Baralts when Carlos's brother resigned his embassy post in Ottawa to protest Castro's growing repression. A government tabloid in Havana bannered, "Baralt Traitor!" across the front page of the next day's edition.

The family found itself under constant surveillance. Carlos's father was forced to resign his position at the university in disgrace, and the family's home was raided and searched by government agents.

Carlos, then twenty-four, made plans to flee to the United States. He told the government he was just taking a short vacation. Maria Menendez begged him to take her son. Even though Jose was just sixteen, his mother feared that the boy's outspoken criticism of Castro was drawing the attention of spies. Carlos agreed, and on October 7, 1960, the two young men escaped to Hazleton, Pennsylvania, where Carlos had relatives.

Jose carried with him a lifelong hatred of Castro. Lyle and Erik said that throughout his professional life Jose harbored an ambition to run for high political office in Florida and then—somehow—kick Castro out of Cuba.

The rest of Jose's family asked, one at a time, so as not to tip off the government, for permission to "visit relatives" in America. Marta left and then Terry.

"I left with a round-trip ticket, supposedly on a week's vacation," Terry recalled.

She traveled to Carbondale, Illinois, where Carlos's parents had resettled after leaving Cuba, and where his father had become a visiting professor in Southern Illinois University's Latin America and philosophy departments. Not long afterward she married Carlos.

Following the abortive Bay of Pigs invasion on April 17, 1961, it became much more difficult to leave Cuba. Visas had to be obtained from other embassies after the American embassy shut down.

Maria managed to get out in August 1961. But Jose's father hung in, unwilling to give up everything his family had built. He held on for another year, until the Cuban missile crisis brought the world to the brink of nuclear annihilation. Then the senior Menendez said a final good-bye to his friends.

"It was hardest for Father," Terry said. "He had a public accounting firm. He lost everything, including our home, to the government."

By then it was almost too late. The family patriarch got out only with the help of a friendly immigration officer who remembered the great soccer player. "At the time my father left, it was with only what he had on," said Terry Baralt. "None of us could leave with any money."

In Hazleton, Jose, now a refugee, shared an attic room with Carlos Baralt in a drafty old farmhouse rented by the Coxe family, who were cousins to the Baralts. Trudy Coxe was eleven years old when Jose came to live with her family.

Later the director of Ocean Coastal Resource Management under President George Bush, the young girl adored Jose. "He was very funny, very smart, very charismatic," she said.

Jose joined the high school's swimming team. Hazleton, which used to send twenty thousand men to dig coal every day until the mines started closing up in the fifties, is in northeast Pennsylvania. It is bone-chilling cold in the winter, and the summers can sometimes be little better, with highs in the fifties not uncommon.

In short, this was not a fertile training ground for Olympic swimmers. Ray Saul, then sports editor of the *Hazleton Standard Speaker*, covered all the meets in the cavernous old pool under the gym, built in 1928.

"It's a dungeon," said Saul, now the managing editor. "It was hotter than blazes because it was built over the coal-heating system. When you came out you were sweating."

Saul remembered Jose Menendez as a good swimmer but not the best on the team. Lyle Menendez would later inflate his father's accomplishments by proclaiming that he had broken the Olympic record for the breast stroke. Burnishing the family legend was something of a habit with some of the Menendezes. The desire to be first and best was so strong that when it came to a conflict between the fantasy of greatness and the reality that they were not always on top, it was reality that gave way. Erik Menendez liked to brag that his mother was "like Miss Illinois or something." In fact, she won a civic organization's beauty contest in her Illinois hometown.

Jose had problems during swim meets because he kept getting disqualified for using the wrong stroke. Though Jose would later be known among his detractors for a philosophy that amounted to "Lie, cheat, steal, but win," Saul ascribed his swimming mistakes not to cheating but to Jose's unfamiliarity with the language. "He would go along a while and do something wrong in the stroke because he didn't understand," he said.

If Jose's athletic career was less successful than his family recalled years later, the new boy's school career was still remarkable. Coming from a foreign country and one of only a handful of minority kids in the blue-collar area, Jose quickly became one of the most popular kids in school. He dated frequently and was one of those most sought out for companionship at Third Base, a café across the street from school where the jukebox blared teen anthems.

"He was one of those people who was friends with everybody," said Howard Sugarman, now a service technician in town. If he was lonely or depressed about losing his home and his family's money and status in the social ranks of Cuba, he didn't show it. He decided his life in Cuba was over and, in his hardheaded way, figured there was little percentage in bemoaning his loss.

The picture of Jose Menendez in the 1961 yearbook Janus shows a good-looking young man with big ears and features that would show up on the face of his son Erik. The photo caption testifies to the mark he made on the school in only a year: "The 'Mightiest Merman' . . . historically intelligent, practical aspect toward life . . . our 'Casual Cuban Casanova' . . . Oh! those eyes . . . something money can't buy—one good guy."

Ceremonies of the Dead

Three days after the murders, the bodies of Jose and Kitty Menendez were wheeled on identical stainless steel tables out of a special secure room for homicide victims in the coroner's office east of downtown Los Angeles, where eighteen thousand autopsies are performed a year. They were washed with sponges and moved into one of two brightly lit operating chambers, where they were parked next to a counter on which surgical instruments and a scale to weigh organs are located.

Dr. Irwin Golden began working at nine-thirty, reconstructing in cool, institutional language the savagery of the attack and charting the trajectories of shotgun blasts that blew out chunks of flesh the size of golf balls.

Dictating into a tape recorder, he turned his attention first to Jose's body, while Zoeller and several other Beverly Hills detectives looked on in queasy discomfort. The external evaluation revealed a "well-built, well-nourished" Caucasian male identified by toe tags.

The first wound Golden examined was the killing shot to the head. He called it a "gaping laceration," five inches by four inches, large enough for an adult to thrust his fist into the wound. The brain had been "predominantly eviscerated" and was placed in a separate container.

This wound produced two exit wounds, one on the right ear and another on the right temple. "Subsequent autopsy shows explosive decapitation, with multiple comminuted fractures of the calvarium and base of the skull," Golden noted. Comminuted means pulverized into powder, a term that conveyed the frightful power of the weapons.

There were multiple fractures of the facial and jaw bones, with "deformity of the face and abnormal mobility," referring to the angularity in the facial features that Erik observed. Twelve lead pellets were recovered from the cranial cavity, irregularly distributed along the path of the wound. This was a contact wound, and soot was found in the cavity.

It was hardly necessary to add, though Golden did because he was following rigid procedures, "this is considered an immediately fatal shotgun wound."

The rest of the wounds would not have been fatal, at least immediately. Golden described the two shots to the right arm, one just below the shoulder that fractured the humerus, and the other to the right forearm.

The trajectory of the shot to the left elbow was back to front. Since Jose's arms were crossed, this could have been one of the first shots, delivered from the side as the killer walked around to the front of the couch to face him, firing as he came. Five pellets were recovered and sealed up in what is known as a projectile envelope.

The blast to the lower left thigh, just above the knee, was a "through and through" wound that left a three-inch hole and fractured the left femur. A sixth wound was noted, to the upper chest, but Golden was suspicious of it. "This wound is listed separately, but appears related to the shotgun wound(s) of the right upper extremity; by manipulation of the right upper extremity the wound path may be brought in relation to one of those shotgun wounds."

Golden found bleeding into the body's tissues along all the wound paths, meaning the heart had still been pumping blood. This meant the wound to the back of the head was not the first shot, as authorities at first believed. Golden said he could not determine the order of the shots.

The clothes were examined. Jose's sweatshirt and shorts were blood-soaked and riddled by shotgun pellet holes. He was wearing leather shoes, and there was so much blood that even his socks were coated with it.

The examination of the internal organs began with a Y-shaped incision in the trunk of the body. In the stomach Golden found chewed, semi-solid food, though he could not identify it. He also found several things that Jose would have been glad to know had he lived. He had been worrying about his heart since January, when he rushed to the Beverly Hills Medical Center with a painful attack of what may have been angina. Jose feared the demands made on his heart by his over-charged personality, his job, and his intermittent exertions on the tennis court, where he was every bit the competitor he was in the boardroom, even though he was a mediocre player. But Golden found the cardio-vascular system to be in good shape, with "minimal atheroscle-rosis" of the aorta.

The rest of the internal inspection read like a physical exam for a man in his twenties. The liver was "not remarkable," the gall bladder was unobstructed, the prostate unenlarged.

The cause of death, concluded Golden dryly, was "multiple shotgun wounds . . . There was evidence of close-range firing, with the shotgun wound of the head identified as a contact-type wound."

The autopsy of Kitty's body began about eleven o'clock and extended until past two because of the time it took to examine the barrage of wounds she suffered.

"The body is that of an unembalmed Caucasian middle-aged female who appears the stated age of forty-four years," Golden began. In fact, Kitty was three years older. When the family had moved to California, Kitty had lied on her driver's license application to hide the fact that she was older than her husband. Age was, in the vernacular, an issue for Kitty. She battled it furiously. She dyed her hair, had a facelift, and in the months before her death had begun painful electrolysis treatments on her face.

An even bigger issue was her weight. She went to the gym several times a week with Karen Wiere, with whom she had been close friends since she and Jose moved to California in 1986 to take the job at IVE. "He's around so many pretty women," Kitty told Karen, her green eyes narrowing. "It happened before." It, of course, was her euphemism for an eight-year affair Jose swore was over. Even to her close friend she could not bear to mention the name of the longtime mistress, the hated Louise.

The autopsy revealed Kitty was losing the weight battle. At five feet two inches, she weighed 165 pounds at death.

Like Jose's, Kitty's clothing was washed in blood. The blood on the bottom of the shoe was examined, a small but compelling testimony to how desperately she fought for her life. She would have had to have been bleeding badly at the time to spill blood onto the rug where she could step in it. Yet she had pulled herself up and tried to stagger off, only to be brought down again in a hail of gunfire.

The examination of her wounds began with the blast to the left cheek, which had torn a one-inch hole in her face, fractured her upper jaw, and dislodged several of her upper teeth. These were found loose in her mouth. There were pulverizing wounds to the skull, fractures of the lower jaw, and pellet wounds to the tongue. This shot also lacerated the brain.

There was an abrasion near the wound and the discovery of soot and wadding confirmed Golden's suspicion that this was a contact wound. As opposed to all of Jose's wounds, and most of Kitty's, birdshot was found in this wound, apparent evidence of reloading.

The other birdshot wound was also to the left side of the head, striking the rear of the neck and extending upward to the left ear. This glancing wound was not as serious as the first and would not have been fatal.

The next wound was a shotgun blast directly in the face. The pellets opened a four-inch-wide wound extending from the right cheek across the nose to the left cheek. After smashing through the nose, the orbital bones containing the eyes, and the upper jaw, the pellets intersected the path of the birdshot in the first wound and buried themselves in the brain.

The last head wound was a shot to the right side of the face entering the lower jaw and extending to the collarbone. The pellets fractured the upper jaw and knocked out more teeth. Now Golden discovered something. Looking closely, he felt this wound, or the one preceding it, might be related to a wound of the right hand that almost severed Kitty's thumb.

"By manipulation of the right upper extremity," said Golden of the hand wound, "this wound may be [placed] in apposition to those two wounds."

Some investigators theorized Kitty had extended her hand to block the coming shotgun blast in a last, vain effort at self-preservation. That would make the wound to the hand the killing shot, since either of the two head wounds associated with it would have been fatal. The other shots were mere gratuitous violence.

But there was one thing wrong with this theory. Most people extending their hands to block an incoming projectile put their palms out. Yet the exit wound to the hand was on the palm side, not the back of the hand. This would mean that either Kitty extended her blocking hand in a strange position, or she did not extend her hand at all. Perhaps instead of sticking out her hand in defense, she was cowering, with her hand over her face. Or perhaps something more was at work. Maybe she did not want to see what was about to befall her. Something about the scene, something even more horrible than the approach of her own death, caused her to blind herself.

Next to fall under Golden's inspection was a wound to the upper right arm that shattered the humerus. By moving the arm, Golden was able to bring this wound into alignment with a wound to the right forearm, and he concluded these were related. The exit wound five inches below the shoulder was nearly an inch wide.

This would not have been fatal, but the broken arm would have been incapacitating.

The last of the fatal wounds was the one to the left breast.

The final three wounds were all to the left leg. One shattered the large leg bone at the hip, the second was the graze wound of the calf. The last wound, to the knee, was odd because it was back to front. The other leg wounds were front to back. This meant that either the body, or the killer, was in a different position when this shot was delivered.

Perhaps this wound was the one that brought her down after she leaped up from the couch to escape the carnage in the family room? In trying to run, she might have presented her back to at least one of the attackers. Or was this delivered after all the other shots, a coup de grace by the mob, which according to popular legend liked to shoot its enemies in the knees?

Golden inspected the organs. He found the heart in good shape, but the lungs were congested. Kitty had been a smoker for years, and it had been a source of problems in the household.

Erik, she had confessed to a friend, had ordered her not to smoke at his tennis tournaments. It embarrassed him to see her in the stands with a cigarette dangling from her mouth. "I forbid it," he said. But she could never quite kick the habit, especially when she was on a diet. A cigarette and a Sprite went well together.

Golden's analysis revealed the path of each shotgun blast and helped the investigators to begin forming images of the murders. In their minds the cops began seeing shadowy pictures of men moving around the family room while the television blared in the background. The shadows fired their guns until they were smoking, reloaded, then stood over a mortally wounded Kitty and fired again. But these shadows did not have faces.

* * *

The final ceremonies of the dead commenced with a memorial service at the Directors Guild of America on Sunset Boulevard on Friday, August 25. The service was one part testimonial, one part publicity event with news cameras outside, and one part show of corporate solidarity. Several of LIVE's executives were on hand to prove that the company was prepared to carry on without their departed leader.

The service, jointly administered by Jose's company and Erik and Lyle, was also meant to show that Jose was a valued member of the film community. This was partly a pose. He was only a peripheral member of the film set, and Sylvester Stallone, beefed up in classic Rambo condition, which tested the seams of his dark suit, was one of the few famous Hollywood names to show up. It was ironic because Jose secretly disliked Stallone.

Stallone's renegade Vietnam vet movies had made many millions of dollars for Carolco Pictures, which owned 49 percent of Jose's company. At the time of the service, Carolco had in production two new movies, *Total Recall* and *Terminator 2*, that would solidify the company's reputation for carnage done in high style. More than one person noted the irony of Jose's connection to a film company that had become rich specializing in just the sort of gore that cops saw in the Menendez mansion.

The service was set for eleven, but Lyle and Erik were late. Three hundred guests milled around the foyer, growing more irritated at the delay with every passing minute. Finally, an hour late, Lyle and Erik, dressed sharply in sport coats and slacks, hurried in through a side door.

Among those greeting them was John Mason, a music industry attorney and longtime friend. He had helped Jose land the job at LIVE by introducing him to the bosses at Carolco. Mason noticed that Erik looked disoriented. His face was red and puffy. Mason chalked it up to nervousness. "I don't think either one of them had been in a position of speaking to so many powerful people before."

But Lyle looked cool and in control. "He was shaking hands and talking to people and assuring them that everything was okay," Mason said.

For Lyle, the ceremony was as much a coming out as a farewell. The world at large had known him only as Jose's kid, who stood politely by his father's side while Jose hung his arm around his shoulders and bragged about his boy's accomplishments on the tennis court, or asked if you had heard he was attending Princeton now. But Lyle was about to prove he was more than a smiling puppet. He had felt himself growing, stretching, adding years of maturity in the few days since his parents' murders. He felt ready to take his place at the head of the family, to show everyone that there was another Menendez to be reckoned with.

Lyle had been carefully taught by Jose about his family's special history and coached in the philosophy of excellence that Jose lived by. Lyle used to complain about how difficult it was to be Jose's son and the high standards he set, the long hours of demanding athletics each day, followed by intense intellectual study and debate, all directed by his father. It had been the kind of training a young Alexander received. But now that the hour was at hand for him to assume his rightful place, Lyle realized it had been worth it. "These twenty-one years have been like a basic training for life," Lyle would say.

He was determined not just to carry on without his father, but to assert himself as his father's legitimate replacement, just as a monarch's son would step forward at the king's death. Jose Enrique was to be replaced by Joseph Lyle (Joseph was his first name, but everybody called him Lyle).

"I pretty much recall him saying at the time that he wanted to take over the position of Jose," said a family member.

Following the serenely confident young man, the crowd filed into Theater One, which resembled a contemporary movie hall with red velvet curtains and plush seats. Light contemporary music was playing. The service was deliberately kept simple. The two-page program said nothing about the murders, noting only that Jose and Kitty "Entered Together Into Life Eternal" on August 20, 1989. A more traditional service was planned three days later in Princeton, New Jersey, where the family had lived for a decade and where Lyle was attending college. The bodies were not present at the memorial service. They were to be cremated.

Standing at a lectern bearing the guild emblem of a stooping eagle, Erik spoke touchingly of his parents. He wiped tears from his eyes from time to time, but never broke down, which would have embarrassed this crowd. He didn't speak long, but his words showed such power and unaffected poise that the corporate executives settled into a respectful silence.

The brothers called to the stage a small parade of business associates and relatives. The dead woman's brother, Brian Andersen, a developer from Downers Grove, Illinois, remembered that he had given her the nickname Kitty when she was a child because she was always tagging along like an adoring house pet. Her real name was Mary Louise, but few people called her that.

Erik and Lyle hugged each speaker.

Karen and Pete Wiere, who had befriended the Menendezes shortly after their move to California three years earlier, were sitting in the crowd. Their son, Steve, who, like the Menendez boys, was a tennis player in the amateur ranks, sat nearby. He did not much like Erik and Lyle, considering them "bad dudes" for some reason he wouldn't explain to his parents. But even he was awed by the unfolding scene. "There's no way I could stand up and talk about you that way," Steve murmured to his mother.

Afterward, Pete Wiere waded through the crowd of well-wishers to shake hands with the boys. He was an easygoing, balding real estate salesman who had negotiated the lease of LIVE's Van Nuys offices, a deal so lucrative that he thanked Jose by buying him a pistol autographed by Roy Rogers.

"Your mom and dad would be very, very proud of the way you handled this," Pete told Lyle and Erik with feeling.

"Thank you, Mr. Wiere," both replied respectfully. They invariably addressed him that way, as Mr. Wiere, looking him right in the eye. It had always impressed him. He knew it must have come from Jose's enforcement of an Old World code of behavior brought from Cuba. Many immigrants, Pete knew, tried to bring their children up with the conservative values of their homeland. He also knew many Americanized children of immigrants rebelled at the regulations, since their friends often have much more freedom. But the Menendez boys had not seemed in the least uncomfortable with Jose's strictures. A part of Pete had always been a little jealous. The Menendez boys were home every night for dinner, and they never left the house without a hug and kiss for their parents. His own kids did little more than call out, "I'm outa here" on their way out the door.

Now, in their grief, the boys had shown him a completely new and even more impressive side. "I couldn't believe two people of that age could handle [the service] that well. The performance was so incredible."

One of Erik's best friends, Kevin "Casey" Whalen, a big, beefy football player with auburn hair whose nickname among Erik's crowd was the Wizard—Erik was the Shepherd—approached the stage to offer his condolences.

"Thanks," Erik said. "We're staying at the Hotel Bel-Air for a few days. Why don't you come on over later and we can talk?"

Casey showed up that evening to find Erik and Lyle ensconced in a $1,300-a-night hotel room with a private spa outside on a deck.

"What's with the room?" Casey asked, impressed.

"My dad's company put us up here," Erik said simply.

LIVE was concerned for the safety of the brothers. Since no one knew why Jose and Kitty had been killed, it was impossible to know whether the killers would come after the boys next. Nobody wanted them staying at the Beverly Hills house, even though security guards were stationed all over the property. Besides, Lyle didn't get along with the guards. They considered him imperious, nicknaming him "Ice Man."

Despite the official silence of the police about possible suspects, press speculation was settling on the mob. Two names had already shown up in print. One was a former pornographer, Noel Bloom, who the Department of Justice said was an associate of a capo in the Galante crime family. Jose and Bloom had had a falling-out after Jose was hired to run Bloom's failing video business, International Video Entertainment. Menendez fired many of Bloom's handpicked loyalists, isolated Bloom himself by taking away his responsibilities, and finally forced him out.

The other name being linked to the mob and Jose was Morris Levy. Just before the murder Jose's company had purchased the BackZack Corporation, which owned the eighty-one-store Strawberries chain of audio and home-video stores in the Northeast. Levy was a principal shareholder in BackZack, and some said Jose had made a fool of Levy in the sale. An FBI affidavit filed in federal court in New York quoted an unnamed informant as saying the Genovese crime family owned an interest in Strawberries.

Spokesmen for Bloom and Levy denied they had anything to do with organized crime or the Menendez murders.

But Jose's sister, Marta Cano, added fuel to the speculation, according to news accounts, in an interview following the memorial service. "Because of his success, he probably was stepping on too many toes, which some people didn't like," Marta was quoted as saying about her brother.

Erik picked up on the same theme that night. "Strawberries wanted to bump my dad off," he said, according to Whalen. Erik was sure the police were looking into that angle.

"If I found who killed my parents, I would have to go to

jail because I would kill them," Erik muttered darkly, Casey recalled later.

The mood in the hotel room that night was solemn. Several other friends of Erik's came by, and nobody seemed to know exactly what to say. Lyle was busily packing for the funeral service in Princeton, and after he left for the airport in their mother's Mercedes, Casey and Erik ordered food from room service. Casey had spaghetti and Erik, as was his habit, for neither brother ate red meat, ate chicken. Then they climbed into the spa. The soothing water seemed to loosen something in Erik. He broke down.

"I'm so sad, I'm so sad," he sobbed over and over, staring into the hazy night sky.

Casey felt inadequate to help. He mumbled supportive, forgettable phrases, while his friend moaned out his loss and grief.

Casey and Erik hadn't known each other long, but they had a special closeness which Casey referred to as being "on the same page." After meeting in their senior year at Beverly Hills High School, they had found they shared certain beliefs, such as a respect for women. Both thought it was rude the way so many guys these days fail to open doors for their dates. Lyle had the reputation as the family ladies' man, but a friend recalled Erik turning on his answering machine one night and hearing messages from a dozen different girls.

Erik was always doing imaginative things to impress girls. Once he had a friend interrupt a restaurant full of diners to deliver flowers and read a poem he had written to a waitress. Another time he dressed up as a clown to win back a girlfriend with whom he had had a fight. When she got off her plane at L.A. International Airport, Erik handed her balloons, one of which said, "I Love You." Afterward, in his oversized shoes, he flopped out into the street to show off, and when a cop threatened to give him a ticket, Erik said, "You wouldn't give a ticket to a clown, would you?" Then he kissed the startled man on the cheek.

His sensitivity came from his mother, with whom he had been especially close. Not long before her death, she had sat Erik down for a heart-to-heart talk.

"She told me all about her childhood," Erik said later. He was sure she had some premonition of danger. She talked about growing up in Oak Lawn, outside Chicago, a merchant's daughter with dreams of a broadcasting career. She had even left a note lying around referring to her imminent death, though that might have been another of the thinly veiled suicide notes she had written when she was feeling desperate and unloved and wanted Jose to pay more attention to her.

Erik treasured that private conversation with Kitty like some secret present she had left behind just for him. For weeks after the murders, even in the midst of some business meeting to settle the estate, the mere mention of Kitty's name could provoke uncontrolled sobbing and moaning in Erik.

In memory of his mother, Erik wrote a poem called "Castles in the Sand." The message was a sad one, about a woman who tried to hold her family together. "My mother was always building castles in the sand to be blown away by the wind," he wrote.

Erik and Casey stayed up talking until 4:00 A.M., when an exhausted Erik finally collapsed into bed, all cried out.

Princeton University considers itself to be a community for students in the old sense, when young men and women looked to institutions to take care of them in every way while they were away from home. The university wants its charges to feel that they are part of an extended family, a policy that works so well that those who attend the college go back years later to hunt for the initials they carved into the tables at the historic Nassau Inn, which once played host to the signers of the Declaration of Independence.

So it did not come as a great surprise that Lyle chose to have the funeral for his parents at the university chapel, even though he had tried desperately to convince his father to let him drop out of Princeton. Its academic standards were impossibly high, and he had been frequently in trouble there.

But one thing Lyle had learned from his parents, who were skilled entertainers, was how to stage an event. And the chapel was a gorgeous building, just the proper setting for a funeral.

The interior walls of the Gothic brown stone chapel are lined with oak paneling carved from trees in Sherwood Forest, the legendary home of Robin Hood.

The service attracted several hundred people, many of them parishioners from St. Paul's, where the Menendezes worshiped when they lived in the Princeton area. Though the Menendezes were not religious—often ducking out the back after the service started for pancakes at a nearby restaurant, then returning just in time to file out with the rest of the parishioners—they made appearances at Christmas and Easter. The mourners filed into the church through the west doors, under the great stained glass window of Hope, depicting Christ at the four rivers of paradise.

To officiate, Lyle had turned to Father Brendan Scott. Two years earlier, Scott, then one of Princeton's spiritual advisers to the students, had helped defend Lyle against accusations that he had violated the campus honor code by plagiarising another student's paper. Despite Scott's impassioned appeal, Lyle lost his case and was suspended for a year.

Scott thought Lyle got a raw deal in that case and readily agreed to help in his time of need. Scott read for several minutes from scripture, but the longest portion of the ceremony, about thirty minutes, was set aside for Lyle. He ascended the pulpit, looked from face to face, and began speaking in a firm voice.

His mother, he said, had not only made her sons feel loved but made sure the household ran smoothly. "When we moved . . . she did every conceivable detail herself to make the house comfortable to live in," he said, according to accounts.

Lyle brought up something that had been a sore point in the Menendez household, Kitty's mammoth renovation at the family's fourteen-acre estate in Calabasas. Jose had purchased the house—five bedrooms and a lighted tennis court—when they moved to California. Kitty spent tens of thousands of dollars remodeling it, putting in a waterfall, even moving the huge rectangular pool a couple of feet. But the project seemed unending. Jose was frustrated and so was Kitty, who spent many of her mornings on the phone fighting with contractors. "I wonder if we'll ever get to live in it," she had said wistfully to friends.

"They were awfully close to finishing a week or two before they died," Lyle said of the project. "It is a shame," he added, that her fears of never getting to live in it came true (in fact, Jose intended to sell the Calabasas house after the remodeling was finished).

Then, Lyle read a letter written to him by his father.

"Dear son. Thank you for your very thoughtful and moving letter," Lyle recited from memory, barely looking at his notes. "As you know, to me the family [is the] most important thing in my life and I hope it will be in yours. I can't tell you how much I miss not being able to speak to my father. . . , I miss him a lot.

"Ecclesiastes 4:10 states: 'For if they fall, the one will lift up his fellow, but woe to him that is also [alone] when he falleth; for he hath not another to pick him up.'

"As we have discussed in the past, we are the heirs to a very special heritage and with that good fortune comes duty and responsibility. I know that you sometimes worry about your future. I have total trust in both you and Erik, and have no concerns about your future and your future role in your country.

"I urge you as you go through life and enjoy the fruits of your work and the good fortune of your heritage to think of your family, your country, and your fellow citizens. I believe that both you and Erik can make a difference. . . . I believe that you will!

"I encourage you not to select the easy road. I urge you to walk with honor regardless of the consequences and to challenge yourself to excellence. The future does not belong just to [the] brightest but also to the more determined.

"I extend to you and Jamie my congratulations and my good wishes. Perhaps next summer we should have an engagement party."

This was a reference to Lyle's engagement to Jamie Pisarcik, a standout tennis player herself. Jose's congratulations had been a long time coming, because Lyle's parents had been less than enthusiastic about a match with a woman five years his senior. Like Jose, Lyle seemed to gravitate toward older women.

Lyle continued reading: "I am sending you two books that I thought you might enjoy reading. One is *Empire* by Gore Vidal. Vidal is a very leftist individual but an excellent writer. I will be reading this during my upcoming holiday (will miss not having you with us). The other one, *Against All Hope*, is by Armando Valladores. It is important because it serves as a witness to human courage.

"I have to get back to work now," Lyle read. Then he stopped and added tenderly: "That was so typical of him."

It showed his priorities. First his family, then his work.

Father Scott has a special interest in comparative literature, so he notices the arrangement of words and the way they are said more than most people. He thought to himself as he listened that the letter was written by a man who loved his son and deeply respected him. And the way Lyle read it indicated just as strong a love in return.

Others might have noticed the formality of the letter. It was filled with Jose's motivational language, and there were almost too many reassurances that he was confident his sons would do well in life. The remark about the future not only belonging to the bright could have been interpreted as a comment upon Lyle's lackluster performance in college.

Though it may have been inadvertent, there was a powerful symbol in the choice of verses from Ecclesiastes. The book is all about vanity and the folly of pursuing riches instead of wisdom.

When Lyle descended from the pulpit, he was embraced by Erik. Too emotional to deliver a eulogy, Erik managed to choke out, listeners said, "Lyle and I love you all, and we hope you will be our extended family."

After the service, Lyle went off to have dinner with an attractive dark-haired young woman who had been his first girlfriend. In the bloom of love in high school Lyle and Stacy Feldman had even planned to marry. In fact, Lyle had been so eager that he had started talking about china patterns only a short time after they started dating. This had been too overwhelming for Stacy, who was naturally shy and delicate. When she broke off the relationship, Lyle promised to give her a fur coat if she would come back to him, but she refused the present. They remained friends, and when Lyle and Jamie fought, as they did frequently, for Jamie was a strong, opinionated woman who knew how to stand up to Lyle, he called his old girlfriend for advice.

Now Lyle unloaded on her. He was exhausted and keenly feeling his new responsibilities as head of the family. "I don't know if I'm ready for all this," he told her.

He worried about Erik. "He keeps breaking down."

They recalled some of the good times they had had together and talked vaguely about the future. Lyle told the young woman that he wasn't going to go off to live a playboy life on his dad's money.

"It would be revolting to just take a large sum of money and just either blow it or live just comfortably," Lyle said later on the subject.

Stacy didn't know what he intended to do. Lyle himself was still uncertain, although plans had begun to take shape in his mind. He was already thinking about how much more money he could make if he took his inheritance and invested it right, or started a business. He had always had good ideas. Now he had a chance to show what he could do.

"The impression I got," she said, "is that he wanted to do something to make his father proud of him."

Patterns

Jo McCord was upset. More than upset, her pride was hurt. It was the winter of 1963, and she had stopped off to visit her mother in Watseka, just in time to hear the latest rumor sprouting amid the long, even rows of corn and soybeans that stretched across the Illinois flatland like some kind of leafy army on the march.

The story was that the McCord girl was pursuing John Koonce, a local man seventeen years older and only recently separated from his wife. Not even divorced yet. The tale had credibility because Jo had already proven her daring by going off to a big-city college five hours away in Carbondale, where she dressed in black and let her hair fall in her eyes like a New York folksinger.

Making things worse, McCord had rolled into town for the weekend with Koonce in tow, along with two other friends, Kitty Andersen and a male friend of John's. They were all students in the Southern Illinois University radio and television department on their way to Lansing, Michigan, to broadcast SIU's basketball game back to Carbondale. There was nothing romantic about the trip, but Jo knew no one would believe it. She was embarrassed and angry that people would think she was a man-chaser.

"Well, we'll just fix that," Kitty reassured her friend. She had a plan that would save Jo's reputation and give the busybodies something to talk about for weeks. She offered to dress up like a sex kitten and hit Watseka's night spots, including the bowling alley in the basement of the Elks Lodge, on the arm of John Koonce. Jo would have John's friend Jerry as her escort.

Kitty's scheme to scandalize the townspeople didn't surprise Jo. Kitty was wildly exotic. She starred in campus plays, wore stirrup pants when pedal pushers were the rage, applied fiery lipstick, and colored her dark hair a sultry brown. Kitty didn't talk at all about herself or her family, which only increased the sense of mystery around her. She didn't seem to care a bit about all the young men who, in McCord's words, "fell in rows" at her feet.

The two women explored the closet of McCord's mother, who was "kind of a siren" herself, according to McCord, and found a pair of spiked heels, a low-cut black dress that fit Kitty's voluptuous body like Shrink Wrap, and a billowy white wig that was a cross between a hairpiece and a headdress. Kitty strolled into the bowling alley that night with an airy smile, her hips swaying like a bridge in an earthquake. Her large breasts threatened to erupt from the dress at any moment, and every bowler in the place turned to witness the contest between flesh and fabric.

"She got the biggest kick out of it," Koonce recalled. "She flounced around." Then the foursome went over to a dance hall outside town and caused another sensation.

"It seems a pretty silly prank to me now, but it's another example of how Kitty was," Jo McCord said later. "Always ready to go along with the gag, always with a wide but quiet smile on her beautiful face."

One rumor was squashed and another was started. But Kitty didn't give a damn what other people thought. She proved that later on when she fell for Jose Menendez, whose fractured English made him the butt of campus jokes.

Nobody who read about the murders a quarter century later would have recognized Kitty Menendez as a woman who would court scandal. At her death she was portrayed as a shy housewife who followed two steps behind her powerful husband. There was some truth to this. At the big Hollywood gatherings Jose enjoyed so much, Kitty could retreat into a shell of intimidated politeness, hiding behind thick blond curls and a broad, thin-lipped smile. To her powerful California friends she was the perfect businessman's wife, friendly, pretty, and intelligent enough to know that most people didn't care how intelligent she was. They spent time with her only to get an angle on her husband.

But this portrait fell short of describing a woman who was a uniquely complex personality. Much about Kitty seemed contradictory.

She could be shy, yet she had an eccentric, outrageous side that was more than willing to flout the rules, as she did in Watseka and as she would do repeatedly with her sons. For one thing, she was an aggressive, heedless driver who, according to some accounts, crossed entire states at speeds above ninety miles an hour. When Erik began dating, she made a phony ID card on a copy machine so his first girlfriend could go drinking.

For years Kitty did her sons' homework for them, which might explain the fact that they were lousy spellers and that Lyle seemed hopelessly outclassed at Princeton University. She didn't think there was anything wrong with these little larcenies. People often had to cut corners to get ahead. It just proved they wanted success more than the rest of the sheep.

She was self-sacrificing in the extreme, spending hours in the car every day driving Erik and Lyle to their tennis lessons. She did more for them, said one friend, than any mother "ever, ever did."

Yet she was lacking in the softer arts mothers are expected to practice. She had little sympathy for children who whined and cried over scraped knees. Nearly as competitive and demanding as her husband, she pushed her sons hard to achieve.

She was fun-loving, scatterbrained, disorganized, always dashing around, always arriving late, but doing it with such flair and good humor that nobody could be angry with her. Yet she battled depression and drugs and suicidal thoughts for years. Surrounded by friends, she sat home alone many nights reading self-help books, waiting for Jose and writing sad, self-destructive notes.

"This letter is not easy to write, but I feel I must somehow try to help you understand how impossible it is for me to continue," she said in a letter apparently written not long before a suicide attempt. The letter discussed the betrayal she felt upon discovering Jose's longtime affair, and how, despite her struggles to go on, she could not fight anymore.

"I fought as hard as I could, not so much for our marriage as I did for our children. They are the sole reason that I lasted this long. . . . You were my prince who would take me into our castle and build a mote [sic] shielding me from all the hurt I felt as a child. In this last year, I realized there are no princes or castles—only real life."

When friends tried to describe this many-sided woman, they often ended up sounding confused. "She was probably the most aggressive female I have ever known, but soft," mused a Princeton friend.

The contradictions in her personality gave her a changeableness that made her a good partner for a man as fixed as Jose. While her husband clawed his way up the corporate ladder, Kitty took on a dozen different roles to keep the family functioning. She performed them all with a dizzying, high-wire act kind of ditzy anxiety that threatened to bring everything down on her head and left others breathless. The atmosphere of impending chaos in which she lived her life was reflected in her house, which was often a mess, with newspapers, books, tennis gear, and occasional droppings from Chipper the ferret spread here and there.

The most important roles in her life were wife and mother. Both were challenging jobs in this family, because inside her home Kitty was not an equal. "Jose ran the household in a traditional Latin way, where the father was dominant and the wife played a subservient role," acknowledged one family member.

In fact, in many ways Kitty's importance in this competitive household fell below Lyle's. Jose made sure his elder son had all the money he needed. He carried around a credit card at fifteen and lavished jewelry on his girlfriends. In his room at any one time, he might have a thousand dollars lying around. But Jose kept his wife in the dark about family finances. While her husband was earning more than $1 million a year, Kitty worried that the family was so short of cash that she feared spending $100 for a leather coat.

This lack of status was most obvious at the dinner table, where Jose conducted his nightly seminars that covered everything from arms control to ballot propositions. Both boys were expected to participate in these intellectual sparring sessions, which were designed to toughen their minds the way the grueling tennis practices that Jose commanded hour after hour toughened their bodies. These discussions over steak and potatoes were a part of the warrior training for Erik and especially Lyle, who as the first born son in this traditional Latin family bore the responsibility of carrying the family's banner whenever Jose should lay it down.

Kitty's participation in these brain trusts was not welcomed.

"No one would pay much attention to what Kitty would say," said a friend of Lyle's, Donovan Goodreau.

But although Jose was the outsider of the two of them Kitty was the more original. He was the quintessential success-driven immigrant, from his conservative politics to the big black Mercedes parked in front of his Beverly Hills mansion. What made Jose unusual was not his big dreams—a kid with a knife outside a convenience store has similar dreams—but his ability to realize them.

Kitty was raised to a conventional life in a conventional midwestern town. Yet she was the one who challenged convention, who read a poem with an anti-war theme at the local VFW post beauty contest—and won anyway. And she was the one with guts enough to choose as her mate a man who appeared to be one of the most ineligible bachelors on campus.

Kitty grew up in Oak Lawn, Illinois, a town of about 61,000 that sits like a benign growth south of Chicago. Today it is a place of long, flat, traffic-choked streets filled with nondescript brick shops and surprisingly few oaks.

A flat and utilitarian community made of asphalt and concrete, Oak Lawn does not look inviting, but for a brief period it was a kind of mecca.

"It was just a little town on the Wabash railroad," said Fred Dumke, a former mayor. "After World War II was when we had the growth. Fellows in the service returned and started looking for homes to raise families."

While they once enjoyed the excitement of living in Chicago, where it was a short walk or cab ride to a good restaurant or to a brightly lit hotel for dancing, young parents of modest means developed reservations about raising their families there, especially as the neighborhoods on the South Side became blighted.

Oak Lawn seemed like a good refuge. It was near enough to the city for an evening trip in, and far enough out to be removed from the growing social problems in Chicago.

Between 1950 and 1965 the population grew 600 percent to 49,084.

Unaware of the future problems that would be created by urban sprawl, merchants schemed to attract even more people. During the Oak Lawn Round Up, a community carnival with a Wild West theme, "prospectors" dug in mounds of sand named after famous gold mines in search of $500 down payments on new houses.

Oak Lawn was a middling town, without the glamour of Lake

Forest or some of the other Chicago suburbs. And in the burgeoning community the Andersen family had a certain status.

Charles "Andy" Andersen owned a heating and air-conditioning shop and was active in civic affairs. There were four children. The boys were Milton, nicknamed "Spike," and Brian. The two girls were Joan and Mary Louise, the much loved baby of the family. But Mary Louise quickly became Kitty. Although her older brother tagged her with the name, it seemed to be such a perfect fit to her happy, tagalong personality that her real name was nearly forgotten.

"The only time she was Mary Louise was when somebody was mad at her," said childhood friend Nancy Dittrich. And it was hard to be mad at her.

Despite the family's position in town, life was not as cozy as a fifties sitcom at the Andersen house. As a small child Kitty witnessed violence in her own home. Andy beat Mae in front of the children, sometimes hitting her so hard she fell to the floor. He also hit the boys, which was nothing very unusual in those days, though his brand of corporal punishment sounds extreme even by those standards. Once, it is said, he threw one of his sons through a wall.

Mae took her beatings without complaint, apparently, because it was Andy who decided to leave the marriage before Kitty even entered school. After Andy left, Mae was humiliated and, according to one source, suffered a nervous breakdown and was hospitalized for a time.

Andy remarried several years later, and the fact that he and his new wife stayed in town caused some talk. Mae Andersen, a concert pianist, took a night job in a clerical capacity with United Air Lines at Midway Airport and raised her children herself. She never remarried; nobody remembers her even dating. She never complained about her lot to outsiders, and within the family she came to be regarded as a minor saint for bearing up under the weight of her responsibilities. But the experience embittered her. Friends who visited Kitty in the small frame house on 91st Street remember Mae as crabby and distant. "She kept the house shut up dark," said Audrie Peters.

There were reports in the neighborhood that Andy, even after remarrying, returned to see Mae from time to time for sex, though others deny it. Neighborhood children teased Kitty when they saw her father coming around, and all this had a powerful effect on her, convincing her that divorce was one of the worst things that could happen to a woman. Not only had her mother been abandoned by her father, she was so bereft and desperate that she was forced to take him back as a part-time lover.

This portrait of Andy differed greatly from the warm, smiling Chamber of Commerce stalwart who was so highly regarded by the rest of the citizens in Oak Lawn. Kitty hated her father and refused to speak to him for years, even though friends who knew him in his new family told her he had become a wonderful and kind man. Years later, when Kitty's own marriage was in turmoil, she said she "married a man just like my father in disguise—the very man I tried to run away from."

Mae's crabbiness—depression is what they would call it today—was only worsened by a dependence on alcohol.

Making things more painful for Kitty, Mae leaned on her daughter for strength, confessing her hopelessness. "Throughout my [early] life," Kitty wrote later, "I lived with a tormented mother who bared her soul to me, and I could always feel her hurt but was powerless to help her. . . . I lived in a broken home and knew of no other like mine."

This increased her resolve to be strong and independent and never to put herself in a position where she could be made a fool. "I felt different from everyone else . . . and never allowed my feelings for any boy to run deep enough to hurt me," she wrote.

Kitty never let on that she was having a hard time at home. Besides a strong reliance on her friends that sometimes seemed like dependence, her only eccentricity was a deathly fear of spiders. "She would scream" if she saw one, said Peters.

In the fragmented household Milton and Brian felt a special responsibility toward their baby sister. As with Jose, also the youngest child, she was spoiled and developed a pampered child's belief that life should be arranged for her pleasure.

Milton used to complain to his mother that Kitty got everything. But she was the baby, and he understood in the end.

She wasn't smug about her status, though, for she was able to put others first. Kitty idolized her brothers, following them around, learning athletic games and developing a competitive spirit. Her infectious nature made her welcome among the older children.

"She was the kid sister," recalled Milton, who has become a leader in Oak Lawn civic affairs and owns a camera shop in town.

She took dancing lessons as a child and did well in school, though she was hardly the brainy type. She liked having fun more than anything, and people were naturally drawn to her, said Dittrich.

"Everybody knew Kitty," she said. "Kitty was very popular. She was easy to laugh with, a fun person."

Among the interests she listed alongside her tomboyish yearbook picture in high school were the Dramatics Club, the Pep Club, and the Poster Club, one of those organizations dedicated to building school spirit that died out in the more activist sixties.

Kitty was a product of the Midwest in the fifties and used to love dancing the jitterbug to the jukebox that was always playing at the Lucky Horseshoe, a café right out of *American Graffiti*, filled with bebopping teens. She worked as a waitress in one of the local drive-ins.

Her sense that she didn't fit in, though, gave her a rebellious streak. She joined a group of girls who called themselves the Party Dolls, in honor of a popular dance tune at the time, and they were a bit wild compared to most girls. Kitty's nickname was Fat Cat. Another Party Doll was called S.O.B. because those were the initials in her name. The Dolls drank a little and ran around a lot.

When she was only fourteen, Kitty began to "borrow" her mother's 1956 Plymouth while her mother was at work. Then she and her friends, one of whose fathers owned the local tavern, the Town Tap, would go cruising. Kitty liked to drive out to Hickory Hills and see how fast she could go up and down the wooded lanes. This lust for speed and danger was something that Kitty carried with her into adulthood.

If any of her friends worried they would get caught, Kitty pooh-poohed them. "Nothing's going to happen," she said with the certainty of a girl who felt that fate would not dare trouble her.

Around this time she and her friend Nancy retired to the bedroom in the Andersen house with a bottle of wine, Kitty's first introduction to a vice that troubled her off and on throughout her life. They drank so much—while Mae slept peacefully in the other room—that both girls became sick.

"Whenever I go out now and there's a lot of wine around, I think of Kitty," said Dittrich.

She also was popular with the boys. "She had no problem with that," commented Milton.

She had natural good looks and an attractive personality, with a memorable giggle, though she was not, in the vernacular of the time, a knockout. She wore her dark hair up in tight curls, and she did not spend hours applying makeup in front of the mirror. "She wasn't into that kind of thing," said Dittrich. "But everybody knew her because she was so outgoing."

She also didn't mind taking up unpopular causes. A member of the Party Dolls became pregnant, and authorities tried to have her dismissed from school. But Kitty stuck by the girl. "The couple wanted to get married, and Kitty was supposed to stand up for them at the wedding," said Peters. "But the priest wouldn't let her."

Kitty graduated from Oak Lawn High School in 1959, but was not ready to settle down with any local beaus. In fact, her experience at home made her suspicious of domestic life. She wanted to be a career woman.

While Milton went to war in Southeast Asia as a Green Beret, Kitty enrolled at Southern Illinois University, becoming one of the first Andersens to go to college. But Kitty felt so guilty about leaving her mother behind that she went into therapy in college.

SIU's drama and communications departments had good reputations. Kitty loved the theater and had already been in a number of high school plays. "She was a forceful reader," said her brother Brian. The love of performing was a trait she would pass on to her son Erik, who would later try to break into modeling.

Kitty went to work for the campus television station, WSIU, mostly behind the camera, remembered Jo McCord, who was her roommate in her senior year. McCord was the host of a children's show on WSIU called "Chimney Corner."

To McCord, now a reporter for the *Journal* in Kankakee, Illinois, Kitty was something special. "She was glamorous, quiet, and mysterious," McCord said. "She was one of the choicest young ladies in our group."

Around this time the Johnson-Phelps VFW Post and Auxiliary went looking for young girls to vie for the title of Miss Oak Lawn. Kitty signed up for the pageant, which was held August 11, 1962, in the post hall.

"The girls entered were really outstanding as far as talent and looks went, and the judges themselves admitted it was difficult making a choice," wrote a reporter for the *Oak Lawn Independent*.

Eight finalists were chosen, including two candidates whose talent involved presenting "high style" hair fashions, two girls who modeled dresses they made themselves, a girl who sang "Misty," another who played "Moon River" on the piano, and one who pantomimed "The Girl from Wolverton Mountain" in a hillbilly costume.

The eighth finalist varied from these unintentional caricatures of the pre-feminist woman by performing a reading of Amy Lowell's melodramatic poem "Patterns."

About a woman whose lover has died in war, the poem concludes:

> I shall go
> Up and down,
> In my gown.
> Gorgeously arrayed,
> Boned and stayed.
> And the softness of my body will be guarded from embrace
> By each button, hook, and lace.
> For the man who should loose me is dead,
> Fighting with the Duke in Flanders,
> In a pattern called war.
> Christ. What are patterns for?

This frank expression of yearning sensuality had far greater depth and emotional power than the superficial pop entertainments and pantomimes of her competitors. Kitty's passion was still held in check—this was the early sixties, after all—but it was straining for release.

"What is summer in a fine brocaded gown," she intoned. "I would like to see it lying in a heap upon the ground."

A month later, Kitty was named queen and told the newspaper that she hoped to work in television and radio as a producer and director. These were heady, courageous ambitions at a time when strong women were not often seen in front of a camera and never in a position of power behind one.

But McCord didn't believe this was really Kitty's goal. Despite her deep distrust of men, her roommate thought Kitty's effervescent independence was a mating strategy. As the popular Doris Day movies of the time showed, a modern young woman was smart and savvy and able to take care of herself. Kitty was very much like the women Doris Day played: ambitious in a perky, self-contained way, independent, pretty in a curly-top fashion, and maybe a bit square. But that squareness only made her more attractive because she seemed solid and sensible and the kind of person who would be a good anchor for a man.

In her senior year Kitty had lots of boys hanging around,

including the male star of most campus plays. But Jo McCord doesn't remember her taking any of them seriously. She was, without knowing it, waiting for just the right man, the one who would loose her from the stays and hooks of her past.

Following the jaunt that scandalized Watseka, Kitty even dated John Koonce for a time. They went dancing, and once doubled with Guy Mitchell, a fifties singing star whose version of "Singin' the Blues" was a big hit. Mitchell's wife was a Scandinavian beauty queen whose well-proportioned figure had appeared in the pages of *Playboy* magazine. The two women attracted a lot of comment on campus. "People went around saying that was four of the biggest boobs anybody ever saw," Koonce said. When Kitty heard the jibe, she laughed as well. But she and Koonce were never serious about each other.

Then, suddenly, the exotic young woman who had vowed to keep her relations with men on a superficial level was hit by "a velvet bulldozer," said McCord. She and Kitty were living at the time in a cramped mobile home only eight feet wide and forty feet long, with a rotting picnic table out front. Kitty came home one day with a dreamy look in her eyes. "I met this guy," she said. "He's a swimmer."

The bulldozer was a young Cuban on an athletic scholarship from the East, Jose Menendez. Jose had met Kitty after going to work as a crew member at the campus television station. She offered to help him adjust to college life and to translate for him.

Kitty had been seeing someone else, but that young man was no match for Jose.

Their backgrounds could hardly have been more different. He was the scion of a noble family that had lost its station and became wandering immigrants.

She was the proper, if somewhat unconventional, midwesterner.

"We were so disappointed when she fell in love with this Cuban who could not even speak English," said McCord. Kitty's friends were stunned that she would care so little for the smart, good-looking American boys who courted her and instead choose this *immigrant* from Cuba.

Reflecting a racial bias that permeated American life, Jo's and Kitty's other friends assumed nothing good could come of such a relationship. "We thought, 'what a waste. She's a choice catch,' " said McCord.

The couple's behavior seemed to justify her friends' doubts.

Keety and Hosee, as they were secretly called by Kitty's friends, spent all their time together, reveling in each other.

"She would look at him and giggle," Jo said.

All night, every night, while Jo McCord tried to sleep in the bedroom, Jose and Kitty would be in the living room of the tiny trailer, playing Jo's collection of steamy George Shearing records on her beat-up old hi-fi.

"They would play those records over and over again," Jo recalled.

Then the next day Kitty would fall asleep at the master control board at the television station.

Within weeks the smitten couple made plans to marry. Though in time both sides of the family would become close, there was opposition to the match. Jose's family thought he was too young to get married. But he wrote that "if I'm old enough to live on my own at sixteen, I'm old enough to get married at nineteen."

There were plenty of other obstacles: the hostility of friends, language and cultural barriers, and the differences in their status. Kitty was among the elite on campus while Jose was an untouchable, a freshman and a foreigner.

But there was something fated in the match. To Jose, Kitty was more than an attractive, passionate, exotic woman. The daughter of a shopkeeper, she was a product of the American merchant class. By winning her, he staked a claim on something fundamental about his new country. Relatives recognized this.

"She was his first acquisition," said one Menendez family member.

Jose fulfilled an ideal for Kitty as well. She sensed there was more depth and power in this younger man than she saw in her more privileged classmates, for whom success in life was guaranteed if they just didn't screw it up. Jose would have to fight for what he wanted, and the coming battle ennobled him to her. He was made of knight-in-shining-armor material, as described by Amy Lowell. Jose, after all, had aristocratic roots, Old World charm, and a warrior's spirit.

I should see the sun flashing from his sword-hilt and the
    buckles on his shoes.
I would choose
To lead him in a maze along the patterned paths,
A bright and laughing maze for my heavy-booted lover.
Till he caught me in the shade,

And the buttons of his waistcoat bruised my body as he
    clasped me,
Aching, melting, unafraid.

Though the marriage would be tested many times, and although Kitty never completely recovered from the discovery
late in their marriage that Jose had been consistently unfaithful
to her, her passion would never weaken. "After twenty-four
years together I am still crazy about you," she wrote late in life,
several months after discovering her husband's longtime affair.
"I remember so much how excited I was when we first started
seeing each other after our 'official' meeting at the late show in
Carbondale. I have those same feelings for you today. These
last ten months have been the most difficult in my life, and even
through the pain, I know down deep how much I loved you.
Somehow we've come this far, and I only hope we have learned
and grown together. . . . I love you, Jose, with all that I am and
want to be. I love you. I want us to enjoy living together, to be
totally free with each other, and one day I hope you think of me
as your closest friend as well because you are and always have
been mine."

After the murders a friend told the dead woman's family that
Kitty loved Jose so much that she "would not have wanted to
live without him." Though that might have sounded callous,
Kitty's sons knew what Lee meant.

"Jose was Kitty's hero," said Lyle.

Following their marriage, Jose moved into the trailer. He
didn't do much more than fawn over his new bride. They barely
had enough to eat, surviving on peanut butter. McCord was
sure they would be condemned to a life of poverty.

Even though Jo McCord turned out to be wrong, she can't
shake a troubling image of Jose and Kitty together, one that
seems to have confirmed her doubts about the match. McCord
pictures Kitty and Jose sitting together, looking deeply and
lovingly into each other's eyes. But as she concentrates on the
image, she sees Kitty leaning away ever so slightly. She has a
wide but uncertain smile on her face, like a child being offered
candy by a stranger and who remembers her mother's warning
just before she gets into the car. Jose is straining forward,
grinning broadly. "He is making a questioning sound that really
means she has no choice but to agree with him."

6

Success

Those who knew Jose Menendez at Southern Illinois University found him to be unprepossessing. When he wasn't hunched over some piece of equipment at the television station, bleary-eyed from staying up too late in Kitty's trailer, he was hovering nearby while she talked to her friends. Silent, with a serious, vacant look on his face, he looked more like Kitty's bodyguard than her lover.

When he didn't understand something being said, which was often, the vacant look would slowly turn angry, and his face would darken like a field blackened by fire. His brow would furrow, and the air filled with tension. He would try to get Kitty away.

This withdrawn, stolid young man had little in common with the charismatic boy who had made such an impression in Pennsylvania. People there had seen him as a leader, and they don't recall him having any trouble with English. In Illinois he was mute and sullen. The only thing that could explain this change is that Jose felt vulnerable. It was true, he had made a striking woman fall in love with him, but the disapproval of her friends was palpable. He sensed their dislike and correctly traced it, in part, to his race. This was conservative, midwestern America. The civil rights struggles were still under way in the South, and the Watts riot, symbolizing the hopelessness of America's inner cities, was still a year away. In the words of one of Kitty's friends, her choice of a Cuban mate "was like marrying a black man," and everyone knew without saying it that that was the worst thing a young white woman could do in 1963.

Even twenty years later, at Kitty's high school reunion, the story went around the banquet room that Kitty had married "some Mexican" who worked at RCA. Everyone who heard the story assumed he was working in the stockroom.

This disapproval was especially difficult for someone as full of pride as Jose to accept. His self-assuredness faltered, and he failed to make any mark in Carbondale. He was not an outstanding student. And athletically he appears to have been a washout. Though McCord recalled him going around without his shirt, she doesn't remember Kitty ever going off to a swim meet. He is absent from yearbook photos of the team.

It is no wonder, then, that he arranged to leave Carbondale soon after Kitty's graduation. His parents were in New York City, so it was natural he would want to return there, taking Kitty from her turf to his.

He might have run away, but not quite with his tail between his legs. When he showed up as an accounting student at Queens College in New York, the fawning gigolo was gone, replaced by a man consumed by ambition. Perhaps it was New York's crackling energy, or perhaps it was a result of his embarrassment in Illinois, but something had unleashed him.

One of his teachers recalled Jose Menendez many years later as an ambitious student who "would batter me for a better grade." When he came up after class one day to ask what he had to do to improve, the question sounded like a demand.

Menendez was struggling financially. He told the instructor he would have to wait until payday for a three-dollar class expense. Though Jose was working part-time in a local supermarket, the couple's main source of income was Kitty, who was teaching in the Bronx. This was a low point in their fortunes. They lived frugally, though not exactly hand to mouth.

But it was this period that Lyle apparently was drawing on when he claimed later to college friends that he was born a ghetto child. He liked to portray himself, according to the friends, as a "street kid," with a savvy understanding of the bargains and compromises one had to make to survive downtown. This was all pure fantasy, part of Lyle's flair for self-romanticization, which was every bit as strong as Jose's. Lyle was not yet born when his parents were struggling to make their way.

"Lyle doesn't know what poverty is," said a family member.

While still in school, Jose was hired as a trainee by the big accounting firm of Coopers & Lybrand. According to his sister

Marta, Jose had a remarkable talent for figures. He passed the demanding CPA exam at twenty-one, even though "he never studied for it."

"The worst thing that could happen is I could flunk it," he said of his decision to take it a year early.

After he passed the test, Coopers & Lybrand gave him a ten percent pay hike, and Jose found himself making $25,000 a year, a very good salary in 1965. He and Kitty moved into a comfortable apartment in middle-class Queens, where Lyle was born on January 10, 1968.

Jose's first big chance came when he was sent to audit a Coopers client, Chicago-based Lyons Container. "He was carrying around the books, not a very important person," Erik said later.

Lyons was struggling at the time. After sitting through a lengthy board meeting, during which the directors wrestled with restructuring plans, Jose was asked for his opinion.

"Frankly, I don't think it's going to work," he said with typical bravado. "I have my own plan."

Even taking into account his sons' habit of inflating family history into myth, the spectacle of a young man barely out of college telling the paunchy directors of a respected American corporation that their ideas were all wet was remarkable. One can imagine the arched eyebrows as Jose began speaking, laying out the remedy he had prepared in advance for just such a moment. By the time he was done, he had not only convinced the board of directors that their ideas would not work, but also had convinced them that they must have this young prodigy on their team.

Lyons implored Jose to come aboard as an executive. But he was reluctant to move back to the Midwest, from which he had only recently escaped. So he boldly told Lyons' management that if they wanted him they would have to pay him a huge sum, $75,000 a year.

Jose's staggering demand revealed his other genius. He could not only read and understand a company's books better than the people who ran it, but he seemed to know instinctively how far an opponent could be pushed. It was as though he could see their fears, doubts, and weaknesses laid out face up like playing cards. Later this ability was made to serve his darker side when he used it to humiliate and terrorize.

When he returned to New York, he told his family about his

audacious demand. Then he had a good laugh. He doubted the company would meet his salary.

He was wrong. Lyons hired Jose, and at his price. In 1969, he and Kitty moved to Hinsdale, outside Chicago, and Kitty became a full-time mother. Indifferent to concerns over nepotism, he brought in Carlos Baralt, his brother-in-law, as an assistant.

In a year Jose turned Lyons around. Revenues nearly doubled to $5.5 million annually. Jose became chief executive. At twenty-six, he was a genuine wunderkind, a man who could raise corporations from the dead.

Two years later, though, he and the chairman of the board became embroiled in a proxy fight over the future direction of the company. Jose was forced out, along with Carlos. This would prove to be a pattern. Jose could perform miracles. But over the long term his vertical management style, which concentrated all authority in his hands and forced even senior executives to report to him on a daily basis like office boys, wore thin. At one of his companies the joke was that he personally signed every purchase order.

Jose's next opportunity came when he was hired in 1971 over almost eight hundred other applicants to be comptroller of the Hertz Corporation, the car rental giant. Jose moved up quickly, becoming chief financial officer in the car-leasing division within a year. Then he was promoted to general manager.

"I never knew anyone who worked harder, worked more toward goals," said Robert L. Stone, the Hertz chief executive at the time.

It was at Hertz that Jose developed a reputation for abusing subordinates that would stay with him throughout his career. Still in his twenties when he arrived, he began to fire people wholesale.

"He single-handedly handed to Hertz's competitors the best and the brightest in the business," said Adrian Bulman, one of Jose's mid-level managers. "He alienated people, and he didn't seem to care. I'm surprised that in an industry as tough as this one, somebody didn't punch him out."

In fact, somebody came close. A salesman being vilified by Jose one day set his rate book afire and threw it in Jose's face. Another man was driven into retirement by Jose's abuse. He left behind a missive: "Dear Jose, I quit. Fuck you."

One coworker recalled a time Jose was introduced to a lower-ranking colleague. He took an instant dislike to the man's curly hair. "I don't like your hairdo," Menendez declared. "Change it."

The man was too stunned to offer anything more than a weak defense. "This is what God gave me," he stammered.

"I don't want to see you with that hairdo again," Jose snapped and stalked off.

Warren Hudson had been in the textile business, but heard from a friend that car leasing was a "good cash business" and that there was plenty of money to be made. He went to work for Hertz in Atlanta, leasing fleets to corporations in the Southeast.

"My first encounter with Jose was almost pleasant," he said. They met in the teeth of a New York blizzard over coffee and doughnuts. In those brief minutes Hudson felt he was sitting in the presence of someone extraordinary. Jose's manner was overbearing, filling up the space between them and using up a good deal of the air in the doughnut shop. The man's mind worked with such precision that Hudson could almost see the gears gliding smoothly past one another.

"He remembered everything he had ever seen or heard in his life," Hudson recalled.

But his admiration for Jose was short-lived. He said he "would have gladly killed Mr. Menendez myself."

A source of Hudson's hatred was a quarterly business review meeting in New York. These meetings were legendary for the quantities of corporate blood spilled. Sales managers from across the nation were summoned to report on their progress meeting their goals.

"Weeks before the meetings, people prepared and started taking Valium," said Hudson. "People would get hives getting ready."

Nobody could prepare better than Jose Menendez, who was known to plan seating arrangements ahead of time to make sure certain people would have the sun in their eyes. He made it his business to know everything about every salesman at the meeting, as well as his territory. He frequently traveled the country under assumed names gathering intelligence. He liked to show up unannounced in some out-of-the-way place and demand an accounting from his representative on the spot if he saw too many cars sitting unleased.

The sales managers preparing for the quarterly meetings were especially nervous because they knew that Jose would demand hard numbers, proof that objectives were being met.

He had neither interest in pie charts nor patience with a sales manager who said he had worked hard but the numbers had not fallen his way. Hard work didn't matter to Jose. Results did.

"Where's my money?" was his bottom-line question.

Hudson took the floor at this meeting to deliver his report and began talking about the success he was having implementing what he called the Limited Maintenance Lease agreement. Unfortunately for Hudson, not long before, Jose had decided that title did not sound grand enough and changed it to Major Maintenance Lease agreement. This was deceptive because despite the name change, the terms of the lease did not change.

The third time Hudson referred to limited maintenance leases, Jose stopped him and switched on the lights. Twenty-five pairs of eyes blinked and adjusted to the fluorescence as Jose tore into Hudson.

"Did you leave your brain in Charlotte?" Menendez demanded. "Is everybody else in Charlotte as fucking stupid as you are?"

Then he polled everyone in the room, one by one, asking each if he or she was as "fucking stupid" as Hudson. The straw poll took twenty minutes, and it was finally decided that nobody in the eastern United States was that stupid. Hudson sat with his head down, silently enduring the assault.

Finally Jose allowed Hudson to continue. But just as the shaken man began again, Menendez stopped him, unable to stand the sight of him. "I don't want to hear any more from you, sit down," Jose ordered.

Hudson's hatred of Jose was so strong and enduring that after Jose's death, he sent a note to Lyle: "Having worked under your father and been on the receiving end of more than one of his tirades and having been witness to his destroying people in business meetings, actually reducing grown men to tears, I was wondering if I could ask you a question? . . .

"I was just wondering if Jose was a whimpering piece of shit when the other guy(s) had the big guns and all the power on their side, or if he was still super macho, Mr. Arrogance and spit in their eye. . . .

"When all the stories came out about the Beverly Hills police department 'interviewing' everyone who might have a motive for killing Jose, I called them to ask why they never contacted me . . . and lots of other Hertz people. . . . I explained to them that I would have done the job for nothing, but at the least, I wanted to shake the hand of the actual killer(s)."

Jose Menendez had few close friends in business. He was too proud to let people break through the barricade he was building around himself. He needed the wall for several reasons. For one thing, his talent and ambition separated him from most other people. Then, his race separated him even more from the uniformly white male culture that prevailed at the higher elevations of corporate America. It was a culture he could never really be a part of, no matter how hard he tried to lose his accent or how many companies he turned around. When he did let someone in, he often came to regret it.

Once at Hertz, he was screaming down the hall at someone, and a friend with whom he had gone fishing yelled at him good-naturedly, "Jose, why don't you just jump up on the desk and piss to get everyone's attention?"

Jose was profoundly humiliated. "Damn it," he fumed. "I let you get close to me, and I'll never do that again."

Jose's word was good. After this, his idea of letting down his hair was repeating one of the several versions of the story of his life, over a single glass of wine at the end of a day of business meetings. He fancied the story was inspirational and might encourage others to work harder. But its real purpose was to awe his listeners and show them they could never measure up to Jose Menendez.

"He made a comment one time about winning and always being the best," said Hudson. "He came to this country with nothing and intended never to let that happen again."

Menendez's desire to win led him, over the years, to employ business tactics that went beyond ruthless. Admirers argued that Jose was simply reaching for every advantage available to him and sometimes, yes, he reached too far.

A top Hertz associate once argued with Jose that while a strategy he was proposing would make the bottom line respond in the short term, within two years it could backfire to the company's disadvantage.

"We won't be here then," Menendez replied.

During the oil shock of 1979, inflation soared and Hertz suffered a cash crisis. Menendez decided to unilaterally raise the lease fees on Hertz customers.

"I raised the possibility of going to customers, explaining the deal and asking them to let us bill them a dollar more a month," said Mike Christian, an area vice president for the Southeast and mid-Atlantic states.

Instead of going to the customers for help, Jose raised the

rates by almost four percent. "Legally, there was no basis for it," said Christian.

If customers complained, Jose backed off. If not, the assessments stood. "From a strategic standpoint it was handled badly. There may have been a question of fairness," Christian said.

Jim Sanders, a division vice president, recalled that even in the small things, Jose's desire for an edge consumed his sense of fair play. Jose once tried to delay a bonus Sanders had coming. When Sanders began demanding his money, Jose tried to get him fired.

By 1979, at thirty-five, Jose had grasped the plum, executive vice president in charge of all of Hertz's U.S. operations. The family purchased a two-story home on a lake in Pennington amid rolling green hills outside Princeton. A major attraction was the tennis court out back, facing Honey Lake. Neighbors woke up many mornings to the sound of tennis balls being hit back and forth by two young boys and the occasional plunk in the lake when one of the balls landed in the water.

Allen Fite, small fleet sales manager for Hertz's Atlanta region, said that for many people who knew Jose when he was a young lion, his death was not much of a surprise.

"It was kind of funny," said Fite. "When this happened, people were calling other people within Hertz saying, 'You didn't do it, did you?' "

"The joke was, when he was killed, everybody needed an excuse to prove they were not in L.A.," said Sanders. Others, however, said there would be so many suspects among the people who had been broken by Jose over the years that the police would never solve the crime.

Jose's stint at Hertz ended abruptly in 1980, when the president of the company left and another man was brought in over Jose as president of U.S. operations. Jose Menendez was reassigned to the entertainment division of the parent company, RCA. But before making the appointment, the top brass wanted to see whether the buttoned-down Menendez could get along with the less formal West Coast music crowd.

They dispatched him to Los Angeles for a meeting with five of the top entertainment attorneys in town, including John Mason, who represented the Beach Boys, Belinda Carlisle, Randy Travis, and others. The group dined at the Beverly Hills Hotel.

"I thought Jose was just wonderful," said Mason. "We talked

about music, politics, entertainment, business. We had a warm friendship until his death."

It was natural that the two men should hit it off. Jose was a Republican and harbored aspirations to move to Florida someday and run for political office. Mason was also a conservative whose penthouse office on the beach in Santa Monica featured framed pictures of him with presidents Ronald Reagan, Gerald Ford, and Richard Nixon.

In 1981, Jose was handed the job of reversing the long decline of RCA's record division.

The record division was "considered a joke" in the industry, Mason said. One company executive called RCA a "retirement home for failed superstars" because the label had signed huge contracts with a stableful of one-time stars, such as Kenny Rogers and Diana Ross, who were past their prime. Rogers was said to be getting $4 million per album.

When he moved to RCA, Jose Menendez knew nothing about music. He didn't know the groups, and he didn't know such basics as the importance of touring to the success of an act.

But he figured that he hadn't known much about the auto rental business when he went to Hertz. And he had energized that venerable company by injecting a lot of new blood and cleaning out the dead wood. Of course, there were those who said that Jose's accomplishments at Hertz and everywhere else were like the actions of a tornado striking a town. By ripping up whole blocks and flattening the business district, he certainly eliminated some bad neighborhoods.

Jose saw his first job as selling RCA to its own disheartened employees. He gave a succession of old-fashioned, bell-ringing speeches about how much RCA meant to him and what its people could do if they pulled together. Even in the cynical eighties, when the idea of corporate loyalty became as outmoded as the family prayer before dinner, Jose was effective.

"I've seen the guy bring people to their feet screaming at company meetings," said Don Ellis, a vice president for U.S. and Canada under Jose.

While Jose didn't mind reigning by terror, he also was able to command great loyalty when he turned on the charm. His inner circle was so dedicated to him that it was said of one colleague at Hertz, "He would have blown up the fleet if Jose had asked."

"He had the ability to make people feel really good and really bad," said Ellis.

Ellis wound up in New York as a result of one of Jose's power plays. Ellis had been running the RCA operation in England. Jose said he needed him stateside, but Ellis was uncertain.

"You know, Don, I would be uncomfortable if someone running the company in an important place like the United Kingdom was not smart enough to see the importance of a job in the U.S.," Jose said.

Ellis caved in, but soon came to regret it. He was unavoidably late one day for a business meeting chaired by Jose. There had been a train accident on the line from Connecticut, where Ellis was living, which stranded two hundred thousand commuters. Through a herculean effort Ellis managed to find an alternate means of transportation and arrived before the meeting was over.

"I whispered to Jose what had happened," said Ellis. "I was a senior vice president, and I shouldn't have had to explain at all." But knowing Jose, he knew he should.

A half hour after the meeting was over, Ellis received a memo "incorrectly worded in pidgin English"—Jose's male secretary was not allowed to correct his boss's poor grammar—"telling me, 'When I call a meeting I expect you to be there.' "

Ellis was disgusted. He resigned a short time later.

Jose had a deep sense of personal dignity. John Ford, another vice president at RCA under Jose, said Menendez once told him about the time his father had made him wear short pants to a Boy Scout meeting. The other kids made fun of him.

He ran home, humiliated. "I've never forgotten it," Jose told Ford in an unusually candid conversation.

This pride, which caused him to inflate an ordinary childhood incident into some kind of psychic crisis, was part of what drove him to achieve. But it could lead him into self-destructive combat with people he didn't need to alienate.

Not long after Jose's arrival at RCA, New York entertainment attorney Paul Marshall was invited to lunch in the RCA executive dining room with Jose and Bob Summer, who as president held the top job at the RCA record division. Jose served just below him.

"I was asked to meet the budding genius," growled Marshall. "I didn't like the son of a bitch. When he comes in, sounding like Señor Wences [the puppeteer from the *Ed Sullivan Show* who had a comical Latin accent], as a mark of politeness, I spoke Spanish. I got yelled at."

Jose was hurt that the other man obviously noticed his accented English.

"Whazzamatter, can't you speak English?" Menendez snapped.

On another occasion, Marshall outlined a deal he had completed for RCA. Around the executive suite there were murmurs of approval. "I sat back in that glow an attorney has when his clients are satisfied," Marshall said.

"This guy [Jose] said, 'I guess you didn't work very hard on this one.' " Marshall turned to the chief counsel and said, "Who the fuck is this guy? The results are spectacular."

Jose said, "Why are we being so nice?"

"You don't run a record company like a used car business. I know that's your business," Marshall responded snidely.

He couldn't understand Jose's behavior. "Why did he take me on? First of all, I was richer than he was. Jose was so nasty on both occasions, I gather he was not pleased with being Cuban."

Marshall recalls the eerie response he got when he told RCA's chief counsel about Jose's perplexing behavior. "He who lives by the sword dies by the sword," the man said.

Of course, Marshall, a rich New York patrician, was just the sort of person Jose *would* take on. Jose was unable to resist trying to bring down such men, who he felt looked down upon him, even though he lusted to be exactly like them.

Surprisingly, in a man known derisively as a bean counter, Jose excelled during his time at RCA at artist relations. He sensed instinctively that art could not be made on a production line, and he resolved to do whatever it took to keep artists happy.

One of his first moves was to resign the Eurythmics, the duo led by pop diva Annie Lennox. Shortly after he signed on at RCA, Menendez called Eurythmics manager Gary Kurfirst, a man with a long and colorful history in rock 'n' roll. Kurfirst had run the Village Theater in New York (before it became the Fillmore East), promoted Bob Marley, and managed the Talking Heads.

"I'm taking over at RCA, and I want you to work only with me from now on," Menendez said. This was a classic bit of Menendez bravado, since Jose did not hold the top job in the record division. It revealed his apparent intentions to move Summer out of the way, as well as his cavalier lack of concern over whether his remarks might get back to Summer.

When it came time to resign the group, Jose and Kurfirst had lunch at the Russian Tea Room. The deal, said Kurfirst, "had to be a ton of money. I asked for $10 million firm for five albums and a high royalty."

"I'll think about it," Menendez said noncommittally.

The negotiations took place in the wake of critical acclaim for Lennox's brassy vocals and on the strength of several hit records. The timing was good for Kurfirst.

A few months later, Kurfirst was awakened at 2:00 A.M. in his room at the Sunset Marquis Hotel in Hollywood. The desk clerk said Jose Menendez was downstairs. He had made up his mind and had to see Kurfirst immediately.

"He wanted privacy, so we went into the kitchen, which was closed," said Kurfirst. "We were stealing ice cream out of the freezer, standing and eating out of bowls and talking. He gave us everything we wanted. That was quite a number back then. Maybe Paul McCartney and Stevie Wonder got numbers like that, but at this time the Eurythmics had only had a two-year career. Usually they'll give you $2 million for an album, but for only one at a time."

Lennox went on to win wide respect, but the band did not develop the staying power of a McCartney or Wonder.

"He saw the Eurythmics as [a guaranteed sale of] one million" albums, said John Ford. " 'Ship it,' he would say.

"It didn't work out that way. There are times my promotion people would say, 'Is he crazy? You want us to put how many out?' "

"I think people might have laughed about his ignorance of the business," agreed Paula Batson, who worked under Jose in public relations.

"In some cases he didn't do bad deals," said Ford. "The trouble was, he was in love with the entertainment business."

Another band Jose made a point to being on good terms with was the Jefferson Starship, a longtime RCA rock band that had stayed with the label, according to band manager, Bill Thompson, because the record company always treated the artists well. This was in part because the band for years was one of the only successful rock acts on the label.

"I sold more records for RCA than anybody but Colonel Parker," Thompson said, referring to Elvis Presley's manager.

Jose's stewardship at RCA coincided with one of the band's most productive periods. The Starship had three hit single records—"We Built This City," "Nothing's Going to Stop Us Now," and "Sarah"—and their biggest-selling album in ten years. If Jose's predecessors at RCA worked hard to keep the band happy, Menendez made it his mission.

"I was on the golf course in Kalamazoo and I got a phone call," Thompson said. The voice on the other end of the line was Jose, taking the time to personally deliver good news. "I wanted to let you know 'We Built This City' went from number five to number one."

Jose's willingness to spend money on artists was vital to the success of the Starship at this time. Just before the release of the best-selling album, "Knee Deep in the Hoopla," a rival band tried to lure singer Mickey Thomas away. This was a serious threat. Thomas was lead singer, along with Grace Slick, and a crucial member of the band.

"If Mickey had left, we wouldn't have put out those hits," Thompson said flatly.

Thompson went to Menendez and said he needed some cash to keep Thomas from defecting.

"Jose was wise enough to go along," said Thompson. Within two weeks a deal was struck with Thomas to keep him with the Starship. Jose handed over $100,000.

Over the years Thompson dealt with sixteen or seventeen different executives at RCA who struggled to bring respectability back to the label. "Out of all the guys I dealt with, he had some of the biggest success," said Thompson.

He did, however, make one serious blunder, according to his critics. While by this time Jose was taking pains to obliterate his accent and most other ties to his Latin culture—friends routinely called him Joe—he was able to see that the growing number of Latinos in America was an untapped market. His attempt to exploit this market led him to go after the Puerto Rican singing group Menudo.

He was on to something with Menudo because the boom in salsa music was just around the corner. Latin radio was to grow four hundred percent in the eighties. But Jose's ignorance of music, as well as a basic disinterest in the difference between art and artifice, led him astray. His vision of the first Latin superstar was built on an outmoded and discredited stereotype, the manufactured teen idols of the fifties and sixties, who were not so much artists as wavy-haired puppets for an army of Tin Pan Alley songwriters and promotional men. The archetype was the Monkees. Like Menudo, they were a group of cuddly boys with a prefabricated pop sound. Menudo had even less integrity than the Monkees because its membership changed whenever the performers reached age sixteen, considered too old to appeal to the pre-teens that made up the core of the group's audience.

But Jose, who traveled frequently to Latin America in search of talent for RCA, was thrilled by images of thousands of young Menudo fans swaying to a peppy Latin beat. He felt sure the group could be a hit in America too.

So he offered the group, in the words of one RCA veteran, "the moon."

"The word around the office was that he paid close to thirty million, including the jet that belonged to the late Shah of Iran," said Tony Sabournin, who was in charge of regional marketing in RCA's new Latin division.

"He screwed up the whole deal. It was very unrealistic," said John Betancourt, the head of promotion at the time. "I heard they got half the country, airplanes, millions and millions of dollars."

Others scoff at the $30 million figure. "I don't think it was near that," said Steve Wax, Jose's West Coast consultant. Others put the value of the deal at below $10 million.

Whatever the price, Jose was putting his reputation on the line with Menudo and the new Latin presence he was giving RCA. He set up a regional office in Miami to be closer to the booming Latin beat. Menendez built a "classy operation," said Sabournin, providing everyone with cars and expensive suits.

After signing Menudo, Menendez arranged a lavish press party to introduce the band to the American music establishment. The Plaza Hotel event was attended by seven hundred and fifty people, recalled Carlos Barba, president of a Latin television station at the time. After the press conference everyone retired to the ballroom, where Jose and Kitty danced.

"They were a very happy couple," Barba recalled.

Menendez watched over the group's every move. He attended concerts with his sons to chart fan reaction and worked hard to spoon-feed the group's pop pablum to American kids. He also tried to Americanize them. They played the Jerry Lewis telethon, performed the music on a string of B movies, and went on a thirty-five-city tour of the United States.

But Menudo flopped. The generation of young Latins in America might listen to the group on the radio, but they didn't rush out to the record stores to buy their albums. The band's reputation was later sullied by news accounts in New York and

Puerto Rico alleging that several members of Menudo had been sexually abused and plied with drugs and alcohol.

Wax said Jose "would joke about" the abuse allegations connected with Menudo.

Given Jose's need for control—"Define your universe, then control it" was one of his mottos—it was inevitable that he would come into conflict with Summer, the president of the record division.

As Jose began to assert himself, the tensions between the two were so poorly hidden that rumors of the executive suite hostilities circulated freely around the company (Summer declined to talk about Jose's tenure at RCA). The man who suffered most from the infighting was probably John Betancourt, the head of promotion.

"I had a problem," said Betancourt, a brash-sounding man who took pride in his good relations with talent. "Bob Summer signed artists and Jose signed artists. My problem occurred when Jose told me not to work on Bob Summer's projects."

That order displayed an amazing chutzpah, because it showed Jose was willing to take Summer on head to head, without any subterfuge or apparent fear.

The order put Betancourt in an untenable position. He sat down with Jose to try to work things out, telling him he was being put in the middle.

Menendez didn't care. He had no interest in seeing things from Betancourt's point of view. To Jose, showing concern for the other person was a dangerous first step on the way to vulnerability. After that came weakness and defeat.

"Jose was from the school, if you weren't his guy, you were fucking him," Betancourt said. "There was one very nasty meeting where it became very clear that if I didn't screw Bob Summer he was going to ruin my career."

That's when the rumors started, said Betancourt. Menendez told artists and other executives that Betancourt was unethical. "Even Yoko Ono called me and said Menendez went out of his way to slander me."

Jose began firing Betancourt's employees. The Babylonian finger was writing on the wall and its message was clear: Betancourt was on his way out. When he finally left for a job at another label, Jose's campaign against him had worked so well that Betancourt never collected thousands of dollars in severance pay.

After Betancourt left, Jose accused him of stealing RCA

executives for his new bosses. This technique of hounding an enemy virtually to the grave was another Menendez tactic. Betancourt said Jose was not satisfied with firing someone he didn't like—he wanted to destroy the person.

"Jose felt there were no laws for him."

A representative of one of RCA's biggest acts said Menendez was willing to go beyond spreading rumors to get rid of people he didn't like. This man said Jose planted a large quantity of drugs in an unwanted employee's desk, then called the man on the phone. "I can do that anytime I want," Jose boasted.

Cowed, the employee quit flat.

Others doubt this story. They say the assassin's knife in the dark alley was not Jose's way. He didn't mind disemboweling opponents, but he did not act in secret, and he hated anything to do with drugs.

As they did elsewhere, Jose's ethics came under scrutiny at RCA. The accusations were not serious enough to warrant firing or prosecution, but they were the kinds of things that people who disliked Menendez anyway could say were proof of an inability to see a clear line between right and wrong.

One questionable act was his practice of shipping too many albums to record stores. This made the bottom line look good in the short run. But these large numbers would evaporate later, when the unsold records were returned.

The company was forced to take back $25 million in returns in 1986 alone, said this source. "There were unopened boxes everywhere."

Jose was not the first to engage in this practice. "It's not unique, but it's not proper," said one RCA executive.

RCA insiders argued about the relative success of Jose's tenure. Some thought he did a good job bringing more visibility to the label and at least trying new approaches instead of throwing money at failed superstars as his predecessors had done. He also saw the future in Latin music.

"He did an incredible job running RCA," said his friend John Mason. "Jose lived for RCA Records. Everywhere he went, he would say, 'This is the greatest company. It's going to be number one. People would say, 'Don't be ridiculous.' "

As it turned out, people were right.

The bottom line, said Batson, was that whatever Jose Menendez did, the one thing he did not do was turn RCA around. He could not restore the company to the glory days when Elvis and Nipper, RCA's trademark pooch, ruled the pop charts together.

Still, by 1985, at age forty-one, Jose had risen to executive vice president and chief operating officer responsible for worldwide operations for RCA/Ariola. He headed the subsidiary's video, direct marketing, and manufacturing operations. Once again he had reached the executive suite with amazing swiftness. And once again he was headed for a fall.

The Corrected Jose

While in Princeton for the funeral service, Lyle made a point of looking up some of his college friends returning to school for the fall semester.

One of them was Glenn Stevens, a tall, serious boy whose nickname was "Steamboat." He had known Lyle only a few months, but they had shared everything and spent most days together hanging out in Lyle's small dorm room in Gauss Hall.

Glenn knew his friend had to be torn up inside. He tried to find a way to let Lyle know he cared for him and that he wanted to share his pain, but it wasn't easy because Lyle didn't seem to be in any pain.

Finally, on the second afternoon they were together, Glenn asked awkwardly, "How ya doin'?" Lyle pondered the question.

"Well," he said thoughtfully, Glenn recalled, "I've been waiting so long to be in a position like this that the transition came easy."

Glenn was startled by his friend's answer. He had expected some kind of choked expression of loss, maybe even a burst of tears. But Lyle didn't show any of that. Even more surprising was Lyle's reaction when Stevens asked if he was going to try to help the police track down the killers. He was not interested.

"My father wouldn't want me to pursue it," he said carelessly, according to Stevens.

That wasn't like Lyle, Stevens thought. He remembered how Lyle had vowed to get revenge on the student who had turned him in for cheating. He was going to have the boy's legs broken, Stevens remembered.

Only a week after his parents were killed, Lyle seemed ready, and able, to put the murders behind him. A rapid metamorphosis had taken place. Always reserved and even a little shy at times, Lyle was now stronger and more in control. When he walked, he held his head more erect, his manner was more businesslike and abrupt, and his tastes more refined. "His demeanor, his walk, were entirely different," said Sheldon Pierce, who managed the Bedens Brook Country Club in New Jersey, where Lyle began taking meals. "He was more confident."

This was more than the rapid maturing of a person in crisis. As Glenn Stevens noticed, Lyle didn't seem like a person who was heroically bearing up under the weight of a great loss. Just the reverse. He seemed freed in some way. There was a buoyancy to his step and a new cockiness in his dealings with other people.

Eerily, the new Lyle bore an uncanny resemblance to another man of business—his father. Lyle commented on the phenomenon later on. "There was initial hysterics, and then, after that night [of the murders] was over, I just entered into my dad's sort of mode. Like an ESP sort of thing."

As strange a concept as that is, Jose would have understood it and even approved of it. He had certainly planned for it. Lyle was to be the corrected version of Jose.

Business associates recall his exact words on the subject. "You are my son; you must be me."

Jose's life had been messy. He had clawed his way to the top of American business and crushed many people's careers and spirits along the way. Though he did not regret what he had done any more than a lion regrets tearing out the throat of an antelope, he was smart enough to see that there was another way to be. Jose, who read voraciously and understood history, regarded himself as a revolutionary, and a revolutionary always has blood on his hands. It was left to later generations to consolidate the new ruling family's power, and these rulers often went down in history with reputations for great generosity and were much beloved. In Jose's dynasty, Lyle was to be the Sun King, who would be reared perfectly in perfect privacy, with the best tutors and the best discipline. Lyle would attend the right schools, drive the right car, date the right girls, and find his rightful station in life, with Jose's guiding hand at his back all the way.

Training Lyle's mind and soul had been Jose's real avocation, far more so than shepherding the boys' tennis. Far from being an end in itself, athletics was just a part of the training. That's why he lectured his firstborn for hours at a time on history and statecraft, describing in detail, for instance, how he would have crushed the Chinese revolution. Then he quizzed Lyle some more over the dinner table. Lyle was a great experiment, a child raised so carefully and attentively that he would literally be a kind of *ubermensch*, man raised to a higher power.

There were two parts to Lyle's relationship with his dead father. One part of him wanted to be exactly like Jose. The other part of him was in more conflict. This part was struggling to break free of his father. He talked about surpassing everything Jose had done, and sooner than Jose had done it.

John Mason saw this competitive attitude in Lyle. "He wanted not to follow in his father's footsteps but to exceed what his father accomplished," said Mason.

Mason served as a kind of adviser to Lyle and Erik in the weeks after the murders. They all met several times in Mason's office to discuss the boys' future plans. Erik was often in tears. He was torn between going on to college at UCLA, as his parents had wanted, and devoting all his time to tennis, to see if he could break into the professional ranks. "I wish I had my father to help me make these decisions," he moaned.

There seemed to be no ambivalence in Lyle. Now that he was free to pursue his own goals, he wanted to take on the world, just as Jose would have wanted. Within days of his parents' death he was riding around Princeton in a limousine with two bodyguards. He shelved plans to finish college and began planning a business career. He also went on a whirlwind shopping spree that equipped him with all the tools a budding entrepreneur needed to command the respect of other men of business: a flashy car, a rack of designer label clothes, and personal jewelry that communicated status and power.

He was in a hurry. He told friends that a man had only so many years when he had the energy to prove himself, to put in the fifteen-hour days it took to reach his goals. And he had already wasted several years in college, working for a degree he knew was irrelevant.

Just four days after the murders, he and Erik walked into Slavics Jewelers on Santa Monica Boulevard in Century City, a section of Los Angeles just outside Beverly Hills where steel and glass high-rises line streets as wide as rivers. Maryellen Mahar stepped up to help her customers, who wanted to look over some Rolex watches. They discussed metal content and debated the assets of various models, Mahar recalled later. The reason she could remember it so well is that a sale like this one didn't walk in every day.

Even in West Los Angeles, "one doesn't often have a single sale for $14,000 or thereabouts," Mahar said.

The two young men finally selected an eighteen-carat gold Gent's Rolex President that cost $11,250. To go with that, they added a stainless steel Submariner, and another stainless steel Rolex.

Then the brothers grabbed a few money clips and presented Jose Menendez's American Express card for payment. Mahar recognized the name immediately. Though every day in Los Angeles seemed to bring some fresh outrage to be digested and forgotten in time for the next news cycle, the story of the Menendez murders had caught the public's attention like no other recent case.

While the transaction was being completed, Lyle asked to use the phone. The sales clerk recalled the conversation because it was so curious. She plunked the phone down on the counter and listened as Lyle called his uncle Carlos and said he planned to wear the watch to a memorial service scheduled the next day.

This was the service in Hollywood. Some of the town's elite would be there, and Lyle wanted to impress them. Carlos didn't like the idea.

"I don't think the relatives will understand," he said loud enough for Mahar to overhear on the other side of the counter.

Disappointed, the young man hung up and concluded the transaction. Generously Lyle asked his younger brother if he wanted the gold Rolex. Erik declined.

"My dad didn't like that, you know, it was showy," he said later.

Money funding their shopping spree came from several sources, including Jose's personal life insurance policy, which was $650,000. Additionally the Menendez estate, valued at approximately $14 million, could be used to obtain bank loans, even though the estate itself would not clear probate court in Santa Monica for months.

The main assets of the estate were the fourteen-acre property in Calabasas and the Beverly Hills mansion. Subtracting loans against the homes, both properties had a value of $5.7 million.

Also, Jose had about 330,000 shares of LIVE Entertainment Inc., which had been selling in the $20 range. Finally, there was a large personal inventory, which included automobiles and antiques.

But when loans and estate taxes were subtracted, Lyle and Erik stood to inherit not anywhere near $14 million. The figure was closer to $2 million each.

This was no small inheritance, but it fell far short of the largesse friends said Lyle and Erik expected. One friend said Erik expected to inherit $90 million. He and Lyle were supposedly convinced their father had hidden $75 million in a Swiss bank account. Neither Erik nor Lyle explained how Jose Menendez could possibly have amassed that kind of fortune. It just seemed reasonable that their father would have accumulated far more than $14 million. Nobody believed more wholeheartedly in Jose's legend than his two sons.

During the same week that they purchased the Rolexes, Lyle and Erik met with LIVE executives at company headquarters in Van Nuys to go over assets they might receive from the company.

Their uncles Carlos Baralt and Brian Andersen were on hand as they hashed out Jose's financial situation. The subject of a $5 million life insurance policy that Jose was to have obtained through LIVE was brought up. "I'm not sure you are aware of this," began Roger Smith, Jose's second in command at LIVE, a heavy-set man who parted his sandy hair in the middle. Because Jose had never taken the physical, the policy was not valid.

A silence ensued. Then Erik asked in a level voice: "And the $15 million policy in favor of the company. Was that in order?"

It was. LIVE had taken out what is known as a key man policy on their prized executive. Such insurance policies were not uncommon among big corporations, who used them as a hedge against exactly the sort of unexpected tragedy that befell Jose. Somehow he had never gotten around to having the doctor over to check him out for the other policy.

"That anything could happen to Jose never occurred to Jose," said a company official.

This incident may have caused hard feelings among the Menendez clan, especially since the $15 million payout gave LIVE its biggest quarter since the firm's inception. Some family members who had been ready to blame the mob for Jose's death began hinting that anyone interested in finding his killers should look among his supposed friends and associates at LIVE.

In the immediate aftermath of the murders, however, LIVE did not abandon the brothers. The company paid the tab for expensive hotel suites in Beverly Hills. The company also picked up the bill for Lyle's bodyguards when he flew to Princeton for his parents' funeral.

Richard Wenskoski, a former New Jersey police officer who was manager of investigations for the D.B. Kelly agency, spent virtually every hour of the day with Lyle in late August and early September, riding from one shop to another in suburban New Jersey. Lyle reclined in the back of the limousine and chatted with friends on the cellular phone like the corporate lion he was already becoming.

One of the first stops was the John Wood Porsche dealership just outside Princeton, fronting a small forest on traffic-choked U.S. 1. The arrival of Lyle's limousine and bodyguards attracted attention, but the sight did not particularly startle anyone because employees are used to young, rich athletes cruising in with entourages to shop for top-of-the-line transportation.

Lyle wandered among the sports cars until a silver 1989 Cabriolet caught his eye. It was a special edition model commemorating the German automaker's twenty-fifth anniversary. Porsche built only three hundred of the convertibles for sale in the United States.

Lyle drove the car several times before he made up his mind. He asked for a discount, and a few thousand dollars were knocked off the price because the car had been driven some.

The final price tag was $64,273. Lyle paid cash.

Now that he had a flashy car and jewelry that would make anybody sit up and take notice, Lyle set out to enrich his wardrobe. He had always been a good dresser, unlike Erik, who Kitty used to laughingly call a "fashion flop" in his mismatched sports jackets and preppie shirts. What Lyle wanted now was a different kind of style, something that communicated grace and power. With Wenskoski trailing behind him, watching for assassins, Lyle walked into one shop and bought a thousand dollars' worth of shoes in a few minutes. On another excursion he selected three thousand dollars' worth of undergarments, socks, suits, ties, and shirts.

He bought five expensive silk shirts—at $89 apiece—in the space of about fifteen minutes at Tom Tailor, a clothing shop on Princeton's Palmer Square.

Michael Schmidt, the assistant store manager, remembered Lyle as cocky. "He tried on the shirt in every color—beige, mint, olive, black, and lavender—right in the middle of the store before a mirror, and not in the fitting room, to see if they suited him."

Then Lyle sauntered behind the sales counter and helped himself to candy in a bowl next to the cash register that was meant for employees.

"That's kind of arrogant, isn't it?" Schmidt asked.

Lyle had always been on the cocky side, but he was developing a distinctly imperious way about him. A friend whose mother had been a waitress chastised Lyle in a restaurant one day for being so nasty to the server. Lyle said his father taught him that.

"They're here to serve me," he explained.

Occasionally Lyle would have the limousine veer away from the Princeton shopping district and head off to Cranbury, where his uncle Carlos lived. Lyle told Wenskoski he needed more money. Though the two brothers were the only beneficiaries of the will, Carlos Baralt was the executor of the estate and thus controlled the fortune, something that greatly irritated Lyle. He told friends he didn't want anyone controlling him anymore.

The bodyguard walked him to the door of the Baralt home and waited outside while Lyle went in to talk to his uncle. Then, fortified once more with cash, they went on their merry way. And merry it was, Wenskoski said.

Less than two weeks after his parents' death, Lyle struck Wenskoski as "happy-go-lucky, carefree. As a matter of fact, the more money he spent, it seemed the happier he was."

He suddenly broke off his shopping on August 31. He told Wenskoski he had to fly out to California on an emergency. It was "something concerning a will on a computer," Wenskoski learned.

Lyle was gone only a day. When Wenskoski picked him up at the Newark airport the next day, he asked how things had gone. "Everything worked out fine," Lyle said happily, once more in the grip of credit card fever.

During the time Wenskoski was guarding him, the two men stayed in adjacent rooms at the Hyatt Hotel in Princeton. One night as he was dressing for dinner, Lyle noticed the bodyguard slipping his gun into his holster. He asked about it and Wenskoski showed him his Browning 9mm, 13-shot chrome pistol.

"Can you get ballistics off a pistol?" the young man asked.

Sure, Wenskoski replied. Lyle asked how ballistics analysis is done. Wenskoski explained that the barrel of every gun has markings inside that are unique to that gun. The inside of the barrel is machined to make the bullet come out spinning. So every gun with a machined, or rifled, barrel leaves its imprint on the projectile. If one can retrieve a bullet, it can be matched up with the gun.

The process is just as effective in tracing weapons as fingerprints are in tracking down crooks.

"Can you get ballistics off a shotgun?" Lyle asked.

No, Wenskoski said. Shotguns have a smooth bore in the barrel. Satisfied, Lyle went off to eat.

Wenskoski's job ended abruptly on September 4, when Lyle told him he was no longer in danger. His uncle, he said, had contacted a mob figure and some sort of a deal had been made. Lyle didn't explain how his uncle, a soft-spoken gray-haired businessman who lived in a small house in a New Jersey suburb, would go about contacting the mob, or what deal he could possibly have made to remove a sentence of death from his nephew's head.

The fact was, Lyle had gone up to New York with Stevens to meet the mob, or the closest thing around. Lyle believed the man he met through Stevens was a real mobster because of the way he talked—"very rough"—the way he dressed, the fact that he drove around in a Lincoln Town Car, and the way people who came to see him at the Italian restaurant where he hung out hugged and kissed him.

It was just like in the movies, which was Lyle's only familiarity with the Mafia, as with many other things. Lyle had gone to see the man because he wanted to get a message to the organization. He was worried that the mob had heard all the speculation about the Mafia being involved in Jose's death and might think Lyle had fueled it. Fearing they might try to come after him, Lyle told the guy with the Italian name that he was not cooperating with the police and he hoped the man might get the message out so that no other Italians with difficult names came looking for him.

"Could you let people know?" he asked.

His fear that the Mafia would get its feelings hurt may seem silly, but it showed how simple and naive Lyle was in some ways. Jose had for years regulated Lyle's life to such an extent that nearly every hour in the day was accounted for. There had been no time for normal outside activities, and as a result Lyle had missed vast storehouses of ordinary, mundane information. He often seemed to substitute movie scripts for life experiences. In the movies the mob didn't let insults go unpunished, so Lyle felt he had reason to fear retaliation.

Lyle's spending didn't stop with Wenskoski's departure, and it began to concern his relatives. If he hadn't changed his mind and backed out of some real estate deals he had contemplated early on, he would have managed to burn his way through $700,000 in a matter of weeks. That was startling enough, but his advisers were just as concerned about the foolishness of some expenditures, such as Lyle's penchant for flying first-class.

"My father flew first-class," Lyle explained quietly, holding Jose up, as usual, as the ultimate arbiter of good business sense.

"But when he did it, somebody else was paying" was the reply, referring to Jose's business trips. "When he went on vacation, he flew coach."

"Oh," said Lyle.

Even though Lyle's family was concerned about the amount he was spending, they were not overly troubled because he had decided to go out and blow a little cash. They felt a young man who suddenly had become wealthy should indulge himself a little. After all, this was a man who had had a bank card when he was a teenager.

Lyle told an interviewer after the murders that the spending was "consistent with the way I've lived most of my life. I like quality things. If there is a car that I like, and it amuses me, then I will spend a little money on that. That's the kind of person I am. I don't feel it's ostentatious, I just enjoy it more."

His family, particularly his two uncles Carlos and Brian, also felt that Lyle's spending was his way of dealing with the grief of his parents' deaths. While some people were shocked by the lack of emotion he displayed over the murders, his relatives knew that he kept his feelings bottled up. In his family's eyes, using up money was the one way he could express feelings that his father had taught him to hold inside the way a warrior does. Even in the most casual family pictures Lyle had held his jaw tightly together, as if the mere act of smiling would give too much of himself away. His eyes were set close and as dark as oil.

This emotional blankness unnerved some people outside the family. Erik's friends often felt uncomfortable around him. "Just to look at him gave you a cold feeling," said a girlfriend. It wasn't that they felt he hated them, but that he had absolutely no feelings about them, not even that basic commonality one human being shares with another simply because they are members of the same species.

But his family insisted outsiders did not know the real Lyle, who had a sense of humor and an abiding love of family.

After outfitting himself with the proper clothing and transportation, Lyle felt ready to mount his assault on corporate America. He and his father had always planned to go into business together, but now that was impossible. Lyle would carry on alone. Well, not quite alone.

He gathered some close friends around him and pressed them into service as officers of a new company, Menendez Investment Enterprises, located in a 2,160-square-foot office complex in a Princeton shopping mall, Lawrence Commons. He rented the place for $3,000 a month and filled it with the right furniture, expensive wooden desks and file cabinets and the like.

Somehow, though, he never moved in. The office sat unused as a testament to Lyle's flair for creating the proper setting, if not for substance. It was as though he were a preadolescent playing a game of big business—dialing the phones and putting his feet up on the big oak desk—in dad's office while he was out. The only difference was, the money was real.

The friends he asked to come into business with him were part of a small group of campus athletes, several of whom had themselves run afoul of the authorities at Princeton.

The group included Stevens, a hockey player named Greg Guest, a footloose Californian named Donovan Goodreau, and a boy who had just returned to Princeton in the second semester of 1989, following a year-long suspension. Lyle, who was ranked sixth on the varsity tennis team, was the unofficial leader of the group.

"Those were Lyle's groupies," said a Menendez family member. "Glenn the most stable of the group by far. Greg was the arrogant guy. They were all lined up by Lyle's charisma, a tremendous amount of charisma," said that man.

"Lyle was good at establishing a power relationship," observed David Bros, a short, preppy-looking boy with an economics background who became secretary of the corporation.

Lyle's power over others derived from his ability to be in absolute control of himself at all times. But along with this rigid self-control, he had a sympathetic ear and ready advice for young men who were having problems or felt uncertain about their future. Lyle was able to draw upon a lifetime of aphorisms culled from the personal improvement philosophy of his father, and he used these to help and encourage his friends. Shored up by Jose's absolute confidence in him, Lyle was not consumed by inner doubts about either himself or his future, at least not outwardly. This was why he was especially good at imposing himself on weak and needy people, who found in Lyle the missing parent they had lost in a divorce, or the older brother they always wanted.

Bros especially noticed how effectively Lyle manipulated his brother. "Whenever the two were together, Erik was totally submissive," Bros said.

Lyle's business team was a strange one, not only because they were so young and thoroughly inexperienced. None had known him more than a few months. And none of his team had any clear business skills.

Lyle asked Glenn to be chief executive officer of MIE. Stevens said he was at first hesitant to sign on. He wanted to stay in school and get his degree. His family was not rich enough to indulge him if he decided to throw away his Princeton career.

Lyle offered a six-figure salary. When Glenn was still uncertain, Lyle took his friend under his wing and offered him a little advice. "People who are most successful are the ones who take chances," he said, according to Glenn's account.

It might have been the old man himself speaking with Lyle's voice. Jose believed that a man must overcome his fear or he would never crawl out of his hole and see the wider world.

Lyle sweetened the deal by setting Glenn up in the condominium outside town that Jose had bought for him just before his death, as an inducement to return to Princeton in the fall. Glenn finally caved in and agreed to take a year off from school and go to work for Lyle.

He found out that being Lyle's employee had its costs. The boss began ordering Glenn about and referring to him in the third person when Glenn was in the room. "That's what I keep Glenn around for," he joked one day about some menial job that needed doing, Glenn said.

With his team in place, Lyle mounted his assault on corporate America. Lyle moved on several fronts at once. He went to work on a land-development deal in California's San Fernando Valley, as well as a mini-mall venture in Hamilton Township, New Jersey. Every day was a blur of business meetings. On a typical day Lyle arose early, went to see a lawyer, then an architect, then another lawyer in the afternoon. "In a way," said Bros, "he was kind of a square. It was all business, business, business."

Lyle was not afraid of making enemies. "Let them sue me," he said in his best corporate shark manner if someone advised that he could get into trouble over an ill-planned deal.

He didn't take well to advice anyway, his friends learned. "What are you trying to tell me?" he would snap if he didn't like what he was hearing. It was a signal to shut up, and one more bit of evidence that Lyle would never again take orders from anyone. He had had enough of that.

"Don't ever tell him what to do," Glenn Stevens warned Bros.

None of the land-development deals came through. At the last moment he backed away from committing himself.

Lyle's long-cherished dream was to run a restaurant. That was something he used to talk about doing with his father. Now that Jose was dead, Lyle began to look around Princeton for opportunities. His eye settled on Teresa's Pizza, which did a bustling takeout business on Nassau Street, across from the big flagstone gates of the university. Lyle strolled in one day and brashly informed Venanzio Momo, the thirty-year-old co-owner of Teresa's, that he wanted to buy his business.

"Money talks," replied Momo, a stocky, fast-talking easterner, more New Yorker than Princetonian.

Lyle invited Momo to dinner at one of Princeton University's many eating clubs, each of which had its own flag flying. Lyle had briefly stolen them the year before, his uncle said, in what the relative regarded as a college prank. Dial Lodge was located in a crumbling, musty-smelling mansion that was noisy with the sound of heavy young feet tramping up and down the creaky wood staircase. Momo found Lyle to be cocky, but "not any more or less than any other entrepreneur with $500,000 in his pocket."

Instead of buying Momo out, Lyle tried to get him to join his team as a consultant. The talks went on for a while, then Lyle turned Momo over to his associates, Stevens and Bros.

The talks continued. All kinds of ideas were kicked around, but nothing concrete developed. Momo began to feel that these young men didn't know what they were doing. "I ended up feeling like a kid in a man's world. I felt [Lyle] was somewhat lacking real proportion and dimension in life."

Soon afterward the relationship went downhill when Momo learned that Lyle was standing outside his shop trying to lure away his drivers. Lyle had decided to invest in a competing restaurant, and he wanted to expand its delivery business. So he parked himself on the sidewalk outside Teresa's with a wad of $100 bills, which he was using as scratch paper to write down the names of Momo's drivers, Momo said.

Momo was enraged. He confronted Lyle. He called him "a real asshole."

"That's not the way to establish good rapport with your neighbor," Momo said later. "It's cutthroat."

Momo's drivers were not impressed by Lyle or his wad. He also offended them with an offhand racist remark that revealed his class-consciousness, one said. Trying to impress them with how much better he would treat them, he said "we have Mexicans" to do the menial chores around the restaurant.

Lyle decided to invest in Chuck's Spring Street Cafe, his favorite childhood eatery and a popular stop for the university crowd. Chuck's was an informal shop designed like a cafeteria, which served spicy chicken wings—a batch of one hundred for $26.50—and salads.

When the deal was consummated, Lyle told a local weekly newspaper, the *Princeton Packet*, that he had tasted his first buffalo wing at Chuck's when he was in the eighth grade at the Princeton Day School. It was love at first bite.

"I had my first wing and I could barely eat another—it was so hot. . . . But it's an addictive taste."

He also pointed out, in a bizarre aside, that the restaurant was located "only a few hundred yards from where my mother is buried." His parents' ashes were located at Princeton Cemetery, also the final resting place of Aaron Burr and Grover Cleveland.

Lyle apparently didn't realize how odd this sounded. His parents' ashes were just another landmark in his soon-to-be storied life. He understood coincidence. He seemed to have a harder time with tragedy.

Lyle paid $550,000 for Chuck's, which Momo called "ridiculous." It was worth maybe $200,000, he said.

The family tried to intervene. Carlos Baralt asked John Mason to talk to Lyle. Mason dutifully advised Lyle against buying Chuck's, saying "the restaurant business is not a good business to speculate in." Mason spoke from the unpleasant experience of having once owned a restaurant.

Lyle thanked him for the advice but ignored it. "Lyle Menendez thinks he can succeed at anything," Mason said. "His father told him he could succeed at everything, and he had a father who could and did succeed at everything."

Carlos Baralt authorized financing for the purchase in the hope it would give focus to Lyle's chaotic activities.

Lyle's key employee was the restaurant's longtime manager,

a short, earnest Greek named Gus Tangalos. When he talked to Gus about the business, he frequently brought up his father's name. "I wish I could have brought you out [to Beverly Hills], so you could see how one could talk so much less and mean much more," he said. Tangalos recalled Lyle challenging his brother to recall quotes from their father, the way old pols reminisce about the words of a departed party leader.

Lyle wanted to put his stamp on the business immediately. He expanded the home-delivery hours from midnight to 1:00 A.M. and changed the name to "Mr. Buffalo's." Other merchants thought it was crazy to sacrifice the name recognition built up by Chuck's over many years. "In this industry, you pay for the goodwill," Momo said. "It didn't make any sense to me."

"Lyle was on an ego trip," said one of his friends.

He had business cards printed up with the Mr. Buffalo's logo on them. But a snag developed over the restaurant's outdoor sign. Because the restaurant was in a historic district called Princeton Borough, any changes in the appearance of the building had to be approved by the town's Preservation Review Committee. Months after the purchase, the sign had still not been changed.

After buying Chuck's, Lyle announced plans to open a second outlet in a nearby Princeton-area plaza. He was also studying locations in Westwood, near the UCLA campus, and in New Brunswick, the home of Rutgers, the New Jersey state university.

But Lyle was ahead of himself. Chuck's was losing money, according to Bros. One reason was that Lyle was allowing his friends to freeload off him. They would come in and load up their trays with wings and then sit for hours eating and drinking, all on the house. Gus finally got fed up and dragged Lyle downstairs into the basement one afternoon. "The honeymoon is over," he told him.

Lyle didn't like what he heard, but the next day he acceded. "You're the boss," he said.

One day Lyle's red Alfa Romeo, the one his parents had given him as a high school graduation present, was dented in an accident in front of the restaurant. Lyle was crushed when he saw it, Tangalos remembered.

"This was my father's graduation present," he groaned. "I'm not supposed to take this car out. I wanted to give it to my son."

Family was tremendously important to him, Tangalos saw. At

the same time, though, he could be shockingly disrespectful. Bros was amazed when Lyle made a joke of his father's death.

"Maybe that's his way of dealing with" the loss, said Bros. "Or maybe he doesn't care."

Lyle honored his parents' memories in the abstract, as admirable people who had helped him prepare for his life's work. But he seemed to have less feeling for them on a more conventional level, as the people who had raised him. It was as though he understood the concept of parents, but had no idea what it felt like to have any himself.

Erik's behavior at times revealed a similar dissonance. Not long after the murders, he asked an old high school friend out on a date. She warned him she would have to be back early. "I don't have to worry about that anymore," he joked, according to the young woman.

There were even times when Erik and Lyle seemed to think their parents' deaths had a positive side. They were a kind of good omen that promised success. "All great men had no parents," Erik is said to have told a friend. He mentioned Adolf Hitler.

Theories

While Lyle and Erik were trying to get on with their lives and fulfill the greatness their father had predicted for them, the men and women at the Beverly Hills Police Department were trying to organize what looked like an extremely difficult, if not impossible, investigation. On the front lines of the inquiry were detectives Zoeller and his partner, Tom Linehan, a dour-looking detective with a quiet manner but an observant eye.

Zoeller and Linehan tried to do their jobs the way they had learned them, using methodical, unimaginative police work to eliminate suspects and run the killers to ground.

But this was not an ordinary case, and the pressure for an arrest built rapidly, despite department attempts to shield the investigating officers from outside pressure. Though the common wisdom, and the opinion of some organized crime experts, held this was a mob hit, Zoeller and Linehan weren't so sure. There were lots of other possibilities in this case. Jose had had his share of enemies. Everybody, it seemed, had a horror story about Jose. He was abusive in the boardroom, aggressive on the tennis court, and even social gatherings at home could turn nasty. Once he had ended up in a wrestling match with Kitty's brother Brian, according to another family member, during a chess game. Brian had accused Jose of moving his pieces around when he went to the bathroom, and Jose lost his temper.

Zoeller realized the problem wasn't too few suspects but too many. Calls were coming in to the department every day, suggesting entirely new avenues of investigation, some crazy and some intriguing. None could be dismissed.

One rumor suggested Jose had been running drugs to South America. That's why he had opened the RCA office in Miami and spent so much time scouting south-of-the-border artists. That's how he got rich, according to this theory. Nobody could amass a $14 million fortune on the strength of Jose's résumé alone.

Another wild theory was that Castro had sent some thugs up to snuff out Menendez because the Cuban dictator had heard of Jose's plans to move back to Florida someday and run for public office. "His main goal," said Erik, "was to get Castro out of Cuba and make Cuba a territory of the United States, like Puerto Rico."

Gang graffiti found on an alley wall behind the mansion suggested yet another avenue of inquiry. Almost two years earlier, Erik had suffered three broken bones in a run-in with the members of a San Fernando Valley gang. This had been followed by threatening phone calls at home and reports that strange cars were prowling the Calabasas neighborhood where the Menendezes were then living in a rented house, awaiting the renovation of the fourteen-acre estate.

Still, it strained credulity to imagine that the bloodbath in Beverly Hills was due to an old gang vendetta.

Two men whose names were high on every list of suspects were record company mogul Morris Levy and Noel Bloom, a legendary figure in the shadowy world of adult entertainment. Both men had had business dealings with Menendez, and both were said by law enforcement authorities to be mob-connected.

Levy was a self-made millionaire who had owned a string of nightclubs in the forties and fifties, then become president of New York-based Roulette Records, a well-known hit factory in the fifties heyday of rock and roll.

A federal court jury in Camden, New Jersey, convicted Levy in 1988 of conspiring to extort money from John LaMonte, a Philadelphia-area record distributor. Levy was sentenced to ten years in prison and fined $200,000.

FBI documents filed in the case said government agencies believed Levy had been involved with organized crime for twenty years. According to court records and law enforcement officials, Levy was an associate of Vincent (The Chin) Gigante, the reputed boss of the Genovese crime family, one of New York's five major organized crime groups.

Levy maintained a sense of humor about his supposed mob ties. "The only thing I know about organized crime is my five ex-wives," he said in an interview in October 1986 with writer William K. Knoedelseder, Jr.

Not long before his death, Jose's company spent $40.5 million to purchase from Levy the BeckZack Corp., which owned Strawberries, a ninety-store record chain in New England, New York, and Philadelphia.

In some quarters it was said Jose fleeced Levy, making the deal on highly favorable terms because Levy needed cash to cover his legal expenses.

As speculation about Levy grew in the media after the killings, LIVE issued a public statement saying the Strawberries deal was clean. "Given Mr. Levy's previous history, the due diligence process for the purchase of Strawberries was unusually careful and exhaustive," the company statement said.

Besides questioning Menendez family members about the deal, Zoeller went to organized crime experts to check out Levy. There didn't seem to be much there. Levy and Jose had never even met during the negotiations, and Jose had only got involved directly, as was typical for him, at the very end when the deal was nailed down. Company insiders disputed allegations that Menendez took advantage of Levy. Some said he paid more than necessary.

Bloom, who owned the company that eventually became LIVE Entertainment, was a more colorful figure. A slender, forty-seven-year-old man who was laid-back California from his office uniform of jeans and a sports shirt to the long, styled hair that nestled against his shoulders like feathery plumage, he was Jose's spiritual opposite. Whereas Jose was buttoned down and conservative, Bloom was flamboyant. He was partial to mirrored shades, drove a Ferrari, and is said to have stocked his private tank with $50,000 worth of exotic fish.

Their relations were strained almost from the day that Jose Menendez was brought in to take control of the finances of Bloom's company in 1986. They were locked in a nasty court battle right up to the day of Jose's murder.

If it had not been for the fact that Bloom's business was so repulsive to Jose, he might have admired the man's vision, for Bloom was a true innovator who had been brought into the sin game by his own father.

Bernard Bloom had begun publishing girlie magazines, or in the trade, Nudie Cuties, in the fifties. His son, Noel, eventually joined the family business. "He talked me into coming to work for him," Bloom said in an interview. "My father got me into the adult business. My mother worked there too," he laughed.

The arrival of the videocassette recorder in the mid-seventies would change American viewing habits, and Bloom was among the first to see its potential for the sex business.

"I said, 'This has got to be the future.'"

Noel Bloom transferred his collection of 8mm films onto videotape. His company, Cinema Classics, became one of the largest in the sex business. No longer did a working man need to satisfy his appetite for vicarious sex in some squalid inner-city theater, with the attendant risks of becoming a crime victim. He could go down to the local video store, rent *Debbie Does Dallas*, and take it home for the night.

The conversion from film to videotape also meant X-rated movies could be made far more cheaply, and as a result video pioneers such as Bloom amassed fortunes. He lived in Hidden Hills, a place of lavish estates so removed from the rest of the world that there are no streetlights in town. One set of offices leased by one of Bloom's companies in Woodland Hills contained a Jacuzzi large enough for ten, a full bar, and a room with a ballet barre in it.

Easy money always attracts the eye of the mob, which began leaning on the porn brokers for payoffs in the late 1960s, according to a 1980 Pennsylvania crime commission investigation. Eventually the Gambino, Galante, DeCavalcante, and Colombo crime families became involved.

The U.S. Department of Justice in 1986 identified Bloom as an associate of Michael Zaffarano, a capo in the Galante family and the family's "West Coast representative."

Bloom firmly denied any involvement with mobsters.

"You can't confuse the fact that there are a lot of jerks out there, a lot of jerks on the street. Those are people who gave the adult business a bad name," he said. These jerks, as he put it, were not real mobsters, just punks and hustlers trying to make a few bucks by throwing a scare into some people.

As Bloom became more successful, he began to distance himself from pornography. He broke his operation into two parts, one distributing the X-rated material, while the other began bidding for film rights to mainstream movies. The heart of his mainstream operation was International Video Entertainment (IVE).

But trying to operate in the big-budget film world was an expensive, dangerous game. An estimated $20 million in debt piled up on him in the mid-eighties. Asked later if he had been headed for bankruptcy, he paused. "I don't want to think so," he said. But "if you read all the articles and all the things [Menendez] said, you'd say yes."

After meeting Peter Hoffman while bidding on the Roman Polanski film *Pirates*, Bloom sold a 25 percent interest in his company to Carolco for a $25 million line of credit. He was to remain on the board of directors with Sylvester Stallone.

"Part of the deal was that they would bring in a financial person, which I was to approve," Bloom recalled.

That person turned out to be Jose Menendez. Jose was available because he had lost out in the corporate power struggle at RCA. He had been angling for years to take the top job, but in December 1985 Elliot Goldman, an individual with considerable experience in the record industry, was brought in as president and chief executive of RCA/Ariola.

"Jose was shocked," said John Mason. He was "put in a position with no place to go."

Goldman decentralized management and repudiated Jose's business practices. He believed "the record industry had moved beyond shipping a lot of product and having to take it back."

Miserable, Jose called Mason and said he was thinking of moving west. Mason put him in touch with Peter Hoffman, who offered him the job as financial manager at IVE. When he left RCA, said a family member, Jose parachuted out with $500,000.

Bloom at first found Menendez to be charming and an easy man to like. "He seemed like he had a hell of a background. He was a nice guy. We spent a day or so together."

The glow did not last long. Menendez quickly set to work trimming the fat he perceived in the Bloom operation. As was his wont, he trimmed with a cleaver, slashing the company payroll from 500 employees to 175.

Longtime associate Ralph King said IVE "was a travesty. We let go a lot of employees because it didn't take a rocket scientist to see that the next largest [video] company only had fifty employees."

Bloom was powerless to stop the carnage. "I couldn't run around the company protecting everybody," he said. "He would find a way to show that those people were inadequate for any reason. Everything we did before was wrong, and everything he was doing was right. And the people that worked for me were totally humiliated."

Bloom tried to mollify Menendez in hopes of moderating his

policies. He offered to help him find a good deal on a car for Lyle. "He wanted to do it on his own," Bloom shrugged. "He paid more."

Menendez wasn't satisfied with improving the bottom line. He wanted to take control of the creative end of the company. That was the area that Bloom felt was his territory. Bloom talked to Hoffman, who reassured him. "It'll work out," he said.

It didn't. Jose demanded that the videocassette-duplicating plant, Creative Video Services, stop doing work for adult companies. "Within a few months we had them go somewhere else," Bloom said.

Asked whether any of the porn companies might have been angry at being dropped, Bloom demurred. "They weren't asked today to leave tomorrow. They were given enough time" to find other duplicating plants to do the work.

Lyle Menendez said in an interview that his father mounted a personal campaign against Bloom himself, taking his office and his company car. Bloom denied that, but admitted that Menendez "wanted everything his way, right, wrong, or indifferent."

Finally Bloom had his fill. "I said a couple of times, 'I can't work this way. Buy me out.' It got to the point, life is too short."

On January 8, 1987, *Daily Variety* announced that Bloom was leaving and that Carolco was taking over the remainder of the company. No terms of the deal were announced, although it was understood that Carolco had agreed to take on Bloom's debt and pay him $1.4 million.

When the final $500,000 installment was not paid, however, Bloom filed suit.

Lyle said Jose felt Bloom "had overvalued the company. So he felt he didn't have a legal right to ask for what he did."

Bloom interpreted the move differently. "It was something that was done, I think, to be nasty."

The suit went to trial shortly before Jose was killed. Despite the fact that the money involved was not significant, Jose Menendez took time to testify in court against Bloom.

"During the court case my father could be somewhat sarcastic," said Lyle. "Obviously he was a brilliant man, a brilliant negotiator. I've been told it was pretty vicious the way he belittled Noel, and basically made him look like someone who wasn't credible. And the other guy [Bloom] got tongue-tied and really embarrassed, really embarrassed."

Lyle relished talking about the way his father had humiliated the other man. He said Jose had been scheduled to testify again when he was killed.

"It's my belief [Bloom] didn't want to go through it again, and he was tired of it and it was a personal thing," said Lyle.

He said his father was not a cautious man, "but he probably would have been more cautious if he had known how Noel was feeling. So I just think Noel decided to settle the score."

Bloom vehemently denied having anything to do with the murders. He pointed out that he had won the lawsuit. A superior court referee in deciding the case accused Jose's company of a "squeeze play" against Bloom. The only phase of the case remaining was the appeal, and there was no need for Jose to testify again.

Only a few days after the murders, Bloom received a call from an associate of Jose's on his car phone stating that Carolco wanted to settle the suit. "He said they felt bad about all the bad publicity I was receiving over this," Bloom said. "The only way they felt they could make it up was to end the lawsuit."

Bloom wasn't sure this was a good idea. "This is not going to look very good," he said. "maybe we should wait." But Carolco would not hear of it. "They rushed it through. It was done within days," Bloom said.

As Bloom feared, this only increased the speculation about his possible role in the killings.

Because of the split between him and Menendez, Bloom was expecting to hear from Beverly Hills police detectives soon after the murders. But days went by and he heard nothing except third-party rumors that the cops were asking a lot of other people questions about him. He grew increasingly nervous, fearing that the cops were taking their time coming to see him because they were building a case against him.

When Zoeller called him for an appointment two weeks after the deaths, Bloom was almost happy.

"What took you so long? I was feeling bad," Bloom said when Zoeller walked into the Beverly Hills law office of John Weston, Bloom's attorney.

He was anxious to explain that he had no idea why Menendez had been killed. He didn't like having his name in the papers. He had kids now. In fact, he had been moving so far into the mainstream that his company had entered a winning float in the Rose Parade a couple of years before.

The interview lasted only an hour. Surprisingly, the detectives seemed mainly interested in anything Bloom could tell them about Menendez's personal history. Bloom did not feel that they were particularly suspicious of him.

"They didn't even ask me what I was doing that night" of the murders, said Bloom.

He said he felt bad when he heard about the killings. Kitty, he said pointedly, was "a very nice lady."

There was another reason for police to consider a possible link to the pornography business. It involved the mysterious white hatchback that had been seen in front of the Menendez mansion the night of the murders.

A similar car had been seen at the scene of another murder notable for its violent excess. Only a few weeks before the Menendezes were slaughtered, a small-time X-rated filmmaker named Teddy Snyder had been shot nine times on a quiet residential street in the San Fernando Valley.

His pregnant wife, Sharon, said all he told her before leaving was that he was going out for a drive.

Snyder was no big fish in the world of sex. With his medallions, flashy jewelry, and broad New York accent, he was a caricature of the stereotypical skin dealer. He and his cigar-smoking pals were legendary for being the first to arrive and the last to leave the big adult video conventions held every year in Las Vegas.

But Snyder was known to organized crime experts because the company he worked for in the valley, Video Cassette Recordings, Inc., did business with a man identified by federal prosecutors as a high-ranking member of the Lucchese crime family.

Police on both cases began consulting with each other, trying to sort out whether Snyder and Menendez could ever have crossed paths. Some law enforcement officials speculated there could be a power struggle going on in the pornography business. Perhaps Jose had got caught up in it when he called a halt to the duplicating work LIVE was doing for adult entertainment companies.

But as much trouble as Jose had stomaching Bloom, it was difficult to imagine him in the same room with Snyder.

Zoeller was mostly a by-the-book kind of cop. His manner was straightforward, and he didn't play games in interviews. But he also had an imagination and a sense of humor, though his jokes tended to be a bit on the corny side. So when he sought out Pete Wiere, Jose and Kitty's Calabasas friend, Zoeller tossed in an oddball question: "First impression, what was your reaction when you heard about the murders?"

"I have no basis for this, but I wonder if the boys did it," Wiere replied, surprised at himself.

Zoeller also was surprised. He asked Pete why he thought that. Pete couldn't explain it. It made absolutely no sense. Lyle and Erik seemed so loving with their parents. The only thing that kept going through his mind was that he had always thought Lyle and Erik seemed almost too good to be true. Too polite, too deferential to adults. Something seemed off about that. He had known some other kids who were as well mannered as the Menendez boys. In every case, when they were out of their parents' sight, they became wild hell raisers, as though they were spitting at the world.

On September 17, Zoeller and Linehan flew to New Jersey to interview the brothers' uncle Carlos Baralt and aunt Terry. Seated in the living room in Cranberry, Zoeller complained that he had not been able to talk to Erik and Lyle. They were not returning his calls. He was frustrated and, though he didn't say this, becoming a little suspicious. Terry, a kindly, plump woman with short, curly hair, said, well, Erik is upstairs. She went up and brought him down. Then Lyle drove up with his friend Greg Guest. Suddenly Zoeller had the interview he had been waiting weeks for, only he was unprepared for it.

Realizing this was his chance and he had better take advantage of it, Zoeller sat the boys down, one at a time, in the living room and tried to remember all the things he wanted to ask. He and Linehan were just searching for reasons why anyone would want to kill their parents, he said.

Then he directed the conversation to the night of the killings. Zoeller asked Erik and Lyle whether their parents had a habit of falling asleep in front of the television, a crucial point if someone had planned to surprise them.

"My dad would fall asleep in a movie like that," Lyle replied. He said his mother's insomnia made it harder for her, but if she was real tired, "which I'm sure she was from the fishing trip, she might fall asleep, you know. They definitely—they usually hold each other on the couch"—Lyle had a strange habit of referring to his parents in the present tense even after they were dead—"and then sort of lay there with the lights out, so if we're in the room watching it, they'll often fall asleep, you know."

Zoeller nodded. Erik asked if the police thought the killers could be people his parents knew.

"To us, going into the room with the experience that he and I have," Zoeller said, trying to keep the conversation going, "is that it's somebody they knew because it doesn't appear that either one of your parents struggled with them."

Erik reflected on his mother's anxiety at the time. He said that when they had first moved into the Beverly Hills house, nobody had ever bothered to lock the gates. Everyone assumed they were safe in Beverly Hills. But near the end Kitty suddenly became frightened. He mentioned a note she left referring to her expected death.

Zoeller asked for the ticket stubs to the movie they had seen the night of the murder. They didn't have them, they said.

The detective then turned to Lyle and broached a dangerous subject because it showed that the cops were eliminating no one as suspects, including the boys. Had there been any problems between him and his parents? Zoeller asked.

Not really, Lyle said. There had been a fight with Kitty the night before the murders, he noted. But it was no big deal. It was about Kitty's penchant for locking the doors to the house. "I got mad at her because she makes you wake her up to unlock the door. She knows I forget my keys," he grumbled.

Edging further into sensitive territory, Zoeller said Jose's longtime secretary, Marzi, had told him something he wanted to get Lyle's reaction to. She said that only a few days before the murders, Kitty had called her to complain that Lyle had kept her up all night on the phone.

Lyle couldn't remember the incident, but thought it might have been the same time he got mad at her over locking the door. As the discussion continued, Lyle said, it broadened into a conversation about his girlfriends. This struck a chord with Zoeller, who knew both Jose and Kitty had been upset at some of the women Lyle was seeing. His relationship with Jamie was off and on, and he was seeing a leggy model on the side who was ten years older.

Lyle admitted that he and his father had different attitudes about women.

"I would give women the time of day and, ah, get into relationships. And he pretty much felt women were sort of bimbos. Certainly the ones that I would just date at my age and so on."

The truth was, Jose feared Lyle would be taken advantage of by a gold-digger.

"It's just the money," he had told Lyle. The best policy, he said, was to "only marry her on the weekends."

Well, Zoeller said, he had to look at everything. All sorts of areas.

Lyle agreed. "Yeah, because, ah, you know, I don't believe the organized crime thing until I see something. You know?"

"That makes two of us," Zoeller said with feeling. "And I haven't seen anything."

In the weeks after the murders, the *Los Angeles Times* assigned two reporters full-time to what some were calling the Mansion Murders case. Ron Soble had covered the federal courts for many years and had developed good sources in hard-to-penetrate federal law enforcement agencies. John Johnson had done a number of stories looking into Los Angeles' billion-dollar porn industry. Each had more than fifteen years' experience in journalism and had worked almost every beat there was on a newspaper, from education to covering the White House.

Like Zoeller and Linehan, Soble and Johnson at first concentrated on the mob theory. They interviewed Bloom, whom they found surprisingly engaging and thoroughly nonplussed at being thrown into the middle of a murder case. They also tried to keep tabs on the progress of the police inquiry.

When nothing much came up, the reporters set up an interview with the grieving sons. The story they planned was a portrait of two young men suddenly thrust out on their own in a horrifically brutal way. How were they bearing up under the weight of their loss?

The interview took place in the family mansion on a cool afternoon. Lyle Menendez, dressed in a stylish blue-and-white exercise outfit, greeted his guests at the locked security gate and ushered them into the sunken living room. Artworks collected by Jose and Kitty graced the walls.

Lyle shook hands diffidently and guided his guests to one of the two white sofas. Across a wide coffee table of rich, dark wood, Erik sat erect on one end of a matching sofa while Lyle slouched nearby with athletic nonchalance. The sun slanted in through three cathedral windows at their backs.

"If the focus of the story is the investigation, really, I want no part of it," Lyle began bluntly. "Because I'm really tired of this investigation."

Surprised, Soble, a low-key man with sandy hair and a loping kind of walk, asked for an explanation.

"I've read so much trash," Lyle said. "There are so many rumors. There is no evidence, one way or the other, about anything. And it's pointless to sit here and try to guess, two months after the fact, again, what could have happened."

His voice was flat. This was surprising because the reporters had expected to hear bitterness, or anger, or anything. But he didn't seem despondent, just devoid of emotion.

But after saying he didn't want to discuss the investigation, he voluntarily began musing about what may have led to his father's death.

"I believe he died because he wouldn't, you know, I believe it was organized crime and I believe he died because he wouldn't cooperate with such activities."

"But you're just guessing," Soble pursued.

"It's more than guessing," he said firmly. "I know the values that my dad lived by throughout his life. He didn't waver, ever."

In saying this, an unmistakable sense of pride crept into his voice. This was a man who admired his father, surely.

Then he speculated about who might have had a reason to want him dead.

"It could have been somebody small whose feelings were hurt along the way, who personally was pissed off about the way things were handled and wanted to clear his own aggressions."

Somebody small was Lyle's way of saying someone who didn't count much, a low-level number on the payroll whom Jose had inadvertently squashed like a bug somewhere along the line. Lyle seemed to have picked up his father's acute sense of class, his way of dividing the world into people you must impress, those you bested in business, and those you kicked out of your way like tin cans.

But he really didn't give that idea much credence in the end. He had a pretty good idea of who would like to see his father dead: Noel Bloom.

"We don't know that Noel did it," Erik said.

But Lyle would not be denied.

"I feel confident that what I have educatedly guessed at is correct," he said. "I think the police are aware that that's a big lead."

Lyle also said he believed some of his father's business associates were not cooperating with the police, perhaps out of fear of soiling the corporate image. He was asked if perhaps his father's old allies simply wanted to put the painful episode behind them.

"I think so," he replied. "Erik and I would like that as well. We don't want to be threatened anymore. Finding out who it is, Erik and I are probably not going to be able to do anything about it. To find out who it is and not be able to do anything is probably worse [than not knowing].

"So it's a hard thing for Erik and I to decide whether or not we want it solved. It would be great if whoever did it went to jail. But it really doesn't help us in any way. The loss is much greater than the benefits of finding out who did it."

This was so bizarre that the two reporters exchanged glances. It was one thing to want to get on with your life. It was another to hope that the murder of your parents remained unsolved.

As Lyle did with friends, he made it clear he was going to move in and take over his father's place in the family. But he said he would not be riding Jose's coattails.

"It's not my intention to take on my father's vision, what he wanted to do with his life," he said. "Each man has his own vision. The only thing we can't do is let him down as far as what he would want us to achieve. I would want this generation to do so much more than the last one," he said, warming to the subject. "The last one was cut short, really. The baton has been passed. We feel that. There was always a great energy in the family and the feeling of moving forward, and it's sort of like, and I do get the feeling, like the baton was passed. I do feel like I need to carry on the burden."

Erik, who had been sitting quietly and letting his older brother carry the burden of the interview, spoke up.

"The past that we've seen in both of our families is so great that there almost is a lot of pressure, there is a lot of pressure to become great. My father was such a great man he gave us a great base to work on."

The sons recited the familiar story of their father's meteoric rise in corporate America, complete with a dramatic account of his achievements. But the accomplishments had come at a high price to Jose and his family.

"My father suffered from being a perfectionist," said Lyle. "It carried over into his home life, and it was sometimes difficult for Erik and me.

"So much so that he really couldn't do something well enough. It wore on him physically. And it wore on him tremendously mentally. And it wore on us. He needed to be the top in just about everything.

"You could see the stress in his face, and you could feel the stress around him," he said. "People feel stress around Erik and myself. You become very demanding. He really felt that he was always right."

As Lyle spoke, he remained detached, as though he were trying to understand his father as an intellectual exercise.

"It was difficult because you had to be a great tennis player and be great in school," Erik added with more energy.

"It was hard for us back then. But now we look back on it and we love the fact. We would not have wanted any other father."

Lyle said he was glad to have had as much time as he did to study at his father's feet.

"I am happy to have been twenty-one when it happened."

No, he didn't cry a lot after the murders. "I didn't relate well to the people around me. It was larger than life to me."

Erik tried to help him out.

Other people, he said, "didn't understand my father. They didn't live with him for eighteen or twenty-one years. My brother understood the loss and how great it was. And how many achievements. It's a man who would have changed our society."

Again and again the brothers focused on Jose's value to the world, to his friends, to everyone but his own sons. They both readily expressed pride in his accomplishments, along with a respectful awe over them. But as far as his listeners could tell, there was little love in the words.

Now that their parents were dead, the brothers were facing a new world. Could they responsibly handle their newfound wealth and status? More than that, were they emotionally prepared to deal with the world as adults, without the guiding hands of their parents? It turned out they had a plan, and Lyle's jump into business was just a part of it.

"I'm going to pursue a professional tennis career," Lyle said.

There was no certainty he could make it. But tennis, after all, had been the one thing that had cemented the family together over the years.

"We had planned I would take next spring off," Lyle said. "This is a planned situation. It's going to be sooner than expected."

But others were not as sanguine about Jose's attitude toward Lyle's tennis. One of Lyle's friends said father and son had argued over tennis and over Lyle's desire to leave school. Lyle had never received a ranking higher than 63rd nationally, and he was past the age when he should have made his vault to the top, if he was ever going to do so.

Jose had known this too. "Lyle's father was so pissed off at Lyle because he wanted to quit college and play pro tennis," said the friend.

But Lyle and Erik could see only that if they would ever make it, now was the the time to try.

"We have a unique opportunity," said Lyle. "We have two kids who put a lot of time into tennis. We have financial backing" from their inheritance.

"It's going to be a struggle," Erik admitted. "But hopefully in two years you'll be doing an article on us."

The interview was at an end. After shaking hands with the two brothers, Soble and Johnson walked out into the sun and stood in the street for a moment, feeling awkward. Johnson leaned against his car. Finally Soble expressed the thought that had been in both their minds throughout the strange, stiff, businesslike conversation.

"They did it," he said.

Teach Your Children Well

As with everything else, when it came to raising kids, Jose had a plan. Kitty did her part. She bore him two sons. She could not have done better, and throughout her life the boys would be trophies that she could point to as proof that she had accomplished something.

"I know our boys will always be most special to you," she wrote later on to Jose. "They are special—my gift to you."

And how beautiful were these boys. Lyle was round and his hair was black and his eyes were dark and all-seeing. Looking down on him after Kitty brought him home from the hospital, gazing deep into the eyes and past them, Jose knew he could mold him. As with a fine colt, he could see the power and breeding in him.

This boy was destined to be great, greater even than Jose himself. And Jose dedicated himself to fulfilling the boy's destiny. No effort would be spared toward that end. That was his pledge. That was his definition of love.

Jose's approach to child-rearing, which Kitty readily adopted, was competitive and driven. He encouraged chance taking, demanded toughness, and didn't coddle weakness.

If the boys cried or stuttered, and both of them did, or fell and hurt themselves, the parents' approach was straightforward. They patched them up, ordered them to stop the stuttering, and got on with their lives. More careful mothers were horrified at the way Kitty let her sons test the edges of safety, running helter-skelter into the street and through stores on shopping trips. Kitty's policy was that the damage done to your personality by being fearful was worse than any damage that might be done to the body through injury. This indulgence could be irritating for other diners in restaurants, who found their meals interrupted by screaming children running from table to table. "They're just being boys," she would say.

Implicit in this was that they were being Menendez boys, which meant better, faster, bolder, and more powerful. Boys with such blood in them needed to express themselves, even to run roughshod over more common people.

But when it came to their training, there was no room for fooling around. Because Jose's plans for his sons were grand, his planning was meticulous, covering every detail of their early years. There were regulations covering what they could eat, who they spent time with, what they saw when they took vacations—monuments in Washington, D.C., of course, to understand civic history—and even what they read and thought about.

When they were small, the boys were not encouraged to have friends over. There would be plenty of time for that later on. A bunch of undisciplined, slobbering, dirty-faced kids running around the house would just interfere with what Jose was trying to do. Other boys lived chaotic, undisciplined lives. Jose did not want his sons tainted by that at an impressionable age. He wanted time for his lessons about life and strength and personal combat to seep deep into their souls, the way water trickles down into subterranean basins, becoming purified as it falls.

Every hour of the day was to be accounted for and used to best advantage. Some relatives were troubled by this. When was there time to be children? they asked. But Jose had a vision, and nobody would be allowed to interfere with it. What he was giving his sons was better than a childhood. It was a life worth living. He expected outsiders would not understand and appreciate what he was doing, because they were ordinary people. But his sons would.

And they seemed to. Lyle once wrote to Erik, "He bore two brilliant children, only two [and] they carry his name and his pride."

The problem with Kitty and Jose's plans for their children was that they didn't take into consideration the needs and desires of the objects of those plans, their sons. Could they be everything they were meant to be?

Jose did not ponder such impenetrable questions. He had grown up too pampered and self-centered to think deeply about others. He never considered that the children might not be up to the task. Negative thoughts, he knew, and Kitty believed this too, were self-defeating. If you defeated the thoughts, you could win any battle. They did not wonder if this was really true or just true for them.

One day a friend, Faith Goldsmith, asked Jose, what if the boys could not be as successful as he intended?

"What would you do if they were not? What would you do if one of them had a learning disability?" she asked.

"That would never happen," he said. "My child could not have a learning problem."

Goldsmith persisted. "Just hypothetically speaking," she added, "just what would you do? Would you be able to accept it?"

Jose was firm. "I would never have a child like that. That is not a possibility."

Another problem with Jose's grand design was that it failed to recognize the fallibility of its designers. Jose and Kitty never considered the possibility that they themselves might be the fatal flaws in their own diagram.

Jose's vicious streak was his greatest flaw. It was partly a result of his insecurity at being Cuban in a business world dominated by Anglos, which caused him to delight in humiliating incompetent Anglos while at the same time begging for their acceptance through his efforts to Americanize himself. Though he disdained the ostentatious presentiments of some rich people, a relative said he kept a book on his shelf about how the rich behave.

He showed his vicious side almost eagerly to Lyle, letting his son see how he had not only bested opponents but rubbed their noses in their own humiliation.

There was a kind of corruptness in this. He preached to his sons about honor and enterprise and doing the right thing for one's family and country, while privately behaving as though it was all right to treat people badly if they deserved it.

Not that Jose and Kitty didn't have assets as parents. Countless times over the years they sacrificed themselves and their time for their sons, whom they loved truly and deeply. But perfection is a dangerous thing to strive for. If you demand it in others, fate has a tendency to be merciless with you as well.

The models Jose used in training Erik and Lyle were ancient warrior societies such as Rome, which began training children in the military arts when they were young. Jose substituted sports for arms.

In Rome, as in Jose's household, every male child, past puberty or not, was firmly under the control of his father. More than this, the boy's father was his judge and could privately sentence him to death. Further, sons needed their father's consent to begin a career.

Not surprisingly, as a result the crime of parricide—the murder of one's parents—was not uncommon in ancient Rome. A young man who knew that he could only be really free with his father's death often resorted to hastening that event.

"During the civil wars," according to the writer Velleius, "the loyalty of wives was greatest, that of freedmen less great, that of slaves not insignificant, and that of sons nil, so hard is it to bear the postponement of hope."

Goldsmith met Kitty, whom she knew as Mary Lou, in 1965, when Kitty was teaching third grade in the Bronx at the same school where Goldsmith taught. Jose was attending Queens College at the time. Goldsmith and her husband and Kitty and Jose became fast, dear friends, spending many evenings together playing board games and teaching each other bridge.

Faith valued Kitty because she was absolutely unintimidated by anything in life, and she made Faith believe she could be anything she wanted. Kitty was athletic, smart, outgoing. She seemed to be able to rise to any occasion. Once someone threw smoke bombs into the museum where the women were watching a show. It was Kitty who leaped out of the audience, stomped out the smoke, and then lectured the vandals who threw them. But Faith noticed that winning and being first were so important to Kitty that she even cheated at Monopoly.

When Lyle was born, the family lived in Jamaica Estates, New York. This was the time Lyle referred to when he told friends he was poor as a child. That was a fabrication, but there was not much money left over after the bills were paid. Kitty had to return to work only five weeks after Lyle's birth. By this time Jose had found a nighttime bookkeeping job at a local market, but that was not enough to feed a family on. As many other women were beginning to do, Kitty went looking for child care for Lyle. Jose's mother, the stately Maria, was living in New Jersey, and she pitched in as well.

Lyle was advanced as an infant, standing up at five months, walking at seven months, and riding a bicycle by age three. He was also into everything. Motherhood was a trial for Kitty. She had never prepared herself for the implications of sharing Jose—of whom she was already so possessive that she referred to him as "my husband" in front of his own family—with anyone else.

And Kitty lacked some part of what women are unfairly assumed to have in excess, that enveloping, nurturing instinct. Her own mother had been so dependent on her that she had never learned some of the basics about mothering. She continually tried to make up for it with self-sacrifice, but the cuddling and cooing did not come naturally. So there was a carelessness about her as a mother. As infants Lyle and Erik walked around the house with droopy diapers that Kitty didn't get around to changing.

While Lyle was still a baby, Kitty and Jose took up skiing, a sport they became devoted to. They would drive over to Maria's house on Friday, drop Lyle off for the weekend, then return on Sunday to pick him up.

Lyle was spending so much time with other care-givers at this time that Kitty came up with what she thought sounded like a clever way to cut costs and solve the problem of finding dependable baby-sitters, Goldsmith said. Because she knew this was an unusual idea, she tried it out on Goldsmith one day. What do you think, she said, about sending Lyle to live with Maria fulltime during the week? Kitty and Jose would visit on weekends, on their way out to the slopes.

Goldsmith was shocked. So, quite naturally, was Jose, who immediately quashed the idea. He was not going to hand over his precious son to someone else, even his mother.

The family moved to Hinsdale, Illinois, when Jose took the Lyons job, his first big break, about the time Erik was born. They were now just a few miles from Kitty's hometown, where her brothers were building their own lives.

Erik was born in 1970, and he could not be contained. He would dash out of the house, churning his tiny legs across the street into a big field that had not yet come under development. He was heading for his uncle Carlos and aunt Terry's house on the other side of the field—Jose had hired Carlos Baralt at Lyons.

Erik would be carried back to Jose and Kitty, who laughed indulgently. This was the way boys were supposed to be, unbridled, heedless, courageous.

In the early years in the Midwest there was not much pressure in the house. The boys were babies, and Kitty had her family nearby. Jose was struggling to reach the executive suite at Lyons, but the pace of life was slow and the family was as contented as it ever would be. In fact, it was about this time that the family began to acquire a reputation as the perfect nuclear unit, with a successful father, a dynamic mother, and two anointed children.

But from the beginning there were flaws in the portrait of perfection. The family had moved back to New York, in the suburb of Monsey, after Jose landed the job at Hertz, when Jose's sister Marta and her husband, Peter Cano, visited. Lyle was just five when Jose reprimanded him one day for his supposed hyperactivity.

Jose stood up, grabbed Lyle, "and just looked at him right in the eye and said something to him that I couldn't hear," Peter Cano said later. Lyle "wet himself," Cano said, and Jose escorted the "pale and trembling" boy to his room.

Cano yelled at Jose, "That's no way to raise a child." In response, Jose hit Lyle in the chest with his closed fist. If Cano didn't like it, Jose replied, he could leave. Cano gathered up his wife and five children and drove off.

About this time, cousins began requesting permission to spend summers with the Menendezes, where they could see the perfect family in action. When Brian Andersen, Jr., the son of Kitty's brother, came to stay in the early seventies he quickly realized that things were not as perfect as they seemed. He recalled lying in bed and hearing Kitty and Jose arguing loudly. Sometimes she cried and Brian saw bruises on her the next morning. One was on her biceps, a telltale mark because Jose had a habit of grabbing his sons by the arm muscles and squeezing them, hard, when he wanted to get their full attention.

Brian saw the family had a set of rigid, military school-style rules to govern their home, restrictions about friends, leisure activities, even the food they ate. Jose and Kitty knew the boys would be star athletes, though they didn't yet know the sport, so they decided the brothers should eat only high-protein meals.

This was also when Jose began turning dinnertime into a series of advanced seminars. While the questions he posed would later deal with highly technical arms-control discussions and the like, at this point he was satisfied with challenging them on the major news events in the day's newspaper. Erik was allowed to join in, but the pressure was mostly on Lyle, and if he could not come up with an answer he was required to put down his knife and fork and find the answer in the paper or in the encyclopedia on the book shelf, Andersen said later.

If Lyle took too long researching, Jose chided, "You've lost five dollars for me right now." To Jose, time was, literally, money. As time went on, Lyle would prepare for dinner like an oral examination at school, making notes ahead of time and rehearsing his lines.

If Lyle did poorly during the dinnertime quiz, Jose would sit the offending boy opposite him in a chair. Then he thrust his face up to the boy, just inches away, and made him talk about his mistakes. Sometimes he would touch foreheads with him, seeking an even tighter bond, a kind of disciplinary mind link. Lyle could not move or look away, while Jose fixed him in a gaze that seemed to search the child down to the cellular level, as though he were scanning for character flaws the way a computer searches its memory, byte by byte. These intense sessions could last five minutes or a half hour. Later, they would last even longer.

The next level of discipline, if they talked back or committed some other transgression, was to send them to their room— they shared a room in Monsey—and the door would be locked. If they moved too slowly or resisted in some other way, Jose grabbed them by the biceps and squeezed. Sometimes he went into the room with them, locked the door, and delivered a lengthy lecture. When Jose was in there, no one was allowed to go near the room. They would be closeted there as long as it took for Jose to make himself clear and, more important, for his sons to accept his argument. Not just with words, that was not enough. Jose had to be convinced they acquiesced on the deepest spiritual level.

Jose used a belt for the most serious offenses, for the boys were, in the vernacular of the times, real handfuls. They always seemed to be into some mischief. They were never able to sit still, and they had a habit of breaking things around the house. This errant heedlessness infuriated Jose, who believed at his core that a person must be in control of himself, even a very small person.

When Jose was applying the belt, Kitty turned up the TV. Sometimes Jose would come home, sit in his favorite chair with his newspaper, and listen as Kitty filled him in on the day's events. Then he would remove his belt with a snap and put it on the couch for display.

If Kitty was worried about Jose's mood when he came home from work, she would try a technique that was frequently used by sitcom television families at the time. She gathered her boys and whoever else was visiting out on the landing, arm in arm, where they greeted Jose with warm, appreciative smiles.

Jose's Old World attitudes about manliness revealed themselves to their worst effect when he taught six-year-old Erik to ride a bicycle. He refused to allow Erik to use training wheels because he believed that would make his son look like a sissy.

So Jose sat Erik on the bike, then gave it a good push down a small incline that led into a cul de sac outside the Monsey house. The bike would wobble, Erik sobbing in fear, then topple over, spilling the boy onto the asphalt. Once Erik cut his elbow badly, which left a scar.

Brian Andersen tried to intervene, but Kitty stopped him. Kitty didn't always agree with Jose's methods and sometimes challenged him, especially when it came to Erik, who was the weaker child, more dependent on her. But there would be no interfering with Jose on those occasions. Learning to ride a bike was too important.

Finally, after several days of failure, Jose took the bike and threw it in the garage and forbade Erik to play with it anymore.

Whenever they were hurt or punished, Jose was firm about them not crying. "A corporate man does not show emotion," is the way Andersen described the attitude.

If Lyle ever started to break down, Jose would say, "Lyle," and the boy straightened right up. Often he would glance at his father as he talked. If he detected disapproval on Jose's face, he would suddenly take the opposite point of view. Over time Lyle so effectively squashed his emotions that he came to appear to some people not to have any. His eyes grew expressionless and his face blank, especially around his father, where he became almost a dutiful robot, according to visitors.

The pressure of meeting Jose's demands began showing on the boys in other ways. Erik and Lyle developed stutters. Erik's was bad enough that he was sent to a speech pathologist. The boys also developed stomach pains and had a habit of teeth grinding.

Both boys also seem to have developed nasty tempers. If Lyle objected to some punishment his father meted out, he would fume about it, then go out in the yard and pound on a tree. More frequently he would abuse his stuffed animals, of which he had a large and growing collection, particularly favoring Sesame Street characters such as Cookie Monster.

Sometimes the fits of temper would come on him with no warning. Lyle would be playing with his stuffed toys, then suddenly fly into a rage and begin tearing them apart, arm from arm, leg from leg.

Lyle liked to animate his stuffed animals. Each had a name, and Lyle would make up elaborate stories for them to act out in his imagination when he was being punished for one infraction or another. Sometimes he used Cookie Monster to threaten Erik, which scared him. If Erik wanted to get back at Lyle, he would throw Cookie out the window, which upset his brother tremendously.

Kitty also had a temper, but she exercised it differently, in a more self-destructive way, befitting her personality. When she had finally had it with her children's shenanigans, she would stand in front of the kitchen sink, scrunch up her face, and bare her teeth. Her hands would clench into fists, and her knuckles would turn white with fury. Then she would open the cupboard and began throwing coffee cups, saucers, breakfast bowls, and glasses into the sink, where they would crash and break into small pieces.

"I would run into the kitchen and go, 'Kitty,' which would snap her out of whatever she was into," Andersen said.

Sometimes when things got tense, Kitty would go to the cabinet where she kept the Valium. After taking a few pills, she calmed down. When a friend confronted her about it, she said, "This is how I get through the day."

Kitty also developed a drinking problem. It's not that she drank so much. She was never a hard drinker, but she was a determined drinker. She liked to pour Grand Marnier, Liquer Galliano, or Cuarenta y Cinco into her coffee. Later, she favored cognac, and felt proud that she got tipsy on such a high-class brand of alcohol. As time went on, the drinking would begin in the afternoon and continue on into the evening. She began to hide her drinking from Jose, not because she feared he would forbid it but because it was becoming an issue in the home.

"Put it away," she would implore Terry Baralt when she heard Jose coming. "He doesn't like it when I drink." Jose would tease her about it, smiling all the while in that leering, sarcastic way he had when he found someone else's weakness.

Some of Kitty's frustration was jealousy over the fact that Jose spent so much time with the boys, particularly Lyle. Because he was away so much working, when he came home, she looked forward to cuddling with him as she had when they listened to jazz in the trailer back in Illinois. But Jose was consumed by two things—his work and raising his sons right—

and there was not much time left over for Kitty. A third interest, other women, would soon intrude.

"Children drive a wedge between a husband and wife," she said on several occasions in front of others. Sometimes she even wished she had never had children. They were so hard to handle, and they seemed to do things that would intentionally make you mad.

Brian Andersen was something of a mischief-maker around the Menendez house. He was caught smoking, and another time he cut off the tops of flowers in the yard to show his anger over something, he said. But he was nearly run out of the house when he hit Lyle in the face during a rock-throwing exchange. Lyle's face swelled up. When Kitty saw it, she was shocked and considered using a razor blade to slit the skin so the swelling could go down. But Lyle cried and begged her not to, and Andersen refused to get the razor blade.

Kitty's reaction was nothing compared to Jose's. He told Brian he was going home, then sent him to his room and locked the door. Kitty called Brian's father, but Jose eventually relented and allowed the boy to stay on, Andersen said.

The parents' rage was understandable, given the fact that Jose put Lyle on a pedestal as a nearly perfect, physically flawless child. They were frightened, maybe overly so, that the injury might interfere with Lyle's sight. Besides, they felt with justification that the older boy had no business luring a much younger child into such a dangerous game.

Jose did not exempt his own family from his expectations. If relatives did not meet the rigorous standards he set, they found themselves frozen out. A class consciousness was drilled into Erik and Lyle early. Visitors recall Jose and Kitty telling both boys that they might not like having their parents decide for them who they could spend time with, but it was important even from a young age to be with the "right people."

As Kitty had been with the Party Dolls, and as she would remain throughout her life, she was an extremely poor driver. Sometimes she piled the boys into the car and told them they were going for a ride, which meant racing along the highways and back roads at top speed. This was her way of releasing tension, blowing it off like exhaust.

Everyone in the family, it seemed, could have used a driving instructor with an independent brake. Kitty had a rash of accidents, especially near the end of her life as she grew more distracted and fearful. Jose accumulated tickets and his license was suspended at least once, and Lyle, when he got his license, was equally aggressive. His license was also suspended, authorities said. Erik, who began driving in California, was no better. He had so many car accidents that he learned to supplement his $180-a-month allowance by asking for money to fix his car, said a friend. The friend recalled Erik asking Kitty for money one day for an accident that never happened.

"Without even checking, she gave him $500," said the friend.

When Kitty and Jose moved back to Monsey from the Midwest, they reestablished contact with the Goldsmiths. Kitty and Faith became as close as ever.

But Faith, who had three daughters, was critical of her friend's carelessness as a mother. Faith recalled Kitty allowing Lyle to walk on a ledge above the porch at the Monsey house when he was still young. "He's not going to fall," Kitty assured her in the same way she had assured her college friends when they worried they would get caught in her mother's car.

Kitty had a theory: "Children, when you leave them alone, learn to defend themselves."

If there was one continuing frustration for Jose, it was Erik's babyish ways. The once heedless boy had, under Jose's demanding instruction, retreated and become a fearful, intimidated child. To Jose, the best way to root this out was to blast it out. A family picture taken when Erik was an infant shows him hanging by his arms from a chin-up bar, his face contorted in a cry of pain and abject fear. Behind him, Jose is laughing.

Jose locked Erik in his room when he was two for crying.

Erik was so fearful as a child that he had a habit of checking all the dresser drawers and the closet in his room for monsters before he went to bed. It didn't stop his periodic nightmares, but it made him feel better. One night Jose surprised him by dropping a witch's mask out of the closet when Erik opened the door.

Kitty applied the same hard medicine in an attempt to break her younger son of being a mama's boy. In this family Lyle and Jose were on a different plateau. Kitty and the less strong-willed, more easily intimidated Erik were on the next tier down, and so Erik was to some extent Kitty's project.

Once the two of them were in a shoe store, and Erik fell and cut his head. Kitty refused to fuss over the boy. She finished buying her shoes before taking him out to have his wound sewn up.

When Erik started school, Kitty became concerned because

he was not at the top of his class. This was just elementary school, but she expected him to stand out wherever he went. Goldsmith said Kitty asked her what she thought of the idea of holding Erik back a year so he could be on top in the next class. Faith thought that was crazy.

Showing how far Kitty was willing to go in the pursuit of success for her sons, she once asked Faith to get her copies of a placement test that Erik was going to take. As a teacher, Faith could get them, but she refused.

Kitty considered herself an honest and moral person. She justified her little larcenies on several grounds. One was that Lyle and Erik had to work so hard to measure up to Jose's demands that they didn't have time for their studies.

Second, helping with homework was a way for Kitty to prove her importance in a family that valued accomplishment beyond anything else. Her education gave her status in the family.

But aside from all Kitty's rationalizing was the simple fact that her husband would not accept second best from his sons. So they were as first-rate as she could make them.

Another relative who wanted to see what life was like in a perfect household was Kathleen Vander Molen, who visited from Arizona in 1976, when Erik and Lyle were six and eight.

She was fifteen, the fifth child of Kitty's older sister Joan. She was supposed to spend the summer there, but left after two months, she said, because she was so unhappy.

Kathleen noticed how regulated the family was, even on casual outings. By this time Jose's plan for his sons was in full swing, and their days were beginning to conform to a rigid schedule that kept them busy from morning until night.

Jose had not decided what sport his sons would play, but he naturally gravitated toward swimming, because it had been his sport. The boys began taking lessons, and on the weekends Jose took the family to a public pool. Kathleen swam and dove where she liked. But Jose watched over Erik and Lyle as they practiced swimming strokes over and over.

10

Tennis

Tennis can be more than a way of life in the affluent, picturesque middle New Jersey countryside, where fourteen historic communities are clustered in Mercer, Middlesex, and Somerset counties.

For some it is pursued with a religious zeal. There are almost as many tennis courts hidden behind spacious homes as there are basketball standards gracing backyards in Indiana. A new resident who wants to install a court has more than a dozen tennis court construction firms from which to choose. What's more, there are nine private indoor tennis clubs in the area. This is critical in a climate with harsh winters, since top players must practice year round.

Since the population in the three counties adds up to little more than 122,000, these statistics speak volumes about the enthusiasm with which the locals approach the game.

"Tennis boomed here before it boomed nationwide," said Colleen Cosgrove, a coach, recalling the emergence of local stars such as Jay Lapidus, Ted Farnsworth, and others. "It has one of the highest concentrations of courts per capita in the nation."

It was in this setting of winding back country roads and rambling, historic brick and frame homes that Lyle and Erik would hone tennis skills that would bring them national recognition and where they would put into action the achievement-oriented philosophy of their father.

With Jose's income growing steadily at Hertz, the family moved from Monsey in 1978 and settled into a new housing

tract, Elm Ridge Park in Pennington. It is a sprawling development of $500,000 homes on large, wooded lots grouped around
brackish Honey Lake, only a few miles from Princeton University. The intellectual center of this Robert Frostian locale,
Princeton was established as the College of New Jersey in 1746,
and was the place where Albert Einstein lived his last years
speaking out for pacifism.

There is a Thoreau-like serenity about the place, and the
simplicity of a small town. On warm weekend afternoons couples
with sweaters tied around their necks wait peacefully in long
lines outside the local ice cream parlor, or share mugs of beer in
the historic basement tavern in the Nassau Inn, with its richly
detailed Norman Rockwell mural of Yankee Doodle riding his
horse.

The Menendezes represented the influx of "new money" into
an area where an increasing number of New York commuters
and high-tech industries were overwhelming the old order.
Condo developments were springing up, and the newcomers
brought energy and an itchy kind of abrasiveness that didn't sit
well with the Princeton life of reflection and settled comfort.

"The people who lived in our neighborhood were vice presidents, not your bluebloods," said Irene Elkins, a friend of the
Menendez family, whose husband was an executive with the
Atlas Corp. Instead of inheriting wealth, "most of us made our
way up."

The husbands rose early, rode by limo or train into New York,
and returned very late, unless they were traveling, in which
case they might not return for days. In this atmosphere, responsibility for running the household fell on the wives, who learned
to be emotionally and materially self-sufficient.

Kitty had stopped working now that Jose earned enough to
support the family. She still dreamed of a broadcasting career,
but Jose would have none of that. He demanded that she stay
home and be a wife and mother. She threw herself into the job
with energy, but it was often thankless. Jose was away so much
that every small and large task around the house fell on her
shoulders. At Christmas, Kitty could be seen scrambling around
on the roof of their two-story, Tudor-style house stringing the
lights. When Jose landed his big job at RCA, she installed a tape
player in his car so that he could listen to new groups on his way
to work. Kitty accepted the long hours Jose was spending in
New York, and the nights he never came home at all, as her
investment in his career.

Kitty was a joiner. Besides signing up at the Bedens Brook country club, set on a large, park-like tract of land among rolling hills, Kitty helped form a gourmet food group, an antique group, and arranged trips into New York to see Broadway plays. She even started an exercise group in her basement.

"If there was a big party and your husband was out of town," said Elkins, "you were included. We did everything together."

But Jose was never keen on social engagements that had no payoff, so he routinely refused them. Once Lyle said later, he told his father that marriage was a two-way street, and Jose should try to be there more for his mother.

Jose relied that in a relationship only one person could be in control, and he would rather not be married than to sacrifice that control. Lyle was shocked to hear this blunt dismissal of his mother.

Kitty didn't feel neglected at the time. Only later, after she discovered Jose's philandering, did she come to regret the freedom she gave her husband and the accommodations she made to him.

"I always found strength in my independence," she wrote later on. "Maybe too much independence isn't healthy for a marriage. I would have sensed what was happening years ago if I felt more dependent on him."

Besides, this was a time of trial for Kitty. As Jose battled his way up the corporate ladder, her task was to accomplish a far more subtle transformation. She was determined to make the Menendezes, increasingly comfortable financially, acceptable in the eyes of the guardians of local society. This was not a task especially suitable to Kitty's personality. She was too raw. Her small-town roots showed in her face and her plain hairstyle. Like Jose, her unskilled competitiveness was out of place among the local gentry, who seemed not to have a leaf out of place on the family tree.

But what she had in excess was energy, and so, armed with Jose's vision, she threw herself into carrying out her part of the plan. She captained a tennis team at the country club and raised money for the Princeton Community Tennis Program. She became transportation chair for the women's pro tennis events held at the Princeton Indoor Tennis Center, where she was responsible for driving around celebrities when they came to town. Kitty insisted on exclusivity with the stars, guarding her job so jealously that she flew into a rage when someone else attempted to pick Martina Navratilova up one time.

Eventually she and the rest of her brood became a part of the local society, but they were always kept at a certain distance. The attitude toward them was reflected in the words of a onetime neighbor who, after the murders, talked about the family with barely hidden disdain in his carefully modulated voice. The Menendezes, he made it clear, were pushy, noisy. He complained about their dog, Tristesse, a big black hound that barked all the time. And he described parties they had given as though they were native gatherings.

Jose's growing success was both a blessing and a curse. The family was more and more comfortable, yet the success allowed his worst characteristics to flourish. Friends only made things worse by fawning over him. Kitty, as a result, tried to provide a balance.

"I saw how well he gratified his own ego," she wrote in another letter. "That's why I never stroked him. I wanted him to keep his feet on the ground. He must have hated that when everyone else kept stroking him."

Lyle and Erik had no chores that anyone could remember. Just as it had been in young Jose's household, athletics was all-consuming.

When they were young, the boys swam and played soccer. In fact, as a nine-year-old, Lyle was on a team that won a New Jersey state championship.

Erik appeared to favor swimming and, at nine, set a Mercer County age group record for the breaststroke.

But to some outsiders, the boys did not seem to be having much fun. One former coach remembered seeing the two boys being dropped off at the Bedens Brook swimming pool by their mother almost every morning in the summer of 1980. Dressed in her white polyester stretch pants, Kitty would bid them a good day and drive off.

While not ostracized, the two brothers were not included in the roughhousing and socializing of other children at the country club pool. Instead they swam together, huddled together, and talked or played tennis together. Lyle was willful, a "brat," according to this coach, who said he was always testing the rules.

"He always seemed to do things that would piss you off," the coach said. "He would look for ways."

Then if he was caught, "he would always look for reasons. He would never take the blame."

Erik just hung back and in general appeared a very "sad"

child. "Erik seemed like the type of person Mrs. Menendez would pick out the clothes he wore that day. He was always dressed a little, he wasn't one of the cool kids."

In the late afternoon Kitty would pick up her sons. Or, if Jose arrived, a strange drama would often be acted out. Jose would swim laps, and even if Erik was exhausted from swimming all day, Jose would make his son get back in the water and swim with him, lecturing him all the while about how he was not breathing right or doing something else wrong.

The reaction of the boys when Jose arrived was not the joy of sons looking forward to having fun with their father. The looks on their faces, recalled this coach, were "here comes discipline."

Jose's behavior was even more extreme at Erik's swimming meets. Jose was not satisfied with just doing well. At the end of a race, while the parents of other children who had done far worse were congratulating them on doing a good job, Jose would pull Erik from the water and dress him down in front of the other team members.

"He would practically humiliate him in front of his peers," the coach said. "Then he would put his arm around him."

If Erik found this message confusing, he didn't show it. He merely grew more introverted.

"Erik had so much less self-confidence because everything he did was never good enough," according to the coach.

While Jose berated Erik, Kitty stood off to the side, keeping her own counsel.

"It was surprising to me how incredibly overbearing Jose was and how uncommunicative Kitty was," the coach said.

Lyle had been playing tennis and taking lessons since he was five years old. But when he was about eleven, Jose decided that his sons should excel in either tennis or soccer. It was his view that a person could not do both without sacrificing some performance in one or the other sport. Having fun was not enough to justify the investment of time and energy. Who could have fun if they weren't the best, anyway? Jose could not imagine it.

The brothers chose tennis, and Jose brought his formidable intensity to the hard court behind the house on Honey Lake in Elm Ridge Park. He read dozens of books on technique and became personally involved in their soon-to-be rigorous training.

As early as six-thirty in the morning, Erik and Lyle would be out in the chill air with their father. Jose would hit balls to them, barking out instructions.

"Higher," he would yell loud enough for neighbors to hear. "Follow through."

Sometimes the brothers would volley between themselves; other times Jose or Kitty would feed a ball machine. Sometimes Jose would serve to Lyle, and he refused to coddle him because he was small. He served to him as hard as he did to an adult, and the balls would bounce off the boy, sometimes leaving bruises.

Then there were after-school practices at private facilities such as the Hopewell Valley Tennis Center. If they weren't playing in weekend tournaments, the practice routine would be two hours of hard, solid practice, followed by thirty or forty-five minutes off. Then another two hours on, followed by another short break. The day would wrap up with two more hours of practice. Water, iced tea, and frozen pops were all the sustenance they took during these sessions.

After this grueling practice Jose, Erik, and Lyle would storm into the house and head for the shower upstairs. They would all shower together, soaping up and talking over the things they had done wrong on the court. Then they toweled off, slipped into bathrobes, and retired to the den next to the master bedroom. While his sons sprawled on the floor, Jose instructed them in history, often Roman history, emphasizing the military conquests of the world's greatest empire and the discipline that allowed heavily outnumbered Roman armies to destroy their foes in the forests of Germany and the green fields of Gaul. While they talked, they had to watch where they sat because a succession of ferrets, most named Chipper, had the run of the house. The ferrets left droppings, and Kitty, never an efficient housekeeper, did not clean it all up immediately. Neither did anyone else, who, as usual, assumed that either Kitty would do it or no one would.

Talking like this, relaxing with his boys after a hard day of work, was what Jose loved to do. He liked to present his ideas about things and have others listen. Erik and Lyle were the best of audiences. They lapped up everything, becoming convinced their father was the most interesting and powerful man on earth. Loving their adulation, he did nothing to discourage them.

Naturally, the boys worried that they might not be able to live up to Jose's expectations. He was so awe-inspiring that they felt they could never be what he was. Don't worry, Jose assured them, the family they came from was so dynamic that success was built into their genes, just as speed is built into a racing car.

The power they needed was there, all they had to do was call on it.

This made Lyle feel better about his future, more confident. "It's a proven thing," he told others.

Jose hired a succession of private coaches. When they arrived, he kept a watchful, anxious vigil from the picture window in the downstairs living room that faced the tennis court. But he didn't stay there long. He would anger the instructors by rushing out and giving orders in the middle of a lesson.

Bill Kurtain, a tennis coach at the Hopewell complex, located off a rural road in the Princeton countryside, was one of the first of many private coaches Jose hired to tutor his sons.

Beginning in about 1980, Kurtain tutored Lyle twice a week, charging $25 an hour for lessons, sometimes on the Hopewell courts, other times on the Menendez family court.

Kurtain recalls that Lyle was a talented young player, but Jose's intrusive manner was self-defeating. There were days, Kurtain said, when Jose would rush out and interrupt. "Excuse me a minute, Lyle, this is what I want you to do."

Kurtain resented that. "Wait a minute, Joe," Kurtain would say. "Were working on certain things here."

Firmly Jose would tell him, "I see these kids doing these things at other tournaments, and this is what I want him to do," undermining the coach in front of his student.

"Lyle needs a big shot," Jose would say.

"Something big," Kurtain recalled. "Well, Becker and Lendl have that, but Lyle was eleven years old. He needs fundamentals before a big shot. I told Joe that."

Kurtain attempted to work out a deal with Jose so that he wouldn't interrupt so often. But it just didn't work out. Finally Kurtain threw up his hands and quit. "I thought here he's paying me to teach the kids. This is my line of business. You know, if you want to do it, do it yourself."

Off the court it was another story, Kurtain said. "Joe was always very outgoing and very friendly." Kitty would often bring sandwiches and iced tea out to the court.

While Kurtain found Jose's involvement an irritation, others found him a shrewd student of the game. He counseled a friend of Lyle's, Ed Fenno, himself an outstanding young player, to position his body inside the service line so that he could hit a hard-to-return slice across the net.

"He taught me a lot of strategy," said Fenno. "Lyle's real coach was his dad even though he had other coaches. Those other guys simply implemented what Jose wanted more often than not."

Despite the power struggles, Lyle showed great promise, developing an aggressive, serve-and-volley, all-court game, though some outsiders described it as joyless and mechanical. Erik, on the other hand, was a baseline player, perhaps fitting his less aggressive personality.

By 1985, Lyle, then sixteen, won the United States Tennis Association's Boys' eighteen-and-under championship in the Middle States region, which encompasses several eastern states. Erik took the Middle Stages Boys' fourteen-and-under crown, the first time two brothers had won in their respective age categories in the same year.

As the brothers' fame spread outside their region, tennis became more than an avocation. The family began traveling to tournaments in various parts of the country. Kitty became a one-woman taxi service. For a year, every day she drove an hour each way to Philadelphia, where one of Lyle's coaches lived.

To attain this level, "Do you have to make [tennis] your major recreational activity? Yes," said Warren Kimball, former president of the MSTA. "Do you have to become obsessed? No way."

People who knew Jose at this time saw him put tremendous pressure on his sons to win. Even when he was on the road, he kept tabs on them. Once, according to an associate's account, Jose called Lyle from an airliner while jetting abroad. He pushed him "very, very hard," so hard, in fact, that his offended seat mate chastened him for being so tough.

Lyle took to carrying Jose's favorite motivational text with him in his tennis bag when he competed in tournaments. "I was not delivered unto this world in defeat, nor does failure course in my veins," he could recite. He coaxed friends to learn the sacred teachings of Mandino.

The pressure showed itself in temper tantrums that both boys threw on the court. Mostly Lyle would quietly, if unenthusiastically, with that same robotic acquiescence, accept the coaching of Kurtain and others. But once in a while Lyle's temper would get the better of him, and he would explode, hitting balls as hard as he could against the fence, one after the other.

"We'd be trying to work on certain things, and he'd just take five balls and he'd just blast them as hard as he could, and they'd hit the back fence with obviously no intention of hitting the court," Kurtain said.

At other times Lyle lapsed into a stutter.

The stigma of losing became almost unbearable. Kurtain recalls the brothers throwing their rackets when they missed a key shot in a tournament. "They might even be winning a match, they'd miss a shot and they'd go nuts," he said.

Even in tournaments both brothers had conduct problems on the court, involving screaming and racket throwing. A USTA official noted that there was "a record of complaints" filed against the brothers in 1986 and 1987, but no action was ever taken against them.

Another tennis friend said Lyle and Erik were never considered very good sports on the court. Often they would call for line judges to watch a match. And Lyle would go one step further, he said. If Lyle thought an opponent was cheating on him on line calls, "he would call for the tournament chairman."

From the stands, Jose could be heard urging on his son. Lyle didn't like it, but there was nothing he could do to stop it. Once, when he got older, he decided he couldn't take any more and spoke back. Jose was making fun of him for favoring a sprained ankle during a practice session at a local tennis club, said Lyle. Reaching a boiling point, Lyle responded, "Why don't you just shut up?"

Jose turned red, grabbed his son by the arm, and steered him over to his limousine, parked behind some trees. He threw Lyle in the back and "punched me straight in the face. Don't ever embarrass me like that again or I'll kill you," Jose said, according to Lyle.

Lyle's lower lip had been split open, and blood was spilling on his shirt. "Is that perfectly clear?" his father asked.

"Yes," Lyle replied.

Even before tennis star Mary Pierce went public with allegations of abuse at the hands of her father, the pushy tennis parent had become an American archetype. There was disagreement about where Jose ranked in the pantheon of abusers. Some coaches who worked with Lyle and Erik said he was one of the worst, most abrasive of them all, brutal, belittling and insensitive. He even made the boys practice on Christmas day.

But others said Jose was aggressive but never out of control. At a tournament in Ojai, California, Erik's high school coach saw a different side of Jose. The coach, Joe Trahan, was forced to disqualify Erik because he took too long at lunch and missed his match assignment by thirty minutes. Erik flew into a rage. "I cannot believe that you would do that," he screamed, said Trahan.

Jose counseled his son. "Mr. Trahan was right." He walked Erik around the baseball field until he cooled off.

Lyle, at least, seemed to understand his father and his need for success. On occasions Jose would berate Lyle in front of other family members, and Terry Baralt would rise to Lyle's defense, ordering Jose to back off.

But Lyle would just smile. "Leave him be, Aunt Terry," he said. "It's all right."

The parents also developed a reputation for bad behavior at their sons' tennis matches. Some suspected Jose of coaching from the sidelines, which is strictly forbidden. Kitty would not hesitate to challenge a tournament official's call if she felt her sons had been shortchanged.

A Middle States Tennis Association official said the association's committee reviewed the conduct of the parents to see if any disciplinary action should be taken, but in the end it was decided to let the matter rest.

Erik's tennis game lagged behind his brother's. But Colleen Cosgrove, one of Erik's private coaches, was impressed by his talent. "He was probably one of the most creative tennis players I've ever coached," she said.

Erik wouldn't just try to perfect a forehand shot, she said. He had to have a number of different forehand shots, including one that developed into an effective drop shot.

As Erik got older, Kurtain said, he showed "more of a temper than Lyle did."

Lyle also knew he was a top tennis player and wasn't shy about saying so. He told a Princeton journalist in 1986 that tennis is "an individual sport, and like anything else in life you have to use all your energies to be successful. That's one of the things that separates the real good players, like . . . myself."

This was vintage Jose, only without the subtlety.

At the end of his four-year high school tennis career, Lyle had lost just four times in eighty matches. He won the state prep schools singles title in each of his last three years at the school and finished his senior year with a 20–0 record.

More important, Lyle was regularly ranked by the USTA in the top sixty or so players in the country in the eighteen-and-under class. Erik rose even higher in the national rankings and had been rated 44th nationally in 1990 when he decided to try his skill in the professional ranks.

As their success grew, the pair began to attract attention from the press in the bigger cities. A Trenton newspaper called Lyle "one of the best players in New Jersey the past few years" with "a strong serve, solid ground strokes, and excellent court speed."

The columnist also noted that Lyle had begun to control his temper more on the court. "Last year, Menendez's emotions sometimes affected his play, but he has learned some self-control for this year," he wrote.

One of Lyle's coaches at school, Rome Campbell, agreed.

"I think he's matured a lot," Campbell told the newspaper. "He's started to handle tight game situations with self-control. And he's always had the shots."

To Jose, it seemed that his plans were being validated. The critics could say what they wanted about him, but the proof was on the court and in the won-lost column.

He didn't have to answer any of the busybodies. Success did its own talking.

Found: In Trouble

Erik and Lyle had sports in common, but their relationship went far deeper. Although they had their disagreements, like all brothers, people who knew them were struck by the depth of their kinship. Nobody else could understand what it was like to be the son of Jose Menendez.

"Their bond appears to me to be the best brother bond I've ever seen," said Erik's friend, Noel Nedli.

They were very different. Lyle was the dominant older brother, while Erik was more vulnerable. Different as they were, there was something that bound them tightly almost from the beginning. If their earliest memories were of their father talking, urging, commanding, their next memories were of each other. They drew together for companionship, for solidarity in the face of their father's control, and, not least, for completion. For each had blank spots that needed filling in.

Erik was timid and insecure as a child, greatly lacking in the Menendez self-confidence that often crossed into arrogance.

Lyle developed the self-assurance and cockiness that marked him as the rightful heir to Jose's legend. For this reason, and others, Jose favored Lyle so much that relatives called Erik the "throwaway child."

Unlike Jose, Lyle was understanding of Erik's insecurities and fears. Because he had his feelings locked away, he could be a rock for his younger brother.

But there was an unnerving, dispassionate quality in Lyle that cut him off from other people. Whether this was something he developed in response to Jose's demands that he not show weakness was not clear. People who met him were struck by the blankness in his eyes.

Erik, on the other hand, rescued wounded animals from the highway, and his sensitivity showed up in the poetry he wrote to friends. He felt bad if he broke a branch off a tree. Lyle, it seemed, gravitated to Erik, seeking this connection with simple human feelings that had been stolen from him.

Postcards that Jose mailed to his sons from Hamburg, Germany, demonstrate the differences between the two brothers and their roles in the family. To Erik he wrote, "I trust that you are not crying much," referring to an unknown problem, perhaps Jose's departure.

Lyle, he is sure, is being good and is "taking good care of Mama."

Alone, each had failings, each felt he could never really measure up to his father's hopes and demands. But together they made one person who was everything Jose would have wanted in a son. Powerful, creative, sensitive, and supremely confident, the boys in combination were the corrected image of Jose that he was bent on creating. Better than Jose.

They were not physically demonstrative with each other; Lyle hated that hugging crap everybody did these days. But he and Erik had a closeness on a level that was almost instinctual. With just a word they could communicate volumes of thought. Their minds seemed to flow on similar wavelengths. And Lyle had an entrancing way of speaking that was as lulling as a piece of music. You could listen to him for hours, and some friends did. He was so persuasive he could make the most outrageous things sound reasonable.

When they were young, Jose was always forcing them into contests, in everything from tennis to seeing who could get his teeth brushed and into bed first. Lyle usually won. Jose would encourage Erik on, sometimes making fun of him.

"Why can't you be more like Lyle?" he was told.

In the words of one law enforcement expert, Erik became the "family bun boy," the one who accepts second place as his lot. When they got in trouble later on, Erik took the blame. After all, Lyle was the anointed firstborn, and nothing could be allowed to block him from achieving the success Jose planned.

Over the years, friends of both brothers would note the devoted, almost irrational awe in which Erik held Lyle. Lyle got the girls, Lyle won the trophies, Lyle had a great body.

"My brother's such a stud," he told friends. When one friend met Lyle he was surprised because Erik's body was much more leanly muscled. It was like he was under a spell.

"My brother's a god," Erik told a girlfriend one day. "I worship the ground Lyle walks on."

The girl couldn't understand it. Like some other friends of Erik's, she thought Lyle was trouble, or, in her words, "seriously psycho."

Where this devotion verging on worship came from is unclear. Perhaps it was a result of the fact that Jose was too remote for his younger son to approach. Jose was an overwhelming presence, almost like a god to his sons. And like a god, he got inside them and manipulated them on the deepest levels. Lyle, on the other hand, was reachable, and he even tried to intervene on his brother's behalf sometimes when Jose was punishing him, which only raised Lyle's stock in his younger brother's eyes. Lyle understood Erik's dependence on him, and he traded on it.

"Never think for a second that I favor anyone over my brother," Lyle wrote Erik later on, when both their lives were on the line. "It is not our place to judge each other. Only to support each other. I can tell you for sure that you will not last for long in a life isolated from me."

Over the years Lyle also learned to manipulate his father. Jose was vulnerable because he believed he knew Lyle as certainly as anyone can know anything. After hundreds of hours of soul-scouring conversations, he thought he had explored every tunnel that twisted away from the main cavern of Lyle's personality. But Lyle dug some tunnels his father never found, and he hid things in them. Friends said both brothers learned to lie to their father. If Lyle was caught cheating in school, he had an explanation, a good, detailed one. Jose, who was so tough on his son but who loved him more than anyone, including Kitty, believed his son and then went after the school.

Lyle, said one family friend, had his father "wrapped very tightly around his little finger."

When the family moved to Pennington in 1979, Jose enrolled his sons in the Princeton Day School, a highly competitive prep school that sends many of its students to the best Ivy League colleges. Tuition is $12,000 a year.

The campus is large and green, and it seems to sit on top of the world, surrounded by a thick wood. Its colonial-style buildings are solid, and the atmosphere is quiet and scholarly, almost like a monastic retreat. One teacher said it reminds him of American public schools in the fifties.

Fittingly, the official school vehicle is a Volvo.

Erik and Lyle were average students at best, even with Kitty's aid. In fact, before they went to visit relatives, there would be a family meeting at which Jose would lay down rules about what could and could not be discussed. One thing that could not be talked about was the boys' classroom performance. Protecting the family's well-rehearsed image was vital to Jose.

Lyle's problems in school began almost as soon as he enrolled in the sixth grade. Patricia Cross, his teacher, found him not very prepared and lacking in concentration. He failed to hand in assignments, and his first report card carried a 4-B grade, which was "marginally bad," Cross said.

Midway through the school year, Jose and Kitty made an appointment to talk to the teacher. They arrived late, about 10:30 P.M., and Cross was on her way out to the parking lot to go home.

"They accosted me, 'Where do you think you're going?' kind of thing," she said later.

Cross has taught about 30 years, but she had never been spoken to the way Jose Menendez talked to her that night. He was belligerent, demanding. Jose was mad because he felt the teacher was failing to appreciate his son's abilities. He blamed Cross for the low grade. "I was his teacher and I should teach him" was his attitude, Cross said.

"My son can do better. You will make sure he will," Jose concluded bluntly.

The whole confrontation lasted five minutes, but Cross was flabbergasted. On Lyle's next report card, Cross raised his grade to a 3-B, in part because she had been intimidated. She also resolved to avoid the Menendezes from then on. Her experience was not unique. Jose and Kitty developed reputations as "problem parents," Cross said.

Sandra Sharp, another teacher, said both boys had learning problems, but Jose would not accept that his sons could be flawed. "Jose said his son was perfect," Sharp said. "He was going to be the best tennis player in the United States, and he was going to be the best student in school. And he expected perfect grades because he had a perfect son."

Sharp noticed the work that came from home was always better than the work in class.

Lyle also was in trouble at school. PDS, as it is known to

veryone around town, frequently held bake sales to raise
money. Many students hated them, and Lyle, said a friend, used
ne of the sales as an occasion to play a joke on the school
dministration. Whipping up a bit batch of chocolate, he dipped
rdinary dog biscuits into the mixture and produced a chocolate-
overed dog treat.

He carried the biscuits to school as his contribution to the
ake sale. Customers dug in hungrily, which surprised the friend
ecause the biscuits looked exactly like what they were, dog
iscuits covered with chocolate.

"People were eating them," the friend laughed. "They
veren't bad."

The school administration, however, failed to appreciate the
umor and gave Lyle detention, which amounted to performing
hores around the school grounds, according to the friend.

Another time Lyle was caught cheating at PDS. He had an
xcuse. He blamed his parents for putting too much pressure on
im. The school administration called Kitty and Jose in for
conference.

Both boys lagged behind their classmates in terms of matu-
ity. Lyle wet his bed and was still playing with stuffed animals
vhen he was fourteen. Kitty continued helping him wash his
air in the bathtub at the same age.

There were increasing signs that there were serious problems
netasticizing at home. Another cousin, Diane Vander Molen,
tayed with the family several summers and for a year beginning
a 1982, when the Menendezes were living in Pennington.

Erik and Lyle were about twelve and fifteen, and Diane was
wenty-three at the time. All three were playfully wrestling
round one night. Suddenly, without any signal, Lyle and Erik
egan undressing the young woman. Working wordlessly, as
hough they knew each other's mind without speech, they tied
er up and stripped off her blouse.

All the time Diane was screaming. Suddenly the attack
eased. It was eerie. The two boys had attacked her packlike,
vith no warning, and then, without explanation, the assault
nded.

There was another attack around the same time. On this
ccasion Diane and Lyle were alone in the family room, located
ff the kitchen. Kitty and Jose were out for the evening. Erik
vas asleep upstairs.

The cousins were lying parallel to each other on the couch,
vatching a movie, when, again, with no warning or words

being spoken, Lyle climbed on top of her and began fondling her breasts.

Diane froze. She said nothing while Lyle worked intently. She hadn't enticed him. Nothing was said. He had just struck. Just as in the other attack, this one suddenly ceased when she finally broke free of her hypnotic state and moved.

She never told anyone about either incident at the time.

Lyle's first real romance occured when he was fifteen. What made this relationship notable was that it was every bit as weirdly innocent and chaste as the previous attacks on his cousin seemed bizarre and sexually perverse.

Stacy Feldman was dark-haired and sweet, on the quiet side. The daughter of a Princeton car dealer, she was Lyle's equal in terms of rank and status in the community.

Stacy was a tennis player, manager of the men's varsity team. The number one singles player on that team, of course, was Lyle Menendez. At first, when she saw him only on the team bus traveling to and from meets, Stacy thought of Lyle as a "typical jock," kind of obnoxious. But as she got to know him, she saw his funny, sensitive side.

Within weeks they began dating. Their first date was to see *Raiders of the Lost Ark*, an action movie, which Lyle always liked. Seeing movies was the one experience that was not filtered through his parents, so Lyle was a devoted video fanatic. And, it seemed, he became so enraptured by the images on the screen that he took in uncritically much of what went on up on the screen. His favorite movie, according to a friend, was the Al Pacino remake of the old gangster movie *Scarface*. Set in modern Miami, the movie focuses on a Cuban immigrant who rises to power through drug dealing and a ruthless willingness to kill anyone in his way, including close friends. It was *The Godfather* with an extra helping of blood.

Lyle loved to watch the movie at home with all the lights off and the sound up very high. "I love *Scarface*," he told one family friend. It's Al Pacino's "most enlightening role."

Stacy and Lyle grew so close so quickly that friends remember feeling Lyle was unfriendly. If Stacy was talking to friends, Lyle would come up and stand there waiting for her to finish. He stood only a few feet away, not saying a word, staring intently until she broke free.

Others noticed this strange behavior in Lyle. Alicia Hercz, who taught Spanish at Princeton Day School, said Lyle came into her tiny office. While students passed in the hall outside her

The Menendez family portrait: Lyle, Kitty, Jose, Erik.
(WAYNE WILCOX STUDIOS)

Lyle Menendez, the handsome, athletic, firstborn son.

Erik Menendez, always considered the more emotional brother.

A proud father
and his sons.
Jose with Erik (*l.*)
and Lyle.

The Menendez home
outside Princeton, New
Jersey, was a beautiful
wooded spread that
now serves as a public
recreation area.

A mother
and her sons.
Kitty with Lyle (*l.*)
and Erik.

Erik in his father's Mercedes on the day of his graduation from Beverly Hills High School.

The Menendez mansion in Beverly Hills. It had a swimming pool, guest house and, of course, the required tennis court. (*Los Angeles Times* PHOTO/RICK MEYER)

Upon graduation, Erik was provided with fashionable two-wheel transportation for commuting to UCLA.

The defense team: (*l. to r.*) Jill Lansing, Leslie Abramson, Michael Burt, and Marcia Morrissey. Lansing and Burt represented Lyle; Abramson and Morrissey represented Erik. (YAEL SWERDLOW)

The prosecution team, Pamela Bozanich (*l.*) and Lester Kuriyama (*r.*), was backed by Beverly Hills police detective Les Zoeller. (YAEL SWERDLOW)

Terry Moran, Court TV reporter, provided daily commentary for millions of viewers. (YAEL SWERDLOW)

open door, Lyle sat down and stared at her, without saying a single word.

Hercz tried to manufacture a conversation. "How are you?" she asked. No response. "Do you need help with your homework?" No response.

She grew increasingly uncomfortable, but Lyle continued to sit and stare. This went on for forty-five minutes. It was as though he were in a trance. Nothing Hercz said could pull him out of it. Finally he just got up and left. The same thing happened a second time, and Hercz finally mentioned it to Kitty. After that Lyle never came back.

Lyle and Stacy fell in love. They walked around campus hand in hand, which was against the rules. Campus authorities didn't interfere because they felt these two awkward kids needed each other.

They were voted "most married" on campus, a fitting honor because they discussed marriage. As Lyle did with the stories he made up with his stuffed animals, he got into the marriage fantasy very deeply. He wanted to rush out and pick out china patterns, and they even settled on names for their kids.

"We were pretty naive," Stacy said. "We were both interested in it. We had discussed it, definitely."

Lyle spent heavily on Stacy, buying her roses every Friday and an assortment of jewelry, including bracelets and an emerald heart pendant. He also buried her under a whole family of white teddy bears, which they called "pookies." His stuffed animals gave him comfort on those days when things were bad at his house, and he thought they would be good for Stacy as well.

To her, the family seemed close. "My parents were getting a divorce when I was with Lyle," she said. The Menendezes included her in family gatherings, and Stacy grew close to Kitty, the workhorse around the house. "She did everything," said Stacy.

The sons had few responsibilities beyond succeeding in school and on the tennis court. Others were hired to mow the lawn. Lyle once tried working in a Princeton restaurant to earn a little extra money. When he got his $33 paycheck, he sniffed, "I could find that going through my laundry bag." He quit after a few days.

Stacy spent two Christmases at the house and remembered the whole family gathering to attend midnight mass. They exchanged gifts in the morning. One holiday Lyle bought her a huge teddy bear. Erik and Lyle received a computer.

But Lyle was never a committed student. He found school a waste of time. "He said to me one time he was not sure he wanted to go to college," said Stacy.

Lyle used to talk about opening a restaurant with his father. In his senior year in high school, when he was finally able to drive, he spent almost every afternoon at Chuck's Spring Street Café, munching on the spicy chicken wings.

Stacy and Lyle were considered square. "These kids went to the prom and came home early," said Robert Watson, the father of one of Stacy's friends: "If they walked into a party and saw an ounce of cocaine on the table, they would turn around and walk out."

Finally Stacy decided to call off the relationship. She realized she was too young for marriage, and she ended it after she went away to college.

"There were a lot of things I hadn't experienced," she said.

Lyle was hurt and responded with a grand gesture. He offered to buy his girl a fur coat if she would stay with him. He even made a $150 down payment on it. She turned him down.

His relationship with Stacy had the same innocent, sweet, dutiful uprightness about it as his dealings with his parents. The boy who wanted to marry Stacy was the same boy who kissed his parents when he left the house and addressed other adults with excruciating politeness as Mr. or Mrs.

But his classmates saw something else. In the Princeton Day School yearbook when Lyle graduated and prepared to go off to college, students mocked one another with funny predictions for the future. For Lyle, the question, "Can you imagine him . . ." was answered, "Doing manual labor." In a school where not one graduating student would probably ever do manual labor, that is a remarkable commentary.

"Intrigued by . . ."

"Money" was the answer.

"Found . . ."

"In trouble" was the prognostication.

One source of trouble that threatened to interrupt the Menendezes on their way to enshrinement with the Kennedys and Rockefellers as a great American family was the near collapse of Jose and Kitty's marriage, and Kitty's plunge into despair.

She had always given him all the freedom he needed and desired. Jose had taken full advantage of it, acquiring a string of mistresses over the years. His longest-lasting relationship was an affair he began in about 1978 with a dark-haired, self-confident executive woman—in short, Kitty's opposite.

The two traveled together and even entertained as a couple at the woman's Manhattan brownstone. Jose's friend Steve Wax attended a party there one night and watched Jose play the urbane host for his paramour.

Jose cared deeply about Louise, but there was never any thought of leaving Kitty. Wax served as a warning for Jose on that score. His divorce had cost him his house, his money, everything. "When you come down to it, you exchange one problem for another," Wax told his friend. It was best to keep women at arm's length.

Jose was not willing to part with his growing fortune in an acrimonious divorce.

But while Jose had no serious plans to run off with the mistress, there were also no plans to end the relationship. Louise was good for Jose's ego. She loved to listen to him talk, and he loved to talk. And she didn't ambush him with stories about his sons' latest troubles as soon as he walked in the door. Mostly, she didn't cling to him and demand more of his time than he felt like giving.

For some time Kitty was none the wiser about Jose's indiscretions. He lulled her with false, yet convincing, claims of faithfulness. He feigned shock and outrage to his wife at the number of colleagues who kept mistresses on the side. Jose portrayed himself to his wife as an excessively dutiful husband, just as Erik an Lyle were excessively dutiful sons.

But gradually Kitty became suspicious. The late nights and last-minute calls claiming he had to have a drink with a business associate finally got to her. Many nights she sat home in New Jersey, looking out over the lake, waiting anxiously for Jose to arrive from work. One friend said Kitty would sometimes drive into Manhattan and scour the streets for Jose.

Kitty uncovered one of his trysts in about 1981, and walked out of the house for a few days. Relatives talked her into returning. The script for his perfect family did not include a broken marriage.

"He did not indicate he loved her," said Jose's brother-in-law Carlos Baralt. "He needed her to be a part of the family unit, to be there for the kids . . . help him as a wife."

Finally, in 1986, just about the time Jose's career at RCA was ending, Kitty discovered the long-running affair with Louise. Jose also decided to make a clean breast of things with his wife and admit his other dalliances. After the family moved to California, Kitty had lunch with an old friend, Myra Ford, whose husband had worked for Jose at RCA. "Were you ever aware of Jose straying on me?" Kitty asked pitiably. She mentioned the names of five women.

The revelations had serious consequences for Kitty. Always subject to depressive moods, she spun downward out of control. Her talk of suicide became serious enough for her East Coast therapist to set her up with a counselor in California when she and Jose moved west for the job at IVE. She began taking large doses of Imipramine, an antidepressant, and Xanax, a tranquilizer. She revealed to Lyle that she was in such despair that she was taking thirteen pills a day.

She also wrote a series of sad, rambling, suicidal, self-pitying letters to Jose, her therapist, her sons, and, sometimes, to nobody.

Taken together, the letters, collected after her death, draw a portrait of a woman who felt worse than betrayed. She was not just a fool, but the worst kind of fool because she had always known this is what men were like. That's why she had resolved not to let any of them get close enough to hurt her the way her mother had been hurt. Then she did and she suffered for it, just as she knew she would.

"For twenty-four years," she wrote to Jose, "I lived in a dream. I tried so hard to keep my marriage complete but didn't know how. I guess I thought giving you free reign [sic] to succeed in your career regardless of how lonely it was at times was my way of being strong so that you would never have to worry about us. I thought if I concentrated on the house and our boys—their grades and sports—that you would feel fulfilled. I guess I was playing the wrong keys and was deaf to the music. For half of those twenty-four years I was both deaf and blind. . . . Reality I see as pain. It's not a world I choose to live in.

"You never were mine really. You were anticipating your time with her. I could go on and on (so many times when I was at East Brunswick with the boys I would call you around 6–6:30 and you would cut me off telling me you were going to be late for cocktails with someone before a business dinner). . . . You are a brilliant, aggressive, soft-hearted man, and I am truly in love with you even as I write this. . . . In the end, all I really wanted was to be as much [of] a friend as Louise. I wanted to be able to comfort you like she did. . . . Believe me, you were and are my only love and truly my best friend. Thank you for that. I take with me the spirit of love that I hold dearest—that of my children and you."

That apparently was written not long before a suicide attempt in which she was briefly hospitalized for a drug overdose. Elsewhere, she wonders if she will ever be able to trust Jose again.

"It's 12:30 and I just finished crying," she begins in another letter, this one not addressed. "I felt so alone and fearful I just couldn't control it. I pictured myself shooting a gun (the rifle in the closet, to be exact) into my head. . . . Why am I writing all this? I hate it when Jose is gone. I go crazy in this bed by myself. Why can't I be strong and independent?

"I wish I could trust him again. I would feel so much more connected to him if only I could truly know him. I once thought I did, but obviously I didn't. Why am I so much in love with him? I hate him for what he did to me. I hate myself even more. I really think I could die now. I've given my boys whatever values I could to help them succeed in life. But they must never think I deserted them. It must always be viewed as an accident. My pain is not their fault. . . . I can't believe I'll ever regain the strength and security I once felt—without it who am I? I deplore what I've become."

Fifteen months after the affair had ended, Kitty wrote a less pained note to her West Coast therapist, Lester Summerfield. It shows her struggling to regain the balance in her marriage.

"Well, Lester, I spent from 5–6 p.m. contacting Snowbird Ski Lodge and the Canyon racquet club arranging for a ski vacation the week before Christmas for our two sons and us. Then I made dinner, folded a load of towels, and have been relatively mindless of my problems. I also read an article or two or three in women's magazines, re: the usual. My husband just called to say he'd be at least another 2 or 3 hours at the office. I was light and jovial on the phone, and he told me how much he loves me. It's now 7:45 and I really would like a drink, but for now settled for a brand [sic] muffin—the only thing I had to eat today. I'm settling for a Sprite and some cigarettes. Erik should be home soon. I wonder if he has had dinner. He may need help with an English essay tonight. Perhaps a drink wouldn't be wise. It seems when Jose doesn't arrive home within a reasonable hour expected, I need the comfort a drink supplies.

"11:22 p.m. My son, Erik, came in at 8 p.m. I fed him and helped him with his essay. When he fell asleep on the sofa I teased him until he was awake enough to type his essay before going to bed. I showered and got into bed. Went downstairs and fixed a light bourbon and Sprite. Got back into bed [with] a cigarette and five minutes later, 11:35, Jose called to say he was going to have a quick drink and be home within the hour. My mood shifted and I was no longer mindless of my thoughts."

Kitty didn't make any effort to hide her shame from her sons. Erik heard her crying night after night in her bedroom. He felt terrible, but he never asked her about it. In his family, pain was kept secret, even if it was a very public secret. But Kitty's despair affected her sons deeply, making them resent their father for what he was doing to their mother. Still, Kitty wouldn't leave and make a new life for herself.

"My parents' divorce," she told her children, "ruined my childhood."

Jose also considered leaving her when he moved west. There was probably no better place in the world to be footloose and single than in Hollywood. In the end, she and Jose decided to stay together, and he gave her a new Mercedes convertible on Mother's Day after moving to California. But she never really trusted him again.

And she became obsessed with Louise, once even flying to New York from California to stalk her. She stood outside the woman's building waiting for her to come out, and took pictures of her when she did. From her first therapy session with Dr. Summerfield to her last, not long before the murders, Kitty invoked the name of Louise as though it were a curse.

12

The Screenplay

The Los Angeles basin is one of the world's most crowded bits of earth. Millions of people are camped elbow to elbow in stucco apartments, or backed up, bumper to bumper, on one of a dozen freeways. These are well-worn images of Smog City. But people who move to Los Angeles are often surprised to find a mountain range, covered with trails, rattlesnakes, coyotes, and even a puma or two, sitting right in the middle of the metropolis like a bear on an ant's nest.

The Santa Monicas, parts of which in the past few years have been set aside as national park land, rise in West Los Angeles, then coil and tumble westward into Ventura County, separating the coastal city of Malibu from the more populous inland valleys. Here and there, highways snake through the canyons to the beach. There is Topanga Canyon, with its eccentric old art community holed up in shacks perched over the road like aging, scruffy blackbirds, and farther west there is Malibu Canyon Road. Wealthy suburbanites have been colonizing this area, building big white cement dwellings with green metal railings on their decks that hover over the two-lane road as it twists its way to the ocean.

In these hills are many other roads that circle around the canyons, going nowhere. But there is one narrow, serpentine Stunt Road that brings you to a place unique in the L.A. area. Eight miles on, you come up to the peak of the ridge, and the road drops off precipitously on both sides. There, after parking your car and walking one hundred fifty paces along a dirt path, you can squat down in the dust, with the cattails and scrub, and see two worlds spread out below. Off on one side is the San Fernando Valley, lit up like thousands of marbles illuminated from the inside. On the other you can look far down to the Pacific Ocean as it nudges up to the shore.

This is called The Key, and it was here that Erik Menendez and his best friend, Craig Cignarelli, a brash, good-looking boy with a wave of jet black hair, liked to come. Crouched in the dirt for hours, they made plans for the future. Craig was set on being president, or at least a senator. Erik, his friend said, was interested in a company that specialized in corporate takeovers, sort of like the Billionaire Boys Club. If not that, his mind swinging in a more generous direction, maybe he would found a city for the homeless called Divinity. The ideas sounded fanciful, but these boys were raised to think big. And Erik had serious plans to be able to afford such things.

"I promise you, I'll be very rich," he would tell friends. He intended to make his wealth before he reached thirty, according to the friends, then sail the world.

Sometimes, huddled together in the dust of the mountains, their minds wandering as the wind whipped up the mountain from the beach, Erik's and Craig's thoughts turned in other directions. Then they dreamed of committing the perfect crime, Craig said, one very clever and convoluted, a statement bold enough to make everyone take notice.

Erik met Craig shortly after the Menendezes packed up and moved west in the summer of 1986 for Jose's new job. Jose and Kitty bought a magnificent house in Calabasas, in the western San Fernando Valley, for $950,000. The house was set on fourteen rolling acres in one of the canyons of the Santa Monica Mountains. But the family didn't move in. Kitty decided the house needed renovating, and she took it on as her personal project. A sudden convert to all things southwestern, she decided the house should have a more regional look.

But soon the project grew out of control, and Kitty wondered if it would ever be finished. While work dragged on, the family settled into a rented house on Park Livorno, across a man-made lake from the Calabasas Park Tennis Club. It was one of those neo-Spanish designs with white outside walls and a red-tiled roof. One room was piled high with boxes that were never unpacked the two years they were there. Some boxes that hadn't even been unpacked from the previous move.

Lyle stayed behind to attend Princeton University. He wasn't enthusiastic about going there. He preferred the University of

Pennsylvania, to be near his former girlfriend, Stacy. But Jose dismissed the idea. He felt a Princeton degree was worth far more in the business world. With the connections Lyle could make at Princeton, he would never have to fight his way to the top as Jose had done. There would be no blood on his hands when he began counting his money.

Lyle was living in a big house on Mountain View Avenue in Princeton, which Jose had purchased only a few months before the RCA job ended. It had acreage and its own private lake.

Kitty worried about leaving Lyle behind. She called Jose's sister Terry nearly every day to check on him. Was he studying? she asked. Was he cutting classes?

Kitty was especially concerned about a lithe blond waitress Lyle had met at a local restaurant. Jamie Pisarcik was a tennis player and coached some on the side. Like Kitty, she was older than her man, by five years. Kitty took an immediate dislike to her. She didn't like the way Jamie dressed in casual tennis gear all the time, which Kitty thought was cheap. She also thought Jamie was a gold-digger, which was not true. In fact, Jamie, a strong-minded, independent young woman, paid Lyle's way many times when they went places.

Kitty also complained to her therapist that Jamie was "taking Lyle places sexually he was not prepared to go." Whatever she meant by that, it sounded like she knew far too much about her son's sexual habits.

Before starting school, Lyle went south to Alabama for a time to live with Jamie, who took a job teaching tennis. Jose and Kitty were genuinely alarmed. Jose loved the fact that Lyle was turning into such a ladies' man, but he wanted Lyle to be smart and not get hooked. After much agonizing Jose hit on a plan to break up the relationship. Secretly he arranged to sponsor Jamie on a European tour. He used someone else as the front man, so she went abroad happily for several months, playing on the Satellite Tour, a kind of minor league of tennis. She never knew the syndicate that sponsored her because they thought her game had so much potential was nothing more than her boyfriend's scheming father.

The only hitch in Jose's plan was that Lyle followed Jamie to Spain, Italy, and France like a puppy dog. Kitty didn't even know he was gone, friends said. She kept sending him money, which was forwarded to him abroad. Lyle earned a little extra money stringing rackets for the players.

* * *

During the early months in California, Kitty and Jose's marriage was near collapse. Kitty cried constantly, Erik discovered a note lying on a table one day and, frightened, called Lyle back in Princeton. She was sorry, but she had no other way out, the note read. She had to leave. "I realize now that Jose never loved me," she wrote. "He got what he needed from Louise. I'm sorry to take this way out."

Erik thought Kitty was moving out. Lyle said it sounded like a suicide note. He told Erik to put it back and he would talk to Mom.

When he did, she denied planning suicide. "I have never regretted a single day" of marriage, she snapped. Lyle was stung by his mother's response. Let her stew in it, then. He had been ready to move in with her to give her support if she left his father. He had never thought of Kitty as a mother that much, and now she had lost him as an ally.

Kitty's suicidal thoughts were serious enough that one of her therapists, Dr. Summerfield, thought she should be hospitalized. The problem with Jose, he felt, was only one part of her depression. There was something deeper and more sinister, but Kitty refused to divulge her secret. She would say only that it was "sick and embarrassing."

Another therapist, Dr. Edwin Cox, called Jose in hopes of enlisting him in his wife's cure.

Cox found Jose to be "a very, very strong personality, bright, quick, very dominating. Very much in control of every situation."

Jose said he wanted the marriage to work out, and he was willing to do whatever it took to get Kitty back in step as a wife who took care of the house and children. But Cox found him uninterested in being a friend to Kitty, which was her desire. "Maybe he had emotions, but I never saw them," Cox said.

Kitty's despair did get Jose's attention, convincing him he needed to handle this problem before it went any further. He became a much more considerate husband. Now they held hands openly, and Jose was frankly solicitous of her. He bought her presents and made an effort to be home more. He even agreed to go out with her friends, such as Karen and Pete Wiere, with whom they played tennis on Sundays and often grabbed a pizza. Sometimes he even went shopping with her, something he would never have considered before.

Kitty's new power was especially evident in public, for she

sometimes humiliated Jose in front of others, which at one time would have brought swift and certain punishment.

Once the family was hurrying through L.A. International Airport on the way to a tennis tournament. They were taking along their little mutt, Rudy, but there was a snag and the ticket seller wouldn't let the dog on the plane. Jose volunteered to stay behind and catch another flight with Rudy. Kitty blew up.

"Oh, so you can meet your girlfriend in the bar," she raged. The woman behind the counter blanched and others in line for tickets turned to watch, but Kitty would not be silent. Jose replied mildly:

"No, I'm not that stupid."

Nonetheless, the whole family took a later flight.

Erik enrolled at Calabasas High School as a sophomore. Though a public school, its west Valley clientele was almost as exclusive as the student body at Princeton Day School. Brash, good-looking, often arrogant, they had plenty of money and lots of freedom. BMWs and sport vehicles dotted the student parking lot.

Erik stood out from the first day he arrived. He was probably the only student at Calabasas High who dressed in a blazer. East Coast preppie was the look. He was stiff and formal, and he naturally felt awkward as the new kid in school.

But in California, out from under the comparisons with his brother, Erik soon found his own identity. He gravitated to a small group of boys who were among the elite on campus. They were bright and cocky, and Erik fit right in, developing his own style, which a friend characterized as a bit loud and theatrical, with a rebellious undercurrent.

Kitty had been genuinely concerned about her younger son's sexual orientation, and when they moved to California she gave him six months to find a girlfriend. He made it easily. An older girl, a cheerleader who was voted by her classmates "most likely to become a yuppie," took Erik to her prom.

He called her "chipmunk" and himself "gopher," and he could charm her parents like nobody else. But he turned out to have a side that wasn't nearly as cute. After arguing at a party, he locked her in a room and refused to let her out, she said. She screamed and cried, but he just laughed. Finally he let her out, but she had had it with him.

"He is one of the oddest guys I've ever met," she said. "He's very arrogant, very confident, but deep down he's got a lot of problems and insecurities."

His most serious relationship was with a fellow tennis player from Thousand Oaks, Janice. She was blond, blue-eyed, athletic, the daughter of a college professor, unspoiled and innocent.

Erik told her he couldn't believe he was dating a blond, blue-eyed, California girl. He had always thought he was ugly, maybe partly because Lyle liked to make fun of his big ears. Erik and Jan fell in love, though they rarely said, "I love you." Their favorite expression was "I fond you."

While Kitty saw nothing but flaws in Lyle's girlfriends, she was delighted to see Erik spending time with Janice. Jan liked Kitty too. She was a lot of fun, if a little scatterbrained. Both had the same birthdays, and Kitty treated her like a sister, cooking pasta with her and inviting her on a family trip to the Bahamas. In some ways Jan was closer to Kitty than her own mother.

Kitty gave Jan a credit card one day and asked her to go buy Erik some hipper clothes. Her son, Kitty admitted with a laugh, was a "fashion flop," and she hoped Jan could bring some taste to his wardrobe.

There was a lot of that kind of kidding in the family, Jan saw. The first time they swam together, Jan beat Erik. Jose laughed, "You let a girl beat you?"

"I wasn't trying," Erik replied defensively.

Emulating Lyle's largesse with his girlfriends, Erik bought Jan jewelry, including a solid gold necklace that made her mother jealous. For her eighteenth birthday Erik sent her eighteen roses.

It seemed like a great family, fun to be around, and loving. There were only occasional dark edges. One was Erik's apparent lack of ethics. While Jan was an honest, decent person, he cheated constantly.

His homework was done for him, and he cheated on tests without a second thought. "How can you do that?" Jan asked. Erik knew there was something wrong with it, but never considered changing his behavior until he met Jan, she said.

Trying to make it easier for the two to have sex, Kitty did just about everything but hand her son a packet of condoms. She made a fake ID for the girl so she could go drinking with Erik, who had his own fake ID.

After the family moved to Beverly Hills, Kitty used to call up the girl's parents and tell them it was too late for their daughter to drive home after dates. Kitty put Jan in the room next to Erik's, where dirty clothes were thrown over the sofa and the bed. The next morning she giggled over breakfast, asking them if they had had a good night's sleep. "I heard a lot of walking around upstairs last night," she said.

Erik took Kitty's not so subtle hint. He sneaked into Jan's room and they sometimes slept together, but they never had intercourse.

"We fooled around," she said. "We had the best foreplay. But we could not have sex. It just didn't work."

Kitty didn't let the matter rest. After Erik had been dating the girl a few months, she asked him if he had had intercourse with Jan, the girl recalled. No, Erik replied. "I thought after three months for sure you would have," Kitty said.

One of the best nights of Jan's life was a Christmas party at the Menendez mansion. Kitty arranged it like a ball for a member of royalty. She ordered a fully decorated tree, twenty feet tall, then rejected it because the ornaments weren't quite right. After several others were shown to her, she finally picked one.

There was a pianist in a tuxedo. Everyone, Jose, Kitty, Lyle and Jamie and Erik and Jan, assembled by the front door to greet the guests. "What an awesome family," Jose said proudly as he looked them over.

Kitty extended her hand to be kissed, and Lyle introduced himself and his brother with rigid formality, like a man trying to make an impression. Remember me, was the way it sounded to Jan.

Erik and Janice disappeared upstairs to fool around in his room. But even then, with champagne exciting their blood, they could not have sex. The most important woman in his life, it seemed, continued to be his mother.

"We never figured out why we broke up," Jan said later.

After the killings, Jan had nightmares of Kitty walking up to her with holes in her.

Erik's most important relationship at Calabasas High School was with Cignarelli. Like many other students, he was a fortunate son, well off financially, drove a customized car and dressed in flashy exercise gear. He flirted shamelessly with waitresses, whom he pointedly addressed by their first names, which he read off their badges.

When they snubbed him, he just smiled. He was self-confident enough to withstand rebuffs from people named Suze. In fact, he didn't mind being described as cocky. He felt he had reason to be cocky.

He was a child of Hollywood. His father was an executive at MGM/UA. But he also had a blustery innocence to his cockiness that made him popular at school. He also had a reputation for mystery. At social gatherings he would be there one minute, entertaining people gregariously. The next he would disappear from the party. As did Erik, Craig liked to write.

Cignarelli was also a skilled tennis player, ranked fifty eighth nationally in the USTA's 1988 junior rankings, so it was natural that he and Erik Menendez should become close. Each of them had a romantic vision that he would do something great, if not on the tennis court, then surely in the boardroom.

Both became captains of the school tennis team, and Craig introduced Erik, who was a year younger, to the right kids, especially to some of the best girls. While it was easy to see what Erik could gain from a relationship with Craig, what attracted Craig to Erik was his academy-bred intelligence. Erik seemed different from the other students, more substantial. He thought about things, Craig noted.

Taken with the Book of Revelation in the Bible, Erik was impressed when Cignarelli suggested that perhaps the rivers of blood it talks about in the last days might not be arterial. Oil, said Cignarelli, is the blood of the Earth. That blew Menendez's mind.

It was things like that that drew them together and cemented a relationship. "We could see that somehow we were different," Cignarelli said. "When we're together, we feel like we have an aura of superiority."

According to Cignarelli, other students at school soon came to appreciate this superiority. "People really looked up to us." In fact, Cignarelli said, the two of them began to cultivate pledges to their cult of personality.

"We're looking for those with an intense desire to excel," he said. "It's a unique quality you don't find among lesser individuals. I'm sure I'm at the MENSA level," he said, referring to the club for the mentally gifted.

They even had nicknames for each other. Erik was the Shepherd and Craig was the King. The explanation of the nickname King seemed easy enough to understand in a man who fancied himself a future presidential candidate, but Shepherd?

According to Cignarelli, Erik was more spiritually minded. "The Shepherd leads the sheep, you know," he said.

But some saw another side to Erik's spirituality. In his mind, it seemed, the Shepherd was not necessarily a benign presence who meekly leads his flock to water.

One friend said Erik talked about how the world was changing. "There is a good and there is an evil," Erik said, "and sooner or later they will come together."

Sitting in a hot tub one night, he told another friend that he and Cignarelli were starting a clique, according to this account. The new boy could join, but he should be warned, "I'm evil."

The other boy supposedly became so frightened he got up and left.

Of course, it's not unusual for teenage boys to try to impress people that they are renegades. And it's hard to know how much of this was juvenile romanticizing in a boy who was trying to carve out his identity in a family filled with strong personalities. But one friend took Erik's malevolent posing so seriously that he read books containing "meditations" that would protect him from someone attacking him on a spiritual plane.

When Craig and Erik wanted to get away from the confining social pressures of the San Fernando Valley, they would drive up Stunt Road in Craig's VW convertible.

Reaching The Key, they looked down on the necklace of lights from the strip of multimillion-dollar beach-front homes and specialty shops in Malibu. Out beyond was the inky darkness of the Pacific Ocean.

It was a bracing setting. They would talk for hours about the future. "Erik and I have a real desire to change a lot in the world," Cignarelli said.

But sometimes their fancy would turn in another direction, and they would talk about how one would go about committing the "perfect crime," Craig said. Sometimes it would be a robbery, sometimes a murder.

Then, on New Year's Day in 1988, one of their fantasies took clearer shape, and they decided to turn it into a screenplay. With both of their fathers involved in the entertainment industry, it seemed reasonable to think that if they came up with something good, they could sell it to a studio for production. Jose even promised to show the play around. Maybe this would be the first great thing they would do.

They adjourned for three days to the Cignarelli family's cabin in the mountain community of Frazier Park, located on the eastern side of the Tehachipis as they descend toward Bakersfield and the wide-open farmland in the San Joaquin Valley. Relaxing in the quiet outdoors, their creative juices flowed

freely. They wrote a sixty-two-page screenplay called
"Friends." To build in a sense of the macabre, they wrote by
candlelight, each of them tossing ideas out and the other scribbling them down.

The story is about the self-centered son of a wealthy couple
who commits five murders, starting with his own parents.

Filled with blood, intrigue, fast cars, and ornate wealth, it is a
very dark, modern tale in which the hero is a killer who dies
with a wry smile on his face.

The play, which Erik's and Craig's mothers typed, opens with
the protagonist, Hamilton Cromwell, going through a file drawer
in a darkened room. Cromwell, according to notes scribbled on
the page, would be played by Mickey Rourke.

"He is eighteen years of age, with neatly styled dark hair,"
according to the script. "Eyes are very exotic and defined. He
is a sophisticated, good-looking gentleman of rather large stat-
ure. He gives an aura of a mentally disturbed person yet very
intelligent. . . ."

Hamilton discovers a will and reads it.

"To my beloved son Hamilton, a man I have respected and
felt proud to father, I bestow the Cromwell estate and the
money in my Swiss account . . . one hundred and fifty-seven
million dollars, and the pride of the family, the portrait of
Oliver Cromwell."

The camera pans to Hamilton, who "smiles sadistically."

In the next scene, Hamilton is climbing to his parents' suite,
a weapon called a razor rope dangling at his side.

"A gloved hand is seen gripping the doorknob and turning it
gently. The door opens exposing the luxurious suite of Mr. and
Mrs. Cromwell lying in bed. Their faces are of questioning
horror as Hamilton closes the door behind gently, saying,

"Good evening, Mother, good evening, Father (his voice is of
attempted compassion, but the hatred completely overwhelms
it).

"All light is extinguished, and the camera slides down the
stairs as screams are heard behind."

The murder is left to the imagination. But for Hamilton,
who inherits, as he foresaw, the family estate, this is just
the beginning.

Hamilton's friend Joe appears next, delivering the valedictory
address at his college graduation ceremony. "You, my friends,
are the elite. The future to our nation's continued success
throughout the world. Let's make America proud.

"But they, my friends, are like sheep waiting to be probed by the shepherds that are seated here around me."

This was almost a word-for-word rendering of Og Mandino, Jose's favorite author. I am a lion, Mandino said, not a sheep. There was a critical difference, however. Mandino wrote that the sheep were to be prodded, not probed in some act of spiritual bestiality. Once Erik's nickname, Shepherd, was considered in light of this rendering, the passage had new meaning.

Hamilton is next shown seated at a typewriter in his mansion. "Zoom camera to paper. It reads: 'Five Deaths to Perfection.'

"Chapter 1: Mr. and Mrs. Jacob Cromwell.

"Chapter 2: . . ."

Hamilton, it seems, is an aspiring author who wanted his macabre tale of murder to be as realistic as possible.

Hamilton proves not only to be greedy but extremely sensitive to rejection. When his girlfriend, Martha, leaves him, he pays a call on her with his razor rope. The gratuitous violence and misogynist messages continue throughout the story. At one point a character calls a friend who isn't home. The answering machine clicks on with a recorded message that begins with a woman's cries. "Take her in the back," says a male voice. "Beat her if she won't shut up."

Besides its obsession with blood and its shallow exultation of wealth, the play is remarkable for its lack of moral viewpoint. The only thing consistently seen as good in the story is money. Characters dash around in expensive cars, make a "ton of money" illegally in stocks, and kill without hesitation. The twist, however, is that Hamilton is not killing just for fun and profit. He is setting everything up to frame one of his friends for the murders.

Finally Joe and another friend named Mike track Hamilton to his basement lair, a room filled with ice, in which are encased the bodies of Hamilton's parents and other victims.

In a struggle Hamilton is killed. He dies smiling.

But his plot succeeds. In the denouement Mike is on trial for his life for killing Hamilton and the others. While the jury deliberates his fate, he plays a tape left for him by Hamilton:

"You must understand, Mike, that the price a player pays for failure in the game of life is death."

Mike is convicted. But like any good sport, he shows no emotion as he is led off to await his execution. The final camera shot planned by the authors shows Hamilton's completed book about the five murders. Hamilton's picture, with his sadistic smile neatly in place, is on the cover.

The screenplay demonstrates the friends' belief not only in the blood-for-art's-sake ethic in Hollywood, but also seems to indicate that playing the game well, making the grand gesture, is more important than anything else, including life.

The fact that these young men lived lives of privilege not so very different from the antihero of the story only made their tale more intriguing.

Over time, the original document was rewritten, producing a version forty-one pages longer than the first. Here, Hamilton kills his father, then approaches his mother, in bed waiting for her husband. The son is shot by his mother when he tries to enter her bed. The woman runs out the door, but is caught by her son, who kills her.

Besides the incestuous overtones, the greatest change here is that in this version we are given a hint of a motive. "My father was not a man to show his emotions," Hamilton says, standing over the coffin, a Santa Ana wind whipping his hair.

"I can only hope that he loved me as much as he loved all of you. Sometimes he would tell me that I was not worthy to be his son. When he did that, it would make me strive harder to go further, to prove to him that I was worthy, just so I could hear the words 'I love you, son.'"

With tears welling up in his eyes, Hamilton concludes, "Nothing I have ever done was good enough for this man, and I never heard those words."

As startling as this bitter eulogy would have been to the friends of Hamilton's parents, it was even more intriguing when considered in the light of Erik's relationship with his father.

One of Hamilton's friends approaches him after the funeral in the later version of the play. "We'll survive, buddy," the character says. "Your father would have wanted you to. He knew what a great man you would become . . . even greater than he was. A warrior who has lost his parents is still a warrior."

Craig Cignarelli was fascinated by their creation. Later on, he was frequently interviewed by police. Once he got in a snit and sent a fax telling Zoeller and Linehan he would no longer talk to them.

"As I walk through the valley of the shadow of death, I shall fear no evil," the fax read. That was one of Erik's favorite expressions. Craig added a thought of his own. "And the trail signifies evil."

He signed it, "Hamilton Cromwell."

13

Problems at Princeton

In an egalitarian age, Princeton University relished its elitism. Not everyone could be a Princeton man. In 1987 the average SAT scores for the incoming freshman class was 649 on the verbal section and 695 on the math portion, the highest total in the school's history. The mean score for all college-bound high school seniors was in the mid-400 range on both tests.

But high SAT scores were no guarantee of entry. In one recent Princeton class, only 457 out of 1,115 high school valedictorians were admitted.

Among the other qualities valued in a Princeton student is the ability to stand aside from the pack. But even leadership doesn't guarantee entrance to the tree-shaded campus and the Gothic buildings that house the classrooms. In that recent class, only thirty percent of student council presidents and only thirty-one percent of the editors in chief of high school newspapers who applied were admitted.

The school does try to achieve a certain geographic and ethnic mix. For instance, the admissions office seeks out minority students who have done well on pre-SAT tests.

The 1987 class was six percent black, and eleven percent Asian, Puerto Rican, Chicano, and Native American. A member of that group was Lyle Menendez.

Kitty's friends were always amazed at her ability to get Lyle into Princeton. His grades were just above average, and his test scores, which Kitty could not take for him, were unremarkable. Lyle qualified for special consideration as a student athlete. As the top-ranked player in the Middle States tennis region, he had been recruited by the university's tennis coach, David Benjamin.

But gaining admission to Princeton is in some ways just the beginning of the test. The students quickly learn that they are no longer special.

"By the time you get through freshman orientation, your ego is gone," said one student, according to Samuel A. Schreiner, Jr., author of *A Place Called Princeton*.

"You realize that you're in the fast lane, that all of a sudden you're one of a thousand—or four thousand—stars in some particular aspect of life. In the first few weeks it cuts you down to size, and after that gives you a chance to grow up."

The wonder, according to Schreiner, is not that some students crack under the pressure, but that more don't.

F. Scott Fitzgerald, a Princetonian, addressed the feeling of competition. "From the first he loved Princeton," said one of his fictional characters. "[Its] lazy beauty, its half-grasped significance, the wild moonlight revel of the rushes, the handsome, prosperous big-game crowds, and under it all the air of struggle that pervaded his class."

And now Lyle, who didn't care much about a classroom education, and even less about the wild moonlight revel of the rushes, considering how far his father had gone on guts and grit, was a Princetonian. Small wonder that Lyle was never happy there, never seemed to be a part of the social milieu.

He knew he could cut it in the "real world," but he was not so certain about the rarefied atmosphere at Princeton, where his intellect and vocabulary no longer impressed anyone. Even his wealth and his father's status, to which friends said he frequently referred when meeting someone new on campus—telling them about all the big jobs his dad had—were not that unusual. Lyle was just another face on a big campus with a distinguished history.

Brendan Scott was a doctoral student at Princeton's Aquinas College and a faculty fellow at Wilson College, where Lyle lived, in the fall of 1987. A warm, outgoing priest, he also was on the team of the Catholic Chaplaincy in the area and as a result made it his business to get around to meet new students who were Catholics, to invite them to take part in parish activities.

"I looked on my job at Wilson College as one to be available to a large range of students," he said. "I made sure each of them had my phone number."

Scott had already met Christopher Codik, a tennis player, and through him his reserved roommate, Lyle Menendez.

He found Lyle to be "a quiet kid. He was not particularly huge into social stuff" because he often was flying home on weekends to be with his family, who had recently moved to California.

"I don't think Lyle was disliked," said Scott. "I don't think he was very well-known."

One of Scott's favorite icebreakers with new students was to invite them out to dinner with a few friends. It was designed to be a casual, low-stress situation, allowing everyone to become acquainted while breaking bread.

If the mood was right, Scott would informally let the students know of his role and interest in getting them involved in the campus religious life. Lyle, like other students, was not enthusiastic, though neither was he rude.

"I'll let you know," he said noncommittally.

But even though the two young men were not that intimate, when Lyle was accused of plagiarism in his very first semester on campus, it was to Scott that he turned.

Plagiarism is a very serious accusation at Princeton. Students are required to sign an honor code, and instructors are told not to grade any paper that does not have a statement at the top saying in the student's own hand: "I have neither given nor received assistance" in the preparation of the assignment.

The school's honor system is almost a century old and has become a cornerstone of the Princeton experience. As described by Schreiner, it is, indeed, one of the most serious responsibilities a student can bear at Princeton and one of the most telling character traits the individual can carry away into the harsh world beyond the cloistered campus. Schreiner writes:

The effect of the honor system is better described by Jeremiah S. Finch, a former dean of the college, in *A Princeton Companion*: "The honor system is less a set of rules than a state of mind—that honesty in examinations is assumed—and a common bond among Princetonians." There are no proctors or faculty members present during examinations, and every Princeton student is under obligation to report any cheating that he or she witnesses; discipline under the code is administered by an undergraduate honor committee.

Over the years it has been a heavy burden to bear for seventeen- to twenty-one-year-olds driven by personal and family sacrifices to make a go of Princeton, and there have been a number of heartbreaking incidents where a violation ruined a life. I am personally grateful that I never had to confront the anguish of reporting a fellow student and equally grateful for having witnessed the gallantry of men who failed rather than compromise their honor.

So it was that Lyle ran afoul of the sacred honor system. He had been accused of copying a lab partner's homework assignment in Psychology 101.

Lyle could not have been prepared for the experience of being dragged up on cheating charges. After all, his parents had always done his papers for him. At Princeton, even Jose had pitched in when Lyle had a paper due on the philosophy of Niccolo Machiavelli, the sixteenth-century Italian statesman. Jose dictated it to his secretary, who Federal Expressed it to Lyle. Of course, Jose had substituted his own theories for the philosopher's. The essence of his treatise was that the threat of pain guaranteed loyalty far better than personal trust, a policy Jose employed. Machiavelli's best-known work, *The Prince*, does suggest that the most effective leader is an amoral and calculating tyrant, but his other works were far more republican in nature, and Lyle got a bad grade.

At first Lyle tried to handle the plagiarism charge himself. "He came to me and asked if I would be his defense counsel," said Scott.

Scott listened as Lyle politely explained that he had missed some previous assignments in class and, as a result, could not afford to miss another. Because of his frequent weekend trips home, he often took his homework with him on the plane. On this occasion, however, he lost his notebook with all his notes in it in an airport.

With his back to the wall, he went to his partner and asked to "look at his results," said Scott.

The resulting assignment so closely resembled the work of the partner that the instructor, a graduate student, flagged it and brought it to the attention of campus authorities.

Whatever the truth of Lyle's story—one professor who believed Lyle had no moral sense called him "Lyle, Lyle Crocodile"—Scott concluded that "it isn't so black-and-white" an issue as the university was making it out to be.

Scott agreed to represent Lyle. The hearing before the disciplinary committee, consisting of two faculty members, two administrators, and two students, began at eight one evening and lasted a grueling four hours.

Lyle explained that he had not really been trying to deceive anyone. He pointed out that he had left blank a key section of the assignment which called for a sketch. If he had really wanted to cheat, he could simply have placed a piece of onion-skin paper over his partner's drawing and lifted it whole.

Then he read something to the committee that he said his father had sent to him about ethics, and how important they were becoming, both in school and in the business world. At this time, of course, scandals were rocking the nation's confidence in its leaders as a result of the Iran-Contra investigation. At the same time Oliver Stone's blistering indictment of the corporate boardroom, *Wall Street*, was generating big box office returns.

Jose, according to Lyle, urged him to guard his honor carefully because "in the business world that issue was becoming more strict."

As always, when he was in a moment of crisis, Lyle tried to cover himself in his father's protective cloak. The truth of the matter was far different, of course. When Lyle, under pressure from his aunt Terry, had called Jose to tell him about the cheating accusation, Jose had not taken it very seriously at all.

Jose was sure nothing serious would happen to his son over the cheating incident. "That they would jeopardize his son's life over a lab report was beyond his comprehension," Lyle said later.

For once Jose misjudged the situation. After nearly an hour of deliberation, the committee found Lyle guilty and suspended him for a year.

Scott was disappointed. Even more disappointed was Lyle's father. He flew immediately from Los Angeles for a meeting with the university president. He was granted the meeting, according to Scott, "primarily because he had dropped everything and flown across country to do this."

Jose Menendez based his appeal of the ruling on the contention that the punishment was unduly harsh, that it did not fit the crime. This was just one homework assignment, after all. It would not have been even a large part of Lyle's final grade.

"Isn't it out of balance" he asked, "to put him out of school" for this?

But the university was immovable. One's word must be kept. The authorities informed Lyle that he could return in good standing in a year, and so he was out.

After the suspension, Lyle was bitterly angry at the student he believed turned him in. He ranted, according to a friend, that he could have the boy's legs broken. There is no evidence he ever acted on the threat, if indeed he made it.

Lyle had come face to face with the core of the Princeton personality, and he had failed the test. Still, it isn't hard to believe that Lyle secretly was glad to be rid of Princeton. He hated the work, and he rarely participated in any campus activities. He was so devoted to winning and being first that he couldn't stand to be just another student struggling to make it at a top school. Even after this humiliation his father would not allow him to transfer to UCLA or the University of Pennsylvania. Perhaps Stanford, but nothing else would do.

His father's willingness to go to bat for him with the Princeton authorities did have a large effect on Lyle. With pride he described how his father had dropped everything to come to his aid. "His dad came out and took his side in all his glory," said his friend Donovan Goodreau.

When Lyle's dismissal was upheld, Jose broke down and cried. Lyle had never seen his father cry before. Jose used to tell his son he loved him, but he did it in such an artificial, offhand way that it made Lyle uncomfortable. Here was real emotion.

Like other problems in the household, the family tried to bury this secret inside the fortress of secrecy that their wealth afforded. To most outsiders, even to family, the Menendezes remained the perfect nuclear unit. A husband, a wife, two dutiful sons, all in love with life, all in love with each other.

Jose's sister Marta Cano heard from her son Andy that Lyle had been kicked out of Princeton. She called Jose and, without betraying her knowledge, asked how things were going. Great, she was told.

"How is Lyle doing at Princeton?"

"He is doing great," Jose replied buoyantly.

Crimes and Punishment

Lyle was out of school, but Jose was determined his son was not just going to lie around for a year until his suspension was up. Jose had always worried about giving his sons too many advantages and turning them into rich brats. So he said it was time Lyle learned what it was like to really work for a living. He put his son to work at LIVE.

Lyle got his own office. His job was to review expense reports and to look for ways to improve efficiency, possibly by computerizing the accounts. He was to be treated like any other employee. He had to make an appointment to see his father.

Seeing the way his father operated up close made a deep impression. He saw the way the atmosphere changed and grew tense when his father arrived. Lyle's friend Glenn Stevens recalled the stories Lyle told him later about how Jose would humiliate people, berating them loudly if he thought their ideas were useless.

"I thought, 'How could you idolize somebody like that?' " Stevens said.

One of Jose's favorite targets was Bloom, whom he disparagingly referred to as a "two-bit gangster and a porno dealer," Lyle said. Jose said he was worried that Bloom was so disgruntled over being forced out of LIVE that he might call on some of his alleged mob contacts to get Jose.

But Jose was not one to back down. "I could fuck with him just as bad as he could fuck with me," Jose raged.

Lyle was in over his head at his job. He especially hated reviewing expense reports, knowing that if he flagged any as excessive, his father would take harsh measures. "Knowing my dad, these people could be fired or demoted," he said.

He also said other employees resented him as the boss's son. One of those employees, however, said Lyle was resented more for his lack of effort than his connections to the executive suite.

Jeanie Mason said she worked for Jose as a troubleshooter analyzing Bloom's operation. She also supervised Lyle. It was a distasteful experience. "He would go about the business of appearing to peruse" the documents he was asked to look over, but actually did almost nothing, she said.

Sometimes he would ask Mason a question. Other times they chatted about one of Lyle's favorite occupations, watching movies. What stuck in Mason's mind most about her experience with Lyle Menendez was an event that occurred one day after Jose had left the building. Lyle went into his father's office and sat down at his desk.

For a long time he just sat in Jose's big chair, immobile, staring into space with a vacant, mesmerized expression on his face. It was like the times he had gone into his teacher's office and sat like a mannequin for forty-five minutes. He was playing some videotape in his head of his own making, but Mason could not tell what it was. All she was sure of was there was something seriously wrong with this kid.

"He looks right through you," Mason said later. "Lyle Menendez reminds me of that scene in *Jaws* when Robert Shaw is talking about the sharks, when he says, 'They have lifeless eyes, doll's eyes.' There isn't anything there."

Mason decided this was contained rage. He had so much hatred in him that his only response had been to blank it out. All emotion went with it. What his hatred was over, she did not know.

Mason also felt Lyle did not know who he was. From his behavior she believed that who he really wanted to be was Jose. His hypnotic trance at his father's desk was an attempt to absorb his father by going to the place that was most intimately Jose. And that place, his Holy of Holies, was Jose's office, where Jose cut his deals and shredded his opponents.

Lyle finally left the company after one of Jose's associates went to the boss and complained. Jose asked what they would do with such an employee if he weren't the boss' son. Fire him, he was told. Okay, Jose said, do it.

Meanwhile, Erik was having his own problems.

One day in March 1988, Erik and Craig were playing tennis

on the courts at Calabasas High, set in the brown hills of the western valley. A group of Latino youths from another part of the city showed up. They were looking for a boy who had made the mistake of winning the affections of the girlfriend of a gang known as the J.C.'s, or Junior Crips. The gang was looking to teach the rich white kid a little respect.

As they passed the tennis court, they saw Erik without a shirt. "Nice body, faggot," said the leader.

"Nice face, ugly," Erik responded intemperately.

Craig walked up to the fence, and they spat on him. Erik demanded that the gang members apologize to his friend. One of them came around and punched Erik. More blows were exchanged, and within moments Erik and Craig were being attacked by a half-dozen gang members.

Erik was badly beaten, receiving three broken bones. But that wasn't the end of it. The Menendez family began receiving threatening calls at the Calabasas rental house. Jose thought he saw strange cars with tough-looking kids inside prowling the neighborhood. He hired a security guard at the rented house and quashed any ideas Erik had about pressing charges.

"Do not get involved," Jose told Erik firmly. "We don't want to deal with gangs."

Erik was driving by now and building his own reputation as hell on wheels. He became so well-known that the police in Calabasas knew him by name.

One of his closest friends at the time as John List, Jr., a slender blond boy who lived in Hidden Hills, not far from Noel Bloom. One day John and Erik decided to play a prank on their tennis coach, who had a court at his Agoura Hills home, just west of Calabasas. Just before they were to meet, Erik called John and told him he had had an accident in his Nissan 200SX.

"I thought the whole gag would subside because he totaled his car," John said.

But no, Erik was still ready for fun. John picked him up and they drove over to the coach's house. Sneaking into the backyard, they painted the judge's stand alongside the court a shocking pink.

"Erik was a pretty goofy kid" was all the coach would say about the incident.

Despite private coaching, Erik was having difficulty making the transition into the competitive world of California tennis. His ranking plummeted to near one hundred for players eighteen and under.

Therefore, in the summer of 1988—unlike most other summers—neither brother was hitting the tennis circuit. The summer was hardly uneventful, however.

Two homes not far from the Menendezes, both owned by the parents of friends of Erik, were burglarized. The List house in exclusive Hidden Hills, not far from where Noel Bloom lived, was struck first, in early July. The Woodland Hills home of Michael and Sharon Ginsberg was hit a few days later, on July 15.

Among the items hauled out of the Ginsberg home were Lladro porcelain statues, a videotape recorder, two word processors and a printer, an exercise machine, and an assortment of expensive jewelry. A stick of tobacco and a one hundred-pound safe were also taken. In all, the haul was worth approximately $40,000.

The theft was discovered by a guest at a party thrown by the Ginberg's daughter, Randi. Melissa Heller was in the bathroom with a friend playfully fighting with a bottle of powder. They had had some beer to drink so they didn't notice at first the mess in the room.

Drawers containing jewelry in the bathroom were turned over, and some of the jewelry had fallen on the bathroom floor. "They're really messy here," Melissa joked to her friend when they finally noticed it.

Melissa found Randi. "There's a lot of jewelry hanging out of your mom's closet," she said. Within minutes, Randi was tearfully ordering everyone home.

When his parents left for Europe, John List, Jr., stayed behind to watch the house. List, like many teenagers in similar situations, decided to throw some parties. During the few weeks his parents were gone, he had fifteen of them. "I knew it was time to stop when I drove around the corner coming home from dinner and found sixty people waiting to get into my house," he said.

John invited his best pals, Craig, Erik, and some of the other Calabasas High kids. After Erik's brother, Lyle, came home for the summer, John began to get close to him too. They played tennis several times.

John heard about the Ginsberg burglary, but he did not know his own house had been hit—$2,500 in cash and $50,000 in jewelry was taken—until his parents returned from Europe. One night shortly after they got back, they were grimly waiting at the kitchen table when he came home.

His parents asked him to compile a list of who had attended the parties. Erik knew the combination to the alarm system at the house. John knew, because he had been around so much. He had even spent the night there on occasion. But Erik was one of his best friends. John's father liked Erik too, describing him as "a good-looking, quiet, but not aloof" young man who was "a pleasure to have around."

Near the end of the summer, as John prepared to go off to college at Colorado State University in Fort Collins, he crossed paths with Erik Menendez. They were with a group of ten to fifteen kids parked in a Calabasas cul de sac, all chatting about the end of summer and looking toward the future.

Things were strained, and finally John brought up the burglary. "A lot of people are saying you did it," John said tentatively.

"Things aren't exactly what they seem," Erik replied. Then he handed List one of his poems.

Each line began "I cry for . . ."

It was a perfect symbol for John, whose father said the crimes may have been committed to draw attention, an act of crying out for help.

Veteran Malibu sheriff's detective Imon Mills, the investigating officer, noticed some parallels in the two burglaries. There was no forced entry, and in both cases the parents were on vacation while their children took care of the homes.

But the most compelling piece of evidence was the discovery in the safe of the List house of two pearl necklaces worth a substantial amount of money. The owner was Sharon Ginsberg. It seemed the thief had developed a conscience and decided to return the necklaces—to the wrong house.

Eventually, Mills tracked the burglaries to the doorstep of the Menendez family. On September 16, 1988, Erik gave a statement implicating himself. He said he had had "to make three to four trips to and from the [Woodland Hills] residence, because of the volume of property taken."

The property was hidden in a locker, along with the property taken from the List home.

Though Lyle had been involved in the Ginsberg theft, Erik, according to sheriff's department reports, "emphasized that he is taking full blame and responsibility for both burglaries, and refused to implicate anyone else."

This seemed to fit the pattern between the two boys. Erik took the fall. From Jose's practical perspective, however, it made sense because Lyle was an adult and could have received much harsher treatment than Erik, still a juvenile.

Erik said the crime had grown out of a practical joke. He and a friend had been looking for the keys to the family van, which they intended to move to make the Lists think it was stolen, when they came upon a piece of paper with the picture of a safe and a combination.

The Lists and Ginsbergs were shocked when they discovered Erik was involved. Such a nice person, said Sharon Ginsberg. "What's not to trust?"

Erik was arrested and booked for burglary, then immediately released in the custody of an embarrassed—and angry—Jose Menendez.

A short time later, a rented van containing the stolen property pulled up to the sheriff's department in Malibu and out jumped Jose Menendez and Jerry Chaleff, Erik's attorney. A professorial lawyer whose office fronts the Pacific Ocean, Chaleff is one of the best criminal lawyers in Los Angeles, with a long list of high-profile cases under his belt. A juvenile burglary was pretty small potatoes for him. But as usual, Jose wanted the best for his sons.

The usually commanding Jose presented a very different face to the detective, who remembered him as a person of "very gentle behavior."

Although most of the stolen items were recovered, Jose still had to reach into his pocket for about $12,000 to pay off the Lists and Ginsbergs for property that was never recovered or damaged.

The burglary victims did not press for jail time. As one parent put it, "we were just happy to get our stuff back."

After pleading guilty, Erik was ordered to perform community service with the homeless. It was also strongly recommended that Erik get psychiatric counseling. Kitty's therapist, Dr. Summerfield, recommended a short, energetic psychologist who was well-known around Beverly Hills as a kind of therapist to the rich, famous, and neurotic, L. Jerome Oziel.

There had been another burglary earlier that spring in Princeton, a crime that was not connected with the Menendez boys until long after Kitty and Jose were dead.

Between April 23 and 24, 1988, the New Jersey offices of the Sierra Club and the office of the Princeton Friends of Open Space were entered. A copy machine, an electric typewriter, and an answering machine were taken, with a value of about $1,100.

The offices just happened to have been located in what was known as the Mountain Lakes House at 57 Mountain Avenue in Princeton. This was the same property that Jose had purchased just before the family left New Jersey, and the house in which Lyle continued living for a time when he began attending Princeton University.

Jose had sold the house in November 1987, and it was turned into a historical landmark.

Princeton Township police discovered the house had been entered through a bathroom window on the second floor of the building. The window was broken and the screen had been removed. There was blood on the windowsill, suggesting the burglar had cut himself breaking in.

The police got a break in the case when they heard a strange story from a confidential informant. The informant said he had been riding with the Menendez brothers to the beach one day in the summer of 1988 in Lyle's Alfa Romeo when Lyle slapped an unusual cassette in the car's tape player.

No music came out of the speakers, just voices talking and background noises.

Lyle turned to the informant, the man said, and bragged that what he was listening to was a tape recording of a burglary Lyle had committed at his old house. "Lyle said that he . . . taped the entire burglary," the informant said, according to a police report.

Lyle was never charged with the crime. By the time it was linked to him, he was in jail on far more serious charges.

As summer became fall in 1988, Jose decided to throw in the towel on the Calabasas estate. The fight on the tennis court was one factor. But the burglaries crushed him. In private, just as he had after Lyle was kicked out of Princeton, Jose broke down in tears. Things seemed to be coming apart at the seams. He couldn't understand what was going wrong with his grand design for the perfect family. Kitty was a basket case, and his beloved sons were turning into screwups. He struck out angrily at his boys, saying they couldn't even pull off a crime successfully. Jose meant the remark as a petulant gripe, but Lyle felt his father was showing him that even in crime he could not measure up to Jose's high standards.

"[My] father taunted me during the Calabasas robbery by making fun of Erik and I, and telling us how stupid we were for doing it in ways that left the police all sorts of clues," Lyle said later, according to Oziel. The fact is, they thought they had come pretty close to committing a perfect crime, Oziel said. If their father had not forced them to face the music, they would have gotten away with it.

They apparently told the therapist that they thought the burglaries were nothing more than foolish pranks. But Oziel warned that he saw a pattern developing, and he was certain there would be more crimes. He asked their permission to inform Kitty and Jose about his concerns.

The baffling thing about these crimes was the fact that Erik and Lyle had victimized not strangers but friends, people they valued. Lyle had gone out of his way to be nice to John List, Jr., playing tennis with him. Hamilton Cromwell, who set up one of his friends to take the blame for his murders, would have understood it.

Jose and Kitty went shopping for a new house in Beverly Hills. Despite the family problems Jose's business fortunes were just getting brighter and brighter. Even Kitty was excited at the prospect of living in Beverly Hills.

After making an offer on the Elm Drive house in October 1988, Kitty waited anxiously for word on whether it would be accepted. Finally her agent called. "Kitty, you got your zip code," she was told.

The move to Beverly Hills gave Jose the opportunity to leave behind the problems in the San Fernando Valley, as well as his sons' friends, who he felt had been bad such influences. So when Craig Cignarelli showed up one night, Jose was angry.

Erik took Craig and another friend on a drive around the new elite neighborhood in the family Mercedes. While the boys were enjoying the view, Jose called up on the car phone and sternly ordered Erik home. When Erik arrived, Jose stalked out of the house and began shouting at a very intimidated Cignarelli.

"If I ever see you on my property again, I'll fucking kill you," he screamed.

"Okay, I'm leaving, I'm sorry," Cignarelli replied.

But Erik jumped in front of his friend's car and refused to let him drive off, defying his father openly. "You're not leaving," he said, according to Cignarelli.

What would have happened next is anybody's guess, but just then Kitty came running out of the house. "What are you doing?" she said to Jose, astonished by her husband's behavior.

"Hello, Craig," Kitty said. "I'm sorry."

Cignarelli's friend told him later that Jose was holding a gun at the time.

15

Lyle's Disciples

Donovan Jay Goodreau is a beanpole of a man—tall and slender with a shock of dark brown hair—who never ceases to be amazed by the world's wonders.

A twenty-three-year-old Californian from the San Jose area, Donovan's upbringing in the household of a Silicon Valley computer engineer was comfortable. But it was nothing like what was in store for the impressionable young man.

Following two years of liberal arts and business courses at De Anza College in the northern California community of Cupertino, Donovan's wanderlust spirit got the best of him and he decided to hit the road.

"It was time to leave," Donovan said. "I wanted to make it."

The third week in January 1989, Donovan and his brother's ex-girlfriend took off for the East Coast in his 1974 International truck. After winding his way slowly across country, Donovan rolled into Princeton one cold, snowless day in February 1989. He loved the place immediately. "It was a beautiful place, so I stayed," he said later.

Donovan was attracted to Princeton's cozy intellectual atmosphere, which gave him an opportunity to mix with students about his own age while sorting out his future plans.

Princeton was going through a metamorphosis, trying to adjust to the changing times that had come to central New Jersey. High-tech industry had moved in, attracting a flood of newcomers fleeing the big cities of the Northeast. Blocks of condominiums in cheery colors were beginning to appear on the hills surrounding the old brick neighborhoods, through the town still retained its Old World charm.

Donovan found a waiter's job at T.G.I. Fridays, a restaurant playing to the town's younger population and located near the college community's quaint downtown area, several narrow streets of small shops. Looming over it all are the great flagstone towers of the university.

At the restaurant Donovan met Jamie Pisarcik, an aspiring tennis player who was picking up some pocket money as a waitress. Before long the perennially cash-short Donovan moved into Jamie's third-floor, two-room apartment in downtown Princeton across the street from a bicycle shop, where he also was to do a stint as a salesman and mechanic. A short distance away was another restaurant, Casa Lupita, where he took yet another waiter's position to make ends meet.

It was through Jamie that Donovan met Lyle. "You have to meet my boyfriend," Donovan recalled Jamie telling him. "You're so much alike."

When they finally did meet over dinner one night, Donovan found that Jamie was right. "We wanted the same thing," Donovan said—success.

Almost immediately Lyle took Donovan on a tour of the Princeton campus. Donovan was thrilled. Before long they were devoted to teach other. "I was Lyle's best friend. I spent every hour of every day with Lyle."

Well, almost.

Lyle had school, and it was an extremely important semester. It was his first one back since his suspension a year earlier for plagiarism.

While Jose and Kitty did not like Jamie, their feelings about Donovan were different. They regarded him as something of a flake, but Jose said he seemed harmless enough. And there was a side benefit: Donovan was willing to pitch in and help do Lyle's papers for him. Now that Kitty was so far away in California, she could not be counted upon to keep Lyle's grades from sinking to the far end of the bell curve, and so she was delighted with Donovan's arrival on the scene.

"Donovan is a godsend," Kitty gushed to a friend one day.

Lyle's return to Princeton started off on a sour note when he discovered that he was to share a room at Gauss Hall in Wilson College. Lyle had wanted a single.

Lyle's student adviser, senior Tom Henderson, said that when Lyle saw the belongings of another student strewn about his room, Lyle threw them into the hall. Books, clothes, wall hangings, everything was tossed out like last night's garbage.

"Lyle knew it was a seven-person suite," Henderson reflected. "I do what I want" was his attitude, in Henderson's eyes.

Once again Jose came to Lyle's aid. He wrote a letter asking for a change, and Princeton's housing supervisors assigned Lyle a single room at Gauss, No. 115. He holed up in there, just as he had the year before, avoiding student get-togethers.

Henderson tried to talk to Lyle about his attitude. He walked into Lyle's little room and began chatting, but Lyle said little and rarely even looked at the older student. He didn't even put down his paintbrush. He was painting the radiator black, a violation of school rules, but Henderson said nothing and left the unfriendly student to himself.

But if he was unfriendly to campus officials, he gravitated toward a group of students, several of whom were jocks like him, who became almost disciples to the remote but charismatic Lyle Menendez.

Many friends of the Menendez boys seemed to have a common look and attitude. They were cool, casual, arrogant, and devoted to attaining success and the good life. Their hair always seemed to curl at just the right spot on their foreheads, and their pickup lines rarely failed. But Glenn Stevens appeared somewhat different in that he had a serious side to him.

"I kept pushing Glenn on Lyle because Lyle needed friends, I thought," Donovan said. "Glenn wasn't superficial. He was real."

The friends liked to hang out in Lyle's room, or spend the evening at one of the eating clubs on campus, drinking, shooting the bull, and leaving their studies to the last minute.

Piercing this circle of friends was never easy for Donovan because he wasn't enrolled at Princeton, although he hinted that he might attempt to enter the school in the fall. Still, some of Lyle's friends viewed him as an outsider, almost a stranger, and this attitude was to play an important role in Donovan's ultimate ouster from Lyle's dorm room and then from his life.

"I was almost labeled as a leech because I wasn't in school," Donovan reflected.

He relished a chance to get a rare taste of life at one of the world's preeminent learning institutions. It was fun to tool around the historic campus with Lyle at the wheel of the bright red Volkswagen beetle Lyle had at the time. Suddenly, without ever having to go through the competitive tests and selection process, Donovan found himself living in a Princeton dorm with the elder son of a millionaire entertainment executive from Beverly Hills.

For Donovan, just being with Lyle was a revelation.

Sure, his new friend had quirks. But who was perfect? For example, Lyle just couldn't keep track of petty cash. Jose allocated his son a certain amount of funds in a bank account, but the account was almost always near empty, Donovan said. One day Lyle even found $48 in a pants pocket in a pile of laundry in the VW's trunk.

And they were always playing pranks around the campus, he said. There was the time they followed a pizza truck making dorm deliveries and decided to snatch a pizza and have a feast while the driver was away. According to Donovan, Lyle brazenly ran up to the pizza truck and looked through the various containers until he found the one he wanted, heedless of the danger of getting caught. Then the friends ran off with their catch, laughing.

Something new was always happening when you were in Lyle's company, he said.

Donovan's association with Lyle was practically out of *Pygmalion*. Lyle attempted to instill in Donovan the driving philosophy of his father. Just as Lyle was Jose's student, Donovan became Lyle's as the philosophy of success at any cost or, as it was later described by its harshest critic, "lie, cheat, steal, but win," was to be passed down the generations.

Lyle ordered Donovan to memorize whole passages from the Mandino book *The Greatest Salesman in the World*. And Donovan did it. Months later, he could still recall phrases like "I will persist until I succeed . . ."

Donovan clung to Lyle like his shadow. He told Lyle he was traveling on a shoestring, and from time to time Lyle would loan, or give, Donovan subsistence cash. They frequently spent the entire night out having fun, then came in in the early morning raising hell, waking the other students up, and then Lyle would sit down and try to cram for that day's exam.

"We spent every minute of every day with each other," Donovan said.

Lyle was a dreamer, much more devoted to his future than his present at Princeton. One dream was to open a restaurant. He and Donovan took off for the Rutgers campus in New Brunswick one weeknight and cased the town for hours looking at possible restaurant sites. He had school the next morning, and the two of them didn't get back until 4:00 A.M.

"But that never bothered him," Donovan said. Lyle lived "for now."

It wasn't two weeks after their initial meeting, on a cold day toward the end of February, that Lyle took Donovan to the grave of his grandfather, Jose, who had died two years earlier. The gravesite was located in a cemetery in Belleville, New Jersey, north of Newark, the home of Lyle's grandparents.

As Donovan shivered in his Bermuda shorts on that cold winter day—"I was shaking," he remembered—his new buddy began a long peroration. Donovan described it as "one of the weirdest conversations I ever had with Lyle. I didn't say twelve words."

For three hours they stood over the grandfather's grave while Lyle discussed the burden of emulating his father.

"I'm the only son who can make it in my father's image," Lyle said. Lyle, Donovan said, declared "there was a lot of pressure on him" to meet—and exceed—Jose's incredible track record of rising to the top of every company he had ever managed.

"Sometimes I know I'm not the best role model, especially for Erik," Lyle said softly, seemingly immune to the chill by the welling-up of emotion in him. "But it's what I have to be—to be somebody."

His family, Lyle told Donovan, "was willing to do anything and everything so he would be that person" who could take the baton from Jose as the next leader of the Menendez clan and carry it further.

Lyle expressed regret he had not been closer to his grandfather, that he had not spent more time at the feet of Jose's father tapping into that great man's mind and life experiences.

It was clear Lyle had high expectations. "He wanted more. He always wanted more. So did his father. It was kind of genetic."

Donovan was impressed at the strength of the tie between father and son. It was wonderful how much Lyle loved his father, Donovan said. "And what a father he was. He would always answer the phone when Lyle called him, even at company meetings."

Soon it was nightfall at the cemetery. Lyle said it was time to leave. Donovan was nearly frozen. But he would never have thought of asking to leave on his own accord as he listened raptly to Lyle talking of kings and things and the greatness that was expected of him.

"I would have stayed all night," Donovan said.

This was Lyle at his most mesmerizing, talking in that quiet, lulling, insistent way that made everything sound possible, everything seem reasonable. But finally it was over. Donovan was impressed as he had never been with anyone. In his mind Lyle was the rare individual who was able to understand what was expected of him and to meet those expectations. A great man becoming.

Donovan didn't know how far short of those expectations his friend was falling, or that in private he feared he would never be able to match his father's feats. On the long drive back to Princeton, Donovan sat in silence, listening to the sound of the road and replaying everything that had been said.

Lyle's aunt Terry worried that Donovan wasn't as harmless as he seemed. He did have "impeccable manners and was charming," Terry recalled. But she recalled Donovan reading poems he said he wrote to a gathering at the Baralt house one evening. After a while Glenn Stevens broke in and told Donovan he believed the verses were copied from already published authors. "Oh, really?" Donovan replied. He later admitted making it up.

At one point Terry said Jose took Lyle aside and asked his son, "Don't Donovan's stories sound strange to you, son?"

But Jose didn't try to break up the relationship because Donovan was still too valuable doing Lyle's homework.

Donovan and Lyle became all but inseparable. They quickly developed a routine together. Lyle loved to talk, so they started each day with a really good conversation over breakfast about what they were going to do for the day, what they would accomplish. They stayed up late and rose early.

Donovan Goodreau will never forget the spring break of 1989. It was then that he was drawn into the inner circle of Lyle's family. Donovan drove Lyle to the Newark airport an hour away on the day Lyle left for Beverly Hills. But as soon as Donovan pulled up to the airline terminal and got out of the car, Lyle hugged him and said he was really a dear friend and that once he was in Beverly Hills, he would send Donovan a round-trip plane ticket so that he too could share the sybaritic pleasures of southern California.

Donovan was elated. He was so excited about the prospect of spending a week in Beverly Hills that he quit his jobs at T.G.I. Fridays and Casa Lupita. "This is the chance of a lifetime," he thought, remembering that Lyle told him he was going to have "the best week of my life."

And he did. A few days after Lyle's arrival, Donovan appeared at the mansion and was shown to an upstairs bedroom which would be his room for the week. Jose and Kitty planned to be away for much of that week, cheering on Erik at a tennis tournament in Florida.

The night of Donovan's arrival, he attended one of those celebrated "state dinners" orchestrated by Jose. Donovan said it was like having dinner "in a big boardroom."

Lyle had attempted to prepare Donovan for the experience of having dinner with Jose. There were some rules Donovan needed to be aware of.

"My father is a very intense person, and he might be critical of you because you're a friend of mine," Lyle warned him. "Think about what you say before you say it."

Dinner, Lyle said severely, would be a debriefing session that would no doubt focus on what he was doing at school. Never interrupt Jose, he was told. On a later occasion, Donovan did interrupt Jose when he was telling a story to Terry, and Jose reprimanded him sternly.

Another time, Donovan recalled, he committed a faux pas by getting up from the dinner table to get a glass of milk and was told by the family that the maid took care of such things.

Later on in Princeton, just as he helped with homework, Donovan would help Lyle prepare for these dinners, especially if Lyle knew Jose would be flying in in a few days. Lyle would try out subjects on Donovan. "I would be like his aide," Donovan said. "Lyle would say, 'My father would love to hear about this.'"

On one occasion, Donovan recalled, Jose initiated an "in-depth discussion over missile bases in Germany. Or Jose would bring up the political situation in Bangladesh. I was overwhelmed by this."

The dinner that first night was everything Lyle warned him it would be. Jose was intense and commanding, and Lyle parried his questions with an easy grace developed over years of sparring with his father. Donovan found the relationship between father and son to be oddly careful. If his father asked him how his school work was going, rather than tell him he was failing, Lyle would go into a lengthy song and dance. Lyle "would never tell his father he wasn't dealing well. Instead of showing his father problems, he would show him solutions."

"It sounded great the way he said it," Goodreau said. But it showed Lyle could not tell his father the whole truth.

"Naturally, being in a $5 million house, I accepted everything as normal," Donovan said.

From time to time Kitty would try to add something to the weighty discussion, but she was ignored. All the while the young Salvadoran maid, Flor Suria, glided around the dinner table like a cat.

After dinner, Donovan settled in to watch the big-screen television in the family room. Jose took Lyle off for a serious talk. The subject was a woman named Christy, who had lately replaced Jamie in Lyle's heart.

Christy was a professional model, tall—five feet ten inches—blond, and, to Kitty's chagrin, thirty years old, nine years older than Lyle. If Kitty had a hard time accepting Jamie, who was five years older than Lyle, she could hardly bring herself to tolerate Christy. She was so desperate to break up this relationship that she wondered aloud to friends back East whether she should put Jose on the job. After seeing pictures of the attractive model, her friends urged Kitty not to do that.

But Jose also was beside himself. Lyle's liaison with Christy came at the same time that he had made it known to his father that he wanted to transfer to UCLA for the fall term. Lyle had had enough of Princeton and apparently wanted to attend a campus with more of a social life. UCLA's Westwood campus, hard by the glitter of Los Angeles, fit the bill.

But Jose would have none of that. Or of Christy, for that matter.

For three hours, Donovan recalled, Jose had a nose-to-nose discussion with Lyle. If his older son wanted to leave Princeton and return to California, then he should consider Stanford.

As for Christy, "I could take you to any bar and find you ten girls who will fuck you just like her—just for your money," Jose said. He never deigned to use her name during the conversation.

When Lyle returned to the family room after this lecture, he didn't seem particularly disturbed.

"My father is right in a way," he told his friend. "But my father still doesn't understand Christy."

Lyle had met her in the parking lot outside a restaurant at the Santa Monica Airport. He was in his father's black Mercedes, and looked very good and very young. He asked what she was up to, and she gave him her phone number.

It didn't take long for Lyle to begin using Christy as a sounding board for all his complaints about his parents.

"God, I don't get any money," he would moan, this coming from a boy with his own credit card and access to his father's Mercedes. "And my parents call all the shots."

Christy was sympathetic but not that much. "Hey, you're young and your parents have a right to do it," she replied.

Even though his parents did not like Christy, they welcomed her into their home. Kitty and Christy even cooked together.

But Kitty never warmed up to her. One day the two women were sitting in the backyard, watching Erik and Lyle work out on the tennis court, effortlessly slamming forehands back and forth only inches above the net. It was an impressive athletic ballet, but Kitty had her mind on other things.

"Why are you seeing Lyle?" she suddenly asked, her voice dripping with venom.

"We enjoy each other," Christy replied.

"Don't you think you're too old?"

"Who's the judge on age?" Christy shot back, refusing to give an inch. The remark may have stung Kitty to remember her own marriage to a younger man. She finally let the matter drop.

Christy witnessed the tense atmosphere at dinnertime. "I thought I was in the military," she said, recalling the way Jose conducted his briefings. She saw too little fun and happiness in the house.

Then when she and Lyle would leave, he would be complaining again.

"My parents are so strict."

During the spring break that Donovan visited the mansion, Lyle's parents left on a short trip. The next day Lyle suggested they take in a tennis tournament in Palm Springs. He didn't have tickets, but he told Donovan not to worry because he always found an angle. Street smarts were far better than Princeton smarts.

The sandy landscape was practically a blur as Lyle pushed Jose's 1989 black Mercedes Benz 560SEL past one hundred miles an hour on the way to the resort.

When they arrived, Donovan found Lyle was right. The tournament was sold out, but Lyle brazenly told tournament officials that they worked for the Prince Manufacturing Company, a popular tennis racket manufacturer. He was wearing a baseball cap with PRINCE emblazoned above the bill. Within minutes he and Donovan were sitting mid-court and rubbing elbows with tennis stars and groupies.

"We were really good at getting people to do things for us," Donovan said.

But the week was still young. And there was still Christy. Lyle and Donovan drove over to her beach-front condo in Venice one day for a double date with Christy and an attractive friend. To give Donovan status with these beautiful women, Lyle said he was a Princeton student.

Inside Christy's first-floor condo were professionally done photographs of the tall, thin blonde. The condo itself had a balcony overlooking an expansive beach. At one point Lyle stood on the balcony and looked down at Donovan standing barefoot in the warm sand.

"Don't worry, we're going to have all of this," Lyle said. "All this will be ours someday."

It was perfect theater for Lyle's cinematic life. His devotee stood barefoot below him, while he, the soon-to-be great man, posed with the sun in his face and stars in his eyes.

"I want it now," Donovan reflected.

"Don't worry, we'll have it in time," Lyle responded.

It was one of those intoxicating days in a young man's life. A beautiful beach day in southern California. A gorgeous model. A beach condo. Suddenly Donovan thought, "I don't want to go back to New Jersey."

But, of course, he did use the return plane ticket that Lyle had bought for him. Donovan was just a visitor to this life of luxury. Still, it had been a great week, he reflected on the flight back to Newark. And it had cost him only $60.

He could still look forward to the summer, when he was invited to return to Beverly Hills. Lyle had even bigger plans for his friend. He said they would be going into real estate soon.

"Lyle and I had plans to, I guess, just be wealthy," Donovan said.

Back at Princeton, Donovan's friendship with Lyle was about to turn sour. There had been a series of petty thefts at Gauss Hall. Lyle's on-again, off-again girlfriend, Jamie, and a friend of Lyle's each said $100 or so had been stolen from them. For whatever reasons, fingers were pointed at Donovan.

"Somehow the rumors started that I was stealing," Donovan said.

It was in late April or early May when Donovan was confronted in Lyle's dorm room by Lyle and two friends, Greg

Guest and a boy from North Carolina, Hayden Rogers. Donovan said that Lyle, with "tears in his eyes," did the talking.

"It's $100 today, but what will it be tomorrow?" he asked.

Donovan denied knowing anything about the thefts. In fact, his bicycle had been pilfered just the day before.

"Tell us the truth," Lyle demanded, every inch the inquisitor. Unbeknownst to Donovan, Lyle had steeled himself for this confrontation beforehand by calling his father and asking advice about how to handle the situation. Stand up and be tough, Jose counseled.

"I had nothing to do with it," Donovan replied.

It was no use. Donovan had to go. He was given an hour to leave Gauss Hall. He took a shower, packed up, and left.

On his way out he told Lyle he was going to New York to study real estate. He still hoped he might get back together with his pal.

As he packed, he forgot to grab his wallet, containing his driver's license, Social Security card, and other identification, which was sometimes kept in a box on Lyle's desk.

Since Donovan was a year older than Lyle, it wasn't unusual for Lyle to borrow his license "to purchase alcohol and stuff like that."

Lyle reciprocated, allowing Donovan to use his Princeton identification card so that he could eat in a campus dining hall.

Furthermore, Donovan and Lyle sometimes practiced each other's signatures for fun.

Since Donovan rarely carried his wallet, he simply forgot to pack it along with his other belongings when he left Princeton, leaving behind one of his dearest friends ever. He didn't notice it was gone until he pulled into a gas station in New York City. Reaching for his wallet, he came up with an empty pocket instead. Then he searched his van, tearing open boxes, but found nothing. He called Lyle's dorm room, but his former friend was out.

Donovan forgot about the missing license, got a job managing a restaurant in lower Manhattan, and learned to punch a time clock with the rest of the working stiffs. His fantasy life with Lyle receded like the memory of a movie that is so well done you almost think that life up on the screen could be yours.

Back in Princeton, Lyle held up a leather wallet for Stevens to see. "I kept his wallet," he laughed.

They looked through it and found a Wells Fargo bank card.

"I'm going to try to get my money back," Lyle said, according to Stevens. He said he was going to try to impersonate Donovan and take all the money from the bank account, Stevens said.

As they looked through the wallet, Stevens saw Donovan's California driver's license.

16

Summer, 1989

Jose's close friend, attorney John Mason, threw a surprise birthday party for his new wife, Bianca, at the end of May 1989. It was Bianca's twenty-fifth birthday and Mason wanted it to be special, so he held it at Vertigo, a Los Angeles discotheque with a reputation as a "New York-style" nightclub, which meant that not everyone could get in even though it was open to the public. Doormen chose patrons based on whether they fit the club's sense of style. The club was always open to the right people.

Champagne flowed and the four friends danced until 3:00 A.M. They laughed and drank and drew close together. Jose was at his charming best, entertaining Bianca with lively anecdotes and filling his friend in on his latest activities at work.

Jose was thinking seriously of renegotiating his contract at LIVE. Not long before, he had asked for what amounted to an $8 million deal, and the top men at Carolco had just smiled and shaken his hand. That only made Jose think he had asked for too little. He was now thinking of asking for $20 million more. After all, without him there would be no LIVE.

Both Jose and John were beginning to look beyond their work to the possibility of careers in public service. Mason hoped to run for governor of Nevada, and Jose dreamed of becoming a senator in Florida.

Though Jose was attentive to his friends that night, he did not leave Kitty out, bending close to bring her into the conversation and cradling her on the dance floor as though they were young and just starting out married life again. And Kitty seemed content and peaceful.

Mason never forgot that night and the warmth he felt being in his old friend's company. "I really enjoyed that evening more than any other evening I ever spent," he reflected.

At home, however, things were coming to a head as spring headed into summer. Christy told Lyle she might be pregnant, and Jose went to see the woman, Lyle said later. "He approached her and he paid her and intimidated her into getting an abortion."

Karen Wiere, Kitty's tennis friend and shopping mate, said the amount was $100,000. Kitty and Jose then demanded that Lyle give up Christy for good. Lyle called his leggy girlfriend, whose credits had included posing for the Victoria's Secrets lingerie catalog, to tell her the bad news.

"My mom said I can't see you anymore," he said sulkily.

Christy took it lightly. She would miss Lyle, whom she found to be a true innocent in bed, with a naive sweetness about him. But she knew they would never marry.

"You kind of are under your mom and dad's jurisdiction," she replied.

Once Christy was out of the picture, Jose went to Lyle. "I have the girl you should date," Jose told his son. "She's wonderful and may be going to Princeton."

Charmaine was the daughter of a business associate and, besides that, the 1988 Rose Bowl Queen. A dark-haired beauty with an even, toothy smile who spoke French fluently and played varsity tennis at the exclusive Westridge School in Pasadena, this was a woman who would look good on the arm of an executive.

One of 847 entrants for the title of Rose Queen, when she was asked on a questionnaire what made her sad, Charmaine answered: "The thought of something happening to my parents."

Lyle and Charmaine dated, and the relationship was welcomed like a fresh ocean breeze in the Menendez home. She wasn't too old and she wasn't cheap. A family friend said Jose and Kitty were "wild about" this new young woman. "I don't think Lyle felt the same way," the friend added.

As far as Lyle went, however, this new relationship was about the only good news that summer. When he came home from Princeton after the spring semester, he brought with him lousy grades, including one F. He had been placed on academic probation despite Donovan's help.

Jose was upset. Before Lyle had returned to Princeton he had worked out a deal with his son to lower his expectations for Lyle's academic performance. He was learning to try to not put so much pressure on his son. Just put in a good effort, said Jose. But even then Lyle had fallen short.

"I went to school and I had to work full-time," Jose said bitterly to his brother-in-law Carlos Baralt. "All I'm asking Lyle to do is to pass."

Then Jose and Kitty were informed by mail that the university had also placed Lyle on disciplinary probation after some pool tables had been damaged during a party he threw for his brother and some friends in the student center.

Lyle patiently explained to Jose that it wasn't really his fault. He took the blame for the real perpetrators, he said.

At the same time Lyle's driver's license was suspended— again. The family's privileges at the Bedens Brooks Country Club also were suspended after Lyle took Donovan Goodreau on a rollicking nighttime ride across the golf course in a cart, tearing up several manicured greens.

"They ruined the hell out of everything," said manager Sheldon Pierce. Jose made full restitution for the torn turf.

There were so many problems that Jose and Kitty were baffled. Jose was becoming much less willing to be persuaded by Lyle's cool rationalizations. Desperate to let their sons know how serious things were, they brought out the biggest club they could use to pound some sense into their heads. They began threatening to cut the boys out of the family will.

The will had been written in 1980, before Jose had begun to amass his wealth. In the event Jose and Kitty died in a common disaster, Erik and Lyle got everything.

But now Kitty warned that they would write a new will that would leave the boys high and dry.

"You guys are so irresponsible," Kitty said, according to Karen Wiere.

To friends like Karen, getting tough with the boys was long overdue. She had always felt Kitty was making a mistake taking care of everything for her sons and husband. She paid all the traffic tickets and fixed all the dented fenders. "There were no consequences," she said. Then they went out and got more tickets and dented more fenders.

The threat had first been uttered a couple of years earlier, Wiere said. But as time went on, it was dragged out more and more. It got to the point, said one friend, that the parents would threaten to take the boys out of the will if they didn't eat their peas at dinner.

Jose and Carlos Baralt were riding in a limousine between New York and New Jersey during a stopover on one of Jose's business trips that summer when he confessed he had made up his mind. Jose said he was "very frustrated and disappointed with his kids." He didn't think he could justify keeping them in the will. He wasn't cutting them off or kicking them out of the house, he was just making sure that if something happened to him and Kitty, the boys would not inherit their estate.

There was very little emotion in his voice. It was as though this was something that had to be done, one more tough business decision.

Kitty was more emotional, however, in a separate conversation. "I can't believe my kids," she said sadly. "I can't believe this is happening to us."

In June, Kitty began work on the new will on the IBM computer she kept upstairs in her bedroom.

Meanwhile, Erik hit the road for a season of tennis. Under the tutelage of his private coach, one known as a master at dealing with the psychological elements of the game, Erik's game was coming around. Still, in the three major tournaments in which he participated in July and August of 1989, although he briefly did well, Erik showed he still had a way to go if he was to make his way in the world of professional tennis.

In the United States Tennis Association hard court championships in Burlingame, California, held July 10–16, Erik won his first-round match but lost the second one.

A few days later, Erik flew to the USTA junior clay court championships in Louisville, Kentucky. There he repeated his performance, winning his first match but losing in the second round. In the consolation round, however, Erik won six straight matches, showing outstanding form.

The Louisville competition was particularly rigorous because of the one hundred-degree temperatures, combined with stifling humidity. Every evening Jose massaged Erik's cramped and aching muscles so that he could rest better for the next day's matches.

Then Jose would rise with the sun to warm up Erik on the court before the matches started.

The last—and most important—tennis tournament of the year was the prestigious USTA national championship in Kalamazoo, Michigan, August 5–13. Jose and Kitty were on hand, but Erik's performance was once again nothing to brag about. He won in the first round and lost in the second.

"He may have been exhausted from the extreme heat of the previous tournament," a relative said.

During one of Erik's matches Jose got very upset. His noisy behavior drew a warning from a tournament official, who told him to sit down. After the official left, Erik turned away from his match and told his father to "shut up."

Jose threw up his hands. "I can't stand this. He doesn't listen to me." In her seat, Kitty went white.

After the match, Jose pulled his son off the court, and the two of them went back to the hotel where the family was staying. Pat Andersen, the wife of Kitty's brother Brian, wanted to console Erik, but Kitty restrained her.

Back at the hotel, the two couples were walking down the hall to go to dinner when Pat asked to see Erik. Jose made fun of her but allowed it. Erik was in bed in the dark, and looked very sad. Pat wanted to hug him, but she was told no. Brian stepped forward and gave him a quiet pep talk.

Everyone else went to the table, but Kitty came late and seemed upset, Pat said later.

Around this same time the two women went out walking together and Pat broke the news to Kitty that she was getting divorce from her brother. Kitty surprised her when she said she "wished she had the courage to do that."

Back in Los Angeles, Erik was preparing to move into his dorm room at UCLA, where he was registered in the fall. He had also been accepted at UC Berkeley, but Erik favored UCLA because it had a better tennis team. Jose and Kitty bought their younger son a motorbike so he could tool around the campus and Westwood, a community made up of a network of small avenues only minutes from Beverly Hills.

In order to get Lyle ready for school, Jose bought a condominium not far from Princeton in an area called Canal Pointe. It was a two-bedroom, first-floor unit that looked out on a large grassy knoll. It was thought to be an excellent investment for slightly under $130,000.

The condo was laid out in such a way that there were bedrooms on each end, separated by the living room. It would be ideal for Jose and Kitty because it provided them with their own suite when they visited Lyle at school. They could stay with him without being too intrusive.

Lyle asked Kitty to decorate the condo for him. She was

looking forward to the project, and planned to fly to Princeton and begin work on September 9, six days before Lyle began his sophomore year at Princeton.

But as the summer wound down, tensions in the Menendez household escalated. In a telephone call Kitty's old Pennington friend Irene Elkins noticed "something wrong" in Kitty's voice. She didn't press her friend for an explanation. Kitty was a private person, after all. There would be better times to gently try to find out what was going on when the two women got together again.

Kitty was locking the doors to her bedroom at night, and she kept two .22 rifles in her closet. She also insisted that the boys not take any keys to the house with them when they went out. She kept the keys in a small table in the foyer. This irritated Lyle, who had to get his mother up each night to let him in when he came home late. But something had frightened Kitty, and her need for security seemed to grow stronger every day.

Her fears may have been exacerbated by something the psychologist treating Lyle and Erik, Jerry Oziel, said to her. After telling the brothers that he feared they might commit more crimes, he asked Erik for permission to talk to his parents. Erik gave it. On July 19, Kitty went to her own therapist, Lester Summerfield, and told him she feared her sons might be sociopaths, a psychiatric term for a person who lacks a conscience.

Summerfield's notes from the session, only a month before the murders, were brief and to the point. "Kitty worried about Erik and Lyle . . . concerned for lack of conscience, narcissism, and sociopathy they exhibit . . . wanted info."

Jose recognized too that he might have something to fear from his boys, the sons he had raised with care and trained to build a dynasty on the soil of his new country. Belatedly he began to realize that a king sometimes has more to fear in his own house than from all the plotters and pretenders.

"You know you can kill me if you want to," he told Lyle, according to Oziel. "You can do what you want, but don't think you'll get any money out of it."

The week of August 14, Jose made a business trip to New York City and on Wednesday stayed at his mother's house in Belleville, New Jersey, before flying back to Los Angeles the following day.

Over dinner that night, Maria Menendez recalled, Jose talked again about his cherished plan to retire and run for office. If he could pull off this $20 million deal he was planning, he would be set for life, and so would his family. Much of his decision to remain in Los Angeles had to do with Erik, Maria said. Jose wanted to be nearby while his younger son attended UCLA.

And he talked at length about another dream, of creating a family compound where Maria could live with his family. He had looked at a small island in North Miami. There would even be room for Terry and Carlos and Marta if they wanted to move in.

"He wanted the family to stay together," Maria said. The next day, Thursday, August 17, Jose flew back to Los Angeles.

On Saturday, August 19, the family went shark fishing out of Marina del Rey. But they were not much of a family in the eyes of the crew. Jose stayed toward the back of the boat fishing, while Kitty, nauseous, wandered below. Erik and Lyle stayed up in the front of the boat talking quietly.

When a shark was hooked, everyone came running to watch the men pull in the big carnivore and toss it gasping and dying on the deck of the boat.

Acting Normal

What happened over the next twenty-four hours would be the subject of thousands of hours of police work, litigation, and public speculation.

But after it was over, Erik and Lyle sat on the carpeted stairs a few feet from the family room, where the smoke from their pump-action shotguns was still drifting lazily in the air. The mutilated bodies of their parents lay like shredded stuffed animals on the sofa and on the floor. This, according to law enforcement experts and the psychologist who treated them after the killings, is what was going on in their minds and what they did next.

They figured they might just get away with it. It had been a horrible affair. Blood and flesh flew everywhere, not at all like in the movies. This was three-dimensional gore, not two-dimensional thrills. But now that it was over and the police had not come bursting in the door to arrest them, they began to think they might just get away with it.

It was the perfect murder. They were sure of that. They had thought of everything. Not a detail was out of place.

They had purchased the guns far way, and in a way that the police, even if they went hunting for them, would never connect to Lyle and Erik.

They didn't have to worry about fingerprints. They lived in the house, so naturally their fingerprints would be everywhere.

All they had to do was get rid of the evidence. They got up, went back into the room, and started grabbing shell casings, picking them up from the goo that had been their parents, just in case police could trace them.

Next, they rushed out and jumped in Erik's Ford Escort, parked in front of the house, and drove to Mulholland Drive, a semi-rural road between the beach and the valley. Erik knew the way, but he was too shaken to drive, so Lyle steered the car while Erik gave directions. They stopped on Mulholland, watched for approaching cars, and then Erik jumped out of the car and ran a few feet down the mountainside, tossing away the guns.

As Erik ran back up the slope, Lyle turned the car around. Erik jumped in and they headed down the hill to a gas station, where they dumped their blood-spattered shoes and clothing in a dumpster, along with hands full of shell casings.

Then they drove home. They had intended to go to the Cheesecake Factory to meet Perry, but Erik was starting to fall apart, sobbing and moaning over what they had just done. So they went home and called the police. Even Lyle was shaky. But, thank God, the cops in Beverly Hills are polite, in some ways more like an exclusive security agency for the rich than a police force. "They don't treat everybody like dirtbags like most police agencies" is the way one law enforcement expert put it.

So they didn't press Erik too hard. If they had grilled him, he might have spilled everything right there.

Luck was breaking their way. Not only did the cops go easy on Erik, then fail to give the two sons a gunshot-residue test, they also failed to check out Erik's car, parked in front of the house.

When Lyle showed up at the house the next morning looking for his tennis racket, what he really wanted to do was search the car himself and get rid of any incriminating evidence that they had failed to dispose of in the gas station dumpster. They had been in an awful hurry at the dumpster, watching out for cars pulling in for fuel.

When he arrived at the door of the mansion, he was met by Zoeller, who told him he couldn't go in. The crime scene had been secured, Zoeller said. The cops didn't want anything disturbed. But three hours later, Lyle and Erik were back again. They were used to getting their way, and it was vital that they get a look in the car.

This time they asked a friendly cop outside the house if they could get some things out of the vehicle.

"Sure, go ahead," he said.

Lyle found more shell casings, wrappings for the shotgun shells, and some other things that would have connected them to the killings. While Beverly Hills police were still crawling all over the house, Lyle calmly loaded the evidence into a gym bag and transferred it to the waiting car of a friend.

This might be the same bag that a member of Bel-Air Patrol, the private security force that guarded the house after the police left the next day, saw just inside the door of the mansion four days later.

Charles Dickerson, the chief of the mansion security force, had served in the 82nd Airborne in Vietnam, so he knows weapons. He was standing at the entrance to the house when Lyle set his gym bag by the front door. Sneaking a glance at the bag, he saw a shotgun shell casing in it.

Then Lyle, whom the guards nicknamed "Iceman" for the way he had of looking right through them, came by and grabbed the bag. This was enough for Dickerson. He began carrying a Derringer.

Two months later, while in Mexico on another job, Dickerson ran into Erik lounging by the pool at a Cancun hotel. "What are you doing here?" said a started Erik, looking around nervously, according to Dickerson.

"I'm an international guy," Dickerson replied, striding off.

But the police weren't as suspicious as Dickerson, not at first. And after Lyle cleaned out the car, he felt much better. He didn't think too deeply about what he had done. The images of smoke and gunfire and blood lingered in his mind, but the horror was crowded out, or at least softened, by a growing conviction. If there was anyone who could appreciate what he had done, it would be Jose. If he could have talked to him about it, Jose might even have respected the skill with which the crime was pulled off. The careful planning that enabled him and Erik to take their parents unawares. Just like Jose showing up, unannounced, in some out-of-the-way place to check on some Hertz flunkie.

Now Lyle had taken his father by surprise, had figured out a way to get ahead of him, to outsmart him. It was just like the younger Don blowing away the godfather; it was only business. You had to be absolutely devoted to winning, and you had to ignore sentiment.

Now he had taken what the old man had started and pushed it in a new, yet logical, direction.

The only problem was, Jose was not around to offer his congratulations.

Now that it was done, all Lyle and Erik had to do was act like grieving orphans. That was Erik's department, and he was doing a good job of it. Maybe too good. He looked genuinely broken up and he kept saying things to people that were almost hints that he had killed his parents. Just a couple of days after the murders, he had started to jabber to one of his relatives, who stopped him. "I can believe just about anything," the man said, "except that you killed your mother."

But Erik was not the only remaining worry. The place where they had bought the guns had had a video camera over the counter. They had gone ahead with the sale anyway, but maybe their faces were on film. They called the store and found out they erased the film after three months. That would be August, September, October, November 20. After that there would be nothing to tie them to the murders.

Until then there would be a little bit of anxiety. But really the cops had no reason to suspect them anyway. All they had to do was act normal.

Unfortunately, neither Erik nor Lyle knew exactly what normal was. Their lives had been too cloistered and their thinking processes too erratic. Both of them had that clashing combination of naïveté and callousness that left them strangers among the rest of the world. So they went around trying to act normal in a very abnormal way.

There was the wild spending spree and Lyle's apparent lack of emotion over the deaths of his parents. Then, eleven days after the murders, Lyle did something that would draw the suspicion of detectives Zoeller and Linehan.

Relatives from all over the country descended on Beverly Hills after the killings. While inventorying the house, one of the brothers' uncles walked into Jose and Kitty's second-floor bedroom, and found the computer on a small table next to a white chair.

The man sat down and attempted to pull up whatever information—if any—was stored in the computer. Three file names caught his eye: *Erik*, *Lyle*, and *Will*.

Over and over he tried to get at the information in the files. Knowing how much a dog lover Kitty was, family members tried various dog's names as passwords, with no success.

The first two file names made some sense, of course. Jose or Kitty may have been packaging some information for their sons, whatever it was. It was well known within family circles that

Kitty used the computer for correspondence, an assortment of writing projects, and even for keeping a personal diary.

But *Will*? What was that all about?

The man did not know that Jose had been planning to rewrite his will. But even if a draft of a new will had been discovered in the computer, it would not have been legally binding. To be admitted into probate, a will must be in document form and properly signed and witnessed. An electronic copy just won't do.

News of the discovery in the computer was relayed to Erik and Lyle. Erik, according to one family member, said he would hire someone to comb through the computer. But Lyle acted first.

After attending the U.S. Open tennis championship at Flushing Meadow in Queens, Lyle flew home and, on Wednesday, August 30, turned his attention to the computer puzzle.

He could not get at the three files either. So he decided to call in an expert to go through the computer's hard drive, which could store twenty million characters of data.

Grabbing the Beverly Hills telephone book, Lyle found an ad for a computer services firm that offered "same day guaranteed response emergency service" for computer problems. The firm, founded by UCLA math student Howard Witkin, had been in business for a half-dozen years and had made its mark in software development for corporations.

As luck would have it, it was Witkin, who had just finished calling on a customer in Beverly Hills, who was beeped by his company and told about the emergency. A "Mr. Mendez" needed help recovering something from the family's desktop computer, something Witkin sees about "once or twice a week."

When Witkin arrived at the Elm Drive mansion, Lyle let him through the electronically operated gate. Guards were patrolling the grounds, but the computer expert didn't give them a second thought. Lyle ushered his guest into the upstairs bedroom where the computer was located, and gave the expert the three file names. Witkin assumed the reference to "Will" was to a third person.

"Typically, I would see if [a client] did something stupid like putting [data] in a wrong directory," he said later.

But when he opened the three files, he found that the contents were not readable. There were letters, symbols, and numbers—but nothing in coherent English.

"The files were corrupted," the expert said. "It looked like someone had copied over them, which is common."

Still, the files actually existed, which the professional knew meant there was a possibility—however remote—that some data might be retrievable.

Witkin searched the hard disk, looking through several hundred files for four key words—*Lyle*, *Erik*, *Will*, and *Mendez*.

"No," Lyle said. "You're not going to find *Mendez*. It's Menendez."

Even with the correction, the expert still came up empty-handed.

While this was going on, Lyle was almost nonchalant, wandering in and out of the bedroom, talking occasionally on a downstairs telephone.

"He didn't make it seem [the problem] was a primary focus of his day." Witkin said. "He said, 'See what you can do and let me know.' "

After about ninety minutes, he told Lyle that it could take upward of twenty-five hours to do a complete search of the computer.

"Lyle's response," the expert said, "was that he didn't necessarily have to have the data, he just wanted to find it and get it off because he's going to sell the computer," and he didn't want to take a chance on selling it while it still had personal family information stored in it.

Lyle then asked the expert to erase the disk. The expert did so in a few minutes, using a special program—called WIPE-DISK—which meets the standards of the federal government's National Security Agency for the secure erasure of data.

"I'm experienced in doing this for t government, military, and financial firms," Witkin said. "I'm an expert in erasing."

When the troubleshooter was done, the best computer experts in the world—not to mention the Beverly Hills Police—could not have restored those three files.

The bill for the expert's services was $150, for which Lyle wrote a personal check.

Despite the uneasy feeling the two reporters had gotten during their interview with Lyle and Erik, conducted only a few feet from the empty family room where their parents were shot, the *Times* went ahead with plans to publish a story that would focus on two grieving boys trying to come to grips with the tragic deaths of their parents. At the same time the reporters hoped they might turn up something leading to the killers.

In the interview, Soble asked if they could have the names of the sons' closest friends, thinking they might know something about the family that had not already appeared in the newspaper or on television. Both Lyle and Erik supplied several. Lyle volunteered Glenn Stevens.

Contacted in Princeton, Stevens sounded like a hurt friend, and he was. It seemed Lyle had been his best buddy, "a lot of fun to be with. He's since gone through a few changes since the death of his parents. He's treating me a bit different, to be quite honest."

It seems that the new, dynamic Lyle was too busy for friendship, and Glenn felt shut out. His feelings had been especially hurt when he overheard Lyle saying, about some menial chore, "That's what I keep Glenn around for."

Perhaps that's why Glenn was willing to talk about his suspicions of his friend. "I've been feeling he might have had something to do with" the murders, he said. He also said the police had visited him and also considered Lyle a suspect.

Glenn's suspicions, it seemed, grew out of Lyle's blasé attitude about the murders. The detectives also had been to see him, and he had the distinct impression they did not completely believe the boys' alibi.

Then he mentioned the computer. He said that after Lyle had erased the disk, he had flown back to Princeton and he and Stevens had gone out for beer and nachos at Lyle's old stomping ground, Casa Lupita. Lyle told him about the computer.

When Lyle told him he had erased everything, Stevens was "in disbelief. I just laughed."

Stevens said Lyle told him, "I only could lose" if a new will was found, since he and Erik got everything in the old will.

"To be safe, I erase it."

Stevens also said Jose was angry at his son before the murders. "Lyle's father was so pissed off at Lyle because he wanted to quit school and play professional tennis."

Then the reporter called a friend of Noel Nedli's. Nedli had played tennis at Beverly Hills High School with Erik, who he said was kicked off the team "numerous times" for his rebellious attitude. Nedli would soon move in with Erik in a luxurious condo in Marina del Rey, right next door to Lyle and Jamie. Nedli said Erik told him the police suspected him and Lyle "of being part of whatever."

The journalists decided to put the syrupy feature story on hold. Meanwhile, Zoeller got a call from Glenn Stevens, who described his conversation with the reporter, including the fact that Stevens had said Lyle was a suspect.

"I didn't cause any problems, did I?" Stevens asked.

"No, but doesn't that cause problems for you if it comes out in the press?" Zoeller asked.

"I can work around that," Stevens assured him.

On the afternoon of October 24, Zoeller drove over to the mansion to see Erik. He was hoping to use the reporters to smoke out Erik, or at least to put some pressure on him and see how he reacted. Zoeller wasn't sure that Lyle and Erik were guilty of anything, but his instincts were telling him to take a hard look at the boys.

He began by telling Erik that the reporters were suspicious of the Menendez brothers. "The *Times* is going to write an article and indicate that you guys, and Lyle in particular, is a suspect," Zoeller said.

Erik remained impassive. Inside he may have been nervous, but he stayed cool as he faced the detective. Zoeller continued. "We're concerned also, because you guys just aren't cooperating," he added.

Zoeller was still having trouble getting the boys on the phone. "You guys haven't returned our calls," he explained. "You haven't talked to us at all. We have a lot of questions that you guys just aren't interested in talking to us about."

"What questions do you have?" Erik asked.

Zoeller mentioned the will being erased by Lyle. Erik said he was upset too because he had had his own expert ready to come in and read the will. Zoeller nodded. He said he also had heard they weren't getting along, that when one was on the West Coast, the other was on the East Coast.

"What's the problem?" Zoeller asked sympathetically.

"Lyle is spending the money," Erik confided, the detective said later, "and he's trying to spend my money too. He's being just like my father, and we weren't getting along."

A rift between Erik and Lyle might seem hard to believe, given their closeness. But Stevens had said the same thing. Lyle was "trying to manipulate his brother and get Erik's half."

Zoeller changed the subject, trying to keep the conversation going any way he could. "Now might be a time if there's something you want to tell us. Not saying you were involved with the murder," he went on hurriedly, "but were you guys involved in anything you want to tell us about? About somebody who might have a motive to kill your parents."

Erik kept his cool. The cops believed that of the two of them,

Erik was by far the weaker personality. They thought he might crack under pressure. Zoeller decided to confront Erik head-on.

"Do you think Lyle is involved in the murders?" he asked. "Do you think he hired somebody?"

No, Erik replied, still unruffled. Erik said he and his brother wanted to cooperate with the police, that Lyle would give a call when he got back in town.

Zoeller went away without anything new to work on, unless you counted the knowledge that the boys were having their problems. This might be useful later, but the investigation had not moved forward.

However, as soon as Zoeller left, according to several accounts, Erik got on the phone and called Princeton, frantically looking for Lyle. He got Glenn Stevens. Erik told him he had to speak to Lyle. He said the police suspected them of committing the murders. Erik had been cool and reserved when Zoeller told him about the reporters' suspicions, but now he was apparently panicked and, as always, he needed his brother's strong arm to lean on. But he couldn't find him.

It was only a few days later when Erik rushed in to see his therapist, Jerry Oziel. It was Halloween. Kids all over Los Angeles were putting on their witch costumes and Freddy Kreuger masks. But what Oziel would hear that evening from a tearful, distraught Erik Menendez was a real nightmare brought to life.

In retrospect, Zoeller believed, it was the conversation with Erik on October 24 that brought his latent fear to the surface and caused him to rush off to Oziel, which months later would prove to be his undoing.

The reporters had no idea that the cops were using them to flush Erik. They were concerned with their own project, which had become more delicate. It was one thing for Zoeller to tell Erik the *Times* was going to publish a story naming the boys as suspects, but another actually to write such a story. If the boys were just two of many potential suspects, of no more interest than anyone else, to name them in a million newspapers would be worse than irresponsible. The only justification for focusing on them would be if their behavior was such that it brought them under hard police scrutiny.

So the reporters went to the police to see if they could push their own investigation further along. As they drove out to the Beverly Hills Police Department, each prepared questions in his head. The police had been extremely close-mouthed about their investigation, though Johnson and Soble had previously broken a couple of stories about the case in the days following the slayings.

They were escorted into a conference room at the police station, where they shook hands with Lieutenant Russ Olson, the chief of police detectives. Zoeller and Linehan sat mostly to the side, listening intently as Olson directed the conversation. It was less like a conversation that the early rounds of a fight, when both combatants are feeling each other out.

Each side, it became apparent, was probing for information they thought the other might possess. Olson, a tall, lanky detective who had been a rock 'n' roll musician in the sixties and now satisfied his musical longings by playing in a police band called Unlawful Assembly, said he had to be careful about what he said. "It's tenuous ground we walk with our chief of police," he said, referring to Iannone, who was said to be monitoring the case as closely as a nurse watches a baby in an incubator.

The journalists asked if they had heard about a second will on the computer.

"No comment," said Olson. "What do you know about it?"

"We're aware of it," said Zoeller. "What do you know about it?"

The reporters said they had heard the document had been erased. Then they mentioned the odd behavior of Lyle and Erik, the spending, the lack of grieving. "Are you taking a very hard look at Erik and Lyle?" Soble asked.

"It would be absurd and foolish for us to say, based on what you've told us, these interesting and unique and unusual behaviors by the boys, to say that we're not interested and that we're not looking," Olson replied. "From a professional standpoint, I think it's something that needs to be looked into. You brought out behavior patterns that are not consistent."

At the time the reporters did not know how much they were using the police to get a story and how much the police were using them. It was only later, when advocates for Erik and Lyle accused them of helping the police solve the crime, that they began to suspect.

That accusation was actually groundless. Zoeller already had plenty of his own suspicions. What the reporters unwittingly did for the police, said one investigator later on, was let them know "we were going in the right direction."

The two reporters began preparing a story about the computer, but before they finished it they wanted to have one more talk with Erik and Lyle. Besides the will, they had heard about Lyle's spending spree, and they had even heard rumors about burglaries in Calabasas.

After being ushered into their places in the living room, they found that circumstances had also changed from the point of view of the brothers. Previously expansive, they were more guarded.

Sitting between them this time was Stephen Goldberg, a tall, young Redondo Beach attorney with neatly combed dark hair who was handling the probate of the will.

Lyle was asked how the family was getting along. It was an ice-breaking question.

"We seem a little bit closer now than we were before," he said, slouched in his chair. "We were so busy before. Now we have some free time. The family is much closer, no question."

The questions quickly became more pointed. Lyle was asked about his spending, about the $64,000 Porsche. What did all this mean, the airplane travel, the clothing purchases? Was it, as his uncle said, merely Lyle's way of expressing grief? Credit card catharsis?

"I like quality things," he said.

He said he was seriously thinking of going back to Princeton for the winter semester. Could he concentrate on his studies so soon after his parents' murders?

"I hope so," he replied, pausing. "By January it will have been a long time in my opinion" since the murders.

A crucial part of their alibi on the night of the murder was the visit to the food fair in Santa Monica. The reporters had talked with Lyle's friend Perry Berman, who said Lyle had called to invite him out. They asked how the invitation came about.

"We were invited that day, so we went," said Erik.

Perry called and extended the invitation?

"Yes," he agreed. "We knew him back east."

So when, exactly, had they seen the movie?

Goldberg interrupted, asking where these questions were heading. The level of tension in the room was rising.

Soble said they were simply trying to gain a better understanding of the events that evening so they could learn at what point the killers could have had a chance to strike.

"My only comment to that," said Lyle, "would be that we left early in the evening and we arrived after midnight."

Goldberg suddenly adjourned the interview and took Lyle and Erik out of the room. Even though they returned a short time later, looking agreeable and relaxed, it was becoming clear the interview would not last much longer.

The subject of the second will was brought up.

Goldberg interrupted again. "I really don't want any questions about anything like that," he said.

But had there been a computer program that was destroyed?

"I don't know anything about that," Goldberg added. "And we've got a will and I don't want any problems with it. If you have some information about some other will, I don't want to know about it."

Erik said, "there was no will being constructed. We talked to my mom's closest friend, and they said they were going to start a will." So work had not begun on the document.

Lyle was asked about erasing the files on the computer.

"I have nothing to say on that subject," he said. "My brother has nothing to say on that subject. My lawyer has nothing to say on that subject. It's been made so clear, I don't know what else to say."

Then he was asked about his suspension from Princeton for a year. "No comment," he said.

"Suffice it to say he is welcome to go back to Princeton at any time," said Goldberg.

Why was he suspended? "You've got your answer to that question," Goldberg said firmly, his irritation deepening.

Johnson had been saving a question to the end, for he knew that once it was asked, they would no longer be welcome.

Stevens had told him about a strange conversation that Erik supposedly had had with one of Lyle's friends, Greg Guest, the hockey player. According to Stevens, Erik had asked, "Do you think Lyle could have done it?" referring to the murders.

Reached by phone in Princeton, Guest said of Stevens, "He's kind of talkative, I wouldn't believe much that he said."

Johnson now turned to Erik and asked him about the alleged remark. Did he say, "Do you think Lyle could have done it?"

"I don't think that question needs to be answered," said an outraged Goldberg. "I don't think it should even be asked."

"No," said Erik.

He was asked to explain his no, but the interview was over. The reporters apologized for asking questions like that. Lyle and Erik shook hands at the door.

A few weeks later, Witkin, the computer professional, was relaxing with the newspaper when a headline caught his eye:

MENTION OF WILL DELETED FROM MENENDEZES' HOME COMPUTER.
"Oh, my God," he said to himself while he read the story.
"Will's not a name. It's a will he wanted me to find."

Almost immediately the telephone was jangling in the detective division of the Beverly Hills Police Department. Zoeller listened as Witkin recounted his visit to the Menendez home.

The detectives got a search warrant and seized the computer. But by then it was too late. The files were gone.

18

Closing In

Perhaps nobody knew Erik as well as Craig Cignarelli, the likable, cocky Calabasas High tennis player.

While awaiting fame's thunderbolt, he was attending the University of California at Santa Barbara, where Zoeller and Linehan found him on November 17. Over a table at the Baker's Square restaurant outside the campus, Craig told them a story that they didn't know whether to believe.

Cignarelli said he had stayed with Erik just after the slayings. One day while they were together and chatting, Erik suddenly turned to him with a serious look and asked if he wanted to know how it happened. Craig knew immediately what "it" was.

Erik said he and Lyle had come home to get the fake ID, just as he had told the police. As he was walking back out to the car, he met Lyle carrying the shotguns. "Let's do it," Lyle said.

Erik said he took the gun. "Lyle was to shoot my dad, and I was to shoot my mother," Erik said, according to Craig.

Zoeller and Linehan tried to keep their faces impassive as this tumbled out.

" 'We went into the room, and Lyle pointed his gun at my dad and shot him,' " Craig recalled Erik saying. " 'He then went over and shot him in the head. I was unable to shoot my mom, and she tried to get away. Lyle shot her too. After it looked like my mother was dead, I shot her twice with my gun.' "

Erik said there was blood and gore everywhere. Craig didn't know whether to believe what he had heard. He didn't ask Erik if he was putting him on. They just started talking about something else.

Zoeller and Linehan were elated at this apparent break in the case. If Cignarelli was telling the truth, they now knew exactly what had gone on in that room. But then Craig said something that tripped them up.

"It could have happened."

Playing mind games with each other was a fundamental part of Craig's friendship with Erik. Craig said Erik was the one who said "it could have happened" after the confession, implying that he was pulling Craig's leg. Cignarelli's bombshell was now a firecracker.

Zoeller and Linehan didn't understand Craig's flair for melodrama, so they were perplexed by what they had just heard. But they didn't push Craig to say more, not yet.

They drove back to Los Angeles, and Zoeller met with Pam Ferrero, a slight deputy district attorney with an iron will and a bulldog disposition that she did under the stylish, buttoned-up suits she wore to court. Passionate about mushroom burgers and getting bad guys, she was a top prosecutor in the organized crime unit of the D.A.'s office. She liked to joke that she was like a grade-B movie actress, with a specialty wardrobe for every case. When she did child-abuse cases, she wore ribbons in her hair like a little girl. And when she asked for the death penalty, she wore her white gabardine dress with puffs on the shoulders like angel's wings, as though she had been sent by God himself to conduct this poor, misguided soul to the other world.

Ferrero had been working on the Teddy Snyder murder—the porn broker who had been murdered in the Valley shortly before the Menendezes and in a similarly overstated way—when her bosses asked her to work with the Beverly Hills police.

Zoeller came to see her at the D.A.'s office in the big criminal courts building, which rises over the downtown business district like a cold gray spike. They sat down and talked. Zoeller described the conversation with Cignarelli, with its bizarre conclusion.

It was certainly not enough to file criminal charges on, but it sounded promising, Ferrero agreed. Another attorney in the office suggested asking Cignarelli to wear a body wire the next time he met with Menendez. So Zoeller went back to Cignarelli and asked if he would do so. Surprisingly, he agreed.

On November 29, Craig was scheduled to meet Erik for dinner at a Pacific Palisades restaurant that overlooked the Pacific Ocean called Gladstones 4 Fish, a popular nightspot for young singles in heat. There are heavy cement tables outside under big heating units that look like lampposts, and fat barrels of free peanuts that help the young sophisticates work up a healthy thirst for the exotic drinks. It is just the kind of place Hamilton Cromwell would have spent his nights hunting for girls and murder victims.

Before meeting Erik, Craig drove up to a secluded spot on a hill about a mile away, where Zoeller was waiting in a van filled with electronic equipment. He outfitted Cignarelli with the wire, which consisted of a microphone taped to Cignarelli's chest. Zoeller also handed the young man a checkbook-looking device that had a calculator in it with another microphone. "Put this on the table in front of you," he was told.

Cignarelli nodded. He was playing a strange game, cooperating with the police to entrap his best friend, which fit very well with the kinds of plot twists and back-stabbings he and Erik had fantasized about. But at the same time he didn't like being the one to do Erik in.

Cignarelli met Erik Menendez outside the restaurant. Zoeller drove around to the employees' parking lot, where he listened as the two young men sat down to talk. Unfortunately, there was a strolling violinist that night, and the place was full of the hubbub of half-drunk conversation. Zoeller could barely make out what was being said. They began discussing the play. Erik mentioned some changes he wanted to make in the script.

Craig said reporters had come looking for him in Santa Barbara to ask him about the killings. There were rumors on campus that he was a suspect. "Everybody still wonders about me up there," he said.

Erik replied, "What about the police?"

"I have talked to them," Craig said.

"What'd you tell them?" Erik was nervous now.

"I still think they think I'm a suspect," Craig replied artfully. The police had never told him that.

"Surely you would never have told them anything that I told you?" Erik asked.

And Craig responded half jokingly, "Oh, yeah, I told them you killed your parents.

"Well, did you kill your parents?" Craig followed up nonchalantly, or as nonchalantly as he could manage.

"No, I did not," Erik said firmly.

Erik said maybe he shouldn't have joked around earlier when he confessed. Now he fell back on the well-worn explanations that the killings were mob-related, or done by someone from the company, or maybe a hit team from Cuba.

The two of them then moved on to other subjects. Afterward, they walked outside and the valets brought their cars up. After Erik drove away, Craig said, "Well, guys, I guess that didn't help much, huh?"

The taping session was not a failure, however, because it convinced Ferrero that Craig had been telling the truth in the November 17 conversation.

Did they have enough to file criminal charges? Zoeller asked. Ferrero considered it. All they had was a statement from Cignarelli that Erik had confessed. But then Cignarelli had added that equivocation, "It could have happened."

On the tape, Erik was nervous about Craig's discussions with police. But he denied the crime itself. This was pretty thin material for building a murder case.

There was a piece of physical evidence, but it was highly questionable too.

It involved Greg Guest, the husky hockey player from the small town of Quesnel in British Columbia, who lived on the same floor as Lyle at Gauss Hall and was one of Lyle's so-called "groupies."

Guest, whose nickname was said to be "the Devil," was using Lyle's flashy Porsche Carrera while Lyle was in California, when he supposedly made an unusual discovery. After taking Lyle's black leather jacket out of the Porsche's trunk, he found a spent shotgun shell in one of the pockets.

Princeton police mailed the shell to the Beverly Hills cops. At first the cops were excited. But a weapons expert consulted by Ferrero said the wadding found at the scene of the crime did not match the shell casing. Then Ferrero heard Guest was backing away from the story that he had discovered the shell in Lyle's jacket. Friends of Lyle said Guest may have been playing a trick on his pal. "Greg is a mischievous person who may not have had any concept of what he was doing," said one friend.

In any event, the shell casing seemed to be useless. It was only later that another gun expert told Ferrero that the first expert was wrong, and that the wadding could be matched up with the shell.

So luck was still with Erik and Lyle. It seemed that no matter how careless they had been, the police were powerless to make a case against them. Weeks were passing, and soon the will

would be probated and the two sons would get their parents'
fortune. Then they might leave the country for good. Ferrero
knew time was against the cops now.

But she decided the case against the brothers was still too
flimsy. "That's not enough for a filing" of charges, she told
Zoeller. "We've got to find the shotguns," she said urgently.

Zoeller knew as much himself. The shotguns would tie the
killers to the crime scene. But where to look? The most obvious
way to go about it was to search every gun store in Los Angeles
for the records of the purchase.

Federal law requires a buyer to present an identification card
with a picture before a sale can be completed. The purchaser
must provide his name, address, description, date of birth and
must state whether he has a criminal record. This information is
entered on a two-page form published by the Bureau of Alcohol,
Tobacco, and Firearms. Unlike handgun purchases, which are
filed in a central federal data system, forms covering shotgun
and rifle purchases are retained by the seller. This antiquated
system can make tracing a shotgun purchase difficult.

Zoeller asked the Department of Justice for a printout of all
the gun shops within a ten-mile radius of the crime scene. The
result was testimony to America's fascination with weaponry.
He received an eighty-page list with 320 shops on it.

Zoeller and Tom Linehan and several others from the special
investigations unit did the searching. It could have been done
much faster with a whole team of investigators. But Zoeller from
the beginning believed Erik and Lyle would have been clever
enough to buy the guns in someone else's name.

So Zoeller had to rely on investigators familiar enough with
the case that they knew the names of the boys' pals.

He and Linehan spent weeks driving from one shop to another. Everywhere they went, they showed pictures of Erik
and Lyle.

In early January, Zoeller asked the Fiocchi Company, the
Ozark, Missouri, firm that made the wadding, what shops they
supplied. More shops were searched.

But nothing turned up. Pam Ferrero became so concerned
that she called the court to try to stop the probate proceedings.
"Lady, you have no standing in this case," she was bluntly told.
Frustrated, she hung up, wondering what it would take to get
this case to court.

* * *

Then on March 5, 1990, JuJuJon Rose Smyth, an attractive
dark-haired woman who operated a New Age store specializing
in crystals and volumes of self-help tapes, came to Beverly Hills
police with a bizarre story of love, betrayal, and parricide.

Actually, Smyth called a friend with a connection to law
enforcement, who brought Zoeller over to her house and introduced him as a friend. After Smyth began telling her story,
Zoeller realized this information was too important, and he told
Smyth who he was. Then he began scribbling notes as her story
tumbled out.

Smyth, a thirty-seven-year-old former actress in the Orient
whose mother did astrological work for police departments, said
she was a friend—paramour was the word the press would
use—of Jerry Oziel, the psychologist for the Menendez
brothers.

Smyth, whose tape line included "Insights into the Sensuality
and Sexuality of the Aquarius Woman," said Oziel had asked her
to eavesdrop on the Halloween night therapy session with the
Menendez brothers. She said she had overheard an extraordinary shouting match between Erik and Lyle Menendez. "I can't
believe you did this!" Lyle shouted, according to this account.
"I can't believe you told him! I don't even have a brother now! I
could get rid of you for this! I hope you know what we have to
do. We've got to kill him and anyone associated to him."

Erik, sobbing, replied: "I can't stop you from what you have
to do, but . . . I can't kill anymore."

The session ended when Erik ran out of the office, tears
streaming down his face. Lyle, followed by Oziel, strode past
Smyth and pushed the button for the elevator.

According to a seven-hour taped interview with police, Smyth
said Lyle had pushed the button for the elevator, then turned to
Oziel. "I can kind of understand Erik, but he shouldn't have
done this. . . . Now we'll just have to take care of this."

"Are you threatening me?" Oziel asked, according to
Smyth's account.

Lyle shook the doctor's hand and said, "Good luck, Dr. Oziel."

Oziel was so frightened that he told his wife and kids to leave
their house in suburban Sherman Oaks. He left the house
himself and stayed with Smyth.

Oziel bought shotguns for himself, his wife, and Smyth. After
that initial session, Oziel kept the brothers coming in for therapy
by telling them that he might be able to help them piece together
the things in their family's history that had caused them to

hate their parents. Oziel supposedly had everything on tape, confessions to the slayings and explanations for why they had been done.

Smyth's taped interview also gave the investigators a chilling insight into the two young killers. Smyth said Lyle bragged that for once " 'my father wouldn't be able to put me down or criticize me because I guess I committed the perfect murder.' And he laughed after he said that."

She also said Erik was having regrets, because "Lyle is just like the father and so it didn't really do any good to go through all that because now Lyle is controlling everything. And Lyle has just taken the father's place."

As they listened to Smyth, the investigators might have noticed that she spent almost as much time complaining about Oziel as she did discussing the brothers. At one point she even accused him of rape. "One of the times that we had sex it was definitely rape because I pretended to be asleep and he went ahead and had sex with me," she said.

The conversation was long and often rambling. Zoeller said later that he had been so intent on the information about the Menendez brothers that he didn't realize Smyth might have been trying to report a crime against her. This would come back to haunt them later.

Three days after Smyth's first meeting with Zoeller, attorney Gary Mogil received a call asking if he was available to serve as a special master on a search warrant. Since it was a search of a psychologist's office and home, a master was needed to safeguard the doctor-patient privilege of confidentiality. The law protects the secrecy of anything said between a patient and doctor, except in special circumstances. One of those circumstances is when the patient threatens to harm the doctor or others.

The special master is supposed to be a "buffer between police who want to seize all kinds of evidence and people who may have a privilege," Mogil said later.

He prepared himself by bringing along a dozen manila envelopes—he would need only three—scissors, tape, and extra copies of section 1524, the law governing such searches.

Three locations were to be searched—the house, the office, and Oziel's safety deposit box—and when Mogil arrived with the police at the six-thousand-square-foot house of Jerry Oziel, he was greeted by his wife, Laurel, in her bathrobe.

"What's this in regard to?" she asked.

"It's in regard to some tape recordings that we're here to recover," said Deputy District Attorney Elliott Alhadeff. A serious man with a mustache who handled special trials in the Santa Monica branch office, he had recently been brought in to replace Ferrero. She had been given the thankless task of retrying the McMartin preschool molestation case against Raymond Buckey. Buckey's mother had been acquitted of all but one count, which was dismissed, in the first trial, but the jury had failed to reach a verdict on thirteen counts against Buckey.

The lead prosecutor on the retrial requested Pam, and she agreed to, as she put it, "go down in flames with him." As it turned out, she was right. The jury deadlocked, but Ferrero won high marks for shearing away all the bizarre satanic allegations in the case and trying it like a conventional child abuse case.

"We have a search warrant we're going to have to execute here," Alhadeff said.

"Do you mind if I get dressed?" said Laurel Oziel.

"Absolutely. Go ahead," Alhadeff replied gallantly. She closed the door and disappeared.

"Mind if I burn the tapes?" Mogil asked Alhadeff sarcastically.

"Yeah," said Zoeller. "You should have her open the door."

"Yeah. This is shit," Alhadeff fumed.

The cops and the attorneys managed to get in the door. And when the woman tried to excuse herself to get dressed again, they weren't having any of it. Zoeller said he would allow her to get dressed only if he could inspect the room first. Finally Jerry Oziel arrived, and Mogil told him they were looking for six cassette tapes "with recorded information relating to the murders of Jose and Kitty Menendez."

Mogil said the tapes would be sealed and taken to the court, where a judge would rule later on the thorny issues of whether the tapes would be admissible in court.

Oziel was reluctant to turn the evidence over, but was warned that if they had to, Zoeller and Linehan would "go through every nook and cranny of this house."

Finally the therapist agreed to turn over the tapes under "compulsia" of the court. As they prepared to retrieve them from a safety deposit box, Oziel asked if "you know anyone with the witness protection program?"

"I don't think you'll need that," Zoeller said reassuringly.

"It doesn't work very well, I know that much," Oziel replied. He was so terrified during the search that when his wife brought out a sandwich, he wolfed it down so fast he didn't seem to be chewing.

When they got to the bank, Oziel suddenly became more cooperative. "If you don't get these people immediately, you're going to have a lot more things to investigate," he warned.

Oziel's attorney, Bradley Brunon, urged the investigators to listen to the tapes. "When you listen to the tapes, if you were he, you would want a whole lot of protection." Before Mogil sealed envelopes containing seventeen audiotapes and seven pages of notes to be turned over to a judge for safekeeping, Oziel played portions of each of the tapes for the cops. In grim detail they laid out what had happened that warm summer night. One thing no amount of taped analysis would ever adequately explain, however, was why.

Shock: The Arrests of Lyle and Erik

In early March, one of Lyle's student/business associates, David Bros, a bright-eyed boy with a good head for numbers, became concerned about widespread campus rumors that Lyle was under scrutiny by police in connection with the killings of his parents.

Bros went to the library and read everything he could get his hands on about the case. The matter troubled him enough that he asked Lyle point-blank one day if he had had anything to do with the crime.

Surprisingly, Lyle was not offended. He answered no simply but firmly, and without hesitation. He seemed to understand his friend's need for reassurance. That was good enough for Bros, and the subject was dropped. Business was good at the café, and Lyle's other projects were occupying all the free time of his team of post-adolescent capitalist dreamers, who so far had managed to bring only one project to completion—the purchase of the restaurant. And for that they had overpaid, snickered their rivals.

Lyle flew back to Beverly Hills the next day to take care of business at home. On the plane with him were two of his other associates, Glenn Stevens and Hayden Rogers. Lyle was on his way to try to find out what had happened to $40,000 Erik had given a concert promoter to produce a show called "Soul to Soul." The money had disappeared and the show had never happened.

"Well, if we can't get the money," Lyle said during the flight, according to Stevens, "I don't see why we can't get in the car, the two of us, and go back, one of us driving. Put him in the front seat if we can't get the money, one of us will just take a razor wire and kill the kid and go dump the body somewhere."

Midway in the flight, something happened that made Lyle put aside his anger. He called his café, just to see how business was going. Around lunchtime, he was told, only an hour after he and his friends had left for Newark International Airport, two familiar faces had appeared: Zoeller and Linehan. They had asked restaurant manager Gus Tangalos, who was working at the cash register, if Lyle owned a gun.

The visit was not too unusual. The two detectives had been in Princeton before. At one time Lyle told the *Times* reporters that he and his brother really liked the cops. "Mike and Les, the four of us get along quite well," he said. Even then, that sounded a little hollow, since Linehan's first name was Tom, not Mike. Lately, though, the cops' persistence had begun to irritate Lyle so much that he was considering filing suit against the Beverly Hills Police Department for harassment, friends said.

When Lyle heard about the latest visit, Stevens said, he took a wad of cash out of his pocket and gave $1,400 to Stevens. He also handed Stevens the business card of his attorney, Jerry Chaleff, and said if anything happened to him they should use the money to get him out of jail.

Lyle also said Chaleff "knew everything," as did his therapist, Jerry Oziel.

"What do you mean?" Stevens asked.

"Well, he has some tapes of discussions with me and my brother that he's holding in a safe deposit box. If the police get their hands on those tapes, I'm fucked."

On the morning of March 8, the board of directors of LIVE met in Los Angeles to hear the long-awaited report from Kay, Scholer, Fierman, Hays & Handler. Investigators for the law firm had for months been looking into the company operations to discover whether there was any reason for stockholders to be concerned about whether the killings could be tied to the company. Mason flew in from his home in Lake Tahoe, where Erik had recently visited on a ski outing, for the meeting.

Pierce O'Donnell, a partner in the firm's Los Angeles office, presented an oral summary of the thick, two-volume investigative document. His conclusion stunned Mason. "One of the things O'Donnell talked about was that he had learned from police that the boys were suspects," Mason recalled.

"He suspected they would be arrested in the future."

Even he didn't know that the future was now. Across town, Oziel's tapes were being seized.

Glenn Stevens and Hayden Rogers were relaxing with Lyle at the Beverly Hills mansion. It was a lazy late winter day. Lyle was paying for everything, and life seemed good. The group got hungry just after one, so they piled into Erik's yellow jeep and headed out for lunch. Their destination was the Cheesecake Factory. Just as on the night of the murder, when Lyle was to meet Perry Berman, they would never get there.

A squadron of police was waiting down the street for this moment. They had decided against surrounding the mansion out of concern for Lyle's grandmother, Maria, who had been staying there since the murders, helping her grandsons and keeping the house. In typical Beverly Hills form, they didn't want to lay siege to the mansion and scare the poor lady to death.

The cops were anxious to get Lyle now because they knew he was about to leave town again. They would have liked to wait until Erik and Lyle could be captured together, but some things couldn't be helped. Erik was playing tennis in Israel.

Stevens "thought something was going on" when they pulled away from the house because he saw that a blue Ford with a flashing light had blocked the street at the south end of the block. Lyle brought the Jeep to a halt just short of the car.

He quickly threw the Jeep into reverse and crashed into a blue van blocking his retreat.

The cops were everywhere. They jumped out from behind trees and someone screamed, "Get the fuck out of the Jeep." Stevens looked over and saw one plainclothes officer who was so nervous that "his hand was shaking" as he leveled his gun.

All three friends climbed out of the jeep and were told to lie down in the street.

Stevens was petrified. "I was afraid they were going to fill me so full of lead I would turn into a pencil," he said.

As police handcuffed the three young men, neighbors came out of their homes, just as they had nearly seven months earlier, and stood looking at the trio on the pavement. Then there had been ambulances and gurneys. This time it was guns and handcuffs. Things had come full circle.

Stevens tried to console his buddies. "We haven't done anything," he said. "Stay calm."

Lyle was booked at the West Hollywood sheriff's station and

transported downtown to the Los Angeles County Men's Jail. Glenn and Hayden were released to go back and tell Maria that her beloved grandson had been arrested for murdering her adored son.

Later on the afternoon of March 8, police convened a news conference in a field house in Beverly Hills' Roxbury Memorial Park to celebrate the break in the case.

"I've been in this business for over thirty-three years, and I have heard of very few murders that were more savage than this one was," said Chief Iannone.

Although Iannone declined to speculate on a motive, he said it was "no big secret that the Menendezes had an estate that was worth millions of dollars" and that the two brothers were the sole beneficiaries.

Los Angeles County District Attorney Ira Reiner called his own press conference. He didn't mince words. The motive, he said, was greed.

"I don't know what your experience is, but it's been our experience in the district attorney's office that $14 million provides ample motive for someone to kill somebody," he said.

Reiner also revealed that special circumstances had been attached to the charges, which meant that, if convicted, the brothers could be put to death in San Quentin's gas chamber.

Asked about the seizure of Oziel's tapes, a spokeswoman for the district attorney's office, Sandi Gibbons, said Lyle's arrest was "based on newly discovered evidence and did involve some conversations."

The family took the arrest hard. "Oh no, this is terrible," said Pat Andersen, Kitty's sister-in-law. "I can't believe this is happening."

Carlos Baralt, Lyle's uncle, said the whole family was behind the boys. "We don't in the least circumstance think he is guilty of what he has been accused." He said Lyle was handling the situation as well as could be expected and was expecting to "get out of this very soon."

Meanwhile, in another part of town, the relationship between Jerry Oziel and Judalon Smyth was heading rapidly downhill. "Well, you did what you did and that's what you did," Oziel said in a taped phone call.

"I think there's going to be an intense" amount of media interest in the case. "I suggest you have no comment. Unless you want a number of things disclosed that you don't want disclosed."

Erik was still at large. He was playing in his first professional tennis tournament in Israel. His private coach, Mark Heffernan, was with him.

Some wondered whether Erik would flee. But these people didn't know how much Erik needed his brother, especially since his parents were no longer around to give balance to his world. Erik would have followed his brother into hell, even if it meant leaving heaven to do so.

After hearing about his brother's arrest, Erik called his uncle, Carlos Baralt, in New Jersey. "The best thing to do is turn yourself in," Baralt advised.

Erik also called Jose's close friend John Mason. He couldn't understand why they would arrest Lyle. "We didn't have anything to do with it," Erik said. He said he was going to come back and "straighten this whole thing out."

Erik flew to Miami to meet his aunt, Marta Cano, who lived in West Palm Beach. It must have been a grim meeting. One minute Erik was polishing his game on the international tennis circuit, the next sneaking into the U.S. to go to jail.

"He told me not to worry," Cano said. "He was concerned about his brother."

From there Cano accompanied Erik to Los Angeles International Airport. She had already notified Zoeller and Linehan of their plans.

On the flight back to Los Angeles, he and Cano talked about a lot of things. Erik was exhausted. He had not slept in forty-eight hours. He was especially scared the media might photograph him handcuffed. Erik also said something on the plane that belied his confident assertions that a monstrous mistake had been made, a mistake he would straighten out in a hurry. "I don't know how long I'm going to be in jail," he told his aunt. "It might be my whole life."

Marta replied that she didn't want to know anything. "Whatever you've done, I forgive you," she said.

He looked at her sweetly and sadly, leaned over and kissed her.

The two were met at LAX by detectives Zoeller and Linehan. Zoeller asked Erik to extend his wrists. "Hey, you don't have to handcuff me," said Erik.

"We know, Erik," Zoeller replied sympathetically. "But we just have to do it."

Like Lyle, Erik was placed in the county jail in downtown Los Angeles.

Hollywood was only a step or two behind the cops. Within weeks two networks, ABC and NBC, poured staff and piles of cash into the story and produced Menendez specials for "sweeps" week, television's critical audience measurement time period.

TV miniseries were rushed into development. The only question was, Who would play Lyle? Mickey Rourke perhaps?

As the crescendo built, a friend of Kitty's reflected on the family tragedy. "It makes you feel sad about the American dream." Hard work, ambition, wanting more for your children— "it's what they tell you to do and [Jose] did it. Then this happens."

To avoid the herds of reporters searching for anyone who knew Erik and Lyle, Glenn Stevens, Hayden Rogers, and a third friend of Lyle's, Col Krueger, decided to drive secretly back east in Col's Toyota sedan. "We took a week" to make the drive, Stevens said.

"It was a long drive" and there was a lot to talk about, Stevens said. "We were wondering what was going to happen with all of this. And we felt Lyle had a good chance to be released."

Stevens, who had been so ready before to talk about his suspicions of his friend, was now firmly in Lyle's corner. "They're trying to build a case around Lyle buying a Porsche," he said angrily.

Maybe it was just that now that he was forced to face the fact of Lyle's arrest, he had trouble grasping the truth of it all. How could Lyle have blasted his parents into eternity?

"Lyle idolized his father," he said. "He had such a love for his father."

Despite the official police line that they had a rock-solid case against Lyle and Erik, there were holes in it. For one thing, there was no guarantee they would ever get to use the tapes they had seized from Oziel. A court would have to rule on that issue, and courts are very cautious about invading the privacy of doctor-patient relations.

There still was no physical evidence tying the boys to the crime, which made finding the shotguns more important than ever. Smyth said the weapons had been thrown down a hill off Mulholland, and police went up there to search six different times. The only thing they came back with was a case of poison oak.

But Smyth provided a valuable piece of information about the purchase of the guns. It turned out Zoeller had been searching in the wrong place. The guns, Smyth said, were bought in San Diego, a place Lyle was familiar with because he had played tennis tournaments there.

Zoeller obtained another printout of gun shops and began all over again. This time he went all out, searching day after day. He knew from Smyth that there was a security camera in the shop, but there were still hundreds to check. He figured Lyle and Erik would probably have chosen some small place on a side street, so he started with that kind of store. He stayed close to the San Diego Freeway, the main route from Los Angeles south, on the theory that the boys would not know the area well enough to be driving all around. Once again he showed pictures arranged in a kind of lineup card wherever he went.

The answer was always the same. No, the clerks hadn't seen anyone who looked like that.

Finally, after checking all the mom and pop shops, Zoeller turned in desperation to the big discount stores, such as Big 5 Sporting Goods, a mass marketer of sports and camping equipment. On Wednesday, March 14, he and Sergeant Edmunds, the officer who had politely interviewed Erik and Lyle the night of the killings, were about to wrap up their search.

There were only two shops left on their list for the day. They drove over to a Big 5 store on Convoy Street in San Diego, where Zoeller flashed his badge and requested the ATF records on file in every store. There, on a plain form entitled Firearms Transaction Record, Zoeller found the sale of two Mossberg twelve-gauge shotguns for $199.99 each, on August 18, 1989.

The buyer answered no to the form questions, beginning with, "Are you under indictment or information in any court for a crime punishable by imprisonment for a term exceeding one year?"

The form was signed Donovan Jay Goodreau and listed a San Diego address. To the side of the store's gun section, positioned near the ceiling and adjacent to a management office with one-way glass, was a surveillance camera.

Zoeller knew he had hit paydirt. He's too much a disciplined cop to shout or celebrate. Deep inside, though, a small voice said something like, "Eureka."

On the day after Lyle's arrest, Donovan Goodreau rushed over to the big international newsstand in Times Square, not far from where he worked as a host at a restaurant called Boxer's. On the front page of the newspaper was Lyle's picture. He went numb.

But not as numb as he would be a week later, when he got a call from Les Zoeller. Where were you on August 18, 1989? Zoeller asked, his voice firm and demanding.

Goodreau told Zoeller he had worked that day at the Manhattan restaurant, Boxer's, where he was the manager. Did he have any relatives in San Diego? Zoeller persisted. Donovan was a wreck. Then he remembered. Luckily, he had punched a time clock at Boxer's the day of the firearms sale.

Though the address was phony, the driver's license number on the form matched Donovan's. Goodreau's California license had been missing since the day he had been kicked out of Lyle's life. After seeing a copy of the firearms form, Donovan said the signature was not even close to his. Elliott Alhadeff asked the court to order handwriting samples to be collected from Lyle and Erik to compare to the signature on the federal form. Erik refused.

The Big 5 assistant manager who sold the weapons and signed the federal form was shown mug shots, but could not pick out any of them as the customer who had identified himself as Donovan Goodreau. Police also attempted to lift fingerprints from the form, but came up with nothing.

Still, here at last was a physical link between the killings and the Menendez boys.

Intriguingly, a Big 5 clerk said that whoever had purchased the weapons had called back later to inquire how long the company retained the film in the surveillance camera. The caller apparently got a temporary clerk who said that he believed the film was retained for two or three months. What that clerk did not know was that there was no film in the camera—it was, in effect, a bluff to inhibit would-be robbers.

After Donovan was contacted by the police, he was angry at Lyle. "At first I wanted to kill him. I know why he did this," he said to himself, "he was trying to get back at me."

But then he talked to Stevens. "He told me it wasn't personal."

As bizarre an explanation as that seemed to be, Donovan, the wide-eyed California boy, was willing to accept it. Lyle had done a lot for him, after all, and he shouldn't hate him too much just because Lyle had set him up to potentially take responsibility for murdering his parents.

Reflecting on his relationship with Lyle, Goodreau declared: "Lyle always offered me a lot of stability even though he lived so recklessly. I felt really secure. I really can't put my finger on why. But it was like if I had a problem, Lyle would take care of it. He was charismatic, always fun to be around, never really down. He was constant entertainment."

At the same time, however, Donovan considers his former close friend "the most selfish, self-centered asshole I ever met."

20

Watching the Wheels

The Menendez murder case now entered a new phase, with a revised cast of players. Lyle and Erik and Zoeller and Linehan stepped back and became almost peripheral to the grinding wheels of justice.

The new players were attorneys and judges, and the contest they waged was often an arcane legal one. Much of it would be decided before the two young men, now nineteen and twenty-two, ever went to trial. It would be like a baseball game in which only the bottom of the ninth was played before the fans.

The prosecution would try to get access to as much evidence as it could, while the job of the defense was to knock everything out, particularly Oziel and his tapes. Without them the prosecutors had only circumstantial evidence tying the brothers to the crime.

When the Menendez and Andersen families went shopping for legal talent, they came up with some of the best, and best-paid, criminal defense attorneys in the nation. Chosen to represent Erik—and earning $750,000 to do so—was Leslie Abramson, a tiny battering ram of a woman with a frothy mound of blond hair, the mouth of a longshoreman, and the will to win of a professional athlete. The granddaughter of a Russian immigrant and one-time Communist Party member, she was so imposing, even at five feet three, in her rumpled suits and heels that many judges were intimidated by her fierce courtroom presence. If she didn't like a ruling, she wrinkled her face in disgust and shook her head, daring the court to hold her in contempt.

Possessing a formidable temper, she once flipped off NBC in

a memorable, nationally televised court hallway encounter when they got their cameras in her face.

A passionate opponent of the death penalty, what might have been her most glittering success was her defense in 1988 of a Philippine teenager who had shot his father in the head while he slept. The youth, Arnel Salvatierra, said he feared his father would kill him over his poor grades at Glendale High School.

The case had been in the international spotlight because the day before the murder, the boy's father, Oscar Salvatierra, a Philippine news editor, had received a death threat thought to have been linked to his newspaper's opposition to former Philippine President Ferdinand E. Marcos. Actually, the letter was faked by the son. Abramson convinced the jury that Arnel, originally charged with first-degree murder, was the victim of physical and psychological abuse.

In a ringing closing argument she warned the jury that if they convicted the teenager of first-degree murder, the father's hand "will come out of the grave, and his last act of terrorism will happen with you as his accomplices."

The jury tossed aside the first-degree murder charge and instead convicted the youth of voluntary manslaughter and placed him on probation.

"She's a self-righteous, pontificating tyrant," said Deputy District Attorney Harvey Giss, the lone opponent to succeed in sending one of her clients to Death Row. He said she feels she is on a holy mission to beat back a "Gestapo government" bent on meting out an-eye-for-an-eye justice. But, he grudgingly admitted, "she's as good as they come" in trial preparation and courtroom guts.

"I have no doubt that she would cut my heart out and eat it if that would suit her purpose," said another prosecutor.

The process of finding an attorney for Lyle was more difficult. Jerry Chaleff was the first choice, but he eventually withdrew, in part, it was believed, because he had previously represented both brothers and might have a conflict.

Lyle's primary attorney would be Jill Lansing, forty-five, a slender blond woman with a prim expression on her pursed mouth that reminded some observers of actress Lee Remick. Like Abramson, she had cut her teeth in the public defender's office, and this was to be her first case in private practice. She worked out of a small, no-frills West Los Angeles office, and where as Abramson was bombastic, Lansing was more easy-going.

A liberal activist in her youth, Lansing at one time had worked for Tom Hayden before joining Los Angeles County's Public Defender's office, where she worked between 1975 and 1990. "I'm a product of the sixties," she says. "I had the wonderful experience of living at a time when people thought that something bigger than themselves was important."

Lansing was not comfortable in a high-profile, media-blitz type of situation. But she would be unable to avoid the spotlight. Of the brothers, Lansing said that on the basis of hundreds of hours of research and time spent with them in jailhouse interviews, she had come to the firm conclusion that "they are both incredibly warm, caring, sensitive people."

"The jury," Lansing said in an interview, "will like these boys when they see them. I don't know how they could not."

Lansing's co-counsel, Michael Burt, was head trial attorney in the San Francisco Public Defender's office and an expert in death penalty law.

On the other side of the table was to have been Alhadeff, the balding prosecutor who once had one of the best government jobs in the country—he prosecuted cases at the small court on Santa Catalina Island. Alhadeff was so confident he had a strong case against Lyle and Erik that he had been ready to file the case even before the tapes were seized. He thought the alibi was patently preposterous.

But he and Los Angeles County District Attorney Ira Reiner weren't getting along, engaging in screaming matches in Reiner's office. The D.A. finally yanked him from the case, telling him that after many telephone conversations that "I didn't develop confidence in your ability to prepare the case."

Being removed from the case at least removed Alhadeff from an increasingly tense relationship with Abramson. After a few months they were no longer speaking, unless you count Leslie's angry denunciation, "You're dead meat," when they met one day.

Reiner asked Ferrero to take the case back. "My boyfriend didn't want me to have it," she said. "But since he was my boyfriend and not my husband, I said, 'It's my career. I'll take it.'"

Soon, however, Peter Bozanich, a supervisor in the prosecutor's office, would be her husband. And he would suffer many sleepless nights watching his new wife climb out of bed at three in the morning to log onto her home computer, where she wrote out questions she would attack defense witnesses with the next day.

Ferrero, soon to be Bozanich, was a slight, cerebral woman of thirty-nine who looks like the Wellesley grad she is, with not a hair or a thought out of place. With a cascade of dark brown hair that reaches almost to the middle of her back, and her makeup done to an understated perfection, she looked like she should be relaxing in a club at Marina del Rey before a sail. She seemed the spiritual opposite of the flamboyant, tousled Abramson, but she was, in her own, less theatrical way, just as tough. While not as tenacious, her legal mind was sharper and she was quick enough on her feet to adjust to surprises from witnesses and the opposition.

Together, Abramson and Bozanich would make for a show within a show as they battled over the lives of two young men who, in the prosecutor's opinion, had it all and wanted more.

When the case quickly became a cultural watermark, Bozanich would say again and again that she didn't understand it, dismissing Lyle and Erik as "garden-variety killers." But of course, she did understand it and put in killing hours to wage a determined battle against the four skilled, well-paid attorneys on the other side.

The legal wrangling began on June 16, 1990, when Santa Monica Superior Court Judge James Albracht convened a hearing behind closed doors to hear testimony from Oziel before deciding whether to release the tapes to the prosecutor. There were three tapes at issue. Two of them contained Oziel's dictated notes following the October 31, November 2, and November 28 therapy sessions. The third was the December 11 tape of Erik and Lyle, which had been done with the consent of their attorney at the time, Chaleff.

The law protecting the psychotherapist privilege was well established. Even in cases where a killer confesses to his therapist that he murdered someone, the privilege guarantees that the therapist cannot go to the police. If he does, he can be sued for malpractice.

The reason for the secrecy is that the state legislature recognizes that psychotherapy can work only if the patient feels free to reveal the most intimate and embarrassing details of his life. If the patient hesitates to talk openly for fear his therapist will rush off and tell someone, the relationship is undermined.

But there are exceptions to the privilege. The two main ones are in cases where the therapist believes the patient is a serious threat to himself or others, and if the patient is using the therapist as part of some plan to commit or cover up a crime.

Erik and Lyle were escorted into the courtroom under a heavy guard. Just the week before, the sheriff's department had announced that they had attempted to escape after Lyle's ankle chain was found to have been nearly severed during a previous court appearance.

Although investigators said the links appeared shiny, as if freshly cut, the department announced later that it could not prove an attempt to escape.

Albracht still denied a request that they be allowed to change from their rumpled blue jail jumpsuits into civilian clothes, as they had done in the past. That outraged their relatives, who said the brothers were being paraded before TV cameras in "an attempt to humiliate and bring them down."

Erik's nose was swollen and bruised, the result, they said, of a jail beating that authorities said they were investigating. Relatives also reported death threats against them. Erik and Lyle were being housed in a special unit of the jail, called the Keepaway Cell, and they only came in contact with other inmates infrequently.

Although the public was not allowed to hear Oziel's remarks, the brothers were in attendance and were angry. They told friends that he was lying on the stand.

A few weeks later, Albracht gave Los Angeles County prosecutors a major victory. He said the tapes could be used as evidence against the brothers.

"I have ruled that none of the communications is privileged," Albracht said. He said Oziel had "reasonable cause to believe" that Lyle and Erik "constituted a threat, and it was necessary to disclose those communications to prevent a danger."

Albracht announced his decision from the bench in open court. There was a stunned gasp in the courtroom from family members when the judge disclosed his ruling.

Defense attorneys pledged to appeal Albracht's decision. "If the judge's ruling is upheld, it brings a virtual end to the psychotherapist-patient privilege," Leslie Abramson fulminated.

He said the right to confidentiality belongs to the patient and should not be trampled by a "talkative" therapist.

True to their word, they took the matter to the Second District Court of Appeals, which on March 2, 1991, echoed the decision of the lower court. While threats had not been made at every session, the court held that once a threat is made to a therapist, there is no longer a "genuine therapeutic relationship, the confidential nature of the therapist-patient relationship ceases to exist, and further communications by the patient to the therapist are not privileged."

In the final two sessions, the court said, Oziel had been focusing on issues that might be helpful if they were arrested and tried for the murders—in other words, he was helping them fashion a defense. In doing so, the court said, Oziel was "motivated by self-preservation. . . . The purported 'therapy' was, in fact, a charade."

The decision also quoted freely from the tapes, revealing to the world for the first time that these two young men had indeed murdered their parents. The impact on their family ranged from shock to utter disbelief. While relatives such as Marta Cano stayed in their corner, some members of the family who had once been vocal in their support dropped out of sight.

Once again the defense attorneys promised to appeal, this time to the state Supreme Court.

On June 4, 1992, more than two years after the arrest, the case finally reached that court, which heard arguments in the potentially precedent-setting case in the elegant third-floor courtroom of green marble and dark wood in the Ronald Reagan building in downtown Los Angeles. The case was being closely watched by medical groups. In past cases the high court had held that a threat by a patient and a therapist's subsequent warning to an intended victim could be used to convict the patient of a crime. But the court had not ruled definitively on whether other statements made during therapy sessions—such as a confession—could be used against a patient in court.

Abramson and Burt, who had defended Nightstalker Richard Ramirez and other celebrated defendants, argued for the brothers. They said only the portions of the tapes dealing with the threat should be given to the prosecution.

"I don't think loose-lipped, unethical, self-preserving [people], all of which reminds me of someone I met in this case, should be allowed to disclose" whatever they want to third parties, Abramson said sarcastically.

More than two months later, the court issued its ruling. The court gave the prosecution one tape, the one dictated by Oziel, dealing with the October 31 and November sessions.

The court decided the release of the tape was not barred by the therapist-patient privilege because Oziel believed the brothers were threatening him and others during those sessions. But the court barred release of a tape covering the November 28 session, as well as the December 11 tape of Lyle and Erik.

In those sessions, the court said, there was insufficient evidence of threats warranting disclosure.

Though the prosecution got one tape, Abramson declared victory. "As far as we're concerned, we won," she told City News Service. "My client heard a radio report in jail, saying that the prosecutors had won, and he called me all depressed. I said, 'What are you depressed for? We won.'"

The decision meant no tapes would be played in court, because the defense would not be able to cross-examine a tape recording. Although Oziel would be allowed to testify about the two sessions, the prosecutor, now Pam Bozanich, feared he could be raw meat under the withering cross-examination of Leslie Abramson. There would be little doubt she would drag out his affair with Judalon Smyth, as well as every other secret she could unearth to discredit him.

The real loss was the December 11 tape, which could have been played in court as an exception to the hearsay rule because it contained the defendants' own statements. "We wanted the last tape," Bozanich said mournfully.

But even without it she was confident that the one tape was damning enough to force the defense to change its strategy. Oziel's credibility was shaky, but the defense, she felt, couldn't risk a go-for-broke claim that the boys hadn't done it. So what would the defense be?

"Battered child syndrome," she guessed. In other words, it would be Arnel Salvatierra all over again, only this time with Jose Menendez in the role of abusive father. "They will go for voluntary manslaughter."

"If I were their attorneys, I would go for battered child," she said. "Any family that could raise two kids capable of murder . . ."

Bozanich didn't know all the details of Menendez family life, but she knew enough to know Jose was, or could be, in the vernacular, an asshole. Bozanich said this would be a NHI case, which stood for No Human Involved. Cops often use the term to describe killings of drug dealers, for instance, to indicate their belief that a kind of street justice had been meted out. In this case Jose would be painted as such a brutalizing monster that no one could feel sorry for him. But Bozanich felt the defense would have a problem justifying the murder of Kitty. "She was such a basket case" that it would be difficult to portray her as an abuser deserving of death.

Bozanich remained convinced that Erik and Lyle had intended the murders to look like a mob hit from the beginning. "Notice how both were shot in the left knee," she said. "They didn't do it very well."

As children of the video age, they could not have known that the mob doesn't blast its victims into pieces, nor does it kill wives, nor does it bother to pick up shell casings from the murder scene.

The defense team had grown to a fourth attorney, Marcia Morrissey, who had handled the defense in the Cotton Club murder case. Morrissey, forty-three, was brought in to help with Erik's defense. Another graduate of the public defender's office, her view of the people she defends, who she admits have often done terrible things, is simple and profound: "People are never as bad as their worst moments."

Looking ahead to the trial, Bozanich, who had a raw sense of humor, predicted that "this is going to be an estrogen vortex."

21

Setting the Stage

As far as prosecutor Pamela Bozanich was concerned, things only got more difficult when psychologist Jerome Oziel was attacked in a lawsuit filed by his former paramour. Judalon Smyth accused Oziel, the prosecution's leading witness, of committing physical and sexual assault and fraud, all related to the crack-up of their relationship.

Smyth charged that Oziel had taken advantage of her and lured her into an intimate relationship with him when she was his patient. The litany of accusations included allegations that he threatened, choked, and struck her on several occasions, raped her, gave her drugs, and coerced her into signing a $5,000 promissory note for money she thought was a gift.

Her attorney at the time, Fred Rucker, also filed a complaint with the state medical board. He described Smyth, who, aside from her other interests, published a newsletter for doll collectors, as "down to earth but vulnerable."

Smyth, who operated an audio and videotaping duplication service, said she had contacted Oziel after hearing a self-help tape he made.

Smyth said she had been looking for a therapist, but could not afford Oziel's $150 to $200 hourly rates. Out of that initial contact, she said, developed an informal therapeutic relationship that quickly turned personal. She said Oziel, whose license at the time was on five years' probation for allegedly allowing a former patient to do work around his house in exchange for therapy, called her and gave her some advice. They began having long phone conversations, she said to Zoeller, which she later came to believe were programming her.

She said "what he was really doing with all those phone conversations was eliciting all of my strategies and so, after a period of a few weeks through June, was, I mean, I was practically like in love on the telephone."

She came to believe Oziel practiced a kind of programming that works on a theory that "everyone works on a formula, you know, and they have certain strategies and it's just like [a] recipe with a cookbook, and if you get those strategies and you get them in a certain order, then you can control them with anything because that's the way that the person is wired up in their brain."

So he was "eliciting my love strategies, and my fear strategies, and my success strategies."

Oziel, she said, asked to meet her. When they met, he was too short for her. The reaction was "great. He's not my type. We're just going to be friends."

She said he wanted a hug, but she warned him, "We're not just going to fall into bed."

She asked if he was married and he replied, she said, "not exactly." He said he was getting a divorce, though he continued to live with his wife in Sherman Oaks, and had even drawn up a property arrangement.

Soon after that Smyth and Oziel became intimate. "It was the worst sex I ever had in my life," she told writer Dominick Dunne. "To have good sex you either have to be in love or in lust. I wasn't either. It was awful the second time. The third time was better. I broke off with him four or five times between September and October. Then Erik Menendez came."

Smyth complained that Oziel dragged her into needless danger when he asked her to listen outside the door of his office on October 31. She said he explained that she should sit in his waiting room, posing as a patient, so she could call police if trouble arose. She armed herself with a neighbor's .357 handgun, and stationed herself in the waiting room, which had no receptionist. Arriving patients pushed a buzzer to get into the therapists' offices, one of which was occupied by Oziel's wife, Laurel.

While waiting for Lyle, Oziel ducked outside and told Judalon about his plan, she said. "Judalon, if I let him tell Lyle, and I'm not there to see Lyle's face, to see the psychology of what's going on with Lyle, I'm really afraid for you and my kids and myself."

When Lyle came, she said, he picked up a magazine and asked if she had been waiting long. "You know how doctors are," she replied, then Oziel took Lyle into his office.

She thought to herself, she said later, looking at the handsome young tennis star and elite student: "Any parent would think, What a great catch?"

But as a result of what she claimed she heard at that session, she became "fearful for her well-being, safety and for her life."

Smyth said she suggested calling the police, but Oziel refused. At the same time he told her she was depressed and had suicidal tendencies, she said. He began supplying her with tranquilizers "and other unknown narcotic substances" without a medical prescription. She said that on one occasion he forced her to take large doses of drugs, causing her to become groggy and incoherent. Then he took her to a hospital emergency room, claiming she was suicidal. After she was released, according to her account, he told her the only reason the hospital let her go was that Oziel said he would take care of her.

Oziel took her to his home, where she lived with him and his wife and two daughters for three months, from December 13 to March 4, 1990. He kept her in an "over-medicated state," she said.

During this period, as their relationship tumbled downhill, Smyth said she and Oziel began having difficulties, and he hit her at least twice and forced her on one occasion to engage in unconsensual sexual intercourse. One night they had a big fight, and she called 911. She said he took the phone out of her hand and "yanked it out of the wall."

Finally, on March 4, Smyth walked out of Oziel's home and went to the police.

Jerry Oziel and his wife of twenty-one years fought back, calling a press conference at the Beverly Hilton Hotel, attended by dozens of reporters. Oziel read from a prepared statement that accused Smyth of making "false, bizarre, and defamatory allegations about me both personally and as a professional."

Oziel denied raping or assaulting Smyth, characterizing her as a "woman scorned" who relentlessly pursued a relationship with him in a scenario straight out of the movie *Fatal Attraction*.

A small, round-faced, balding man who hardly looked the part of a Don Juan, Oziel said nonetheless that it was she, not he, who was the aggressor. He denied that Smyth was ever his

patient, saying the relationship began with her business proposal
to produce a series of cassettes with him. Then he played a
portion of a tape he said was Smyth speaking, saying her
motivation for calling him were "the tapes."

He also denied prescribing medication for her but did confirm
she complained of feelings of anxiety and depression "that were
difficult for her to cope with."

Most significant, he denied asking Smyth to eavesdrop on the
Menendez brothers. He said it is physically impossible to hear
any therapy conversation from his waiting room. He said he
always kept the waiting room door shut for security reasons
and, further, if anyone did get in the hall and listened at his office
door, she would only hear unintelligible mumbling.

Laurel Oziel, dressed in a peach suit and betraying little
emotion outside her slightly quavering voice, sat next to her
husband at a long table with a white cloth. She said she was
aware that her husband's business relationship with Judalon at
some point became, in her words, social. "He was honest with
me about this, and we worked together to determine how to
refocus her attention on business—or get her out of his life."

But "an overwhelming event" occurred—the confession of
Erik Menendez—that tied her to the Oziels. "Although she was
only indirectly associated with this event, Smyth expressed
feelings of being distraught and afraid, and she pleaded with us
to let her stay in our home for a few days only."

She paused and looked around at the cameras crowding the
conference room. "Once there, circumstances occurred which
enabled Smyth to threaten the personal safety of my husband,
myself, and even our children. I cannot discuss the circumstances surrounding her repeated threats, but she used them to
force us to let her remain in our home for an extended period of
time. During this time she became increasingly manipulative and
possessive. She campaigned relentlessly to steal my husband.
She tried to convince us that we should separate permanently
for our children's safety."

Then Laurel Oziel released a collection of letters purported
to have been written by Smyth to her husband.

"This feeling I have for you," said one, dated July 26, 1989,
not long after they met. "Is it love, addiction, curiosity? . . . I
believe I'm that woman you've been waiting for."

Later, the tone of the writing was both more confident and
more urgent. "I don't know what it's like for you when we're
apart, but for me it's like being in limbo—you are the magic, the

music, the heartbeat that seduces me back into this life. . . . I function when we're apart, but I live when we're together."

Then a possessive peevishness appears as the writer expresses frustration with roadblocks in their relationship. "I don't want to place limits or expectations, I just want to love you to the fullest each day . . . I know in my heart that this is what is balanced and non-neurotic, so why do you push my panic button by saying things that are limit-oriented? . . . There are some days I could just park a well-fed pigeon right over your head."

After reading their statements, which were handed out to the press in neat packets, the couple got up from the table without taking any questions and left through a rear door.

Bozanich and Zoeller filed out of the conference room with the reporters and the cameramen carrying tripods over their shoulders. The prosecutor rolled her eyes heavenward.

Leslie Abramson would find more women to come forward and denounce the therapist, causing Bozanich to observe dryly that Oziel seemed to have "a fairly devastating impact on women."

Meanwhile, in jail, weeks passed and then months, and the daily routine of cell life settled in. Their neighbors included the Woodmans, another well-known pair of well-to-do brothers accused of killing their parents.

Their eight-by-ten cells contained a toilet, a bed, and a small desk. They were fed in their cells but were taken out for exercise for an hour, three times a week. They got one visitor for twenty minutes a day but rarely got out in the sun. Erik developed a sickly ivory skin color that, with his already gaunt features, made him look cadaverous.

It was a grim life for two young men used to flying first-class and sunning themselves on the beach at Cancun. Erik was frequently in tears in the early months of his confinement, and became so anxious and upset that he began receiving medication, Xanax, a tranquilizer his mother had taken as often as four times a day.

But if their jail life was spartan, it was not all hard time. They were in regular communication with the outside world. In the early portion of his confinement, Lyle frequently called Gus Tangalos to find out whether Chuck's was still doing a brisk business. According to Gus, it was.

"It dropped 32 percent the first week after Lyle's arrest," he said a month after the arrest. "Now it's okay."

Gus was a staunch supporter of Lyle's innocence.

"My gut feeling," he said, "is that the man will be out in six-seven weeks. I'm gonna start taking bets on that. How long can you keep someone in jail when you can't come up with solid proof?"

Lyle's phone habits made him less than popular with his cell mates. Nine of them signed a letter complaining that Menendez, who at one point was apparently assigned the job of passing out food trays and coffee to other inmates, was shirking his job to spend extra time on the telephone.

"Menendez passes out the food trays and coffee when he wants to," said the letter. The complaints said Lyle was allowed four hours of phone time each day, and if the trays came when he was on the phone, he ignored the entreaties of other inmates to give them their food.

"He just stands there on the phone and yells back, 'I'm on a legal call to my attorney. Write a grievance.' "

The complaint also accused him of stealing food intended for an inmate on a special diet. When the inmate complained, Lyle said, "It wasn't there. Write a grievance."

"I know what is going on with this individual Menendez," the complaint concludes. "I know the way he is manipulating staff and has become a total nuisance here on F-row."

Lyle and Erik had plenty of visitors, and a local doctor who had become a fan sent reading material from Book Soup, the illustrious Hollywood bookstore. Erik received an autographed copy of *Jurassic Park*, while Lyle got *Night Manager*, John Le Carré's latest.

Lyle, relatives said, was managing to hold onto his sense of humor. The older brother told friends that he was receiving amorous notes from women all around the country, a frequent occurrence in high-profile murder cases involving handsome young killers. Lyle joked that Erik was getting a lot of letters too. Only his were coming from men.

Erik was caught in an apparent sexual embrace with an inmate, Bozanich said. It happened one day when Erik was escorted to the shower with another inmate. The deputy sheriff guarding them propped the shower door open and wandered off for a few minutes. When he came back, the shower door was almost closed. Inside, Erik was sitting on a chair in the shower with his back to the door. The other inmate was on his knees in front of him. When the deputy came in, they got up, looking embarrassed.

"Maybe they were praying," said Bozanich.

A relative reported finding a note from a male high school friend to him one day while going through his things. "You will always be my sheep and I will always be your shepherd," the note said.

In the early months of his confinement, Erik was seriously suicidal. But he was told by a psychologist that if he died, his brother would have nobody to testify for him, and that kept Erik going, relatives said.

A tall, blond-haired priest began visiting Erik in jail, and through him Erik began revealing for the first time some of the trauma he had supposedly suffered as a child. These conversations would apparently be the seed from which the defense of the Menendez brothers would grow.

Shortly after Lyle's chains were found nearly cut through, sheriff's deputies in surgical gloves searched Lyle's and Erik's cells and confiscated a seventeen-page letter from Lyle to Erik, along with some loose pages of notes.

The notes talked about plans to travel to South America, then to the Middle East. There was also a drawing of a building showing stairwells and doors. Deputies tried to match it with the courthouse, but finally decided it didn't resemble any building they recognized.

Was this part of an elaborate escape plan, complete with schematics? Or was it the fanciful imaginings of two young men who were once again seeing life through a lens? They knew how the jail movie worked. You escape. So, even if you have no intention, or even the slightest idea how to do so, you dream up a fantastic voyage that carries you up and over the cell walls, where you could float free and far away.

The seventeen-page letter, taken from Erik's cell, was a different matter. In it Lyle refers to the fact that Erik had not, so far, done to Lyle what the Woodman brothers had done to each other. One brother in that case testified against the other. That was exactly what Bozanich had hoped Erik would do to Lyle.

Lyle tells Erik that he would never forsake him. "You notice I have not held you talking to Cig or Oziel against [you] even though my entire life is on the verge of destruction as a result of all this. . . . I maintain a certain amount of honor in order to live with myself, and being true to my brother is at the core of that promise."

He also expresses insecurity. "I am not the pillar of strength the papers make me out to be or Leslie thinks I am. I think if Dad could give us one piece of advice as we left the house that night in August, it would be never to abandon each other no matter the circumstances. Never turn against each other no matter the pressure. Be proud of each other and understand that when one acts, the other acts, and lastly understand that the only way you can be defeated in life is if you lose touch in your heart with one another."

Indeed, this sounded much like Jose's motivational language. But to be able to imagine Jose picking himself up out of the gore to deliver this little pep talk to his sons before they left the mansion took a turn of mind outside most people's understanding.

"I am not an ordinary person," Lyle writes. "I do not see things in terms of manslaughter and life terms. I see only win, lose—honor and dishonor. I refuse to give up for Dad's sake. He is watching and I will not disappoint him a second time or Mom by giving up and having their deaths be in vain."

In vain? Lyle writes about his parents as though somehow they had chosen to give up their lives for him. Not at all like he was the one who forcibly wrenched them away.

Then Lyle worried about the upcoming trial. He was not looking forward, he said, to broadcasting family secrets to the world at large. "We alone know the truth. We alone know the secrets of our family's past."

What could this mean? Could it have anything to do with the psychologists spending hundreds of hours with the brothers?

But Lyle admits to having second thoughts about what he had done. "What we did in August was a mistake for what I can tell, and I don't know what to do about it. We are not bad people, we are close, we are compassionate, we are competent."

Jan, Erik's first girl, stuck by him and visited whenever she could. Erik had grown up fast in jail, she said, and become a model prisoner. Lyle, she said, had been in fights and in and out of solitary.

Jan liked Lyle less than ever. The first time she had visited Erik, he had handed the phone to Lyle that visitors had to use to talk to the inmates on the other side of the glass barricade. Lyle stood and stared at her breasts as though he had never seen a woman before. Jan felt violated and told Erik never to do that again.

Erik was trying to stay optimistic. When he talked about the future, he always said "when I get out." Erik warned her there was going to be some gory stuff coming out when the trial started, so she should steel herself for it. But Jan didn't care. She felt she was saving herself for him. She thought about all the ways they had been close and the thoughtful things Erik had done for her. She remembered the way he once had looked at her with eyes full of wonder and said he couldn't believe he was so lucky, to be dating a blond, blue-eyed California girl.

He always thought he was so ugly, but he was really sweet and handsome. Jan, who had dreamed of Kitty walking up to her with holes in her body, now began dreaming of Erik's trial.

In her dream, Erik was convicted and Jan scrambled to her feet and ran to save him. "You don't know him," she wailed.

The Princeton cemetery, where the remains of Jose and Kitty are located, is in a historic section of town a few blocks from historic Nassau Inn on the town square. Lyle talked about erecting a huge family mausoleum where all the Menendez family could be buried. "Lyle had all kinds of plans," said a relative.

Following the arrests, visitors found only two simple markers and some wilted flowers on the graves in the northeast corner of the cemetery. It was a testament to hubris. Jose had dreamed big, opulent, New World dreams. And what they had come down to the end was a plastic headstone.

After it became clear that Erik and Lyle had committed the murders, Marta Cano went to her mother, the stately Maria, who was staying all alone in the big house in Calabasas. The estate was fast being used up by attorneys' fees, and soon the unfinished Calabasas house that had bedeviled Kitty would be all that was left of Jose's fortune. Very gently Marta told her mother that Erik and Lyle had killed their parents. Maria said she would never accept it.

Then she agonized, "They destroyed what I love most in my life."

22

The Trial

It was a year of major trials in Los Angeles, which was fitting since the city itself seemed to be increasingly on trial in the wake of the worst urban rioting in American history and a seemingly bottomless recession. Pundits everywhere were asking whether the sun had set on the palm-shaded California dream.

First came the Rodney King beating retrial on federal civil rights charges. When two Los Angeles police officers were found guilty in April 1993, the city breathed a collective sigh of relief. The verdicts, it was believed, spared the city another bloody riot.

The emotions from that trial had hardly settled when, across a mountain range in the San Fernando Valley, another courtroom drama unfolded. It did not seem to have the same social gravity to it, but people were no less fascinated by the trial of Erik and Lyle Menendez. As the first King trial and resulting rioting served a warning about the dangers of race and group loyalty, the Menendez trial promised to hold up a mirror to family life, at least as it existed in the acquisitive eighties.

On a national scale, there was let-tomorrow-take-care-of-itself economics, which yielded to a recession and a frightening national debt. On a personal scale, there was the image of Jose Menendez, the hardworking immigrant who had bought wholeheartedly into the American dream and climbed over everybody in his path to achieve it. Until only one body was left—his own, lying in a pool of blood.

How could he have raised two children who would plot to kill him? Everyone wanted to know that. Maybe as a lesson to themselves. Beyond that, there was the glamour of it all, Beverly Hills and murder. Over-the-top wealth and over-the-top gore, an unbeatable combination.

The fact that there were two plotters made it doubly sensational. One killer in a family, that's sad and tragic. But two, that's freakish and macabre.

Right up to the beginning of the trial, some of the family had a hard time believing the boys could have done the crime. But as two juries were soon to learn, this was no whodunit.

The first indication of the direction the defense was to take was the thirty-four-page general jury questionnaire. Question 110 asked, "Do you think physical, sexual, emotional, or psychological abuse of children happens in the homes of wealthy families?"

For the prosecution, the guessing game was finally over. Bozanich had long wondered whether Leslie Abramson would gamble that prosecutors didn't have enough evidence to prove the crime had been committed by the defendants. Abramson had held her cards close until the very last moment, but in reality the state Supreme Court ruling that allowed Oziel to testify about what the brothers had told him in therapy had virtually foreclosed a claim that the brothers had not committed the killings. Now it was clear that the brothers would claim they had killed in self-defense. The law says a person can justifiably kill another if he is in reasonable fear of being killed himself.

The defense attorneys were finally prepared to say in public that, yes, they did it. But the motive—and the defense—would be so shocking and revolting that some people who knew the family would draw back in horror, saying that was impossible. Others would say that was the only thing that could explain killings as bloody as these.

A rich family's filthy secrets—if the defense could be believed—were about to be spread out like titillating postcards in an attempt to save Erik and Lyle from the gas chamber.

But proving the boys were in fear for their own lives when they shredded their parents' bodies with buckshot would not be easy. These were not little boys locked in a closet; these were adults who seemingly could have left home anytime. And how would they explain bursting into a room where the television set was on and the two people inside were unarmed?

The drama would play out in a courtroom in Van Nuys, not far from where Jose had leased offices for LIVE Entertainment.

The criminal courthouse is located on a government campus adjacent to the Los Angeles Police Department's Valley headquarters on Van Nuys Boulevard, a seemingly endless ribbon of car dealers, fast food restaurants, and bland retail outlets, worlds apart from the Menendez brothers' playground in Beverly Hills.

The trial would be held in the fifty-four-seat, fourth-floor courtroom of Superior Court Judge Stanley M. Weisberg, a bespectacled, balding jurist with a quiet, scholarly demeanor. The previous year Weisberg had presided over the first Rodney King trial, which had set off deadly riots when the cops were acquitted. The judge had been strongly criticized for moving the case to the mostly Anglo suburb of Simi Valley, where some people felt a black victim like King would have a more difficult time winning sympathy.

A pool of more than one thousand potential jurors was required because two juries would be selected. This was necessary because some evidence would pertain only to Lyle, and other evidence to Erik.

The second jury sat in the audience section, squeezing the number of seats available to the press, leaving some network reporters outside the courtroom, fuming and watching the proceedings on monitors in a converted children's playroom fifty yards from the courthouse, called the Shack. Inside the Shack, the snaking cables that were the veins and arteries that fed the television mind covered the floor. Cartoons and quotes from the trial soon covered the walls. "Let the sleaze fly" was memorialized from Abramson.

"It's a cheap version of *Divorce Court*" came from Bozanich, a reaction to the way every sordid detail of the family history and pathology was to be dragged out and exposed.

On the first day of jury selection, the prospective jurors let out audible gasps when Weisberg estimated the trial might last five months. Many potential jurors demonstrated an unusual degree of knowledge. Lyle "was a leader," observed one. Erik was "probably a follower." "Father was aggressive," wrote another.

Life, observed one potential juror, "is a two-edged sword. To get where you are in life, sometimes you have to do things you wouldn't ordinarily do." This panel member was quickly dismissed by the defense.

Responses to the questions about whether abuse could justify killing one's parents reflected the difficulty people would have weighing the horrific details of this case.

"I don't understand how a child could have such hatred for his own family unless severely abused," wrote one potential juror.

In surprisingly rapid order Lyle's jury of seven men and five women were picked. Erik's jury consisted of eight men and four women. Including the alternates, the juries were made up of clerks and truck drivers, mechanics and secretaries—the vast workaday pool of America. There were five employees of the U.S. Postal Service, including one man whose father had been murdered in 1952.

Some jury members were outside the mainstream. There was a woman who composed film scores, two college administrators, an aerospace engineer. The jurors were split about equally between those who held society responsible in some way for crime and those who thought bad values and hatred and greed were involved.

There was mild surprise among the observers at the predominance of men on the jury. They figured women would naturally be more sympathetic to tales of abused children than men, who are often the disciplinarians in the home. Of more concern to the prosecution than the gender breakdown was the age of the jurors. The average age of Lyle's jury was forty-two, while Erik's was even older, at forty-six.

Prosecutors felt older people, who had been raised before the national alarm bell over child abuse began ringing, would be more willing to give the parents a break.

Marcia Morrissey, one of Erik's attorneys, said the defense got the best jury they could, given that the pool, through some statistical quick, was heavily male and older.

The charges to be weighed by the juries were the most serious that any defendant could face. Under California law, an act of murder, even premeditated and with malice aforethought, does not trigger the death penalty unless what are known as "special circumstances" are attached. The two special circumstances making this a death penalty case were the fact that this was a multiple murder and that the brothers, the prosecution alleged, had killed their parents "while lying in wait."

A third special circumstance, that the brothers had committed the murders for financial gain, had been thrown out by a county grand jury that indicted the two men several months before. But Judge Weisberg allowed the prosecution to use financial gain as a motive.

The public's fascination with the Menendez case was evident the first day, July 20, 1993, a warm Tuesday morning in the Valley. First in line for a seat in the courtroom was Matt Tabak, a thirty-five-year-old screenwriter. "I'm doing research," he said. Another member of the entertainment community, Philip Krupp of Zev Braun Pictures, Inc., was drawn by the possibility of a production about the trial. At least one other project, for CBS, was already under way. The rumor around Hollywood was that the script was virtually complete, and within a few weeks of the verdicts it would be ready to air. At first it appeared CBS' early and expensive involvement would scare off competitors. But as the trial approached, it began to look like a classic Hollywood feeding frenzy was developing. "[M]ove over, Amy Fisher," *Daily Variety* wrote in a front-page story about the case, referring to the so-called Long Island Lolita who had shot her alleged boyfriend's wife. Three TV movies were made about that case, and each earned high ratings. If Amy stirred the public's imagination, Lyle and Erik promised to traumatize it with lurid tales of sex and psychological terror, all conducted behind the thick walls of a Beverly Hills mansion.

Dianne Kramer was standing in line next to her husband, David, who was forty-four years old that day. "This is what he wanted for his birthday," she said.

Inside Courtroom N, Weisberg quickly assumed command of the trial. He would not, if he could help it, allow the trial to take on the side-show quality that sometimes attends sensational cases. He restricted media interviews to a plaza outside the courthouse and warned the attorneys he was going to run a tight ship.

As he prepared to hear opening statements, he said all the attorneys—prosecutors Pamela Bozanich and her colleague, Lester Kuriyama; Jill Lansing and death-penalty expert Michael Burt for Lyle; and Leslie Abramson and Marcia Morrissey for Erik—were "top notch." But the most colorful reputation belonged to the feisty Abramson.

A fiery opponent of the death penalty, the forty-nine-year-old native of the New York City borough of Queens was the show. Abramson had a well-earned reputation for being able to bully prosecutors and weak judges, frowning at rulings she didn't like, sometimes shaking her head in disgust and talking audibly enough at the defense table that the jury could hear her. In the Menendez trial, however, Judge Weisberg would go to the mat with her time and again on issues and scolded her frequently for what he considered rude behavior.

But even a vigilant Weisberg would not contain her. From the first day before the jury, she dressed her client in boyish sweaters and sports shirts, all to show that this was not a man of twenty-two but a boy of twelve or maybe fourteen. If Erik was a boy, she was his mother, or maybe an indulgent aunt. She would constantly pluck threads or fluff, real or imagined, from Erik's shirt or sweater or hair. She kept a hand on his shoulder while whispering a point into his ear. Sometimes, like a proud mother, she leaned back in her chair, crossed her arms, and smiled at Erik, as if to say, "Don't worry, everything will be okay."

This was no monster, she implied by her behavior. This was a misunderstood child who just needed a little good parenting, the kind he had been denied growing up.

Both brothers, particularly Erik, appeared to have lost weight while in prison. Erik's face had taken on a ghostly, chalk-white appearance after so long an incarceration.

Lyle, wearing a hairpiece, was dressed in a white long-sleeved sweater and a pink, button-down long-sleeved shirt without a tie and khaki pants. Erik, wearing glasses, sat at the defense table in a blue button-down long-sleeved shirt and a red tie with a paisley design.

Jose's mother, Maria, her streaked white hair pulled back in a severe bun, and two sisters, Marta Cano and Terry Baralt, were in the family section of the courtroom. During the opening statements, like a statue, Terry looked straight ahead, as if focused on the blank wall to the left of the judge to avoid facing the horrifying accusations the defense was about to make against her brother. Notably absent were members of Kitty's family.

Both defense attorneys, Leslie Abramson and Jill Lansing, wore white suits, while Bozanich came to battle in a bright red suit. She came to the case with a certain ambivalence. She believes in the use of the death penalty, but she is acutely aware of the sharp controversy over capital punishment, the reluctance of many jurors to vote for capital punishment.

"I think the death penalty is appropriate in this case," she said of the Menendez brothers. "But if society isn't willing to do it, why should we bang our heads against the wall?"

In fact, Bozanich, in the weeks leading up to the trial, had been hinting around to Abramson that she might consider a plea bargain. "Are you going to make us an offer?" she said she asked.

Bozanich would entertain, she said, a reasonable offer. But the defense team did not make one. The two sides were always too far apart.

In an unadorned, straightforward way, Bozanich mapped out her case against Lyle Menendez, beginning with his 911 telephone call. "Someone shot my mom and my dad," she said he wailed.

Speaking from a rostrum behind the attorneys' table, the prosecutor described the lies Lyle had told to the police when they interviewed him, putting the blame on his father's business affiliations. Underscoring the brutality, she said there were fifteen wounds, five to Jose and ten to Kitty. Two of the rounds were "contact" wounds—that is, the tip of the shotgun barrel had been placed against the back of Jose's head and against Kitty's right cheek before being fired.

Laying the groundwork for her theory that the brothers had killed their parents "while lying in wait" as the parents dozed, she described Lyle's interview with Beverly Hills detectives. Lyle had said "his father would fall asleep in a movie just like that [snapping fingers]."

Of Lyle's often expressed fears for his own safety after the killings, which compelled him to hire a security guard, Bozanich sniffed, "From what we now know, this hint that his own life might have been in danger because of his parents' killings was a lie."

This was a pattern throughout the trial. Bozanich reminded jurors that if Lyle and Erik could lie so frequently and in such detail to avoid being caught, they could be lying about abuse to avoid a death sentence.

Bozanich smoothly shifted gears into what would be a key component of her case: the spending spree following the slayings. She mentioned the Rolex watch purchases, the Porsche, condos, a restaurant, and vacations in Cancun.

Then, to further buttress her claim that the brothers wanted money, she brought up the computer incident, saying Lyle hired some "little Jewish guy" to erase the computer's hard disk. When they heard her use the phrase, the defense team was furious, believing the prosecutor was trying to inflame prejudice with the jury against the brothers.

Bozanich recounted the conversation with Glenn Stevens and

Lyle's concern that if the police got their hands on his therapist's tapes, "Lyle Menendez would be—and I apologize—'fucked.' "

After the tapes were seized, said Bozanich, "Lyle Menendez's prediction to Glenn Stevens . . . had come true."

"[B]ut for a few mistakes they made," Bozanich concluded. "This was almost the perfect murder."

Before Jill Lansing began her presentation, the defense asked for a mistrial, citing Bozanich's use of the "little Jewish guy" phrase. Weisberg, who is Jewish, said it was a "rather innocuous remark" and denied the motion.

Lansing pinned several color photographs on a bulletin board in front of Lyle's jury. Among them was a young and virile Jose with his tiny sons balanced on his knees.

"On August 20, 1989, Lyle and Erik Menendez killed their parents," Lansing said. Her voice was thin and high, but her words were powerful. "We're not disputing where it happened, how it happened, who did it. We're not disputing when it happened. The only thing that you are going to have to focus on in this trial is why it happened."

The prosecution wanted the jurors to believe greed and a sick desire to commit the perfect crime drove these two clean-cut young men to kill. But she promised to reveal the real reason: fear. Fear of two parents who were so brutal, so manipulative, so sexually perverse that they drove their own sons to the most desperate act of defilement.

Lansing didn't reveal the details of this perversion and this brutality, not yet. She began by painting a picture of lavish wealth that left the two brothers wanting for nothing. Lyle lived in a mansion, drove a new Alpha Romeo he got for his high school graduation, had credit cards with almost no limit when he was fifteen years old. The brothers had the most expensive tennis coaches, took exotic vacations.

Lansing was not just dazzling the jurors. She was trying to show that money could not have been a motive for the slayings. Jose was "on a meteoric rise . . . and things were only getting better."

Now Lansing began edging into the crux of the defense: Jose Menendez's absolute control of his family. "This trial will take you behind the facade of the rich houses, the fancy cars, the wealthy friends and impressive social engagements. It will take you to the life that was experienced by Lyle Menendez and his brother as they grew up."

Lansing said the murders were rooted in events that had taken place years before. The catalyst for the killings was the fear that those old secrets might come out and destroy the carefully manicured reputation of the "perfect family."

Lansing said the catalyst was Erik's revelation to his brother a few days before the killings that his father had been molesting him for twelve years. The revelation disturbed Lyle so thoroughly because he too had been molested by Jose, from the ages of six to eight, the attorney revealed. So Lyle confronted Jose and told him that he knew what had been going on, "and it was going to stop. And it was going to stop now. And his father was going to let him take his little brother and leave the house."

But Jose told him that "he would do whatever he wanted with his son, and that no one was going to threaten him. . . . He made it very clear to Lyle Menendez that this secret would never leave this family, and that the people who held the secret and this power over him would not be allowed to live."

That's when the brothers decided to use the driver's license of Lyle's friend, Donovan Goodreau, to purchase the shotguns. Erik used the license, she said, "because he was physically quite similar to Donovan." Once more, it seemed to some observers, Erik had been maneuvered into the line of fire.

As for the "carefully crafted alibi," Lansing said it never existed. She said Lyle's plan to meet Perry Berman at the food-tasting exhibit provided no alibi because Lyle didn't show up.

Of the killings themselves, all Lansing would say was that things happened "which led these children to believe that they were about to be killed, and they acted."

Her use of the word *children* to describe two adult men was a pattern that would be repeated over and over in trial.

When they were done blasting their parents with twelve-gauge shotguns, the brothers had fully expected to be caught. They figured neighbors would hear and someone would call the police. No one did, so they picked up the shotgun shells, which Lansing said, "seemed like the thing to do."

Then they went to the theater, dumped the guns, and tried to meet their friend Perry Berman at Taste of L.A.

As for the spending spree, Lansing tried to turn a negative into a positive, saying that "if you're going to cover up a crime, you wouldn't begin a few days later by spending a large amount of money on Rolex watches."

Lansing revealed that neither brother had spoken of sexual abuse until months after they were arrested and incarcerated in the county jail, the shame was so great. Then it had to be relayed to them through a family member, and only then, she said, did the brothers begin filling in their lawyers. Witnesses would include experts in child abuse who each had spent more than sixty hours with Lyle Menendez.

Then Lansing answered the question everyone wanted to ask: yes, Lyle would take the stand and tell his story. And what he would describe was a mother who didn't want him, who chased him with a knife, allowed pet ferrets to defecate all over, and made Lyle lie in the stuff under her bed when he was bad.

And a father who wanted to make his older son in his image. As one relative put it, "He was to be the corrected version of Jose. He was to have all of the things that Jose didn't have."

"His son was going to be the prince. He was going to play tennis, have the best coaches. He was going to go to Princeton. He was going to have all the money he needed. He was not going to suffer the degradation of being working-class, which was so offensive to Jose.

"He told his son he was going to be great. He would spend hours with this little child in the basement giving him inspirational talks, passing along motivational material, drilling him on tennis, making him repeat, making him memorize, conditioning him to have all of the thoughts that Jose thought were right, and none of his own."

But Jose, Lansing said, was a bad role model, flouting the law and bragging of illegal acts. He gleefully describing firing people and destroying careers. "He reveled in his sadism. He was the shepherd and the rest were the sheep. [This was] a message that he passed on to his son and made him memorize."

Jose Menendez, Lansing told the jury, was also a violent man. When Lyle was seven and bought junk food at a deli, she said Jose socked Lyle in the stomach.

What's more, she said, "the Menendez family blended sex and violence. The boys showered with their father up to the very end, and their mother, in their teens, was still coming in the bathtub and bathing them and washing their hair."

Between the years of six and eight, while Lyle was playing soccer, Jose began giving Lyle massages, Lansing said. "He told them that this was the type of thing that the Romans had done; that this is what fathers and sons do; that he was special; that this was a special bond that they had. And he began the sexual molestation."

Referring to the picture of Lyle sitting on his father's knee,

Lansing said that the "sexual abuse and violence" by Jose did not happen to the twenty-five-year-old Lyle sitting in front of the jury, but to the child in the picture, and mostly before he was ten years old.

It was time for the lunch recess. Jurors, the public and media emptied into the fourth-floor corridor. A relative bemoaned the tragedy and declared that the estate, which once had amounted to upwards of $14 million, was dissipated. There was a $7 million estate tax bill, the Beverly Hills house had been sold at a loss, and the Calabasas home was not yet sold. The House of Menendez had fallen.

One family member said that when Erik revealed the molestation for the first time, "Lyle was there when Erik described it like a six-year-old." Then Erik's lawyer, Leslie Abramson, was informed. Suddenly a nationwide search for child abuse experts was mounted. The prosecution would always be suspicious of the timing, feeling that the brothers were rehearsing their stories before revealing them to the family. They said they believed psychologists visited the brothers from the first, but only those who saw them later, after the revelations, would take the stand.

Next to speak was Lester Kuriyama, a thirty-nine-year-old prosecutor who looked far younger, slight of build, with a spiky kind of athlete's haircut and an ingenious smile. but Kuriyama was a strong believer in the death penalty for cold, conscience-less killers, which is what he thought the Menendez brothers were. He faced Erik's jury and told them the brothers wanted to execute their parents and not be caught. "They planned what Erik Menendez called the 'perfect murder,' " he said.

Kuriyama said the brothers' therapist, Dr. Oziel, would describe for jurors the stunning confession of Erik Menendez. Oziel would tell them that Erik felt "his father was too controlling. He criticized them. He made them feel inadequate, and prevented them from doing what they wanted to do."

So they decided to kill him. Erik Menendez told Oziel that he had been disinherited by his father and "that this was another reason to get rid of" Jose.

As for their mother, Kuriyama explained that Kitty had to be killed "because she would have been a witness and would have been miserable and suicidal without their father anyway."

Kuriyama attempted to tell jurors that in January 1988, Erik wrote a screenplay. But before he could finish the sentence, Leslie Abramson objected to any mention of "Friends" until the judge ruled on whether it could be admitted into evidence.

"The evidence will show that the defendant, Erik Menendez, went to great lengths to cover up his crime, including lying to police and blaming professional hit men for what he and his brother had done," Kuriyama concluded. "Erik Menendez bragged about committing the 'perfect murder,' and he almost got away with it."

When it was Leslie Abramson's turn, all eyes were riveted on her. She had won long-shot cases before, but defending a man who not only had admitted killing his parents, but had gone on a spending spree afterward would be a test of everything she had ever learned.

In her opening, Abramson expanded on the theme that Lansing had sketched out while outlining Lyle's defense. Lyle had acted the way he had to defend his little brother. Erik needed defending, according to Abramson, because he was the real victim in the family, not the mangled bodies of Jose and Kitty. He was a young man—actually more a child in many ways—who was dependent, fearful, tormented after a lifetime of abuse.

Revealing abuse only after spending a substantial time in jail might look suspicious, Abramson acknowledged. But that didn't mean it was made up, as the prosecution would repeatedly imply. She said the reason he didn't tell the truth about the abuse to Oziel and Craig Cignarelli was that he didn't trust them.

"But what he could not and did not do with them, he will do with you. He will tell you why he killed his parents. He will tell you the entire painful and difficult and complicated story of his life."

Abuse was the key to the killings, the key to the defense. And to understand how Erik could kill, one must see through his eyes every graphic detail of that humiliation.

"The pattern of molestation in which Jose Menendez engaged started out as inappropriate touching and arousal of his young son, and escalated in a carefully calculated pattern of grooming the child for his father's sexual gratification. This pattern included repeated acts of forcible oral copulation, sodomy, rape, and the intentional infliction of pain by the use of foreign objects upon Erik's person. Jose Menendez's obvious purpose was to use his child's body to satisfy his lust. But this sexual exploitation of his young son was also part of a more pervasive characteristic of Mr. Menendez: his absolute need to control and to manipulate the people around him.

"This was a man who enjoyed, to an extraordinary degree, asserting his power over those weaker than himself, especially his boys. . . . Witnesses will tell you that Mr. Jose Menendez thought himself a superior being and indoctrinated his children into believing that he was in all respects perfect; that their family was superior to other families; that their way of life was superior to others; that being rich was all that mattered; that people who were not successful, according to his terms, were sheep; and he indoctrinated his children in an effort to get them to share those views."

Abramson said Jose pulled Erik's hair when forcing his eleven-year-old son to orally copulate him and slapped him repeatedly when he cried after his father ejaculated into his mouth for the first time.

In a slow, mesmerizing, almost deadpan voice she intoned like a death knell the tortures inflicted on Erik by his father. "He used a variety of objects: needles, tacks, wooden implements, knotted ropes. These episodes are what Erik Menendez called the 'dark days.' "

Tacks? Needles? The mind reeled trying to imagine what sort of sexual gratification a man could receive through the employment of these objects. If it was true, Jose must indeed have been a monster. If it wasn't, if all these details were made up to stitch together a phony tapestry of lies, then his son was much worse than a murderer. He was a man who had killed twice. First with shotgun shells, then by destroying his parents' memory.

Kitty too physically abused her son, she said. Up until age fifteen, Abramson said that Kitty Menendez "would periodically make her son submit to her physical inspections of his genitals, which she called 'checking you out.' "

By the spring of 1989, Erik and Jose were growing further apart. "By this time, Erik will tell you that sex was used by his father mainly as a form of punishment. There was no longer any propaganda that it was normal, what the Roman soldiers did. . . . It was clear to Erik that now the sex was a show of force and dominance and nothing else, and Erik Menendez hated himself for not being strong enough to stop it. In May of 1989 Jose Menendez sodomized his son for the last time."

Jose was in a rage over the boy's anticipated failing grade in chemistry.

Los Angeles County Court Judge Stanley M. Weisberg. (AP/WIDE WORLD PHOTOS)

Beverly Hills psychologist L. Jerome Oziel the prosecution's chief witness. (AP/ WIDE WORLD PHOTOS)

While on the witness stand, Lyle broke down when describing how his father had molested him. (AP/WIDE WORLD PHOTOS)

Bozanich questioning Oziel's former girlfriend, Judalon Smyth, who appeared for the defense. (AP/WIDE WORLD PHOTOS)

On the stand, Erik sobbed as he described how his father sexually abused him from the time he was a child up until the killings. (AP/WIDE WORLD PHOTOS)

Abramson with Lyle. It was her style to frequently touch the defendants, brushing lint off sweaters, fixing their hair, until the judge ordered her to act more professionally. (AP/ WIDE WORLD PHOTOS)

Judge Weisberg frequently had to meet with the lawyers to iron out sticky legal issues. (AP/ WIDE WORLD PHOTOS)

Teresita (Terry) Baralt, Jose's oldest sister, giving testimony. (AP/ WIDE WORLD PHOTOS)

Abramson attempted to convince the court that to understand why Erik helped kill his parents, one needed to investigate the abuse he suffered throughout his life. (AP/ WIDE WORLD PHOTOS)

Erik in court. When all was said and done, would he have reason to smile? (AP/ WIDE WORLD PHOTOS)

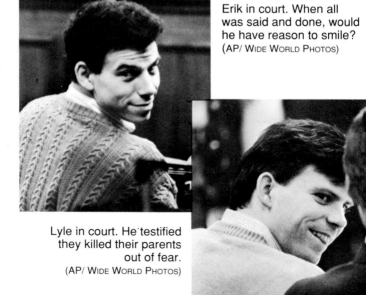

Lyle in court. He testified they killed their parents out of fear. (AP/ WIDE WORLD PHOTOS)

Abramson then portrayed the days leading up to the killings. Erik was looking forward to attending UCLA and getting away from home. But one week before the homicides, Jose announced that Erik would have to sleep at home several days a week so that Jose and Kitty could keep track of his school work.

"Erik Menendez understood immediately what this meant. The sex was going to continue. And all of the hope that he had sustained himself on all of the years, the method by which he pushed away thoughts of suicide, vanished."

Erik revealed his secrets to Lyle, setting the stage for the killings. Over the five days leading up to the slayings, according to the defense, tensions built to an explosive peak.

There would be some problems with this version of events. If Kitty and Jose had intended to kill their sons, why had they invited Karen Wiere over to play bridge? Karen, it turned out, had been delayed on a trip to Santa Barbara, so she called Saturday to say she couldn't make it. Kitty was disappointed. "If you do" get back in time, Kitty said, "come on down."

But the defense would deal with those issues in time. Now Abramson answered a question undoubtedly weighing heavily on the minds of both juries. If the brothers were bent on killing their parents—even in self-defense—why did they have to fire so many rounds into them at close range?

Abramson said one of her expert witnesses would tell the court that rather than the work of psychopaths, the crime scene was "a classic example of the overkill one sees when frightened and powerless people kill those they fear and perceive as all-powerful, the crime scene of abused children who kill their abusers out of fear."

Because Erik's parents were wealthy, Abramson said sarcastically, "the prosecution tells you he did it for the money. What do they say when poor kids kill?"

The diminutive attorney fell into the seat next to Erik, who often appeared near tears during the passages dealing with his father's alleged sexual adventures with his son.

"You all right?" Abramson whispered as she hunkered down for a moment of privacy. Erik nodded. Then, as she would do again and again until Weisberg stopped her, Abramson patted the accused murderer on his arm.

Some time later, Abramson met with reporters. "You know, this case really isn't that complicated," she said.

But it was. And what made it complicated was the Through the Looking Glass quality of the trial. What was true and what was not? Certainly, in any criminal trial there are competing points of view. The defendant says he wasn't there when the crime occurred. The witness says he saw him. Then it becomes a question of credibility.

But in this case the killers admitted it. The trial would be about not so much what had been done on the night of August 20. The defense would put this unusual, driven family on trial for a lifetime of behavior. It would become clear that Jose could be controlling and Kitty was often troubled. But stitched into this fabric of family dysfunction were the most bizarre and sick allegations that can be made against anyone. The juries would have to decide whether the things that seemed undeniably true—Jose's long lectures and harsh coaching techniques—made it more likely that the things nobody outside the family ever saw—the molestation and terrorization and threats of murder—were also true.

23

Opening Salvos

The first prosecution witness was Christine Nye, the Beverly Hills Police Department dispatcher, who had received the apparently hysterical 911 call from Lyle Menendez.

The police tape of the call, complete with attendant chaos and screaming by Lyle to his brother to stay away from the bodies, was played for the jurors, who now knew the whole thing was a manufactured story.

Pamela Bozanich wanted the jury to hear what good actors the brothers could be. Lyle listened impassively to his sobbing voice, resting his chin on his left hand. Erik looked straight ahead, while the jurors bent over written transcripts of the tape recording.

Next up was Beverly Hills policeman Michael P. Butkis, who had been first on the scene. He described the way Lyle and Erik had burst out of the house "yelling and screaming," then fallen to the grass and shouted, "Oh, my God," repeatedly.

No, he told Bozanich, he did not see any tears in their eyes.

Beverly Hills police sergeant Kirk W. West, a seventeen-year veteran, had discovered the bodies during a search of the house. Examining Jose's body, West had noticed that "a large portion of the back of his head was missing."

He thought a shotgun had been used but saw no smoke.

Bozanich strode forward and pinned an eight-by-ten color photograph of the stomach-churning death scene to a brown bulletin board on wheels. When she saw it, Terry Baralt, Jose's younger sister, sitting in the far right corner of the courtroom designated for family, clapped her hands to her mouth.

Bob Anderson, the thirty-four-year-old boatman who worked for Motion Picture Marine out of Marina del Rey, described the shark-fishing excursion on Saturday, the day before the killings.

Anderson said the thirty-one-foot boat left the dock at about four-thirty with the Menendezes, Anderson and a female friend, and a deck hand aboard. It was a windy day and the sea was choppy. The seven-hour charter took the passengers south along the coast to a point off Redondo Beach, then back to Marina del Rey. The Menendezes didn't spend much time together. Kitty got seasick almost immediately and stayed below deck for most of the trip. Jose was at the stern. Lyle and Erik huddled together at the front of the boat.

The brothers "seemed kind of gloomy," Anderson recalled. At one point, though, the boat stopped at a "shark spot" that was home to a large seal population. For the only time that night, Kitty came out to watch the seals frolic in the ocean.

"Everyone was pretty excited," he said.

Jose and Erik each caught one brown shark before the charter put back into Marina del Rey shortly before midnight.

The family's sullenness could be interpreted several ways, and under cross-examination, Jill Lansing tried to put her spin on it. She drew from Anderson that both brothers, wearing only shorts, refused to budge from their station at the bow of the boat.

Upon leaving Marina del Rey, he said, "we actually took a wave over the front of the boat that soaked them. . . . And we couldn't understand why they were standing up there freezing. . . . They appeared to be very cold and shivering."

Abramson told reporters outside that the brothers had huddled in the front of the boat because they feared "the boat trip was a setup to kill them."

As unlikely as it might seem to an ordinary person that Jose would murder his sons during a fishing trip with witnesses around, Abramson said that's what these two young men had believed.

Abramson's case hinged on establishing a growing sense of doom in the eyes of the defendants, leading up to the night of the murder. So what might seem to be the most ordinary acts would be examined through the lens of danger.

Toward the end of the prosecution's questioning of Anderson,

Kuriyama referred to a police report of Anderson's interview with Les Zoeller. When Lansing asked to see the report, Abramson said, sarcastically and loud enough for everyone in court to hear, "Adorable." Weisberg was miffed and during a hastily called conference with the attorneys at the side of the bench, called a "sidebar" because it is out of hearing range of jurors and spectators, gave the first of a series of lectures to Abramson.

"There was no need for that sort of remark. It's gratuitous," Weisberg admonished.

Tensions between Weisberg and Abramson appeared to ratchet toward confrontation on an almost daily basis. At times Abramson's behavior appeared purposeful, in order to grab the attention of the jury, and at others it seemed that she simply could not contain herself.

Anderson was excused from the witness stand. "You may step down and get back to your sharks," Weisberg quipped.

Les Zoeller, the investigating detective, took the stand and Bozanich grabbed the opportunity to show Kitty's bloodstained sneakers. They were minor pieces of evidence, but they were also symbols of the horror of the evening of August 20, and anything the prosecutor could do to put the jury in that room was to her advantage.

She also asked to enter into evidence a portion of a plastic bracelet that had been blown off Kitty's wrist by one of the shotgun blasts. While Abramson's pyrotechnics and tenacity were her best attributes, Bozanich relied upon a thoroughness in trial preparation that rarely left a point unmade. Like Abramson, she had an instinct for the jugular.

These two tough, smart, able women had plenty of reason to appreciate each other, but there was to be little outward respect. Abramson seemed to think of Bozanich as another heartless prosecutor, while Bozanich regarded Abramson as contemptible, calling her "a piece of shit lawyer."

Zoeller, his hair neatly parted in the middle and looking calm and composed on the stand, described the brothers' return to the crime scene at 5:30 A.M. Monday to ask for their tennis rackets. They were not allowed inside because a coroner's doctor was still examining the bodies. The point of this was to show how brazen Erik and Lyle were to come back to a crime scene still crawling with cops and retrieve evidence.

Noting that police had searched every room of the mansion,

Abramson asked Zoeller if he saw any animal fecal material in
the house. The detective said he did not remember. Abramson
was trying to lay the groundwork, even during the prosecution
case, for her contention that Kitty was a lousy mother as well
as a bad housekeeper. The ferret droppings, surprisingly, would
become a running theme, and yet people who had been in
the house frequently said they hadn't seen any mounds of
rodent leavings.

The ubiquitous media became the focus of the court's attention. The trial was drawing international attention and was being
carried into twelve million homes by Court TV, which provided
a daily analysis of the day's events by reporter-producer Terry
Moran, a tall, dark-haired young man with an easy smile.
"People are very plugged into this," he said.

TV cameras trailed the attorneys and the family everywhere.
Lansing told the court the media was stalking her on the street.

"And you have ten, fifteen, twenty people with cameras and
microphones, and you can't walk. . . . You are surrounded by
people. It is an incredibly frightening experience. . . . You can't
move. People are screaming questions at you. . . . And,
you know, I find myself sneaking behind buildings to get into
the courthouse."

Weisberg warned that unless television and radio reporters
adhered to his orders about where interviews could be held, he
would throw the television camera out of the courtroom.

Beverly Hills police sergeant Thomas Edmonds was a silver-
haired, thirty-two-year veteran of the Beverly Hills Police Department. His mustache and low-key manner are reminiscent of
a typical small-town cop from another era, straightforward, easy
to talk to.

It was Edmonds who had interviewed Lyle and Erik at the
Beverly Hills police station in the early hours of August 21, and
he took the stand to explain why the police never had performed
the gunshot-residue test to determine whether the brothers
fired guns.

"They had accounted for their whereabouts. It was too early"
to suspect them, he said.

Erik listened closely, wearing one of a succession of sweaters,
this one long-sleeved and red. He looked a lot like a student on
the first day at a new high school.

Under cross-examination by defense attorney Michael Burt,

Edmonds said his investigative antennae were raised when Erik told him that upon entering the family room he saw and smelled smoke. "I felt if you smelled smoke, it would have to be pretty rapidly after the shots were fired."

This was especially curious since a family room window had been shot out by one of the shotgun blasts. The smoke would have dissipated quickly.

Even so, said Edmonds, he did believe that the shock of the killings had left Erik traumatized. Intrigued by this, Kuriyama asked the veteran detective if he knew Erik aspired to be an actor.

"Objection," shouted Abramson. Weisberg called the prosecution and defense teams to his bench to debate Kuriyama's tactic. Lester Kuriyama looked young enough to be a classmate of Erik and Lyle's, but he had a deep emotional hostility to these defendants. Even more than Bozanich, he was convinced they were liars and manipulators and deserved the worst punishment the law allowed. He never seemed to miss an opportunity to imply that they were phonies trying to con the world. Relations between him and Abramson would grow more and more tense. At one sidebar he looked up and saw her mouth the words "fuck you," said Bozanich later.

"He doesn't have any proof my client is an aspiring actor," Abramson raged, though quietly so the juries could not hear. "The inference he wants to make is my client was acting because he took a drama class at Beverly Hills High School. I think it's outrageous."

Kuriyama said the defense had elicited from Edmonds that the defendants appeared traumatized, and so the topic of whether they were faking was fair game. Weisberg allowed the question to stand.

When Kuriyama asked the question again, Edmonds said he didn't know. If he had, "I would have examined him a little more closely."

Some observers were not impressed by the prosecution tactic. As Edmonds stepped down, a reporter groused in a low voice, "Who hasn't taken a drama class in school?"

As lunch arrived, Erik stood and called to an observer in the audience. "Hi, Arnel," he said.

This was Arnel Salvatierra, whose life Abramson had saved by getting him off on a voluntary manslaughter count after he had shot and killed his Philippine newspaper executive father.

Wearing a short-sleeved blue shirt, jeans, and white sneakers, Salvatierra said he "came to offer my support."

After lunch, the prosecution brought a sheriff's weapons expert, Dwight Van Horn, to the stand to demonstrate the operation of a twelve-gauge Mossberg shotgun. The prosecution team wanted to show that the killers had gone through a complicated thought process to operate the weapons, which backed up the argument that the crime had been premeditated. To fire the shotgun, one has to pull the trigger and go through a two-step pumping process before refiring. The defense objected that the whole thing was prejudicial.

"This is just an excuse to bring in the ugly gun," said Abramson, who was overruled.

That afternoon, Van Horn, sporting a neatly trimmed mustache and wearing a blue blazer, instructed the jurors on how to read a "pellet pattern" to estimate distance from a target when the weapon is fired. He described the function of wadding, a spacing material that "keeps the gunpowder from slipping up from the shot pellets and the shot pellets from mixing up with the powder."

And he described the different-sized pellets a shotgun can fire. A standard load of number seven birdshot would carry 350 tiny pellets in a one-ounce load. About 27 pellets could be packed into a common number four buckshot shell. If 15 rounds had been fired at Jose and Kitty, then hundreds, if not thousands, of tiny pellets had torn into the flesh of the two parents.

Van Horn carefully slid the formidable weapon out of its case. Slowly he began to load six dummy rounds. With the shotgun pointed upward, Van Horn pulled the trigger. The click of the trigger mechanism reverberated throughout the small courtroom. The jurors started.

Yet another confrontation occurred that afternoon between Bozanich and Abramson at a sidebar. Bozanich complained that while she had been questioning Van Horn, Abramson "was shaking and nodding her head while he was answering. And it's very distracting, number one. And number two, I think that it's some sort of commentary on the correctness of either my question or his answer. And I would like it to stop."

Weisberg said he heard "some mumbling," but because witnesses were waiting to testify, he put off for the moment the chore of addressing Abramson's courtroom demeanor.

* * *

Perry Scott Berman was called by the prosecution to testify about the alibi, of which he was a vital, unknowing part. But he ended up scoring a few other points as well.

Two weeks before the killings, Berman had been at the mansion, shooting baskets by the tennis court. Lyle said his parents were upset at him over the Princeton party where the pool table had been damaged.

The atmosphere "was very, very tense," Berman said. There was to be a family meeting that night in the library. It was so uncomfortable that Berman decided not to stay around. He climbed on his mountain bike and rode off.

Asked about the events of August 20, Berman recounted the botched plan to meet Lyle at the food fair and then the call from Lyle at 11:07 P.M. Lyle, excited and "a little jumpy" on the phone, told Berman that he and Erik got lost on the way to Santa Monica but insisted he had to meet Berman. "He wanted to get together that evening to discuss his plans to go back to Princeton in the fall and to talk about his tennis game."

Berman reluctantly agreed to meet at the Cheesecake Factory, but Lyle never showed up.

It was early morning. Shards of sunlight were beginning to bounce around the government campus in Van Nuys, where the trial was gathering momentum. A small line of "court watchers" had lined up in the pre-dawn darkness, as they would throughout the trial, to grab a coveted courtroom seat.

Sometime after the courthouse opened at seven, but well before the scheduled nine o'clock time for that day's session, a solitary figure was allowed into darkened Courtroom N on the fourth floor. Dressed in a blue blazer, a white T-shirt, jeans, and loafers, the young man had dark, carefully combed hair and handsome features. He moved with the grace of an athlete, which he was, and with a sweeping glance took in the room.

He noted where he would enter the wood-paneled courtroom, walking past jurors on his way to the witness box to the right of the judge. He glanced at the tables in front of the judge's bench set aside for the prosecutors, Zoeller, four defense attorneys, and the two defendants. He made mental notes of the public seating sections and the television camera mounted in a back corner near the ceiling that would carry his words to millions of viewers.

Craig Cignarelli was ready to testify against his onetime

closest friend and, like a performer visiting a new theater, he wanted to know what he would face when he took the stand.

When he finally did step into the witness box, he was questioned by attorneys without jurors present as the judge considered how much of his story would be allowed as evidence. As he talked, he appeared to avoid moving his eyes ever so slightly to the left, where Erik was sitting at the defense table.

Judge Weisberg wanted to resolve the question of whether the play that Erik and Craig had written, "Friends," would be described to the juries.

The prosecution wanted to present the play to the juries as evidence that the idea of killing his parents had been in Erik's mind for many months. Abramson said the play was the puerile product of teenagers and had no bearing on the case.

Additionally, the prosecution pressed the court to allow the introduction of Los Angeles County Sheriff's records showing that Erik had admitted to two Calabasas burglaries in 1988, another potentially inflammatory issue. Bozanich told the court that Erik had used the same alibi for one of the burglaries as he and Lyle did for his parents' killings. He said he was at the movies.

Cignarelli described the trip to the family cabin over New Year's, 1988, where the play was written over the next three days. The plot, he said, was simple. A kid "opens up a will, sees his inheritance, and sees that he stands to gain $157 million. Goes upstairs and kills his parents."

Abramson asked if Cignarelli could have been the one who thought up the murder scene. "Could have been, yes."

Weisberg said he would read the play before ruling on whether it was admissible.

On Monday, July 26, before Cignarelli took the stand in the presence of jurors, Weisberg said the screenplay would not be admitted. "The probative value of this evidence is nil" and would "confuse" jurors, Weisberg said.

Abramson was elated. "We're rid of that screenplay at long last," she exulted to reporters in a low voice as she left the courtroom during a short break. That was one victory, but Cignarelli could do much more damage if she couldn't neutralize his testimony. The defense argument that the crimes had been unplanned, spur-of-the-moment acts by desperate young men could be threatened by Cignarelli's testimony that Erik had known he would become rich if his parents were killed.

Cignarelli's attire was now far different. No California casual stuff. He was to testify before jurors, and for the occasion he wore a stylish dark suit, white shirt, and a tie with red and blue stripes. Cignarelli's dress did not go unnoticed by Abramson, who tried to paint him as a preening peacock.

"I take it, Mr. Cignarelli, that you're no wallflower. . . . Is that right?"

"No," he responded blandly.

"In fact, you like attention, do you not?"

"Yes."

Cignarelli recounted his first meeting with Erik Menendez in 1987 at Calabasas High School. Cignarelli was captain of the school's tennis team and knew that Erik was going to be on the team. "We became buddies almost instantly," he said.

And then Cignarelli recounted how he and Erik had gone into the Malibu hills. "We'd go up in the hills and talk about dreams for the future, plans for business opportunities and girls. Just kind of get away from everything that was happening in society and try to dream of a better ideology for the future."

It was here that Craig and Erik had sat in the dust dreaming up the "perfect crime." But Abramson objected to that language and succeeded in keeping it away from the jury.

Sometimes, Cignarelli said, the two friends discussed their business aspirations. "We wanted to start a company which had—it was multifaceted and dealt in inventions and screenwriting—and I hate to use the analogy, but similar to a Billionaire Boys Club type thing with—"

Abramson instantly objected and asked that the answer be stricken. It was the first time the Billionaire Boys Club murder case had been mentioned, and it appeared to startle the defense attorney.

Abramson didn't want her client compared with Joe Hunt. And Weisberg did not want the trial to stray into all sorts of side issues. He struck Cignarelli's answer and admonished the jury to disregard it. But, of course, they already had heard it.

Cignarelli said he went over to the mansion about twelve days after the killings to console his friend. Walking past the security guards, he saw a man working on the family computer in the second-floor master bedroom. Erik "said that his brother had had someone come up and erase a family will," Cignarelli said.

Cignarelli said he was alone with Erik in the foyer when his friend suddenly asked him, "Do you want to know how it happened?" He then recalled Erik's account.

"He said he was coming home from a movie, and that he was going inside to get his ID, a fake ID, to go out to the bars, and he said he went inside and came back outside and his brother was standing there with two shotguns and said: 'Let's do it.' And they walked inside and . . . Erik went up to the door [of the family room] on the left, which was slightly open. And . . . Lyle went up and put his shoulder against the door on the right. And Erik said he looked in, saw his parents sitting on the couch. And Lyle swung open the door and shot his father and looked at Erik and said: 'Shoot Mom.' And Erik said he shot his mom as she was standing up yelling."

This was the first time the jury had been told what went on in the family room, and it varied greatly from the version Erik and Lyle would tell about two terrified young men killing for fear they were about to be killed.

When Cignarelli had testified before the grand jury, he said Erik had not told him why he killed, but had made a curious comment.

"All great leaders had no parents." Erik then modified that statement. "Hitler, Alexander the Great, not that they had no parents, but they had either died or the kids had left home and were on their own and made it themselves."

At trial, Cignarelli was not allowed to testify that Erik thought his parents were holding back his career.

Nor did trial jurors hear about Erik's alleged remark about the size of the estate. Before the grand jury Cignarelli had said Erik thought there was as much as $90 million to be gained from the deaths of his parents, $45 million for each brother—most coming from a Swiss bank account that was never found.

Cignarelli said Erik never told him about any abuse by his parents.

Abramson tried to break Craig down on cross-examination, asking if he had seen Jose "screaming" at Erik on the tennis court.

"No," he said. Jose was "just criticizing and pushing him to do better, like most parents."

"Do most parents criticize their kids in front of other people?" Abramson asked with an edge to her voice.

"In Calabasas, yes."

"Tough parents in Calabasas," Abramson observed.

Cignarelli told Abramson he "wasn't sure if he believed" Erik's confession when he heard it.

"Now, you didn't ask Erik: 'Why did you do it?' "

"No. I know. Everybody comments about that," Cignarelli replied.

Since Craig and Erik liked to play "mind games" with each other, was it not possible that Erik was doing just that with his friend on that Friday?

"That's why I said, 'It could have happened' to the police, because I wasn't sure if at the time he was telling the truth, and I didn't want to be the one to turn him in."

Trying to show Cignarelli as something less than a good friend, Abramson pointed out that Craig had worn a wire for the police to trap his pal.

"And you were willing to help the police to get your best friend arrested, right?"

"That's correct."

"It was a hard thing to do," he said, to tell police "that my best friend killed his parents."

As Abramson neared the end of her questioning, she brought up the fax Cignarelli had sent to the Beverly Hills Police Department when he was mad at the detectives for telling his mother he was leaving school. Apparently, to emphasize that Cignarelli enjoyed playing mind games, she noted that he had signed the fax with the name of a fictional character. Since she did not want to open up the issue of the screenplay, she did not identify the character—Hamilton Cromwell.

"You quote in this fax one of the Psalms . . . 'As I walk through the valley of the shadow of death, I shall fear no evil.' "

"That was one of Erik's favorite sayings, yes."

"It's also part of the Bible. And 'the trail signifies evil' you wrote to the Beverly Hills Police Department?"

"That's correct."

"Does it, Mr. Cignarelli?"

"I told you I was very upset."

"Does the trail signify evil?"

"Sometimes, yes."

Search for Truth

Pamela Bozanich called Donovan Goodreau to testify about the disappearance of his driver's license, which Erik had used later to purchase the shotguns. But the trial suddenly took a sharp turn that once again took the focus off the defendants and placed it on the media. A tall, soft-spoken, forty-two-year-old freelance writer from Miami, Robert Rand, had allowed Lansing to listen to a portion of an interview he had done with Goodreau for a book on the case.

In the interview, Goodreau had said Lyle confided in him, before his arrest, that he had been molested by his father while taking baths with him. It was an unusual practice for a writer to turn over his notes, or tapes, to one side or the other in a criminal case. Rand said he had done so because he wanted a not-for-publication interview with Lansing. Now that Lansing knew about the conversation, she wanted to question Goodreau about it. If true, the tape could support the defense contention that Lyle and Erik, in killing their parents, were acting in fear after years of sexual and mental abuse. And it would undermine the prosecution argument that the whole molestation defense was hatched in jail months after the brothers were arrested.

Under questioning from Lansing, with the jurors out of the room, Goodreau said that toward the end of his stay at Princeton, he and Lyle had a late dinner at a Chinese restaurant.

"School was coming to a close. There was a lot of pressure on him, and we were talking about our plans for the summer and the future. And all the chairs were up on the tables around us. And they were just waiting for us to leave and we just talked. . . ."

Goodreau said he divulged to Lyle that he had been sexually abused as a child by one of his father's friends. Lyle listened intently with tears "welling in his eyes."

"Did he ever tell you that he and his brother had been molested by their father?" Lansing asked.

"No, he didn't," Goodreau replied simply.

Shocked, Lansing persisted, her voice getting tense. "And you have never told anybody that he said anything of that nature?"

"I never told anybody that I said that. I was under the assumption that by his reaction [to Goodreau's story] that he had had problems, but it was only an assumption."

Even after hearing in court the portion of the taped interview with Rand, Goodreau said he still did not recall making such a statement. "I just don't remember the conversation."

Besides playing the tape for Lansing, Rand allowed a Los Angeles television station to play a portion of the interview on the evening news. Rand told the TV reporter that it appeared Goodreau had perjured himself.

Bozanich was livid. She was angry that a writer would inject himself into the case like that, and she was mad that he would go on television and accuse her witness of lying.

Bozanich believed Goodreau had been "fed" information about Jose taking baths with his sons and that he merely had been regurgitating rumors that had originated with the defense when he spoke to Rand.

The next day, she brought Goodreau back to the stand. "At some point since the murders and the arrest in this case, did someone give you information that Mr. Menendez had taken baths with his son?"

"I'm assuming so, from hearing the tape, that I must have heard it from somewhere," Goodreau replied.

The only sources he could think of were Glenn Stevens and Rand himself. He said that after the brothers were arrested, Rand had lunch with him in New York and brought him up to date on the case. Also, prior to the interview with Rand where he disclosed the abuse story, Dominick Dunne had written an article in *Vanity Fair* magazine raising the possibility of sexual abuse as a defense.

Then Glenn Stevens was brought in, also testifying out of the presence of the juries. "Did Mr. Rand ever tell you any information about any kind of a sexual abuse or physical abuse in this case?" Bozanich asked.

"He just had told me a story about Erik and Lyle having taken baths with their father when they were very young, and he had made it explicitly clear that it was nothing inappropriate; that they were very young. And he said: 'Well, I've taken showers with my father when I was young, and I'm sure you have.'"

Stevens said he told Goodreau that Rand had told him about Jose taking baths with his sons. The entire matter of the "baths" had become convoluted and circular. But it now seemed possible that Goodreau picked up the story by way of Rand himself.

Later that day, Bozanich zeroed in on Rand with a barrage of aggressive, belittling questions. She declared there was nothing on the taped portion of his interview that proved Lyle had told Goodreau anything about sexual abuse. Instead, she said, all Goodreau had talked about was the baths. Rand said that was true.

Because Rand had now become part of the case, Weisberg briefly kicked Rand out of the courtroom, and one of his law student researchers had to sit in for him.

Rand said he had done nothing unethical in offering the tape to the defense. "I wanted material from [them]," he said.

A few weeks later, the tape was played for the Lyle Menendez jury, and it was left to them to sort out truth from rumor.

Rand refused to believe he could have been the source of his own story. He wondered privately who had "leaned on Donovan."

Lyle's former bodyguard, Richard Wenskoski, the burly ex-cop, took the stand to describe Lyle's whirlwind shopping spree.

Lyle had been staying at the Nassau Inn near the Princeton campus when Wenskoski got the assignment. Lyle decided to move over to the Hyatt Hotel, and when he moved out of the Nassau Inn, he left behind "a couple pairs of boots, shoes, a jacket, shirts" and underwear. "Leave everything," he ordered. "I don't want anything to remind me. I want to buy new stuff."

Wenskoski was on hand for the purchase of the Porsche, a town house in the Princeton area, and thousands of dollars worth of suits, shoes, shirts, and ties. Lyle rode in a telephone-equipped limousine, while Wenskoski followed in a "crash vehicle."

"If something happened to the limousine, we had a second vehicle to take Lyle out of the area," Wenskoski said.

Wenskoski said Lyle told him "that his parents were murdered by either the cartel or the mob. And he was in fear of his life."

So fearful, apparently, that he asked Wenskoski to get him prices on a bullet-proof limousine.

Curiously, Wenskoski said, Lyle would ask his opinions about purchasing the Porsche, the town house, or even personal items like clothing. "He said that I . . . reminded him of his dad. . . . He looked at me as a father figure."

Finally, on the Wednesday following Labor Day in 1989, Lyle had told Wenskoski that his services were no longer needed.

"He said that his uncle had contacted somebody in New York City, a mob figure, I believe. That was the exact term he used. His uncle went to see somebody in the mob in New York City, and they assured his uncle that Lyle was no longer in danger or his brother."

That was the last time Wenskoski had seen Lyle. During the eight days he had spent guarding Lyle, Wenskoski had never seen any sadness in the young man over the deaths of his parents. "He was normal . . . laughing and talking and joking . . . he didn't look upset."

Glenn Stevens came back to the stand and described the flight from Princeton to California when Lyle had given him $1,400 to bail him out if he was arrested. He also had told Stevens about the tape recordings that Oziel had secreted in a safety deposit box.

"Did he tell you what might happen if that box were revealed?" Bozanich asked.

"Yes. He said, 'If the police get their hands on those tapes'—and I quote—he said, 'I'm fucked.' "

The jurors would not hear another revealing comment Stevens said Lyle made to him. Lyle bragged that he "shtupped" one of his female relatives the night of the funeral service, when he was supposedly mourning his parents and telling friends he wanted to make his dad proud of him.

The witness box can be a lonely place no matter how well an individual is prepared for a trial. An adroit attorney can peel off a person's facade and leave exposed the warts of human frailty. Glenn Stevens had come to court as Lyle's once close friend, a handsome young man with an Ivy League degree who unwittingly became part of a murder case and was testifying as a matter of conscience.

But Jill Lansing was determined to show the jury something different, to raise doubts in their minds about Stevens' truthfulness and his values.

Under cross-examination, Stevens was forced to admit that after Lyle's arrest, he spent the $1,400 Lyle gave him for bail and sold one of Lyle's Rolex watches. Stevens explained that Lyle was "being condescending toward me on several occasions."

"From the time that you went to [the memorial service in Princeton], at least until he was arrested, you were his best friend, his confidant, his business partner, traveled with him, saw him on a daily basis?"

"Yes."

"And it is clear that what you are doing is reporting to the police on a regular basis anything negative you have to say about him; is that correct?"

"Yes, that's correct."

"Now, is that your definition of friendship?"

"I felt it was my duty." Stevens noted that "friendship transcends a lot of things, but homicide is not one of them."

It was hard to say how this would play before a jury. Lansing seemed to be saying that being a buddy is more important than telling the truth about a double murder. She ran a risk that the jury would question her own values.

Lansing returned to firmer ground, producing Glenn Stevens' job resumé. Stevens admitted there were a number of "embellishments" on it. He said he kept the accounting records for Lyle's restaurant, Chuck's Spring Street Café, which did a million-dollar-a-year business. An embellishment, Stevens told Lansing. What's more, Stevens admitted he had been not valedictorian of his high school class.

"And what about the receipt of the Yale Book Award, was that true?"

"I don't believe that's true, no."

Stevens, squirming under Lansing's questioning, said it was an old resumé written by his girlfriend. He said she told him that everybody lies on their resumés.

Lansing asked Stevens if he had a personal code of honor. There was no immediate response. When pressed, he said he did, and he had probably violated it.

Stevens asked for water. During a break, Stevens sought out Bozanich and told her he had also stolen money from the café. "It became obvious to me that he was going to ask me to leave the restaurant and leave me in a state of financial distress. So for a few weeks there, there was a couple of occasions where I had pilfered some of the money from the cash register, and I thought that you should know that," he said. He said he took "a couple hundred dollars" over a couple of months.

Those were hard financial times for him, Stevens said. Princeton was a very expensive school, and his parents had helped him all they could. When he took a leave from Princeton in February 1990 to work for Lyle Menendez, he said he had to forfeit about $2,000 in tuition because he was already two weeks into the semester. He said Lyle had come to his house and sat down with his parents and agreed to cover the tuition. It never happened.

Bozanich appreciated the young man's candor but told him she could not keep his secret from the defense. Her own career would be on the line if she failed to turn over evidence to Lansing, so she sought out the defense attorney and revealed Glenn's secret. His belated honesty exposed him to further harsh questions.

Lansing asked Stevens if he was aware that after Lyle Menendez was arrested in March 1989 that daily receipts at Chuck's restaurant had fallen from $1,800 a day to $500 a day. Stevens said he wasn't aware of this and that his "pilfering" of money from the cash register came later. "I never felt justified in taking the money," he said. "I just took the money because I . . . got vindictive."

Stevens lost his job with a Wall Street trading firm as a result of his testimony.

The defense was scoring points, but the character flaws of the prosecution witnesses did not change the events leading up to the carnage on that warm summer evening four years earlier. Much of the testimony of Cignarelli and Stevens stood unchallenged.

Yet despite this, some media ignored these things and focused on Leslie Abramson and her promise to reveal the Menendez family's dirty secrets. Film of her opening argument, filled with dramatic pauses, when she listed the devices Jose supposedly tortured Erik with, was playing again and again on television.

This was partly understandable because the prosecution case against the two brothers was old news by now. The lurid details of possible child molestation were fresh and uncharted territory. And Leslie Abramson was consistently good theater. Unlike

Pam Bozanich, a reluctant interview subject who was suspicious
of the press, even though her earthly sense of humor played
very well to the cameras, Leslie Abramson had a flair for the
sound bite and an almost unconscious way of doing things that
were supremely visual. One day she complained of dizziness and
almost collapsed into her chair, but did it in such a way that
the courtroom camera caught every dramatic moment of her
slow descent.

"It's an interesting phenomenon how she is able to influence
the press," said one jealous criminal defense attorney who asked
not to be identified. "A lot of us are forceful and we court the
press, and none of us has succeeded in getting the positive
press she gets."

Some members of the Los Angeles County District Attorney's
office had long complained about the kind of favorable treatment
her cases received at the *Los Angeles Times*. And these conspiracy buffs always pointed out that Leslie Abramson had a very
direct link to the *Times*. Her husband, Tim Rutten, was a
writer there.

That was hardly persuasive. Many powerful people are married to reporters. And sometimes couples work for competing
news organizations. It can be delicate, but the partners soon
learn to keep quiet about their work at home. The *Times* was
more vigilant than most news organizations about making sure
its hands were clean, issuing firm guidelines against accepting
gifts, for instance. But the conspiracy buffs at the D.A.'s office
would have had a field day if they had known about a telephone
call from Abramson to the *Times* reporter at the courthouse,
Alan Abrahamson. The attorney allegedly complained about the
story he was writing for the next day's editions.

Abrahamson, who declined to talk about the incident, was
confused. How did Leslie Abramson know what he was writing?
According to reports from several sources at the *Times*, the
reason she knew so much was that her husband, who wrote
about capital punishment for the national desk, had read to her
what is known as the skedline on Alan's story. A skedline is a
brief synopsis of a coming story that a reporter files with his or
her editors early in the day so that they can decide how
important the story is and where to place it in the paper.

Abrahamson, a man with a strong Old World sense of right
and wrong, was shocked and reported the incident to his editors.
The sources said the incident raised a lot of hackles around the
Times editorial offices. Abrahamson received a new set of

instructions designed to prevent future leaks, the sources said. He was ordered to file purposely vague skedlines.

Asked about the incident, Rutten replied, "Go fuck yourself."

The defense would maintain that Lyle and Erik believed their father had disinherited them, so greed could not be a motive for the slayings, as the prosecution alleged.

This made Howard Brian Witkin, an orthodox Jew who wore a skull cap and spoke in a booming voice, a crucial witness for the prosecution. It was Witkin who had responded to Lyle's hasty call for someone to check the document called *Will* on the family computer.

Lyle's uncle, Carlos Menendez of New Jersey, had hired his own expert, Edward M. Hayman, to go to the mansion on September 1, following the slayings, to explore what was in the family computer. But before Hayman could get to the house, Lyle Menendez made his move.

Witkin recalled his conversation with Lyle who didn't want to recover the information in the computer. Lyle asked the expert not only to erase the files, but wanted to know whether he could "make it look as if you were never here."

This comment "made my spine crawl," Witkin said. "I strongly felt, at least subconsciously, there was something very unusual and very wrong."

The next day, Hayman and his eight-month pregnant wife, Deborah, showed up at the Elm Drive house at about noon. Hayman said they were greeted by Erik Menendez, along with Erik's friend, Craig Cignarelli. Erik, he said, "was real anxious about finding any information."

Like Witkin, Hayman found nothing in the files *Menendez* and *Will*. He did detect, however, that someone had erased the files.

"I thought [Erik Menendez] looked sort of worried," Deborah Hayman told the court. "I had no idea why."

As the trial rolled along, the theatrics outside the courtroom began to rival the testimony within. It wasn't just the reporters chasing the attorneys around. One day Al Goldstein of *Screw* magazine showed up with two well-known porn stars, an actress named Jennifer and Ron Jeremy, who looks a little like a lost Mario brother and has probably been in more X-rated movies than anyone.

"I'm fascinated with this trial," Goldstein said. He said he had to see Lyle and Erik in person. "They're really despicable," he pronounced. "It's like looking at evil."

He said he planned to do a cartoon strip in his magazine that would be a takeoff on the popular MTV cartoon series called "Beavis and Butthead Menendez." The strip would focus on the two boys "shotgunning their parents because they want their ice cream."

Taking a similarly jaundiced approach toward the defense was Dominick Dunne, writing for *Vanity Fair*. "At the outset, I must admit to a prejudice," wrote the sixty-seven-year-old Dunne, who himself had lived not far from the Menendez Beverly Hills mansion years earlier when he was a film director. "I feel not an ounce of sympathy for these two young killers, even though I acknowledge that they lived a miserable life with a pitiful mother and a detestable father. I happen to believe in the alternative solution of moving out, but that way, of course, you risk not getting the money, and these kids liked money."

After this article came out, Leslie Abramson seemed to develop an intense dislike of Dunne. A friend of Dunne's, a *New Yorker* magazine writer, came to have lunch with him one day. Passing Abramson's table, she stopped to say hello. "Are you having lunch with that prick?" Abramson said, according to Dunne.

Another time Dunne found a handful of pickets outside the courthouse denouncing him. He was suspicious about whether they had come there on their own, or were brought in, after he walked up and they didn't recognize him.

Following the trial long-distance was one very interested party, Jose's former mistress Louise. Watching the proceedings on Court TV in her Manhattan apartment, she was outraged at the way defense attorneys were trying to portray her former lover as a child molester.

Louise called the prosecution team at the Van Nuys courthouse and said the Jose she had known was nothing like the person being ravaged by the defense. She also said that far from being suicidally enraged over the affair with Jose, Kitty had been very nice to her. They talked and Kitty was most concerned that the affair was, indeed, over.

Bozanich and Kuriyama considered calling the woman to the stand to rebut some of the "dark secrets" being divulged in Courtroom N. But Bozanich was reluctant, worrying that doing so would subject her to the hounding of the media.

* * *

Dr. Irwin Golden, a stocky, balding coroner's doctor who had a habit of answering questions with an impatient "yes, yes" was called on to describe the carnage in the room and to explain how the wounds had occurred. The defense was arguing that the killings had been the result of wild panic, not cool plotting. If so, the shooters had been extremely lucky. Only two shots missed.

Before Golden appeared, Bozanich asked to show the jury an array of death-scene photos, which the defense opposed strenuously. The close-up shots were still-life scenes of terror. Jose's body could be seen slumped on the couch, his head tilted crazily on his right shoulder, his hands on his lap. Kitty's body had been found on the floor next to the couch. Her mouth was open, her right eye and part of her nose had been blown away, and her right shoulder was a bloody mess. Hauntingly, Kitty's left eye remained open, as if taking one last look at her executioner, her own son.

Michael Burt, Lyle Menendez's co-counsel, who had a calm, reasoned, almost scholarly way of making his points, declared that "the cause of death is not in dispute" so the court should bar "the bloody photos."

Weisberg overruled him, saying the pictures were relevant to decide whether the killings had been done out of premeditation or in self-defense.

Ten photos were pinned to the bulletin board, five of the death scene, five taken during the autopsies. Lyle, dressed in a light green shirt and black polka-dot tie, reflected little emotion, glancing at the pictures at times, chatting with his counsel, Jill Lansing, at other moments. Erik was visibly upset. He stole quick glances at the photos, then hastily looked away.

Leslie Abramson put an arm around his shoulders and patted him on the back, asking if he was okay.

Golden said he could not be sure how many shotgun rounds were fired, nor could he be sure which rounds were fired first. Then, with chilling understatement, he went through the wounds one by one. Ten to Kitty's body, six to Jose's, though two of Jose's wounds could have been related.

As Golden went through the wounds, Kuriyama stuck red "wound" dots on a diagram of the male anatomy and green dots on the drawing of the female.

Golden said all the wounds were fired in "quick succession."

* * *

As the trial picked up in tempo and intensity, so did the clashes between Judge Stanley Weisberg and Leslie Abramson. He warned her not to gesture at the defense table, then admonished her to stop shaking her head when returning from a huddle at the judge's bench.

On more than one occasion he threatened to hold her in contempt. Nevertheless, Abramson continued to fight tooth and nail for her client. She was the defense team's leader, on occasion pressing the questioning of Lyle Menendez's witnesses, even though Lyle was not her client. She would never give an inch, never cower, never allow the enemy—the prosecution team—to win a skirmish without a bloody fight.

Abramson was a skillful role player. At one moment she was the contrite attorney, saying she was sorry in an almost whimpering, whispering little-girl voice when Weisberg admonished her. At other times she strutted around the courtroom scowling, her Little Orphan Annie-type hairdo bouncing as she paced from lectern to the witness stand. On occasion her intensity seemed to be too much for her body to bear, and she would fling herself into a chair and ask for a break to re-energize with a quick smoke outside the courthouse.

Her relationship with the media was mercurial. On some days she would sidle up to writers with a toothy grin. On others she lashed out at those who failed to understand how the brothers could kill in self-defense even if their parents had been unarmed.

"We get questions from you as if you're working for the district attorney's office," she spat during one news conference. "We figure, as cute as you all are, we haven't a prayer of getting a fair shot from you guys."

As for the prosecutors themselves, they were the worst. The government always thinks you're lying, she said with contempt. Of Bozanich, she summed up her relentless cross-examination of witnesses for Court TV in a single word—"sneering."

The Great Satan

Jerry Oziel's tape recording was the foundation on which the trial was built, and even before the short, self-contained therapist appeared in court, Abramson served notice that she would spare no effort to discredit him.

"I intend to attack his credibility in every way known to man and God," Abramson told Weisberg. The defense position was that Oziel's tape was not a reflection of reality. He had created it for his own questionable purposes, and Lyle and Erik, unwilling to tell him the truth about their abuse, had told him what he wanted to hear.

The attack on Oziel's credibility began, as it turned out, even before he took the stand. On July 23, only days before his testimony, the state Board of Psychology filed a complaint asking that Oziel's license be revoked or suspended because he allegedly had "engaged in sexual, social, and business relationships with two patients."

The allegations were based on Oziel's involvement with two people identified only by their initials, JS and AK. It was apparent from the complaint that JS was Judalon Smyth, the woman whose tip to the Beverly Hills police had broken open the case.

Leslie Abramson called a news conference to announce the filing of the complaint, which charged Oziel with improperly supplying JS with tranquilizers such as Xanax without a prescription, threatening to have her hospitalized, and forcing her to have sex with him.

Oziel's attorney, Bradley Brunon, said the allegations were

"outrageously false," but the timing of the filing was propitious for the defense, which could now use the charges in the trial.

Leslie Abramson had even more ammunition in the form of a lawsuit filed by Oziel's former housekeeper, Cynthia McPhee, who said Oziel had given her therapy and then taken her to bed.

All of this provoked a prescient comment from Bozanich that Oziel's colorful life would become "a trial within a trial."

Out of the presence of the juries, Weisberg cautioned Abramson about her assault on Oziel. "The way you plan to attack his credibility could corrupt this trial and prolong it for no good purpose," Weisberg said.

In other rulings outside the presence of the juries, Weisberg allowed Oziel to discuss the reason the brothers had come to see him—the thefts in Calabasas.

Abramson argued the matter of the burglaries was a confusing one in this family because the crimes "didn't result in punishment, but in ridicule in not pulling it off. These parents corrupted these kids by giving them very confusing moral [signals]," she said.

She was referring to the statement in Oziel's notes about Jose taunting the brothers for screwing up the crimes. Regardless, the judge said, the burglaries would show "how the parents treated the sons."

Abramson also was extremely concerned about anything she said that would be "waiving the privilege"—the absolute confidentiality existing between therapists and patients—if she asked certain questions of Oziel. If the privilege were waived by a careless question, or answer, involving some other therapy session besides the two opened up by the Supreme Court, other therapy sessions could be handed over to the prosecution.

"I do need to know what the court's understanding of privilege is before I'm going to ask . . . questions," Abramson said.

Weisberg was piqued, saying "it's just like any other issue that's presented in a trial. Counsel don't normally expect the court to rule in advance and give you a preview of what it is your trial strategy should be," he replied.

The defense won one battle when the judge refused to allow Oziel to use the word *sociopath*. More than once in therapy, he said, the brothers had "looked at each other and affirmatively said, 'We're sociopaths' or 'We'd be in that category.' "

Oziel described a sociopathic murder to them as "being a murder that was predominantly a means to an end, something that the murderer believed was a way to achieve a particular end; and it was a planned, premeditated murder; and a way to deal with problem-solving; and that if there were emotions involved with it, they didn't get in the way of needing to accomplish the end; and that once there was a decision that the murder had to be committed, it was committed; and feelings, basically, didn't enter into it in a significant way."

Weisberg called sociopath "a buzz word" that would be "prejudicial."

On Wednesday morning, August 4, L. Jerome Oziel, dressed in a dark, conservative business suit, took the stand.

The forty-seven-year-old Oziel, wearing glasses, looked every bit the textbook professional, and his credentials were impressive. Regarded as an expert in phobias, he had taught at the University of Southern California. The majority of his professional articles, however, deal with sex-related disorders and sex therapy. Without naming any famous names, Oziel admitted he was a popular therapist with a waiting list. Abramson asked if he earned between $300,000 and $500,000 a year, but an objection blocked his answer.

As Oziel began answering the questions of Deputy District Attorney Lester Kuriyama, Leslie Abramson patted Erik on the shoulder.

Referring to his twenty pages of notes, Oziel began by relating the events of October 31, 1989, when Erik Menendez came to his office in an "extremely agitated" mood. Oziel said Erik "felt very isolated and very alienated, and he had lost a lot of weight. . . . He talked about having some nightmares that were very vivid images of his parents being dead, and having images of the scene of having seen them dead."

In fact, a cousin had called Oziel a few days earlier to recommend that he see Erik because he had been lying on the floor and moaning. In the early part of the session, Erik said he didn't know if he wanted to live or die, and that he thought he might need to be on medication. He said he had lost his stability and he was trying to get some structure back in his life by playing tennis every day.

After some time, Oziel said, Erik asked to take a walk. Abramson cut in on Oziel's monologue, obviously piqued because he was talking directly to the jurors. Making eye contact with jurors would only serve to underscore what Oziel was about to relate.

"Excuse me, Your Honor. Is there any particular reason why the witness is facing away from . . ."

"He asked me to tell the jurors and I thought that meant to . . ." Oziel said.

"That's fine," Weisberg allowed. "You may face whichever way you want."

"Okay. And he, after telling me a lot of detail about his depression and his feelings of despair, at some point in the session he asked me to take a walk with him and to leave the actual physical office that we were in.

"So, we did take a walk. We walked outside the office and to a small restaurant called 'Bagel Nosh,' and just used the restaurant facilities there, and then took a walk from the Bagel Nosh to a strip of land that is park-like in Beverly Hills. And we sat on a bench. And for a significant period of time, Erik told me things about his father and how his father was a great man and how he intended to write a book about his father, and that it was amazing his father wouldn't be able to fulfill a lot of the goals that he had, a lot of the ambitions and maybe he could help do that in a book that he would write.

"At some point in the session, as we were sitting in the park, we just discussed going back to the office. And we headed back to the office. And right before we entered the front door of the office building in which I had my office, he leaned back against, as I recall, a parking meter that was in front of the office door, and said, 'We did it.'

"I don't know if he said, 'We killed our parents.' But I asked him, 'You mean you killed your parents?' And he said, 'Yes.' And from that point we went back up into the office."

Oziel told Erik he had feared Erik might tell him that. When they went back up to the office, Erik described the killings in detail, Oziel said. He said Erik told him that the plan to kill Jose and Kitty had its roots "in a situation where Erik was watching a BBC television show or movie . . . that had to do with the theme of the person in the film killing their father. And at some point in the watching of it, Erik called Lyle in the room and shared with him what the contents was of the movie."

The journalists assumed Oziel was referring to the British Broadcasting Corporation. But that was not what Erik meant at all.

Oziel said the plot to kill Jose Menendez was discussed almost casually between the brothers.

"They started discussing what would happen or how it would

be if the person who was a dominating force and a negative force, a very controlling person in their life, wasn't there anymore. And, at that point, it evolved into a discussion about killing the parents, most particularly the father first."

Oziel said that Erik told him Jose "had just been completely dominating and controlling; was impossible to please; had perfectionist standards; that he was controlling of a lot of different aspects of Erik and Lyle's life in a very extreme way; and also that he had been very controlling and very damaging to their mother; and that she was also miserable."

As they discussed killing their father, according to a transcript of the tape, Lyle turned to Erik and asked if he had the "emotional ability" to do the crime. "Erik said he realized at that moment that they were making a clear decision to engage in the murder, and he told his brother 'yes,' " according to the transcript, to which Oziel referred.

In response to Kuriyama's question, Oziel said the brothers decided to include their mother in the killing plan because "they couldn't find a way not to include her . . . and they also began to see the mother as somebody who was very victimized by the father."

So the reasoning was, Oziel continued, that the mother had to die because she would be a witness and because the brothers did not believe Kitty could have survived emotionally without Jose anyway.

"They thought the mother was so miserable that it was—and this is not Erik's words—sort of like a euthanasia situation."

Erik also listed Jose's "near disinheritance of him as an example of one of the things that led to, or was an example of, why they had to kill the father."

Lyle wanted to take a week to plan the crime, "to make sure that it was as perfect as could be." But Erik didn't have the ability to wait, Oziel said. The actual planning of the details of the killings took place a few days before the parents were slain, Oziel said. Then they drove to San Diego and bought the guns.

In describing the killings on the evening of August 20, 1989, Oziel said Erik recalled that Jose and Kitty were "surprised" when the brothers burst into the family room. Erik said he entered the room first, shooting at his father and that "Lyle finished off the job."

Jose said "no, no" while turning away, according to Erik, and was shot as he said that. Kitty was shot next as she began to stand and then fell to the floor. "He (Erik) said that she was moaning and trying to crawl," Oziel said. Then, Erik told him the brothers went outside the mansion to reload their shotguns, and Lyle finished off Kitty.

Erik described a scene of nightmarish proportions, Oziel testified. "There was blood all over the room and. pieces of tissue all over the room," Oziel said. Their bloody clothing, Erik said, was thrown into a Dumpster.

After they came back, they stood and looked at their parents for a long time before Erik became hysterical and ran outside screaming.

Oziel said Erik told him he was having problems dealing with the fact that he was going to be inheriting nearly $15 million, and that his guilt had become so overwhelming that he finally felt he had to unburden himself with the therapist. Still, problems like this aside, Erik nevertheless felt that the brothers had committed perfect killings.

"So basically, insofar as he knew, it was a perfect murder," Oziel said. Oziel elaborated on this, declaring that the brothers got a heady rush out of the slayings. "The fact that they were able to kill the father and complete this act, I think was almost a way of vindicating that they had a level of power themselves to be able to do it. That was their statement. They stated that they'd finally gotten to the place where they did something perfect."

Indeed, Oziel told the prosecutor, Lyle felt the killings were so well done, that even their slain father would have been proud of them. "He knew that his father knew that he should have been killed," Oziel said, "and he also said that he would have been proud of the good job that he (Lyle) did."

At one point during the October 31 session, Oziel said, "Erik was afraid that Lyle would kill him" for confessing to the therapist. Oziel called Lyle and, with Erik listening in his office, told Lyle that "your brother has told me everything."

"What do you mean by everything," Lyle replied, according to the transcript.

"I think I should be circumspect," Oziel replied, "and I think you know what I mean."

About fifteen minutes later, Lyle arrived at Oziel's North Bedford Drive office. Immediately, he said, Lyle began arguing with Erik, questioning his loyalty. Erik's reply was straightforward, Oziel said, declaring that "he needed to confess to somebody, and he needed to confess to me. And he knew that if he had told Lyle about it ahead of time, that Lyle would have said, 'No. Absolutely not,' and then Erik would have confessed anyway, and they would have had a huge fight over that."

Oziel made it clear that he felt himself in danger after the October 31 session. Lyle, he said, said that because Erik had confessed to the therapist, "it wasn't a perfect murder anymore and that it was a very, very big problem for him, that I knew and that I was the only person who had this information. He was very fearful that I would tip the police or tip the newspapers. He didn't believe that there was any way for him to be safe now that I had this information. . . . He was very menacing. . . . He just glared at me and said that he didn't want to have anybody looking over his shoulder, and that's why he killed his parents to begin with."

Finally, Oziel described the scene at the elevator, when Lyle shook his hand and said, meaningfully: "Good luck, Dr. Oziel."

At the November 2 therapy session with the brothers, Oziel said he told them that he had placed his notes of the first session in a safe-deposit box along with a note saying "that if I were to mysteriously disappear or be murdered . . . that the notes that I had taken would be revealed." Oziel said he made sure the brothers understood that because he felt his life was in danger after the first session. Oziel said Lyle laughed at him.

"He laughed and said that I should have felt threatened because immediately after the session he and Erik had sat in Erik's new Jeep, and the first statement that Lyle had made to Erik when he got into the Jeep was, 'Now, how do we kill Oziel?' "

At the November 2 session, Oziel said Lyle asked the therapist if he was frightened. "I said that I really didn't choose to live in fear," Oziel told Kuriyama. Then, Lyle responded: "Neither did my father."

According to Oziel's notes, Lyle decided against killing him because "it wouldn't look too good if I disappeared too soon because, in the event I did, it would start to become obvious that it wasn't too healthy to be associated with the Menendez boys since people who did seemed to die a lot and always with shotgun shells around."

At this session, Oziel said he had a lengthy conversation with the brothers about why they had killed Jose and Kitty.

"Well, basically they hated their father. They felt they had to kill him because he . . . ridiculed them. He put them down. He controlled their every activity. He controlled them in all ways.

He made them feel not adequate. He made them feel inferior. He dominated them."

"The defendants indicate to you that they considered it an accomplishment to have killed their father?" Kuriyama asked.

"Yes. That, most particularly, with how well it had been done."

Jurors then heard Oziel describe Kitty as a victim of Jose's abuse, that she was suicidal and that "they couldn't conceive of her being able to live effectively . . . if the father wasn't there. . . ." In short, he said, the brothers felt that "they were putting the mother out of her misery" even though they also felt that "the mother doesn't deserve to die and shouldn't die."

Moreover, Oziel added, the brothers worried that "if, in fact, they left the mother alive, they couldn't think of any way to be able to kill the father and escape detection."

As the day of the slayings approached, Lyle recalled, his father declared in so many words: "You can kill me if you want to, but you won't get any money if you do."

As Oziel spoke, the jurors listened intently, some taking copious notes. Erik and Lyle showed little emotion throughout the therapist's long hours on the witness stand.

Although the judge had ruled that the jurors could not hear the word "sociopath," Bozanich, in her turn, guided the therapist through a detailed account of the way the brothers planned the crime, a vital element in proving premeditated murder.

"They indicated that the . . . logical, rational, thought-out pattern was, in fact, the one that characterized their acts in relationship to the murder."

Oziel said that after he warned the brothers that he was keeping notes of the sessions, Lyle became anxious. Lyle, he said, made a macabre joke about Oziel's importance to him.

"He made a joke about us having to be very good friends, and that if somebody broke into my house and robbed me and began to shoot me, if I heard a shot behind me and saw the robber drop, I'd probably see Lyle behind saying: 'Have a good night sleep, Jerry.' "

Then, according to Oziel, Lyle suggested putting everything on tape to make sure it was right.

For months after he got Oziel's tape, Lester Kuriyama had carried it with him constantly, slapping it into his car's cassette player at regular intervals to remind himself who he was dealing with. His questioning revealed an intimate knowledge of the document, taking Oziel through every key portion of the tape. But there were narratives within it that the jurors would never hear, but which offered chilling insights into the twisted thought processes of these two young men. One such area was a detailed discussion of whether Erik and Lyle were sociopaths.

On the tape, Oziel, in an apparent effort to keep them from killing him, said he might be able to help the brothers piece together some of the things in their "family constellation" that led to the killings.

"Lyle looked at me and said," according to Oziel, " 'I don't see there's anything to work on, ah, what caused me to commit murder isn't here anymore. I've killed them both.' "

Oziel reminded Lyle that he had thought the "robbery in the Calabasas case with Erik" was a one-time incident, and was "simply foolish behavior." But Oziel said he had warned them then that he saw a sociopathic pattern beginning and that's why he had informed their parents.

Oziel said the brothers didn't think they would commit any more crimes. But they had always known they hated their father because he made them feel inadequate and preached a higher moral level "while at the same time he talked about other people as being sheep and them as being the shepherds."

Still, they saw their father as predominantly moral. "I then asked them how such a moral person could have raised two sons who rose up to murder both him and his wife, and they stared blankly."

When Oziel asked why he thought his father would be proud of him for killing him, Lyle said, " 'He just would have been proud of how well I did it. Also, my father taunted me during the Calabasas robbery by making fun of Erik and I, and telling us how stupid we were for doing it in ways that left the police all sorts of clues as to how it had been done.' "

They thought they had done a good job, Oziel said, and would never have been caught if their father hadn't turned them in. They believed they could commit further crimes and not be caught. When Oziel pointed out that this was exactly the kind of thinking that would lead to further criminal behavior, they couldn't see it. "Then Erik mused that they had both discussed their concern that their children, someday, if they had them, would rise up and kill them as they had killed their parents."

Oziel said it "became clearer and clearer" that each of the brothers was immensely pleased at having pulled off the killings without being caught. "Erik then began to describe that the two of them together formed some sort of a whole that was bigger than the sum of the parts, but that 'went in the wrong direction.' "

Oziel said he used the word *sociopath* several times with them, and Lyle asked what the term meant. "When I described a murder committed in passion and a sociopathic murder, each of the boys looked at each other and looked at me and said matter-of-factly, 'We're sociopaths. We just get turned on by planning the murder. Once we plan it, nothing gets in the way. Once we start, nothing will stop us. Furthermore, we don't think much about what we're doing before we do it. Once we get going, we just go ahead and commit it and make it happen. And we can't change the plan because it's already formed perfectly.'

Oziel said that being sociopaths meant there was a likelihood that they would commit more crimes. "Lyle turned to me and asked what a psychotherapist could do with someone who is so sociopathic that he had no feelings and didn't care whether he committed crimes such as these or not?" Not wanting to say there wasn't necessarily a lot that could be guaranteed, Oziel told them that by working together they could try to prevent further crimes. He said he felt strongly there was a risk that they would commit more crimes "because of the lack of conscience that existed in each of them as people and because of the negative feelings that were extreme and potentially explosive based upon their relationship with their parents."

Lyle struck Oziel as "almost a complete sociopath, with no evidence of remorse whatsoever that I could detect." Erik seemed much less capable of committing such an act without Lyle and was torn up by what he had done to his parents. Lyle wanted to be regularly involved with Erik's continuing therapy, mainly, Oziel believed, "as a way of making certain that his brother did not disclose any further events to me or details to me that Lyle didn't want him to disclose."

Lyle was particularly concerned that Oziel's notes never get read. "He mused about how 'embarrassing' it would be if it ever came out that they had killed their parents. The word *embarrassing* in relation to murdering one's own parents struck me to be a particularly sociopathic term, since it related not at all to any feelings, but simply related to an embarrassment at having been caught doing something that wasn't socially appropriate. The magnitude of what they had done in murdering their own parents seemed to have entirely escaped these two boys. . . . The only notion that they have is that somehow, by killing their father in particular, they had elevated themselves and had dethroned a king and had also vindicated themselves in terms of the father having talked about how stupid they were that they couldn't commit a simple crime like robbery in a correct manner."

On cross, Abramson suggested he was a publicity hound who sought out television appearances. She had a transcript of a conversation between Judalon Smyth and Oziel that showed him discussing his celebrity status in the wake of the arrests.

"You read *People* magazine. . . . Did you read it?" he asked.

"No, I didn't."

"Well, you're not in there, but I am," he said.

"So you love that sort of stuff," she chided.

"Fuck you and anything that looks like you," he said.

Oziel said the remark "had to do with not liking media attention."

Abramson asked if he told Jose and Kitty when they came to see him on September 30, 1988, following the Calabasas burglaries, that he was on probation for allegedly allowing a patient who could not afford his fees to do more than three hundred hours of manual labor around Oziel's four-bedroom house in Sherman Oaks.

"I don't believe I did" tell them, Oziel replied mildly.

Looking over Oziel's ledger cards, Abramson noted that he had billed the brothers $1,300 for sessions on August 23, 24, and 25 at the Bel-Air Hotel, where they stayed after the killings.

"And this is after you called with your condolences, is that right?" Abramson asked, attempting to show him as mercenary.

"No, that is not right," Oziel replied.

"You didn't call with your condolences?" Abramson asked.

"No, I did not."

"You didn't feel badly?" she persisted.

"I didn't say that, Miss Abramson, you know that," Oziel shot back. Personally, he said, he found Jose Menendez to be "condescending" and did not like him. Kitty was bright, educated, sophisticated, but "very passive and anxious and depressed and just not . . . not very efficient or fulfilled as a person."

Abramson asked if the therapist attended the memorial service in Los Angeles for Jose and Kitty and whether he billed the brothers for being present. Checking his records, Oziel said he billed them for that day, too.

Oziel kept his cool and, indeed, seemed almost to delight in playing mind games with Abramson. Time and again he challenged her, declaring she was twisting his words and bending their meaning.

Abramson asked about Oziel's much publicized relationship with Judalon Rose Smyth, the dark-haired beauty who had sued him and received a settlement, according to Smyth's new attorney, Steve Ruben, who specializes in therapist malpractice cases, in the neighborhood of $400,000.

By October 31, the day Erik confessed, Oziel said he was having an affair with Smyth—which Abramson bitingly described as "a relationship . . . which had a sexual component." Smyth, according to police, claimed she was outside Oziel's office when Erik confessed, but Oziel said he didn't recall her being there. Asking someone to listen in on a therapy session would violate patient confidentiality. "Was she there?" Abramson asked.

"I don't recall her being there," Oziel replied coolly.

"So, are you saying she wasn't there? Or are you just saying you don't remember?"

"I don't believe she was there," Oziel responded.

"Well, you don't believe she was there?" Abramson seemed to be flustered at her inability to pin down the witness.

"I don't recall Judalon Smyth as having been there, no."

"Was it raining that night?" Abramson asked sarcastically.

"I have no idea whether it was raining or not," Oziel replied, unperturbed.

"Were you wearing clothes that night?"

"I am certain I was wearing clothes, that's correct, Miss Abramson."

They continued like club fighters struggling for an advantage. Oziel paced himself, ducking and deflecting her verbal punches. Like many a knockout artist trying to hit an agile, quicker opponent, Abramson appeared frustrated as the day came to an end.

The next day, Abramson focused on the events after the confession. Oziel said he called his wife, Laurel, also a therapist, to warn her to take his two young daughters and leave the house. They moved to a neighbor's house. Where did he spend the night? Abramson asked.

"I went to the home of Judalon Smyth," he responded. A smile crossed the face of the brothers' aunt, Marta Cano, watching in court. The fears of the prosecution were coming true. The private life of Jerry Oziel was becoming "a trial within a trial."

In almost a whisper Abramson asked, "And you didn't seek to be with your wife and children to look over them at this time of great danger?"

By this time even the poker-faced Lyle was smiling. He turned and gave a confident grin to Cano. But Oziel had an explanation. He said he didn't want to put his family in jeopardy if Erik and Lyle came looking for him.

Abramson was steamed. "If they were out there lurking, you were about to lead them to your girlfriend, is that right?"

Oziel said that was correct.

At a sidebar conference, Abramson vented her frustration over Oziel's verbal fencing. "See, it's impossible with him, Judge, as I think you've seen, even if you ask a very specific question, to get a specific answer, unless you're the prosecution."

As time went on, and the questioning got more and more personal, Weisberg became concerned about what was happening. "It seems that he will be a specter over this case," Weisberg groused during one sidebar.

Abramson agreed that she was delving into some seedy areas, but it was unavoidable. "I mean, I tend to agree with the court that much of this evidence is melodramatic. But the fact of the matter is Dr. Oziel lives a very overheatedly dramatic life."

Because the prosecution was relying on Oziel, it was vital to attack him with everything she had. "It is our position that ninety percent of that tape he created is a lie."

The defense contended Oziel wanted to control the brothers for his own devious reasons and created the tape to get that control.

Returning to the attack, Abramson pointed out that Oziel had revealed to Smyth what had been said on October 31. "Was it your intention, Dr. Oziel, to have someone go to the police and blow the whistle on the Menendez brothers at that point?"

"I think you know very well that it was not my intention at all to have that occur."

Several jurors were smiling. Oziel said one reason he told Smyth about the exchange between him and the brothers on October 31 was his concern that Lyle and Erik might somehow get inside his home and find materials there linking Smyth to the therapist. There "were very explicit letters" from Smyth to him in which she "expressed a lot of intense feelings. . . ."

"You had an entire bag or bags of love letters in your house from a variety of women at that time, isn't that true?" Abramson asked. According to Smyth, Oziel kept the letters in a bag garbage bag and used them to coach her in writing devoted letters to him.

Oziel denied it.

Abramson's frustration with Oziel grew daily. When Oziel said the brothers "discussed the role that money played in the killing," Abramson shot back that she did not see that subject in the therapist's notes. The transcript of the audio tape, Oziel replied calmly, "does not consist of the totality of all the things" that were said to him.

Oziel asked Abramson if she wanted more clarification. "Just answer the question," she fumed.

Oziel's method of preserving his notes was continually challenged by the defense. Within a week or so of the second session, he had written down what the brothers had said. Then he had destroyed his notes of the two sessions *before* recording them on audio tape. He did this so there would be no written documentation of what the brothers told him in the two sessions. Then, seated on his bed, he dictated into a tape recorder and put the tape in a safe in the bedroom. Normally, he said he wrote out his notes, but he concluded a cassette "was safer."

"Are you claiming that you got every single detail down just right?" Abramson asked at one point.

"I would never claim I got every single detail down just right," he responded. "I think that's an extreme statement."

Abramson ridiculed the so-called plan. "Was the plan," she asked, " 'We'll shoot our parents with two twelve-gauge shotguns in the middle of Beverly Hills at ten o'clock on a Sunday night and hope that later the police will be silly enough to let us go back to our car where we can take the rest of the shotgun shells out?' Was that the plan?"

Following Abramson, Michael Burt took on Oziel on behalf of Lyle Menendez, a tag-team approach to questioning that wore down some witnesses. While Abramson was aggressive and blustery, Burt was smoother and slyer, continually laying traps for witnesses that some blundered into.

Oziel claimed that Smyth was never his patient, and he had never diagnosed her. Burt produced a letter from Oziel stating that Smyth was "incapacitated 8/30/89 by a chronic stress-induced panic disorder" which manifested itself in numbness and tingling.

Oziel said at first he did not recall the letter, then admitted he had signed it as a friend, doing Smyth a favor to help her avoid a small-claims court hearing she was afraid she would lose. Burt triumphantly said Oziel had given false testimony by insisting he never diagnosed Smyth. Oziel denied this was a diagnosis. It was more like a favor, he said "in the context of a friend/girlfriend relationship."

"You didn't sign it, 'L. Jerome Oziel, boyfriend,' did you?" Burt asked sarcastically.

Now wielding Oziel's telephone records, Burt suggested it wasn't Smyth who was fixated on him, as the therapist claimed when he compared her to the character in *Fatal Attraction*, but he who was fixated. Burt noted that one call from him to Smyth on October 6 at 10:58 P.M. lasted for 268 minutes.

"So who's being obsessive here, Doctor?"

"Judalon Smyth," Oziel replied stolidly, if less convincingly.

Bozanich had had it and asked for a sidebar conference. "I think we're getting very far afield, and it's beginning to sound a lot like *Divorce Court*," she told the judge.

The tension between Bozanich and Abramson finally flared into open hostility during another sidebar, when Bozanich complained to Weisberg that Abramson was talking so loudly at the defense table that jurors might hear.

"I'm a little tired of Mrs. Bozanich coming up here like a school child and saying: 'Oh, teacher, she's been bad,'" Abramson complained.

Even if the defense failed to convince the juries that Oziel had manipulated the brothers into telling him a version of the murders that he scripted, smearing Oziel could have another purpose. Showing him as a man who cheated on his wife openly, in his own house with his wife and daughters present, might make him so unsympathetic that the jurors would ignore anything he said. For the defense the opportunity to question Oziel was an opportunity to make a monster—or, as he became jokingly known in the press corps, the Great Satan.

Burt asked the therapist if he suggested to Smyth that she call his wife and disguise her voice, saying, "Hello, Laurel. This is Erik. You're in trouble. I'm going to kill you."

Oziel laughed at the question, which irritated Burt. "You laugh at that?" Burt pounced.

"It—It's absurd. No, I did not," Oziel responded.

Burt told the judge privately that he had a telephone tape of that conversation. The suggestion was prompted by Oziel's promise "to dump his wife" to marry Smyth, who asked on the tape if he would fulfill his promise. Oziel replied, "Why don't you call her up and say you're Erik and threaten to kill her," to scare her off.

Burt asked to play the tape "to effectively impeach" Oziel since he laughed in Burt's face. Weisberg put off the issue. The grueling examination of Oziel was in its fourth day, and the judge was losing patience.

When the prosecution took over the questioning again, Kuriyama asked to introduce Smyth's negative AIDS test. It would show, he thought, that Oziel was not a bad guy; he wanted to protect his wife, so he had had his girlfriend get tested.

This was a stretch, and Abramson mocked that it was "awfully sleazy to get down to AIDS testing."

"I suppose we can have some expert witness come in and testify to the etiquette involved in such relationships," Weisberg declared. "Do you really want to go into the details of the sex activities?"

"Well, Your Honor, with respect to the sleaze . . ." Kuriyama began.

"Let the sleaze fly," Abramson announced.

"What the people are trying to show is that he is a wonderful husband and father," Abramson continued. "We are more than happy, eager, to litigate that issue, and then we can ask him if he had all the other women that he was having affairs with, who were living in his home, tested for AIDS. I suppose we can ask if he wore condoms."

"There has to be some limit to the area of examination here," Weisberg concluded.

Oziel tried to explain what likely seemed to be pretty bizarre behavior to the juries. He said that after the brothers left on October 31, he called his attorney, Bradley Brunon, and told him what had happened. Brunon, he said, indicated that was "almost an impossible situation." He said that if Oziel turned in the killers and they were subsequently released for lack of evidence, "there's an unacceptably high risk that you'll be killed."

That was why he did not go to the police, and why he became drawn deeper into a relationship with Smyth, who he feared would go to the police if he ended the affair.

Both sides had collected writings from Smyth and Oziel, or, as Abramson put it, "They have their little pile of letters and we have ours." At Kuriyama's request, Oziel read aloud some of her letters.

"The seed of our love was there long before we met. It's part of life's plan. Destiny," Smyth wrote. "I, for one, have been saving up a lot of water, lots of food, lots of love. And I want to nurture this to full bloom."

As time passed, Oziel decided Smyth was getting fixated on him and said he wanted to leave the relationship. "Each time I told her that, she—she threatened suicide."

Kuriyama produced an October 16, 1989 "suicide note." In this letter Kuriyama noted that "Smyth leaves you her two kitties" Shantih and Ishi Kitty. Court observers chuckled at the names.

Following the suicide letters, Oziel said Smyth asked him to come over "for a final meeting to give me back the business materials." When he came in, "there was a suicide attempt in progress." She had opened the oven at home and lain down on the floor, pretending to be unconscious.

After this, Oziel moved her into his house, where she stayed until leaving to go to the police.

In response to Kuriyama's closing questions, Oziel said neither brother told him that they were physically threatened by their parents, nor that they killed Jose and Kitty in self-defense.

Now it was Burt's turn to expose a few of Oziel's letters to millions of viewers. The jury, frequently smiling, seemed to be enjoying the mud-slinging.

Burt produced a July 1989 happy birthday letter from Oziel in which he said Smyth was "a new and special friend who feels much, much more familiar than that. I sense your need and ability to care, to be kind, to love."

Oziel said the letter was written during the summer, when the relationship was young and growing. By the fall, he said, he was ready to break it off.

Burt would have none of that. He produced a January love poem. "For like a nymph she strides from the forest at daybreak dressed in white where no other man has truly known her, Judalon."

It may not have been Milton, but then Milton didn't dash off *Paradise Lost* in ten minutes, the time Oziel said he took to write his poem. He wrote it because Smyth complained no one had ever written her a love poem.

While being questioned about the poem, Oziel began laughing. Burt became angry. "Is this whole proceeding humorous to you?"

"Mr. Burt, I never said that," Oziel replied. "I'm laughing at this letter."

"Do you realize in this case that the Menendez brothers face the death penalty?" Burt added.

"Of course."

Oziel's sixth, and last, day on the witness stand saw Burt make a last, concerted attack on the therapist's tape. He asked Oziel if he made the tape to extort money out of the Menendez brothers. One of the defense theories to explain Oziel's behavior was that he didn't go to police because he wanted to get his hands on the brothers' fortune.

"No, Mr. Burt, I did not."

If financial gain was not the motive for the tape, Burt wanted to know if Oziel would agree that he had created it to control his wife and girlfriend, putting them in fear and forcing them to see him as their only protector? Quoting from the tape made covertly after the brothers' arrest, Burt noted that when he arrived, Oziel's first move was to try to give Smyth a hug.

"I don't want any hugs," she said.

"You don't like hugs?" Oziel asked. The jurors must have been wondering why a man trying to get away from a woman would want to give her a hug, even after she had gone to the police against his wishes.

Referring to Oziel's warnings that they could be in danger if they went to the police, Smyth said, "Well, the boys are in jail and I'm not dead. And you said that if I went to the police, I'd be dead in two minutes."

Oziel said, "Guess what, it's gonna be a little bit longer."

Burt accused Oziel of tossing out the threat "for the purpose of manipulating her back into the relationship."

"That's absolutely false," Oziel said. He warned her because the police had told him that even though the brothers were in jail, that "was not a guarantee of any kind of my safety."

As the final hours of his testimony unfolded, it was a piqued Abramson once again complaining to Weisberg at a sidebar conference about Oziel's courtroom demeanor. She said Oziel had been permitted "to make broad, lengthy statements" on the witness stand that the defense was not allowed to challenge.

Weisberg dismissed this complaint. He said he had permitted the attorneys to explore Oziel's relationship with Smyth far more than he originally intended.

"We're basically in the process of creating a straw man for the defendants to blow apart without any attention being given to the underlying facts of this case," he said. Weisberg said he would focus on what the trial was about: the murder charges.

Showing how thoroughly the defense had researched Oziel's background, Abramson even attacked his military record. His vitae stated that he had been honorably discharged from the Army in 1968. Abramson brought out that his Army record consisted only of a stint in the Reserve Officer Training Corps.

Oziel said he was discharged because of "severe food allergies."

Abramson, allowing a dramatic pause, asked, "And this was in 1968, while the Vietnam War was going on, is that right?"

"That's correct." The implication was clear. While 55,000 young men had been fighting and dying in the jungles, Oziel had skipped out on his duty by claiming he couldn't eat with the grunts.

Abramson returned to the theme of the perfect murder. "Show me where it is?" she demanded.

Oziel said the phrase was repeatedly mentioned by the brothers but was not specifically recorded in his notes. He repeated that his dictated notes "were not intended to be an entire, complete record of all eight hours that I had with Erik and Lyle Menendez."

Toward the end of the day, a frazzled Abramson asked for a break. Weisberg refused. "I'm physically uncomfortable. I'm asking for a brief recess," she pressed.

Weisberg gave her five minutes. Following the break, Abramson looked drained. Oziel, as always, looked impassive and unruffled.

Weisberg announced with a slight note of sarcasm, "It's been reported that this will be the last question by Miss Abramson."

"Much to the court's thrill," she shot back.

There was nothing very dramatic about the question, asking about the brothers' attitude toward their family. Oziel said that one minute they described it as successful, and the next a "sham."

Abramson, looking exhausted in her black dress with white

pinstripes and gold buttons on the cuffs, picked up her thick
loose-leaf binders from the defense table and hauled them to a
metal cabinet at the rear of the courtroom. She had relentlessly
pounded Oziel. But he was unmoved. Abramson slammed the
binders onto a shelf in the cabinet. Under her breath she hissed
her contempt for the man.

"Cocksucker!"

The prosecution was nearly ready to rest, but wanted to tie
up some loose ends. One was a leftover issue from Oziel's
testimony that the inspiration for the killings had come from a
television production on BBC that the brothers had seen three
weeks before the killings.

With both juries out of the courtroom, Kuriyama revealed
something that was more the stuff of Perry Mason fiction than a
real trial. BBC stood for the Billionaire Boys Club, three of
whose members had gone to prison in connection with two
murders.

For a year after Oziel's 1992 grand jury testimony that
Erik Menendez had been watching a BBC movie, Kuriyama,
Bozanich, and Zoeller had been searching for the meaning
of "BBC."

They had hunted through the program listings of back issues
of the *Los Angeles Times* Sunday television magazine, donated
by a fellow deputy district attorney who collected them. Nothing.

Meanwhile, Zoeller checked with Britain's Scotland Yard, but
came up empty once more. He also checked public library
microfiche files while Bozanich combed through library copies of
TV Guide. As it turned out, it was Kuriyama's wife who cracked
the mystery.

On Saturday, August 7, just days before the prosecution was
to rest its case against Erik Menendez, the Kuriyamas were in
a video store renting *The Adams Family* film. Suddenly his wife
spotted a video of *The Billionaire Boys Club* on a lower shelf.

Abramson could not resist a sarcastic "Eureka" for the court.
"My wife said, 'You're talking about the BBC movie. Is this
it?' " Kuriyama said.

The discovery was ironic because Zoeller had investigated the
BBC case.

Kuriyama said watching the show "sent chills up my spine.
The similarities between this case and that movie are astounding." He ticked off the parallels in the two-part NBC movie.

• One of the BBC victims was shot in the back of the head.

The victim was then shotgunned in an effort to obliterate his identity.

• Joe Hunt talked about the perfect murder. The BBC killers' alibi was that they had attended a movie the night of the slaying.

• The son of a multimillionaire Iranian who is slain in the BBC production proposes an alibi that his father had political enemies. Erik Menendez raised the issue of Castro engineering his Cuban-born father's death.

• In the BBC movie, Joe Hunt drove a Jeep and wore a Rolex watch. Erik, after the killings, bought a Jeep; and Lyle, four days following the slayings, bought three Rolex watches.

Kuriyama said he wanted to show the ninety-minute film to jurors. "Sell popcorn?" quipped Weisberg.

Abramson was incensed. She called Kuriyama's conclusion "pure speculation." The Menendez family had not been even in Los Angeles on July 30 and July 31 when the film was shown, she said.

Weisberg ruled that showing the film to jurors would prove nothing and refuse to allow it. "I guess we cancel the popcorn," Abramson joked.

Tidying up its case, the prosecution brought in a few last-minute examples of spending. One was the Hotel Bel-Air bill of $8,800 for a five-day stay after the killings. That included $2,000 in room-service charges.

The brothers also nearly bought a $990,000 two-bedroom penthouse in the Marina City Club in Marina del Rey. When they came, said the manager, Lyle wanted to see "the largest condo you have."

Price was no problem. Lyle said he did not like the wallpaper and carpeting in the unit, and asked that some appliances be installed. They also wanted two "well-lit" parking spaces. Erik wrote out a $29,700 check and signed Lyle's name.

They finally decided not to buy the condo and leased two in the building instead. Erik's cost $2,450 a month, while Lyle's, where he stayed with Jamie, was $2,150 a month.

At 3:29 on Friday, August 13, Deputy District Attorney Pamela Bozanich rested the prosecution's case against Lyle Menendez (the case against Erik was rested the following Monday). As he walked out to wait the beginning of the defense case, Lyle, in a long-sleeved white pullover sweater, patted Burt on the back and confidently waved to his aunt Marta Cano.

Going to the Mat

Defense attorneys had a difficult—and critical—bridge to cross: proving the brothers had feared their lives were in imminent danger before they killed their parents. Under California law, proving "imminent danger" was the only way they could be totally acquitted, or have a chance for a lesser conviction through a manslaughter verdict, based on a killing "without malice."

To lay a foundation for such a verdict, the defense team was required to prove two things: that Lyle and Erik had been in fear of their lives or serious bodily injury and that the conduct of the parents would have produced that state of mind in a reasonable person.

The defense intended to produce a detailed chronology of the brothers' lives, going back to the womb, using an array of anecdotal evidence from friends and family to show the insensitivity and brutality of Jose and Kitty Menendez. Only in this way, the defense team urged the court, could jurors understand what had been going on in the minds of Lyle and Erik when they shotgunned their parents to death on August 20, 1989.

This strategy relied upon relatively new legal theories surrounding the battered-wife and battered-child syndromes. But Weisberg appeared to conclude almost from the outset that the defense was aiming too far afield in its effort to show that the family's dysfunctional history, if it existed, had led to the murders.

As the defense began its case, an unconvinced Weisberg said the whole business of abuse was "being blown out of all proportion; that somehow there's some linkage between molestation, if there was one, and the killings that occurred in this case . . . that somehow that establishes a defense in the case."

"It does not surprise me to hear the court express that," Abramson responded. "It does sort of horrify me."

"It doesn't prove anything as far as a legal defense," Weisberg replied firmly.

But Abramson kept grinding away at Weisberg. She declared that the brothers' "interaction with their parents from the second they are born is relevant to their relationship with the parents, just as a battered wife's relationship with the husband from day one is relevant when that evidence is being put on."

The only way to show jurors Jose Menendez's "cheat, steal, lie, but win" philosophy was to weave a detailed, dark fabric of family life, replete with stories such as Kitty engaging in a water balloon fight with a woman at a barbecue in the 1970s that almost turned violent.

The defense maintained that an impossible set of standards left the brothers extremely anxious and fearful, and made it clear that their parents' affection was totally conditional.

But Weisberg insisted that many of the defense's stories were simply too remote. "And the problem is that these things are so remote that the relevance and probative value is very suspect."

Adding to the defense burden was the fact that there was little California precedent for the battered-wife and battered-child syndromes.

One of the controlling cases applying to the Menendez trial was *People* v. *Aris*, in which the defendant had shot and killed her sleeping husband, who earlier that night had beaten her and declared he did not think he would permit her to live until morning. The woman had been found guilty of second-degree murder, and a state appellate court panel affirmed the conviction in 1989.

The trial judge did not admit expert testimony that the defendant was a battered woman, which would have explained her state of mind at the time of the homicide. The appellate court ruled this was an error, but decided the error was harmless.

This case put pressure on judges to allow a wider range of testimony in potential battered-person cases. And, in fact, Weisberg, despite his misgivings, would allow the defense to present an elaborate lineup of teachers, coaches, relatives, friends, and child-abuse experts that analyzed the family back virtually to the day Lyle and Erik were born.

As the trial went on, it was a chagrined prosecution team that began losing patience with the jurist, believing he had let far too much of this suspect evidence in.

Abramson and her colleagues had a second theory of defense as well. Whatever Abramson's success with the battered-child syndrome, Erik and Lyle also stood a chance of avoiding the gas chamber under a theory called "imperfect self-defense." If the brothers had had a sincere but unreasonable fear for their lives when they killed, they could be convicted of voluntary manslaughter. That crime carried an eleven-year sentence, but would still cause the defense team to pop champagne corks.

The controlling case here was *People* v. *Flannel*, involving a defendant convicted of second-degree murder in the shooting death in 1976 of a man with whom the defendant had had a history of hostility. The case established the doctrine that an accused person's honest but unreasonable belief that it is necessary to defend oneself from imminent peril negates malice aforethought, the mental element necessary for murder.

But whether the jury would be able to consider these mitigating factors depended on the instructions Weisberg gave to the jury at the end of the trial, a point one law professor described as "crunch time."

If Leslie Abramson was the quarterback of the defense team, the man behind the scenes, the coach helping to put the strategy together, was said to be Los Angeles attorney Paul Mones, who has spent his career defending parricide cases.

A tall, balding man, Mones, forty-one, had become a paid consultant after the brothers revealed their stories of abuse. His years of professional work have led him to an unalterable conclusion: when parents wind up dead, it is their fault. He is convinced they invariably inflicted unspeakable abuse upon their children.

In his book *When a Child Kills*, Mones provides a comprehensive guide for defense attorneys representing children who have killed one or both parents, including how to select jurors.

Even the appearance of the young people on trial is important, he notes in his book. In one parricide case, he recalled that an investigator had bought the young defendant "a new three-piece, dark blue suit, the right choice for the average defendant in the average murder case." But Mones said it was totally wrong for the sexually abused teenager who had killed his father 'because it made him look older than his years. The jury had to see Tim as he was, a teenager, not an adult."

Mones, the investigator, and the attorney rummaged around and found two sweaters. When the boy put one on, Mones reflected, "he shed five years."

This same strategy was adapted in the Menendez case, where Lyle and Erik appeared in the courtroom almost daily in long-sleeved sweaters of various colors and button-down shirts.

There are more striking similarities between the Menendez defense strategy and Mones' narrative.

Abramson's argument to Weisberg to allow historical testimony echoed Mones' passage underscoring the importance of researching an accused child's history practically back to the womb.

"The parent must be held accountable in death for the abuse she visited against her child in life," Mones writes. "Putting on such a defense demands that the attorney reconstruct in painstaking detail the relationship between child and parent, a process that is both difficult and emotionally draining. In the conventional homicide case, an attorney need only concern herself with events on the day of the killing or perhaps two or three days prior to it. In parricides, an incident that occurred twelve years before the killing is as important as what took place twelve hours before it."

There were other points of conjunction. In Tim's case, a jar of Vaseline and some porn magazines had been found in the house. The Menendez defense team produced a picture of a jar of Vaseline in Erik's room and testimony from one witness who had seen gay porn magazines in the house. Mones also says it is not unusual for abused boys, especially, to hide the abuse, even after they are arrested.

According to the brothers' aunt Marta Cano, Lyle and Erik had intended, following their arrest in March 1990, "to go to jail and never tell the truth" about their father. But a Catholic clergyman who became close with Erik following the Calabasas burglaries convinced them to open up, Cano said.

Then they divulged their secrets to their aunt and uncle, Terry and Carlos Baralt, in September 1990, after they had been incarcerated in the Los Angeles County Jail for about six months. At the time Abramson was in Ireland on vacation.

The brothers did not talk at first, Abramson said, because the Menendez family was "incredibly secret and private. . . . These

children were told that the secrets of the family must be kep
secret, secret, secret."

Mones is critical of judges. "Trial court judges, like prosecu
tors, have not been particularly sensitive to the unique problem
of severely abused kids. Such judges peg the self-defense
standard of reasonableness to that of a strong, healthy male
treating the child as if he killed a grocery clerk during an
armed robbery."

Of course, Lyle and Erik were not children.

Throughout the trial, the defense seemed to be trying to
educate Weisberg, to bring him over to their way of seeing
things. If there were strong emotions in play on August 20
Lansing asked, "where did they come from? And where they
came from was not something that happened the day before, or
the week before; as with a battered wife, where it came from is
a lifetime of abuse. And so everything that happened to them
along the line that is certainly within their memory is something
that they had with them, available to them, on August 20
something that was impacting how they perceived their world
how they perceived the behavior of their parents."

"You could use that analysis relating to fear or anger in any
case no matter who the defendants were," Weisberg responded
"in relationship to defendant and victim, and argue that, well
the jury's entitled to hear the entire life history of the defendant
and the entire life history of the victim so that the jury could
have a better idea and understanding of why the defendant was
angry or why the defendant was fearful or why the victim acted
a certain way."

The prosecutors, Bozanich and Kuriyama, had another reason
to be skeptical of the defense strategy: They felt the sexual
abuse stories were fabricated.

Their position became abundantly clear when the brothers
lawyers called John N. Briere, an associate professor of psychia
try at the University of Southern California's School of Medicine
to lay a broad foundation on the subject of child abuse.

Briere, who never interviewed the brothers, admitted some
children lie about being sexually abused.

"Anyone can say anything under any circumstances," he said
"They could say they see monsters."

Monsters is exactly what Lyle and Erik were going to tell the
juries that they saw in their home. Then the juries would have
to decide whether those monsters were real or not.

27

Pattern of Abuse

The defense intended not only to put Jose and Kitty on trial for their treatment of their children, but the parents' parents, in an attempt to establish a chain of abuse that had surfaced in generation after generation, like a bad gene.

The person they counted on to forge this chain was Marta Cano, Jose's older sister, an auburn-haired woman with a welcoming, though understandably sad smile. Quick to say she loved her family, Marta nonetheless admits she was "the black sheep of the family."

As a child, she rebelled against the family compulsion to swim and was the first to leave home, attending a Catholic boarding school near Louisville, Kentucky at age thirteen. Always headstrong and assertive, when Marta's marriage to Peter Cano had ended in divorce, she had trained herself as a financial planner and raised five children by herself, "with no alimony or child support."

Though she was a Princeton neighbor of Jose's in 1979, ultimately the fifty-one-year-old Cano settled in West Palm Beach, Florida, where she was living when her godson, Erik, flew back to the United States to surrender to police after his brother's arrest.

"I knew from the first day they did it," Marta said later.

Marta wanted to tell the juries about Jose's upbringing: the way he had been spoiled and every whim catered to by his mother, the way he bullied other children even when he was little more than an infant, the way he acted as though he didn't have to obey anybody, the way he grew up self-centered and acted like everybody must obey him. Marta had no evidence Jose was ever abused, but was nonetheless convinced it must have happened, "sometime, somehow, somewhere." She said she loved her dead brother, but believed he had become mentally ill somewhere along the line. This was a view of Jose far different from Jose's other sister, Terry, who knew her brother as strong and powerful but not sick and brutal.

But Weisberg said he agreed with the prosecution that information about Jose's and Kitty's upbringings "is so remote that it's not relevant to any issue in this case."

Frustration showed in the faces of Cano, the brothers, and the defense lawyers, who shook their heads in disappointment.

Though Cano would not be allowed to reach back a generation—that seemed to be Weisberg's arbitrary boundary—she was allowed to talk about the history of the Jose Menendez family going back two decades.

Cano said she was in the Menendez home enough to see how the brothers were treated when they were small. Lyle, she said, was not allowed to express his opinions. "The boy seemed to be very tense, very frightened, very obstructed," she said.

Jose began conducting what Marta called his "monologues" with Lyle when he was just two years old.

Jose's "instructions" to his children were always done privately, away from the family. "Come here. I have to talk to you," he demanded when he summoned Lyle or Erik.

Jose's philosophy, which he hammered into his boys, she said, was, "Anybody can compete, but only one could win."

Often times, she said, when Erik lost a sports contest, Jose berated his younger son, Cano testified, calling him "a sissy . . . that he was not worth his last name."

But Jose did not always reserve his wrath just for Erik. "He used idiot for everybody," Cano said. " 'You're a bunch of idiots. You idiots.' That was his favorite word."

When it came to Kitty, Marta Cano said Erik treated his mother well when he was young and "felt sorry" for her later. As for Lyle, Cano said that Kitty "did not like Lyle."

To illustrate Kitty's carelessness with her two boys, Cano described the time she and Kitty were in a shopping mall in 1972 when the Menendez family was living in Monsey, New York. Erik, then two years old, and Lyle, then five, ran off and got lost. Suddenly, on the public address system, it was announced that the boys had been found and could be picked up at the mall information booth.

"Oh, great," Kitty said happily. "We know where they are, so we can keep on shopping."

As a baby, Erik "was a sweetheart" who "just opened his arms and threw himself at you." But by the time he was about ten years old, Cano said, he became "very distrustful" and would not talk to her. Erik stuttered when he did talk.

As for Lyle, between the ages of two and four, she said the older brother would never talk to her, and would "run away and hide behind the sofa and just peek at me."

When he got older, he used his stuffed animals to threaten people. "He would go around teasing everybody that the Cookie Monster was going to eat them or do something to them."

At fifteen, Cano said his personality changed. "He was very disrespectful to his mother. He would answer back to his mother. He would not obey her."

At one point, Cano recalled, Kitty told her in front of young Lyle that she wished that neither son had been born "because they had broken her marriage. . . . She said, 'My husband only cares for the boys.' "

The environment in which the brothers were raised was chaotic, according to Cano. The Pennington house in New Jersey, for example, was a pigsty, except for the "green room," a visitor's room that was always kept neat and clean.

As for the rest of the house, Cano declared: "There were . . . dirty clothes all over the place. There was animal feces all over the place. There was animal food all over the place, spread out in the kitchen. There were leftovers of food all over the place. . . . Towels were dropped in the bathroom, toothpaste without closing. Everything was just a mess."

Jose's older sister, who was in the house just as much, said outside court that while Kitty was not a great housekeeper, the house was not a "junk heap."

Abramson was putting together a series of questions about Kitty's sloppy washday habits—"piles of dirty clothes and piles of clean clothes"—when Weisberg's patience ran out and he ordered the defense attorney to "move on to something else."

Greed could not have been a motive, Cano explained later, outside the presence of the juries, because Lyle and Erik erroneously believed that they had been written out of their father's will.

"Aunt Marta, we were not the beneficiaries. Our father disinherited us over a year ago," Erik supposedly said when she told them they stood to inherit $14 million.

But Weisberg ruled that jurors would not hear this testimony, noting that the brothers had had time to fabricate the remark.

Cano then faced a sizzling cross-examination from Bozanich. She got Cano to admit that she had deliberately lied to Les Zoeller when he interviewed her in October 1989—telling him this was a warm and loving family. Cano said she wanted to project a positive image of the Menendez household and not that of a sick family in need of therapy.

"I just omitted certain issues that I did not see any reason to reveal at the time," she told Bozanich.

Then Bozanich revealed that when the defense team had first gone to see her, she had painted the same happy family picture.

"And now you're trying to paint a different picture?" Bozanich asked.

Denying that, Cano declared she loved Jose and Kitty and also loved the brothers. She appeared to be near tears.

Bozanich asked her if Jose had any good characteristics. Total dedication to his children was a positive trait, Cano said. "The problem is it became a sick type of obsessive dedication."

Reviewing Kitty's assets, Cano said she "was a tremendous athlete. She was very strong. She could pick up a Christmas tree and move it from one place to the other."

Bozanich was not particularly impressed. The prosecutor then initiated a rapid-fire line of questioning that turned on the fact that Cano had sent her son, Andy, to the Menendez home on the lake in Princeton, New Jersey.

"There were animal feces inside of the home that the Menendezes lived in, is that correct?" Bozanich asked.

"Yes. All over the place."

"There was dirty laundry in the house?"

"Yes."

"Sometimes the defendants wore clothes that were dirty?"

"Yes."

"Kitty didn't really participate too much in meal preparation; the children got their own meals on occasion?"

"The only meal that Kitty prepared was the evening meal."

"Mr. Menendez spoke abusively to his sons?"

"Oh, yes."

"Mrs. Menendez drove recklessly?"

"Yes."

Bozanich paused. "And you left your son there?"

Abramson objected angrily. "That's argumentative," she protested.

"Overruled" was Weisberg's icy response.

At the end of the day, after the jurors had gone, an angry Weisberg demanded that Abramson stop shaking her head negatively in the courtroom when he ruled against her. Otherwise, he would hold her in contempt of court.

"Well," Abramson shot back, her arms folded across her chest like a stubborn child, "the court may be finding me in contempt pretty soon, because I'm finding the court's rulings astonishingly biased. . . . There's only so much unfairness one can bear."

Weisberg did not back off. "You had better behave professionally," he admonished her. "I'm warning you at this time. Is that clear?"

"I heard you. Yes, indeed, sir."

Thus, in fire was the defense case born. It would ultimately last three months and parade more than fifty witnesses to the stand. Of course, throughout, the prosecution insisted there was far more smoke than fire from people so intent on saving the sons that they were willing to trash the dead parents.

Following Marta Cano were a series of witnesses, coaches and teachers and friends, some of whom added only a single anecdote to the portrait. But together they were compiling a kind of Menendez oral history.

There was Stephen Mosner of Royceville, New Jersey, Lyle's soccer coach when he was twelve years old. Jose, he said "almost treated Lyle like he was a thoroughbred racehorse the way he would towel him down after the game." The father, he said, viewed Lyle more like "a property than a son."

Brian A. Andersen, thirty-one, of Lisle, Illinois, described his summertime visits with the family in the 1970s, the fights between Kitty and Jose that he overheard, the "Jeopardy" dinners, Jose's snapping belt, and Kitty's fist-clenching tantrums.

Diane Vander Molen, thirty-four, of Denver, Colorado, provided the first evidence of possible sexual molestation in the Menendez household. Vander Molen, who had stayed with the Menendezes for three summers, said she and the boys were

playing downstairs, where she slept one night in 1976, when
Lyle was eight years old. They were called up to bed, but Lyle
returned a few minutes later. Vander Molen thought he had
come to say good night, but he asked to sleep in one of the
single beds in her room.

"I pretty much brushed him off," she said.

Then Lyle told her that "his dad and him had been touching
each other down there." By "down there" Vander Molen made
clear to defense attorney Lansing that Lyle was referring to
his crotch.

Vander Molen went and found Kitty to tell her what Lyle had
said. Kitty did not believe her and grabbed Lyle by the arm and
dragged him upstairs to his room.

This was potentially powerful evidence. Under cross-examination, Bozanich suggested that Vander Molen had been able to
rehearse the anecdote during three visits to the county jail in
June 1991. Vander Molen said she did not even discuss the
incident with the brothers during her jail visits. Following the jail
visits, some seven months later she told defense attorneys
about it.

Later that day, August 19, Leslie Abramson dropped a bombshell in a conference with reporters outside court. She said Lyle
had briefly abused Erik when Lyle was eight years old and Erik
was about five. "He was just mimicking what was being done to
him," she said.

Sometimes crying, a pregnant Vander Molen also recounted
the sexual attacks against her by the brothers. They were
fifteen and twelve, respectively, when they attacked the twenty-
three-year-old woman, stripping her and, just Lyle this time,
fondling her breasts.

Abramson wanted Vander Molen to talk about other incidents
in Erik's life, such as the time a canoe got lost in a storm and
Erik had to hunt it down in the dark.

Weisberg refused. "We've been beating a dead horse here
with things that are minutia," he said. But Vander Molen's
testimony could not be shrugged off. There were only a few
possible interpretations. Either she was mistaken about what
Lyle had been trying to tell her so many years earlier, or she
was telling the truth about real abuse, or she was deliberately
misrepresenting what she had heard. If so, why?

Jessica Goldsmith, twenty-four, whose parents had been close
friends with the Menendez family, said she was at the Monsey

house one day when Lyle, then eight years old, got himself out on a beam over a stairwell. Hanging there, he got scared because he could not get down, she said, and starting crying.

"You'll learn not to cry," she recalled Jose saying while poking Lyle in the stomach.

Robert M. Clause, Jr., forty-one, of Stewart, Florida, had been Lyle Menendez's tennis coach early in 1987, at the time Lyle was about to enter Princeton University.

Following a dinner at the Menendez house in February of that year in Calabasas, Jose told him, in effect, that he was not to point Lyle toward a professional tennis career. That would interfere with the boy's studies.

"Don't fuck with my son's future. Is that fucking perfectly clear?" Clause recalled Jose saying.

Charles P. Wadlington, thirty-nine, a financial adviser in West Palm Beach, had coached the brothers between 1981 and 1985. Often emotional, with tears in his eyes, he said Lyle and Erik were good students of the game, but he found working with Jose a burden.

Jose wanted Wadlington to teach the brothers how to play psychological games with their opponents. "At the top, it is a cutthroat game," Jose told him.

"They were two of my favorite kids," Wadlington said of Lyle and Erik, choking up on the witness stand. "They were nice kids . . . they were very respectful . . . They wanted to play the game the way I wanted them to, but they couldn't. They had to play the way their father wanted them to play."

Jose finally fired him. Wadlington said Jose "was the harshest person I ever met."

Several witnesses described the brothers' bizarre checking-out behavior.

Alica M. Hercz, forty-eight, the Princeton Day School instructor, described the time Lyle walked into her small office, sat down, and said nothing for thirty to forty minutes.

Douglas Doss, the head tennis professional at the Calabasas Park Tennis Club, where the boys had played, said Erik would do the same thing, "just disappear mentally. He would just be gone."

Finally, Norman Puls said he had noticed a similar mind-set in

Erik when he tutored him at math between 1987 and 1989. "No one was there behind the eyes," he told the court.

Hercz said the last time she saw Kitty was on August 1, 1989, about three weeks before she was killed. Hercz said Kitty was upset because she believed Lyle's latest girlfriend had become pregnant. Kitty's last words, as Hercz and her son escorted her to the front door with their arms around her, were that she wished she had taught Lyle "the facts of life."

Barbara Howarth, who had taught ninth grade English to Erik at Princeton Day School, described Erik's irrational worship of his older brother. Part of the class assignment was to keep a journal, Howarth said.

Approximately seventy percent of Erik's journal was about Lyle, she testified. Howarth noticed that Erik was a very good soccer player, and she asked him why he did not play soccer. "Because Lyle plays tennis," he said.

Jose Menendez had bought the mansion at 722 North Elm Drive from real estate and furniture dealer Mark Slotkin. Slotkin, in turn, had asked the sister of an employee, Mary Theresa Dominguez, to help the Menendez family move into the Elm Drive house. Just before Lyle was scheduled to testify, she told the court that she spotted male pornographic magazines and videos in packing boxes in the upstairs master bedroom and the downstairs library.

Bringing a certain relief to the proceedings was flamboyant Los Angeles cable television talk show host Skip E. Lowe, sixty-two. Lowe said he attended a black tie dinner at the Beverly Hilton Hotel in the spring of 1989 with the Menendez family.

Lowe's date, buxom actress Mamie Van Doren, was talking to Jose when Erik cut in to talk to the actress. "Shut up, dummy," Jose admonished his son, pinching him on the biceps.

Lowe said Erik "turned red," picked up a fork, and started playing with his food.

Bozanich suggested the entertainer might be taking advantage of the nationally televised trial to grab a little publicity.

"I'm on TV every day, so I don't need to be here," Lowe tartly told the prosecutor. "I had something to say."

* * *

When the succession of witnesses had come and gone, a portrait had been sketched and the scenery filled in. A picture was emerging, but what did it all mean? Jose and Kitty would never be parents of the year, that was certain. But, the prosecution complained, plenty of people grow up with rotten parents and don't murder them. What did all this have to do with the events of August 20, 1989?

Lyle Menendez was about to try to answer that question.

28

Lyle and Erik

"It's show time," one of the writers joked the afternoon Lyle Menendez was to take the stand and tell his story.

Though there was something repellent about the comparison, the choice of words was apt. Lyle's ability to tell his story and make the jury sympathize with him would weigh heavily in their decisions about whether to send Jose's firstborn to the gas chamber. He and his attorneys had spent months rehearsing him for this moment.

For the young man who once had made notes before meeting with his father, this would be the performance of a lifetime.

If he was nervous, Lyle, dressed in a crew-neck, navy blue, long-sleeved sweater and a blue button-down shirt, did not show it as he briefly huddled with Paul Mones before taking the stand.

Jill Lansing eased him into what would be nine days of often acrimonious testimony by touching soft as a light snowfall on Lyle's earliest recollections of his childhood in Hinsdale, Illinois. He remembered his puppy, Tristesse, and "running out to my dad and jumping on him and playing in the snow."

He recalled his mother rising early on Christmas day to help an excited Lyle open presents by the ornament-laden tree. And his mom's special gentleness with birds that injured themselves flying into window at the Monsey house. How she tenderly cared for them in a special cage until they were well enough to return to nature.

"Did you love your mom and dad?" Lansing asked quietly, herself a doting mother.

"Yes," Lyle said.

"And on August 20, 1989, did you and your brother kill your mother and father?"

"Yes."

"Did you kill them for money?"

"No."

"Did you kill them because you wanted to pay them back for the way they had treated you?"

"No."

"Why did you kill your parents?"

" 'Cause we were afraid," he said, his voice shaky with emotion. Several times he seemed to have trouble getting out the words through a quivering mouth.

After that dramatic opening, Lansing led her client through the childhood of a boy who had been groomed for greatness from the moment of his birth. Jose, he said, believed "that the firstborn was the one that carried the line. I carried my dad and his dad and his dad and his dad's first name, Joseph or Jose."

From about the age of four onward, sports was all consuming, "my whole life." And Jose was, as Lyle's coaches had already told the jury, a harsh taskmaster. To teach Lyle to excel at swimming and expand his lung power, his father had held him underwater until he couldn't stand it and pushed and pinched Jose to let him up.

Though he hated swimming, he enjoyed soccer, which he played until age twelve. But his father warned him not to become friendly with other players, worrying his son would lose his competitive edge. Jose was furious that Lyle's soccer coach took his players out for pizza even after they lost. "He believed all through sports that the people that win are the ones that hate losing."

Jose was firm about training, which included a rigorous diet free of sugar and junk food. Once, at age eleven, a friendly shopkeeper slipped Lyle a bag of pastries and cookies. When his father found out, he grabbed Lyle by the neck and punched him in the stomach, Lyle said.

Now Lansing guided him out of the shallows and into the deep water of brutal psychological and sexual abuse, the things no outsiders had ever seen, the things Lyle needed to convince the jury were real. Kitty, he said, was bitter that Jose's obsessiveness with Lyle's success in tennis took up all of her husband's free time when he was home. "She would say I ruined her life . . . that she could have been an actress," Lyle said.

"You're a bastard," she raged at him at age seven, he said. "I wish you were never born."

Lyle recalled his father bringing home pornographic films depicting gang rapes, and taking photos of the brothers' private parts when they were showering or changing clothes. Color photos, with the brothers' heads cropped off, were shown to jurors. Lyle said he had never seen the pictures before.

When he was six years old, Jose began talking with him about sex between men. "He would talk about the bonding between men, going into battle or in competitions, mostly with regards to battle and history, and that sexual interaction and touching, hugging, but also sex, was throughout history, was something that men that had gone into battle had done together."

Beginning to cry, Lyle described his molestation between the ages of six and eight. Following sports practices, Jose massaged and fondled him and showed Lyle how to do the same. Lyle said this happened two or three times a week in his bedroom. Then, when he was almost seven, the routine changed.

"We would be in the bathroom, and . . . he would put me on my knees, and he would guide me, all my movements. And I would have oral sex with him."

Lyle, blinking back tears and looking off into space, appeared to be on the verge of breaking down. Lansing, caringly, asked Lyle if he had wanted to do that to his father. He shook his head.

Eventually Jose began using a toothbrush and shaving brush on him. "He'd have a tube of Vaseline, and he'd just play with me."

Then one day Jose raped him, he sobbed on the stand. He cried and asked his father to stop. "He said that he didn't mean to hurt me. He loved me."

Lyle said he went to Kitty, who said he was "exaggerating, and that my dad has to punish me when I do things wrong."

Lyle said that as a child he never whispered a word to anyone about the abuse. Jose told him "that bad things would happen to me if I told anybody, and I told him I never would."

The abuse stopped when he turned eight. About this time, Lyle said he occasionally took Erik into the woods near his house and molested him. "I took him out sometimes, and I took a toothbrush, and I played with Erik in the same way."

By this time Erik, too, was sobbing at the defense table.

And, then, in one of the trial's more melodramatic moments, Lyle looked at his younger brother sitting a few feet away at the defense table and, his voice cracking, added: "And I'm sorry."

* * *

Lyle's first day of testimony was one of the most dramatic that experienced court watchers had ever seen. Some viewers were in tears, convinced that no one could fake that kind of emotion.

In the *Los Angeles Daily Journal*, a legal newspaper, writer Mary Jane Stevenson wrote that several lawyers agreed the testimony was "compelling enough to, if nothing else, keep him off Death Row."

"You would have to be a stone not to be moved by what he was describing," said Southwestern University law professor Robert Pugsley. "But that's a huge step away from concluding that they had a right to kill their parents, which is what self-defense is."

But would the jury care for such niceties in the face of such an affecting performance? And should they?

Back on the stand, Lyle described his talks with Jose. In the Monsey house, for example, they took place in the basement. Jose would sit in a chair, and Lyle would sit hunched over beneath him on a couch with his knees between his father's knees. Jose too would be hunched over, their heads touching. And if Lyle said something that Jose thought was a mistake, he would bump his son's head "not too hard. Just enough."

His father showed him how to withstand pain. Jose demonstrated by putting needles through calluses on his hand until they bled. He also held his hands over candles for lengthy periods of time without flinching. It was a kind of Menendez family rite.

Then Jose introduced his firstborn son to Og Mandino.

"I was not born into this world in defeat nor does failure course within my veins," Lyle recited for the jury, just as he had done for his father. "I'm not a sheep waiting to be prodded by my shepherd. I am a lion, and I refuse to walk and to talk and sleep with the sheep."

Jose's cruelty surfaced in many ways. Lyle said when he did not get rid of a rabbit he brought home from his second grade class, his father beat it to death and left it atop the garbage attracting flies. Lyle put it in a shoe box, and he and Erik went behind the house and, with all of his stuffed animals as witnesses, they buried the mangled creature.

Then he described Kitty's brutalities. To punish him for bedwetting, she would "rub my face in the sheets. She refused to change the sheets. I'd sleep on the floor."

Sometimes, as a child, she stuffed him under her bed in a space so small he could not turn over, and in an area the family's pet ferret used for a bathroom. "It was terrible. And that's why she put me there."

When he was eleven years old, Kitty cut her hand on a glass door and rubbed her bloody hand in Lyle's face, snapping, "See what you did to me?" He said she made him eat dinner with a blood-streaked face.

When he was sent to an overnight soccer camp when he was eight or nine years old, Lyle said he got homesick, and he could hear her voice refusing to accept his collect call.

Some of Lyle's fondest memories were of his stuffed animals, which he began collecting as a child in Monsey, "the worst period of my life." That's when he acquired Cookie Monster and the Sesame Street regulars. They were his faithful pals, and he continued to collect and play with them until he was seventeen years old.

"They all had personalities and names. . . . I acted out things with the stuffed animals and we had different story lines." There were the weak stuffed animals like his rabbits; the more violent ones like Kermit the Frog; and ones who played the role of judges. "And if Cookie Monster was beating up one of the little stuffed animals, then [the judges] would step in. . . . They slept with me on the bed and it was a big deal. It was important."

Then, in tenth grade, he met his first love, Stacy Feldman. Lansing posted a card on the board that Lyle sent her along with roses.

Lyle read for the court and a national television audience the inside of the card, which undoubtedly sent uncounted numbers of sympathizers racing to their Kleenex boxes.

"PS. This gift is sent to you from Pooky, Webster, Cookie, Froggy I and II, Theodore, Pinkie, Dino, all the Teddies, Lambie, medium and little Cookie, Woodstock, Odie, Garfield, King-Kong, all the dogs, including Snoopy the Great Magician, Pandy, Rabby and all the other rabbits, Zookie, The Man, Oscar, all the other rabbits, old and new, Scoobydoo, Bugs Bunny, Kawala, Sammy the Snake, all the lambs, Paddington Bear, Pinnada, Phillie Phanatic, Darth Vader, Robot, other Pinnada, both lions, Shogun Warrior, my fish, Indiana [his turtle], Chipper [the ferret], Velvet [the dog], Eagle, and not to mention me."

* * *

"It was sheer theater, very well done," reflected Southwest-ern's Pugsley. "The defense is doing a very crafty and workman-like job, a fantastic job with what they've got to work with."

Lyle had clearly been well drilled but was not overly prepared and histrionic. He sounded so mild and gentle, his voice slipping into a slightly higher register. And there had been a quality about it, a lulling, soporific feeling that seemed to spread out over the courtroom. Just as Donovan had stood for three hours, freezing in the cold, Lyle's listeners liked to hear him talk. You almost wanted him to continue, to hear that soothing voice.

Bozanich took a dimmer view. "I thought his testimony was compelling," she told reporters outside court, "just as watching Laurence Olivier act is compelling."

It was a powerful story, rich with detail, the kind of detail many people would argue nobody would be able to make up. But then, Lyle had trained for twenty-one years under Jose, and while he may not have mastered Jose's single-minded devotion to winning and hard work, possibly because Jose subtly con-vinced him no amount of hard work would be enough, friends said he did master his father and learn how to tell him richly detailed lies. Lyle, said one friend, was an "extremely compe-tent liar."

Lansing posted a photograph of Kitty when she was Miss Oak Lawn. Kitty was proud of her appearance and asked Lyle when he was seven how she looked when she was topless. She sometimes exposed herself in an open robe.

At the same age, he said Kitty "would wash me every-where"—including his genitals—when he was bathing. And at the ages of eleven and twelve, he said he slept with his mother and would touch her "everywhere" even when his father was sharing the same bed.

"She kissed me, but she didn't touch me," he said. When Lyle decided to stop it "she was furious," and he had problems about it for years—"really for my whole life, because it came out in other ways . . . she felt rejected."

Lyle said Stacy, Jamie, and Christy were his three loves. He said his father was so anxious to get rid of Jamie, however, that he secretly sponsored her through other investors on a worldwide pro tennis tour. After hearing this, Jamie checked with the sponsor and found out that was a lie.

Of Christy, he said that when she told him she might be

pregnant, Jose "paid her and basically intimidated her to getting an abortion." Again Christy denied it.

Lyle testified that when Kitty was at her most irrational and self-destructive, she threatened to take everyone with her. Jose was so concerned she would poison them all that Lyle recalled his father on occasion refusing dinner and taking his two sons out to eat. "I don't trust you" is what he told a furious Kitty.

Despite all of the abuse he had taken from Kitty, Lyle loved her. In a July 1987 letter from Madrid, Lyle wrote:

"Hi, Mom. How are you? Hope you're all right and hanging in there. I often worry about you. You're the only mother I have and would want."

Yet it was Lyle who had applied the final—and fatal—shotgun round to his mother's head on the night of the killings as she attempted to crawl away.

Describing the chronology leading up to the killings, Lyle said the tension built from the Tuesday before, when he had an argument with his mother in the den. In a rage Kitty reached out and yanked the hairpiece off his head. It hurt because he used a solvent to attach it to his head.

"I looked in the mirror. My head was swelling up, and my eyes had tears in them from the pain more than the embarrassment."

Erik was standing in the doorway when Kitty threw the hairpiece back at him. "You don't need your fucking hairpiece," Kitty yelled.

Erik was astonished. Lyle, who had been losing his hair since the age of fourteen, had got the hairpiece in 1987 but never told Erik.

Now that Lyle's secret was out, Erik decided to confess something to his brother. Years earlier, Lyle said, he had learned that Jose was molesting Erik, and he went to Jose and asked him to stop. Jose agreed, Lyle said.

Now Erik, shaking, blurted out that "those things with his dad were still going on."

Lyle said he was astounded and angry. "I asked him if he liked it. I asked him why he didn't tell me a long time ago. I asked him why he didn't fight back." Erik cried and did not answer.

At the time of the confrontation, Jose was on a business trip and was not expected back until Thursday, August 17. Lyle told Erik he would tell Jose to stop molesting him. Lyle said he felt confident because "we held all the cards"—that is, Lyle could threaten to go public with the abuse story and ruin his father professionally.

Lyle told his brother "his life was going to change . . . and he was going to be free."

Lyle spent several hours preparing notes to use in his meeting Thursday night with his father. He was worried that he might cry. "I couldn't let my brother down."

Jose arrived home at 11 P.M. on Thursday, entering the house, as he so often did, "like a hurricane," bags flung to the floor and calling hello to Kitty.

Lyle told Jose he had to talk to him and "he kind of looked at me disappointed." Lyle said he almost never took the initiative to speak to his father. Jose told him to wait in the first-floor study while he went upstairs to see Kitty. Lyle cooled his heels for about forty-five minutes, sitting on a small green couch and nervously glancing at his notes. Then he thought twice about using the notes because "that would be the first sign of weakness."

Jose walked into the study and sat in a chair higher than the couch. He still had his suit pants on, but he had left his jacket upstairs. He lit a cigarette and waited. There were an awkward few moments. Then Lyle blurted it out.

He said he told Jose what he knew "and that it had to stop . . . and that I didn't want to disrupt the family, and I wasn't going to tell anybody. But there had to be some changes."

Jose did not say anything at first. He did not even look at him. He simply continued to puff on his cigarette and play with his ear, as he often did.

"You just listen to me," Jose finally told Lyle, who tried to imitate Jose's voice for the jury. "What I do with my son is none of your business. Don't throw your life away. Just stay out of it.

"Let me tell you what's going to happen. You're going back to Princeton and your brother is going to UCLA like we planned, and we're going to forget this conversation ever took place."

Lyle did not let him finish. He said that for once he put his foot down and swore at his father and called him "a fucking sick person." He ordered him to keep his hands off Erik. To back up his words, Lyle said that if Jose did not toe the line, he would tell "everybody everything about him."

Lyle braced himself for a punch. "I don't think anybody had ever spoken to him like that in his whole life."

But Jose seemed to relax and sat back and looked at Lyle.

"We all make choices in life, son," he said. "Erik made his. You've made yours."

Lyle, speaking in calm, measured language as opposed to the tearful way he had described the molestation, said he tried to tell Jose that he would go public only if Jose did not stop molesting Erik. But he said that his father replied: "You're going to tell everyone anyway."

Jose left the room. Lyle was convinced he had "just made [things] a hundred times worse."

Lyle was now convinced his father would kill them. A short time later, Lyle said Erik came running to him, yelling that his mother knew "about Dad and I." Then Lyle in turn began screaming at Kitty. "How could you not have done anything?"

The mansion had apparently been plunged into chaos, though the maid would say later she never heard anything. Erik told Lyle that Jose barged into his bedroom after meeting with Lyle and accused Erik of betraying him. Erik was "screaming that Dad was going to kill us."

Lyle, after telling his brother about his meeting a few minutes earlier with Jose, agreed that "they could kill us."

The brothers talked about leaving home, but concluded, "Where are we going to hide?" A powerful man like their father, they reasoned, could easily find them and snuff them out anywhere in the world. If they went to the police, the brothers figured, charges might be pressed against Jose, but "then we would be through for sure."

"I think I was the one that said that we weren't just going to stay around waiting to die," Lyle told Lansing.

Lyle described their odyssey Friday in search of guns—first going to a Big 5 store in Santa Monica to purchase handguns— only to be told that in California there was a two-week waiting period. They could not wait that long because they felt their lives were in immediate danger.

The brothers drove toward San Diego. On the way Erik described his father's abuse. "It was very different from what happened with me. It was very much forceful," Lyle said without disclosing details. "It was very sick."

Eventually they stopped at another Big 5 store where Erik used Donovan Goodreau's driver's license to purchase two twelve-gauge Mossberg shotguns while Lyle picked out shells. When they got back home, Kitty told them they were going on a shark fishing trip the next day. Lyle said he thought the fishing trip was a ruse designed by Jose to kill them.

They stayed away all day Saturday to avoid the trip, but when they got home, Jose and Kitty were waiting. After they got back from the trip around midnight, Lyle said he and Erik drove over to UCLA to talk about strategy and did not return until early Sunday morning. Since Kitty kept the house keys to herself, the brothers had to ring the doorbell and wake her up. A furious Kitty let them in. Lyle said she turned on Erik and snapped, "If you had kept your mouth shut, things might have worked out in this family."

Sunday afternoon, Lyle said he went into the family room in an attempt to make "small talk" with his parents. Jose and Kitty were watching a televised warm-up match for the U.S. Open. Lyle said he inquired about a tennis camp that his father had been interested in. Jose replied: "What does it matter anymore?"

Lyle said he took it as another omen—"my dad's sarcastic way of saying you're dead."

That Sunday night, the brothers had another argument with Kitty, who refused to let them go to the movies. Jose appeared, pushed her aside, and ordered Erik to his room to wait for him until he finished watching the movie. Lyle said he yelled at his father that "you're not going to touch my brother."

Jose steered Kitty into the den and closed the doors. "I was sure that was it," Lyle said. "And I just freaked out."

He scrambled upstairs to get his brother. They grabbed their shotguns—Lyle's from the guest house, Erik's from his bedroom. Then they ran to Erik's car and loaded them "as fast as possible."

Lyle and Erik ran back to the den, "hoping to get there when they were not expecting us."

Erik burst into the den first, Lyle said, and he was close behind. The room was dark with the only light being emitted from the television set.

"And I started firing," Lyle said.

"I remember—what I realized was my dad at some point sort of coming forward in my direction. So he was standing. And—and I remember firing directly at him. I believe he fell back. . . .

"My brother was, I guess, firing and there were—there was things shattering and the noise was phenomenal. And we fired lots—many, many times. And there were just glass and you could hear things breaking. And you could hear the ringing noises from the boom. And there was the smoke from the guns. And it was just basically chaos."

Lyle told Lansing that, yes, he had fired a contact round at the back of Jose's head. And he had seen "somebody moving" behind his dad in the shadows toward his brother. And so he ran out to Erik's car and reloaded.

"I ran around and shot my mom. Just reached over and shot her close."

After they were done, their ammunition spent, the brothers collapsed in the foyer outside the den. When the police did not come, Lyle said they returned to the den, turned on the lights, and gathered the shells, which contained incriminating fingerprints.

"Somehow," Lyle said, as though it was a stroke of luck, "we ended up getting all of them."

After establishing their alibi and getting rid of the evidence, they called the police. Erik was in a state of panic, and Lyle did not know if he would hold up under questioning. But he did.

"He whispered something else about that I could stay with what we had talked about," Lyle said. "I really wasn't sure what I was saying, but I was . . . trying to keep with the story that we had made up."

Lyle said he didn't expect to inherit any money. He thought they had been cut from the will. Further, in an attempt to blunt Oziel's testimony, Lyle said the brothers had no plan for a "perfect murder." Indeed, he told Lansing, they never had a plan.

The prosecution had a particularly damning piece of evidence to show the jury. It was an interview with Lyle's former girlfriend, Jamie Pisarcik, who said she was offered a bribe to make up a story that Jose had tried to molest her.

She said that while visiting Lyle in jail one day, he asked her to watch a movie called *At Close Range*. Once again, when Lyle needed inspiration, he turned to the silver screen.

Jamie said he told her there was a scene in the movie where the father of one of the characters sexually assaults his son's girlfriend. If she agreed to say Jose made a similar pass at her, "there was going to be a large sum of money placed in my bank account," she said.

"Who told you that?" Bozanich asked, according to a transcript of the interview.

"Lyle said that."

Jamie responded firmly, "And this is one of the things that started me wondering about the whole thing, but—but I said if that ever happened, I'd go right to the police."

"And nothing was ever said after that, nothing—there was no money put in my bank account; he said, 'That's what I thought you would say."

Jamie concluded the interview by telling the prosecutors, "Mr. Menendez never did anything like that to me."

Faced with this damaging evidence, which cast suspicion on the entire defense theory that Jose was a pervert, the defense did the only thing they could. They introduced it themselves in the hope of taking a little of the sting out of it. It was seriously damaging information, but if Bozanich had introduced it, it would have looked even worse.

Bozanich didn't believe Lyle's story for an instant, and in four days of relentless cross-examination she belittled his account of the killings. Armed with a thick green loose-leaf notebook packed with questions and a clipboard to take notes, Bozanich held Lyle in a steady gaze before she started, like a cat waiting for its prey to make the first move.

"Cross-examination is an art," Bozanich said during a break in the trial. She likes to "set the stage right away" and show the jury if a witness has a motive to lie.

"It's kind of like that old George Bernard Shaw story where he offers the woman a million dollars to sleep with him. And she says, 'Sure.' And then he says, 'What would you do for a dollar?' And she says, 'What do you think I am, a whore?' And he says, 'We've already established what you are, we're just dickering over price.'"

Once again jurors heard the 911 tape containing Lyle's hysterical voice. Lyle smiled at Erik, seated at the defense table, while the tape boomed in the tiny courtroom.

"At the same time that you're crying, you're also lying, aren't you?" Bozanich asked. Lyle said that was so.

"Now, you cried in the courtroom in front of the jury here, correct?"

"Right."

"And that was genuine emotion?"

"Yes."

Bozanich then described all the lies they had told, to the police, to family, to friends. How are jurors supposed to believe him now when he lied for months?

"Basically," Lyle replied, "I've changed a lot in the last two years. And that's in being involved with Miss Lansing and

others. My brother and I trust people a lot more, and we're in a
position where we don't feel we have a choice."

"You almost got away with it, didn't you?" Bozanich taunted.

The prosecutor struck a nerve.

"You characterize it that way, and you think it's funny," Lyle
shot back. "But my brother's and my life was very miserable for
six months before we got arrested. . . . And isn't good now.
And I don't know what's going to happen at the end of this case.
And we may go off to prison, very likely. But, you know, some
good things have come from it."

Lyle proved to be fast on his feet, and he had an ability to
take questions and give rambling answers that allowed him to
make his own points.

The prosecutor described his life of luxury—private schools,
membership in an exclusive country club, a new car, vacations
to the Caribbean for sailing lessons, all the spending money
he needed.

"But I think you indicated when you testified . . . that your
childhood was basically very miserable, right?"

"Um, in—not every moment," Lyle considered. "You know, I
mean certain things would happen one day—you know, as a
child you—you want to be happy. You want to be loved. You try
to have fun. You try to make the best of the situation regardless,
and—and I wasn't just sitting around saying it's miserable. I was
just trying to adapt."

When Lyle put the shotgun to Jose's head, Bozanich wanted
to know, "Where was your mother? What was she doing?"

"In my mind, she was sneaking around the side of the
coffee table."

There was an intake of breath among the observers at the
use of this word. His mother was trying to escape certain death,
and Lyle considered her a sneak.

Bozanich asked if he loved his mother when he put the
shotgun to her cheek. Lyle said he did.

"And was that an act of love, Mr. Menendez?"

"It was confusion. Fear."

At one point Lyle, to show Jose's power, had said he controlled people with hand signals. "What signals did your mother
give you when she was sneaking around the coffee table?"
Bozanich demanded.

If he was scared of his parents, and they had been abusing
him and Erik, why didn't they just leave? Bozanich asked,
echoing the thoughts of many people watching the trial.

"You just didn't do that with my dad," said Lyle.

To some, the rest of Lyle's answer to this question was almost mystical and impenetrable, considering what had happened on the evening of August 20, 1989.

"I wanted to be a part of his life. I—you know, I mean, I loved him. I thought he loved me, and I—regardless of the past, I saw us together in life."

Bozanich rarely let her natural biting wit show, but she couldn't resist needling Lyle, who had said his father harbored political ambitions. "Did you consider that if he killed his sons, that might harm his political career?"

Calls flooded into Court TV as Lyle concluded his story.

"These are very unpopular defendants, even by Court TV standards," said Terry Moran, the affable commentator for the court network, which boasts that it has more viewers than any cable network except CNN.

"People have very strong feelings against them," he said. "People feel the defense is either made up or outrageous."

On the other hand, he said, there were extremely strong feelings among people who had themselves been sexual abuse victims. The first two callers one morning were in tears. As the case continued, it became a kind of phenomenon, a field on which all of America, it sometimes seemed, was playing out an obsession with child abuse.

Bozanich had not broken Lyle down. He had proven to be a tougher nut than almost everyone expected. But she had pointed up inconsistencies, and the remark about sneaking around the coffee table was the kind of thing jurors would remember. All in all, she felt good. But her pleasure was dampened by the criticism she was getting from the commentator hired by Court TV to analyze what was going on in court. One analyst was Gerry Spence, a well-known Wyoming attorney who called himself a country lawyer and had defended Imelda Marcos and white separatist Randy Weaver. Spence set his cowboy hat on the desk beside him and opined that Lyle had done a good job on the stand. He seemed sympathetic and comfortable, always adding a polite nod at the end of his answers like a boy hoping he had done well.

Perhaps coincidentally, Spence said the most effective defendant on the stand is a psychopath, because he does not suffer guilt or any sadness over the crime he has committed. "When I have a very innocent client I rarely put them on," Spence said, because they feel nervous, which can make them look guilty.

Spence criticized Bozanich for allowing Lyle Menendez to run on with answers, telling more of his version of events to the jury. He compared the exchange between the two to a minuet, and said he was missing the "horror and blood and misery and degradation" of the killings.

While generally lauding Lyle's performance, Spence said he was facing trouble as well. Lyle seemed too at ease discussing these horrific acts. "This guy is just kind of, um, he's too unemotional [talking] about the emotional things that would just destroy most of us. I could not imagine talking about blowing my mother's head off as if I was paying this month's electric bill," Spence said. He said this with an almost imperceptible shudder.

Spence slammed Leslie Abramson for her run-ins with the judge, calling this tactic a "losing proposition." To the jury, he said, "the judge is Daddy," and no attorney looks good fighting with Daddy.

Bozanich resented the shots taken by outsiders who weren't watching the whole trial. "I did not sign up to be on national television and have people criticize my work who have not seen the evidence in the case," she said angrily after court one day. She sat erect in a wooden chair in the district attorney's office waiting room. "I don't think a criminal trial should be treated like a sporting event."

Outside the courtroom, the trial was becoming a cultural phenomenon that transcended the dry language of the law. Cocktail parties all over Southern California debated the case, neatly breaking down into opposing camps. The boys were victimized by those horrible parents, said one side. The other side scoffed, what a bunch of bull, they made it all up.

There was no such ambivalence the night *The Tonight Show* with Jay Leno previewed what it said would be a new sitcom starring the Menendez brothers.

Sung to the theme of "The Patty Duke Show," the show's theme song went:

Meet Lyle who's been most everywhere,
From New York town to old Bel Air.
But Erik's not as fancy-free
He spent his time in therapy.
What a dangerous pair!

But they're brothers,
They're murdering brothers, filled with hate,
One pair of matching loonies,
Trying to get Dad's estate.

Where Lyle enjoys the outdoor sports,
A Rolex watch, and a brand-new Porsche
Our Erik likes to spend his time
Planning out the perfect crime.
Now they're in the courts!

Still they're brothers,
These murdering brothers love to kill,
They load alike, they shoot alike,
They plan to share the loot alike,

That's their special skill!
What brothers
Get cut from the will!

As the song played, the camera flashed up courtroom scenes showing Lyle and Erik at the defense table.

The crowd began arriving outside the Van Nuys courthouse at about 4:00 A.M. on Monday, September 27. Some of them arrived even earlier and dozed in their cars under blankets, though they hardly needed them because Los Angeles was in the grip of one of those heat waves that blow in off the desert just when Southern Californians begin to think, and hope, that summer has cleared out of town.

Erik Menendez was going to take the stand, and the excitement of it had been building for days. The popular notion among the thousands glued to Court TV was that there was a good seed and a bad seed in this family, and the good seed was Erik, the soft, emotional, dependent boy who had clung to his mother's legs and rescued wounded birds from the highway.

How would he do on the witness stand? Would he break down, sobbing openly, the way he had right after his parents' deaths? Lyle had already surprised court watchers by showing himself to be a sympathetic witness, at least in the first dramatic days, and now the pundits among the press and elsewhere believed the pressure was turned up a notch on Erik. Some felt Lyle's tears had stolen the emotional impact of what Erik would say, the firsthand experience of being savagely molested for twelve years by his father.

Erik's attorneys were also concerned. Marcia Morrissey, Erik's hardworking co-counsel, said the fact that Lyle went first "made it more difficult" for Erik. They "grew up in the same house and had many of the same stories to tell. . . . But somebody had to go first, and Lyle was the oldest and he went first."

Once more the family "bun boy" had gotten the short end of things, it appeared.

On the Monday morning that Erik took the stand, Abramson came to court in a cream suit with an elegant chain at the back. Her frizzy mat of hair had been puffed out in a glorious fountain of gold. Erik had passed on the boyish sweater in favor of a blue dress shirt with a conservative tie.

He was so skinny that his face had become gaunt. Combined with his heavy brows that put his narrow eyes in shadow, he had a distinctly unsettling, furtive look. And he was so pallid that his attorney felt it necessary to explain to the jury that he had been in jail more than three years awaiting trial.

"How long has it been since you were in sunshine?" she asked.

"Four to six months ago was the last time."

What was the cause of the killings? Abramson asked.

"Me telling Lyle that . . . my dad—my dad—my dad . . ." His voice choked with sobs. His aunt Marta said that when Erik got in this state he might pass out. The judge leaned forward and asked if he could answer the question.

"My dad had been molesting me," he sighed. Then he looked at the ceiling, wiped his eyes, and bowed his head.

This was the only strong emotion Erik was to show all day, and, oddly, it was not nearly as moving as Lyle's words had been. Erik's demeanor throughout his days on the witness stand was jagged and difficult. One moment he would stare out from narrow eyes under his sharp brows, looking dangerous, and the next he would appear wide-eyed and innocent. He looked more mentally disturbed than sad.

Abramson too showed an odd persona. She stood poised at the lectern behind the counsel table and led Erik through his testimony like a rider giving a horse a hard bit to break him. Whenever Erik started to embellish an answer, she interrupted him and fired off a new question. At times it appeared she was dealing with a hostile witness rather than her own client.

Perhaps this was a reaction to the tongue-lashing Weisberg had given her the previous Friday. At a sidebar conference,

Kuriyama had complained that Leslie had been caressing and holding Erik in front of the jury, which Kuriyama worried would make the defendant look even more childlike and innocent.

"I haven't been caressing him," Abramson said.

"Okay. Well, clearly the conduct of counsel in touching and physically reacting to the defendants is an area of concern, not only of counsel but of the court; that counsel are to be acting as professionals, not as nursemaids or surrogate mothers, and that counsel are to refrain from doing just what has been described here," Weisberg said. "The court has noticed it on occasion, and it's inappropriate conduct."

Abramson turned first to the murders. As the summer of 1989 came to an end, Erik said, he was looking forward to going away to college at UCLA. Getting away, he said, "was the most important thing in my life."

But then his father told him he expected his son to spend several nights a week at home, not in the dorm. Erik was devastated because he knew "the sex was going to continue. It made me feel lost, like the hope I had was gone."

As he spoke, Erik sighed frequently, and often lowered his head. But he kept his composure.

He said he began thinking of killing himself, possibly by hanging, driving off a cliff, or slitting his wrists. "I was in a daze. I just wanted to die."

Then Abramson moved into the final days before the killings, covering much the same ground that Lyle had discussed, focusing on Erik's view. For instance, Erik said that after Lyle and Jose had their first confrontation Thursday night, he ran into the den and found his mother watching television.

"What's the matter with you?" she asked.

"No, nothing, you wouldn't understand," Erik said he replied.

"I understand a lot more than you think," Kitty replied. "I know, I've always known. You think I'm stupid?"

"I hate you," he said, and ran out the back door.

Kitty chased him up to Lyle's guest room, where Erik cowered behind his older brother while Lyle argued with Kitty. This was nothing new. "I used to stand behind Lyle a lot," Erik said. "He was braver than me."

Lyle asked Kitty why she never helped Erik stop the abuse. "No one ever helped me in my life," she said.

Erik believed his mother would help his father kill them. "They were very much a team," he said awkwardly. And his mother he found frightening for another reason. He said she seemed to have magical powers. She knew where he went, who he saw, everything he did. It was only after her death that he found a taping system in her bedroom that tapped into all three phone lines in the house. He also found tape recordings, he said, of himself speaking to friends.

These kinds of fantastic thoughts, which might have been more believable in a five-year-old, seemed harder to understand coming from an adult. But a key defense contention was that Erik and Lyle had been infantilized by their father's control, and they were not really the ages they appeared to be.

During the drive to San Diego, Erik described the sexual acts in detail that his father perpetrated. "I told him there were pins and tacks Dad would stick in me and use," he said.

When they bought the guns, Erik had the pick of two fake ID's. He had Donovan's license, as well as another in the name of Richard Stevens. He said students at Calabasas High had birth certificates in phony names, and his mother had told him how to complete the process of getting a driver's license in the other name. But he decided to use Donovan's license and practiced the signature a few times over lunch at a Bob's Big Boy before going off to buy the shotguns at the Big 5 store.

A reporter for the television show *Hard Copy* showed up during Erik's testimony, trying to confirm a strange story told by a woman who had walked in off the street one day. The woman claimed she was a hooker and that Jose had been a client of hers several times. What made him stand out in her mind was his preference for brutality. He liked to choke her, she said.

The rumor around the courthouse was that the show had paid $5,000 for her story.

The story appeared later on television. An editor at *Hard Copy* who asked not to be identified confirmed that the woman had been paid for her story. Asked how the producers confirmed that she was telling the truth and not just making up a story to collect a fat fee, the source said the show's producers checked out the hooker's madam with the Los Angeles police, who confirmed the madam was legit, or as legit as a madam gets. He admitted that didn't mean the hooker was telling the truth.

"I find the whole process of what we do fascinating," the editor said. "At times I'm troubled."

A dull, unaffected Erik picked up the chronology the next day. After his initial burst of emotion on the stand, he had lapsed into a bland mood that was especially surprising considering how well Lyle had done. One writer suggested that Abramson needed to get Erik off the Xanax he was taking in jail for nerves; it was making him flat.

After the fishing trip Saturday, Erik huddled on his bed with his shotgun, listening to his father pounding on the door.

"I was going to shoot" if he came in, Erik said. He didn't really think his powerful father could be killed by mere shotgun rounds, but even if he could be killed, that would leave Kitty still alive to kill him.

Jose finally went away and Erik fell asleep at four-thirty. He was jolted awake a few hours later by his recurring nightmare. "It was about a green face and how it changed into Dad chasing me through this darkness. The dream began with me being real tiny. Everything got larger and larger, and I felt like I was disappearing. I ran to my relatives and asked them to help and they said no. I ran to Lyle and he abandoned me and ran away. I ran to Mom and she was floating in the sky over the roof in the Pennington house."

It ended, he said, "with me falling off the roof of the Pennington house."

Sunday night, he said, he was convinced Jose was going to come up and have one last fling with him before he killed him.

He "only had seconds" to act, he felt, when he went for his gun. Then he and Lyle burst into the room and began firing. "As I went into the room, I just started firing, in front of me, at my parents. I fired as much as I could, every shell I had."

After the firing stopped and the smoke filled the air, he heard a moan from his mother.

Terrified, he scrambled from the room and went out to his car, he said, where he gave Lyle another shotgun shell so that he could finish off his mother.

After the killings, he stared at the bodies. He couldn't believe they were dead, that he had killed them with nothing but a shotgun.

Asked by Abramson if he felt guilty for killing his parents, Erik replied soberly, "Yes, I thought they were these great people that I had killed. I loved them more than I had ever loved them in my life."

Having taken care of the killings first, Abramson turned to the family history to explain them. Erik described how his parents tried to get him over his myriad fears by scaring him, once by locking him in the basement while his father made noises in the dark that made him scream and cry. Another time he described the scene in his bedroom when he was going through his usual nightly routine of checking the drawers of his dresser and under his bed for monsters. A witch's mask dropped on him from a closet, and his father came out laughing. He was also abandoned in a cemetery once by his father.

Abramson led Erik through his alleged history of abuse, which Erik said began at the Monsey house and continued all the way to Beverly Hills. Erik said there were four kinds of sexual games Jose played with him. They were called "knees," "nice sex," "rough sex," and just "sex."

When he was young, he felt his father disliked him. So he was happy when Jose came to him and began giving him massages. Eventually simple massages turned into manual and oral stimulation of Erik's penis.

Kitty began participating in the molestation, making him strip off his shorts so that she could inspect his penis and pop the little blisters she found. She never told him what they were.

After that Jose began forcing Erik to perform oral sex on him while kneeling. Jose told him this is what the ancient Greeks and Romans did to get ready for battle, and Erik called it "knees." When his father had an orgasm in Erik's mouth, he held his son's head and ordered him to swallow.

What started out as a display of affection, to Erik, turned painful when his father began forcing him to have anal intercourse at age twelve. "I thought it was really dirty," he said. Then he asked for a break, looking queasy.

"Rough sex," Erik said, started at thirteen, when Jose began using needles, tacks, pins, and rope. He stuck the tacks into Erik's butt and thighs.

Erik said he hated himself for allowing the sexual molestation to continue. Only once, when he was seventeen, Erik said, did he try to say no to his father. Jose threw him on the bed and put a souvenir knife to Erik's throat that Jose got as a promotion for the Rambo movies. Then they had "sex."

Erik said he gave himself a nickname as a result of the rough sex he endured—"Hurt man." He shared it with some relatives and friends, but did not reveal the ugly meaning. "I just told them I got hurt a lot."

What was probably the lurid high point of either brother's time on the stand came when Erik volunteered that he began putting cinnamon in his father's tea and coffee. He said he learned the trick when he overheard classmates talking about sex.

"I heard it makes it taste better," he said, referring to his father's semen.

Erik was in the seventh grade when he supposedly heard this conversation. It seemed difficult to understand how Erik could have dosed his father's beverages without Jose finding out. Cinnamon was not likely to pass undetected.

Erik also said he began eating lemon on all his food; this was a dietary habit that had been noticed by Erik's friends over the years. It became a "big joke" in the family. The purpose, he said, was to dull his taste buds, "so I wouldn't have to taste my dad's . . ."

Erik said he began to question whether he was gay. His father, despite the sexual games he was supposedly playing with his son, hated gay people.

Erik wasn't the only one concerned about his sexuality. After the family moved to California, Kitty gave him six months to find a girlfriend, he said. The girl he found was the blue-eyed California girl Jan.

Jan said Erik didn't get around to kissing her—on the cheek—until a month after they started dating. Four or five dates later, they "really kissed."

"It was like a new life for me," Erik said. "It was something that I had never experienced before. And suddenly I was actually happy sometimes. I looked forward to seeing her, and I felt really warm when I was with her. And it made me really insecure at times, but it also made me feel more comfortable."

But despite encouragement from Kitty, they could never have sex. "It just didn't work," Jan said.

Erik told jurors that he felt uncomfortable with the girl because of what was going on with his father. When their relationship ended after six months, Kitty ridiculed him. "What, are you not man enough for her?"

Far from seeing Kitty as a basket case or an abuser, Jan said Kitty kept the whole family together. She said she felt like a sister to Kitty during the time she and Erik dated.

Even Erik's early relationship with older brother Lyle had been an ordeal. Recalling his molestation by Lyle when he was five years old, he said that at the time, "I didn't like him. I didn't like him at all."

But when Erik was eight and Lyle was eleven years old, he said Lyle began defending him. As Erik recalled it, Jose took his sons into the middle of a lake in a small sailboat and insisted he and Lyle swim to shore. Jose told Erik there were snapping turtles in the water that had a predilection for nipping swimmers. After Lyle jumped into the water, Jose pushed a reluctant Erik in. About halfway to shore, Erik said he did not think he was going to make it and began swallowing water. Then he thought of the snapping turtles and panicked and began screaming for help.

"And Lyle swam back over and grabbed me and lifted me up in the water, and then just took me to shore, and said, 'It's going to be all right.'"

Jose got mad, but it didn't matter. The bonding process had begun. Erik increasingly turned to Lyle for guidance. Whatever the truth of the abuse allegations, by the time Lyle and Erik burst into the darkened family room on the evening of August 20, 1989, and killed their unarmed parents, the bonding had been long completed. If Lyle perceived that the brothers' lives were in imminent danger, Erik could not think otherwise.

From time to time during the trial, prosecutors received phone calls from men who claimed to have had a homosexual relationship with Erik. Bozanich said Jose was so concerned about his son's sexuality that he drilled a hole in the ceiling of Erik's room in Calabasas to spy on him. Kuriyama repeatedly tried to convince the judge to let him put evidence in front of the jury about these things, but Weisberg refused.

Kuriyama felt it was relevant because the defense was trying to make it appear that Jose was a sexual predator. One witness had testified to seeing gay porn magazines in the house, the implication being that they were Jose's, which could substantiate the claim that Jose might enjoy sex with boys. But if the magazines were Erik's, that might put a different spin on the matter.

Then one day a male photographer sent over to Kuriyama a proof sheet of pictures which showed Erik in a variety of modeling poses. They were not pornographic, just slightly alluring. In one he was shown wearing his tee shirt off one shoulder. Another was a "crotch shot" picture in underwear, taken from below.

The pictures were turned over to the defense, but were never introduced.

Prior to the next day's session, Marie Ballesteros, a reporter from *La Opinion*, the Spanish-language newspaper in Los

Angeles, stopped in the cafeteria on the second floor of the courthouse to grab a cup of coffee.

She sat down at one of the metal tables in the big, sunny room, which looked out over the tree-shaded courthouse square. She had been in the United States less than two years, having come from Mexico. An attractive, dark-haired woman who wore her hair in a pageboy style, she was still learning how to speak English. Her note-taking style, half in English and half in Spanish, amazed the rest of the writers.

She was still learning to understand American customs, and the Menendez trial was offering a close-up look at one of the great issues in U.S. life—child abuse. She was trying to get a grip on the subject, but it was clear from the way she talked that she was from a different tradition.

"In Latin America, the psychological and physical abuse," she said in a heavy accent, "is not rare." She said the kind of domineering father that Jose had been was not that uncommon, either. Her own father, she said, had used strong physical discipline from time to time. Yet he was an educated man. She grew up loving and respecting him.

Sexual abuse, on the other hand, is rare.

When Kuriyama began his cross-examination, he relentlessly focused on the scene in the den, trying to force Erik to describe it for jurors. But Erik had trouble remembering details. "I saw nothing. I mean, I guess that's why shots just went all over the place, out the window, on the side. I just didn't know what was happening."

But the shots did not go all over the place—the brothers had been deadly accurate—and Kuriyama pressed him on that point.

"I just started firing as soon as I came into that room, and whoever was in that room, I was going to fire at," Erik explained. "And I didn't think this is who this is or who this is, and I just—just started firing; and apparently I was mostly shooting at my mom. I didn't know. I wasn't—I wasn't aware. I wasn't thinking about it. All I was thinking is I got to fire every shot of my gun."

There are times when even the most exciting trial begins to drag because of the inevitable legal maneuvering. This trial was no different. During one sidebar conference, some jurors even attempted a "wave" to liven things up.

There was no need for false dramatics when Kuriyama caught Erik in what was arguably the biggest mistake—or lie—of the trial. Kuriyama set up the revelation by having Erik meticulously describe the hunt for guns on Friday, two days before the killings. Erik said he and Lyle drove to a Big 5 store in Santa Monica, where they looked at an assortment of handguns.

What Erik did not know was that a couple of days earlier, a law clerk in the district attorney's office, Thomas Moore of the West Los Angeles School of Law, had discovered that Erik could not have looked at handguns at a Big 5 store.

Erik said he saw real handguns and BB guns in a display case. "I remember asking the man behind the counter which are real and which are BB guns," Erik said.

Again and again Kuriyama came back at Erik on the same point. "Now, these were handguns that you were seeing?"

"Yes."

Taking the bait, Erik described in even greater detail how the handguns were displayed next to the pellet and BB guns. Finally Erik said that they picked out two handguns, although he could not recall the caliber, only to learn that California has a fifteen-day waiting period for the purchase of such weapons. And since the brothers felt they were in imminent danger, Erik told the prosecutor they did not buy them.

"Now, you're telling the truth about everything in this case, aren't you?" Kuriyama asked.

"I'm telling the truth to the best that I can."

"Okay. And even though you've lied in the past, you're telling the truth now, aren't you?"

"Yes, I am."

"Did you truly go to the Santa Monica Big 5 store on the morning of August 18 to buy these handguns?"

"Definitely. Without a doubt I did."

"And you and Lyle actually looked in this case and you selected these guns and you were told you couldn't leave the store with those handguns because there's a fifteen-day wait?"

"Yes."

"Mr. Menendez, did you know that Big 5 stopped carrying handguns on March of 1986?"

A gasp swept through the courtroom. It was an apparent lie of large proportion, although Abramson would later grouse that the media overplayed it.

Erik fumbled for a response. "No. I don't know that. Mr. Kuriyama, there were guns there and we did look at them, and he did say we could not carry them anymore."

Writing the next day in the *Los Angeles Times*, Alan Abrahamson, who has a law degree, observed that such Perry Mason tactics rarely materialize in a real courtroom setting.

"Courtroom testimony, especially from a defendant in a high-profile murder case, is gone over and over beforehand—with defense attorneys spending weeks trying to anticipate every possible question the prosecution might ask," he wrote.

After Kuriyama concluded, Abramson picked up the pieces. Erik told the court he was no longer sure it was a Big 5 store he and Lyle had entered.

Lester Kuriyama wrapped up a long and grueling cross-examination by posting the picture of the death scene on the bulletin board. Amid the blood and gore was paperwork with the UCLA logo on them, as though Kitty had been filling them out.

"If your mother was planning to kill you, would she have been filling out your application to UCLA?" Kuriyama asked. The question was objected to and Weisberg sustained it, but it must have raised a doubt in the jury's mind.

After court that day, Abramson and Bozanich appeared for a brief press conference. As Bozanich walked up to the array of microphones, Abramson advised, "Lipstick, Pam, lipstick."

"No," Bozanich answered peremptorily.

She was asked about Erik's demeanor on the stand. "That has been quite surprising, actually," she said.

Commenting on the UCLA paperwork, she tossed off a line. "You don't kill someone and send them to college."

Then she was asked about the fact that the prosecution had ignored the sexual abuse allegations and focused on the shootings.

"This is not a child abuse case," Bozanich replied matter-of-factly. "It's our contention this is a murder trial."

Abramson stepped up to the microphones next. Where Pam Bozanich had a slight stiffness and discomfort dealing with the press, Leslie Abramson looked comfortable in the spotlight. She was asked about the Big 5 incident.

"Erik Menendez was testifying to twelve years of sexual abuse and eighteen years of child abuse. It's very clear he's not the best reporter of geography."

What had been accomplished over nine days of testimony?

"My hope going in was that he would have the ability to tell what he had to tell. I've been very proud of him. He's been very, very frightened."

She said he was on small dosages of Xanax. "Very small. I know, because I take them myself."

Asked about justice in this case, she replied, "I don't think you should kill child molesters. I think you should do worse things."

Smiling and upbeat, she told Court TV that there had been an "overwhelming outpouring" from the public toward Lyle and Erik, both of whom were receiving "thirty to fifty" sympathetic letters a day at the county jail from individuals around the country.

29

The Experts

The defense was about to move into phase two of its case, when it would try to give a context to the abuses Erik and Lyle said they had endured. A series of therapists would show how a lifetime of abuse could lead to the explosion of gunfire on August 20, 1989.

But first the defense had a couple of final witnesses to talk about bizarre goings-on in the home. The first was Traci Baker, a twenty-four-year-old college student with dark hair who worked as a waitress and had a lilt in her voice that smacked of Val-talk.

She had dated Lyle for three months in 1988 and spent an uncomfortable Thanksgiving at the Beverly Hills mansion. She was having dinner one night when Jose stood up from the table and pushed his plate away. "He said something to [Kitty] like, 'what did you do to this food?' "

Then Lyle, Erik, Jose, and Traci went out to eat at a Hamburger Hamlet. No residue of anger remained at dinner, and Traci Baker found Jose to be an extremely charming man. He inspired her to go to college, she said.

Erik had referred to this incident during his testimony as a case where his mother might have been trying to poison the family. "I would normally eat the food unless I thought there was something wrong with my mother," he said.

From the way Erik described it, the family must have constantly been feeling as if their lives were in danger, wondering if today was the day Kitty would poison them all. And Jose's reaction to the threat of poisoning seemed mild. He meekly got

up and went out to eat, then, after narrowly cheating death,
entertained a guest with charming stories.

An alternate explanation was that Jose was being an insensitive boor by showing up his wife, known to be a lousy cook, in
front of a guest and walking out on her. This kind of behavior
was entirely consistent with him.

Thanksgiving was a turning point in Baker's relationship with
Lyle. She and Lyle had been having sex in the mansion, and
Kitty didn't like it. After dinner, when Lyle left to take a friend
home, Traci stayed around and dozed on the couch. Lyle had
asked her to wait for him, but Kitty came in and confronted her.

"Are you having sexual relations with my son?" she asked.

"Yes," said the startled young woman. She didn't think there
was anything particularly outrageous about the admission; Lyle
was an adult now. Kitty's face contorted in rage.

"I've seen girls like you," she sneered. Then she told her if
she thought she was going to get her hands on Lyle's money,
she should forget it. Eager to leave, Baker began to rise.
Kitty shoved her back onto the couch, peppering her with
more questions.

Finally Traci got up, ran to the guest house, and got her
things, then cried all the way home. "To this day," she said,
"my self-esteem is affected."

Under cross-examination, Baker admitted she was not too
humiliated to call back to the mansion later on to see if Jose
could get her concert tickets to see the Who.

Andres "Andy" Cano, Marta's son, was Erik's cousin, a tall,
young man with big ears and a small ponytail. He said he had
carried a secret of Erik's for many years.

He had become friends with Erik, who was two years old,
when his family lived in Princeton for a time. He and Erik used
to go out into the farm fields behind his house to talk. One day
they saw a helicopter hovering above them and feared this was
the farmer who owned the land coming after them, so they
ran away.

They stopped under a tree, out of breath. Erik suddenly
asked if Andy's father ever gave him massages. Were they
normal? Andy said he didn't know, his father wasn't around. His
mother had been divorced by this time. Then Erik said his father
was massaging his dick. Erik made Andy swear never to reveal
the information.

And he didn't, apparently. Marta Cano said before he testified that he never told her about it.

Under cross-examination, the prosecution tried to attack the young man's story. He frequently pleaded memory lapses. Andy had flown back on the plane with Erik when he turned himself in, and during the ride, he said, he may have asked him if he had been involved in the killings. He didn't remember what Erik said.

The lapses may have looked suspicious, but Andy Cano never wavered in his story about Erik confessing abuse to him.

The defense experts now began to appear in the courtroom. These were the men and women who would take all the amorphous bits of information that had come out in the previous four weeks since the brothers took the stand and shape it into something recognizable. Speaking in calm, melodious voices, these professorial hired guns would take an act that to an ordinary person might look like simple revenge and show that it isn't that simple.

What the defense had to show was that Erik and Lyle had felt their lives were in danger when they burst into the room. And since Kitty and Jose had been unarmed, the only way to show that was to show that their mental states had been altered from those of a normal person by years of mistreatment. Much of the experts' efforts would be aimed at showing a gradual escalation of tension over the five days leading up to August 20, when the boys exploded and went into what one expert labeled "automatic pilot."

The first expert was Dr. Ann H. Tyler, a child abuse expert from Utah. A woman with short dark hair and, at least in the beginning, a cool, confident way of speaking, she said a lifetime of psychological abuse had left Erik Menendez immature and naive. She said repeated abuse can lead to a condition called "learned helplessness," in which victims cannot flee an abusive situation.

The term is a familiar one in battered-women cases, where wives who have been beaten repeatedly are unable to leave their abusers.

A chart with six categories of psychological maltreatment was placed on the bulletin board. The first was *Rejecting, degrading.* An example is saying, "I wish you were never born."

The second was *Terrorizing.* When a child is terrorized, said Tyler, he develops "incredible fear . . . you may fear your life is threatened." The kind of terrorization Erik was exposed to

apparently included episodes where he was left in the basement
or abandoned in a cemetery, as Lyle said was done to Erik once.

Third is *Isolating*, that is, keeping them away from friends
and other outside experiences.

Fourth is *Exploiting, Corrupting*. One part of this would be
giving them the message that cheating is all right to reach a goal.

Fifth was *Denying Emotional Needs*. Leslie Abramson asked
if ridiculing a child for being fearful would fall into this category,
and Tyler said it would.

Number six was *Denying Mental, Educational, or Medical
Needs*. The defense maintained that Kitty ignored Erik's learning
disabilities because she wanted him to be perfect.

Tyler said the parents abused Erik from the moment he was
born, even before he was born. Kitty wanted her second child
to be a girl and bought pink baby things.

"It sets him up for expectations that can never be met,"
Tyler said.

Statements like that drove Bozanich crazy. If everyone who
hoped for a boy and not a girl, or vice versa, was charged with
child abuse, there wouldn't be enough foster homes in the world
to care for all the children.

She bored in on Tyler, and the woman with the easy smile
and confident manner became rattled. Bozanich noted that many
of the worst anecdotes about the family were totally uncorrobo-
rated.

"If the information [Erik] told you was untrue, how does that
affect your opinion?"

"It doesn't affect my opinion," she said. "Erik had no reason
to lie about his abuse."

Bozanich paused for a moment. What about being on trial for
murder? she wondered.

How did Tyler reach her conclusions? Bozanich asked. Tyler,
who continually referred to Erik as "this boy" and occasionally
"this child," said she looked at school and other records. Had
she looked at Oziel's notes? She never asked for them, she said.

"I knew Erik went to Dr. Oziel because of some acting-out,"
she said, referring to the burglaries. She referred to the crimes
as "adolescent burglaries."

Bozanich asked calmly if Tyler thought stealing $80,000 to
$100,000 worth of jewels and other property was "a prank."

As the questions got tougher and more belittling, the witness
began to argue with the prosecutor, prompting Weisberg to

admonish her to answer the questions even if she didn't like them.

Responding to Tyler's use of diminutives to describe Erik, Bozanich asked sarcastically, "Do you think he's a child here?"

"Emotionally, yes."

As the hammering continued, Abramson tried to come to Tyler's rescue. "She's a doctor, it's disrespectful," she said of the way Bozanich was phrasing her questions.

"Overruled," Weisberg said.

"Explain to me how a child suffers abuse at age zero," Bozanich pleaded.

"Pam blew her away," Kuriyama said as the prosecution left the courtroom, wheeling their carts of files behind them.

"I felt sorry for her," Bozanich said. "I wanted to say no hard feelings." Kuriyama, always the tougher of the two, disagreed, saying Tyler deserved it.

Tyler was right about one thing. The naïveté of the brothers did come across frequently on the stand in completely accidental ways that, unlike crying, they would have difficulty faking. There was a kind of softness, a hothouse plant delicacy to them, even when, at times, they were caught off guard by a question and responded with flashes of anger that were quickly covered up. It wasn't necessarily innocent, but it was there. Then there was the fact that they could hold on to that bizarre respect and love for their father even after they had killed him, which also seemed genuine. Somehow they couldn't see the contradiction.

Outside court that October day, Kitty's sister, Joan Vander Molen, made a brief statement to the press. She said she would be testifying soon about her sister for the defense. "This in no way reflects on the love that I have for all the members of my family or on their love for me."

She choked up for a moment. She was reacting to a remark earlier that day by Bozanich about squabbles in the Andersen family over the defense posture.

"We feel that Mrs. Bozanich's comment this morning about their being bad blood among members of our family was very wrong, and not right. And has caused more pain on a family that is already suffering an immeasurable amount of pain."

As she concluded her statement, other members of the defense team gathered around and hugged her.

But the dissension issue was a real one in both families.

Milton Andersen gave an interview to his home townpaper, the *Daily Southtown*, in which he defended his sister against her sons.

The defense, he said, was "bull." He believed Erik and Lyle killed because of greed. He said the defense team visited him in Oak Lawn. "They tried to convince me what bad people my sister and brother-in-law were, but I didn't buy it," he told the local paper. "My sister didn't abuse her children."

Andersen said he visited the Menendezes a few weeks before the murders. They went out to look at the estate in Calabasas and then ordered in Chinese food. Erik and Lyle ordered the food, and ordered far too much, enough food for a banquet, but Jose didn't seem to mind. Another house guest around the same time said Erik and Lyle ordered every item on the menu, and Jose just laughed.

"That's just the way they were," Andersen said. "Everything was lavish."

Far from abusing them, Milton felt that Jose and Kitty had not disciplined their boys enough. This dichotomy appeared over and over again in interviews with people who had known the family. Jose and Kitty were tough and unyielding; Jose and Kitty loved their kids so much they indulged them excessively. Could both have been true?

Milton Andersen has taped a photo of Kitty to the dashboard of his van and says hello to it every morning. He said his greeting is a way of "keeping her in my memory."

The second defense expert was Ann Burgess, a slender woman with a slightly crooked mouth and a way of looking over the top of her glasses when she answered questions.

Burgess, a professor of psychiatric mental health nursing at the University of Pennsylvania, was an expert in crime-scene analysis and had taught at the FBI academy in Quantico, Virginia. She said that after looking over pictures of the family room in the mansion, it was her conclusion that this was a "disorganized" crime scene that could not have been the product of a premeditated murder. She also said the random nature of the wounds, the overkill element of the crime, showed a lack of planning.

Burgess broke the crime into three categories—pre-crime planning, the crime itself, and post-crime behavior. The fact that weapons were removed and the shells picked up spoke to post-crime planning rather than premeditation before the crime, she said.

She said there was a high risk of detection, another element showing lack of premeditation. The factors here were firing the guns in a residential neighborhood on a warm night when windows would be open, and firing so much and at such close range that the shooters would get blood on them.

"Does the fact that the weapons were purchased days before change the crime scene-definition?" Abramson asked.

"No, it does not," Burgess replied.

Burgess then gave a technical description of research into brain function in terrorized people. She said that in such people, something called "genetic recoding" occurs, in which the brain rewires itself to respond to much lower levels of stimulus. This produces a kind of hyper-vigilance in these people, who constantly search their environments for danger.

In other words, Erik had been frightened so repeatedly that he might overreact to what might appear to be an ordinary event, if it somehow cued in his fear response. So walking into the family room and closing the door might seem to a genetically recoded person to be much more ominous than it sounded.

Burgess said there were five factors that heightened tension and directly led to the slayings. First was the order that Erik would have to live at home part of the week while attending UCLA, second was the disclosure of sexual abuse to his brother, third was the confrontation between Lyle and Jose, fourth was the time Jose came to Erik's room and tried to assault him, and fifth was Kitty's revelation that she had known all along of the abuse. At the end, Erik was in full fear response or, in Burgess's words, on "automatic pilot."

Bozanich went on the attack when her turn came. She asked if there was a difference between poor planning and no planning.

"We don't give it an adjective," Burgess said.

It was Bozanich's position that Erik and Lyle had planned the perfect crime, but just didn't plan it very well. This was different than not having a plan. Comparing the killings to a wedding, she said a ceremony may be planned for months, and still the judge may show up late and the food turn out to be a disaster.

"Does the fact that my wedding did not go well mean I didn't plan it?" Bozanich asked.

"One could say there were certain factors that were checked and double-checked, and carefully outlined, which usually goes into a good plan. That's not to say that extraneous factors can't occur."

Bozanich sighed. The point is, she said, the marriage still

occurs. "Dr. Burgess, lack of planning is not the only explanation for a disorganized crime scene."

"There could be other factors," Burgess agreed.

Had Burgess considered the possibility that Erik and Lyle were making up abuse that never happened? Bozanich asked. Burgess said she had, but rejected it.

"Are you aware of the fact that Erik Menendez took his bed with him" when he moved from the mansion into the Marina del Rey condo? Was there not something strange in taking the bed on which his father had sexually assaulted him for years?

Burgess said he needed furniture. "My opinion is this is a crime born out of fear," she said.

Bozanich asked how it could be that two young men with no experience with guns could hit their targets fifteen of seventeen times, despite being in an "automaton rage." When Burgess tried to respond, Bozanich snapped:

"Dr. Burgess, do you know what psychobabble is?"

"No."

The prosecution tactics were angering some people. Lester Kuriyama revealed one day he had received a death threat.

"If he doesn't lay off Erik Menendez," the caller had stated, "I'm going to blow his head off."

As a result, Kuriyama was getting police protection. He had a bullet-proof vest and was wearing it to court some days.

Then a man was seen outside court carrying a copy of the Manson trial transcript. He said, "The judge and prosecution are biased, and people like that should be shot," according to a bailiff. Two security men from the district attorney's office appeared outside court later on, and the man disappeared.

These incidents were results of a highly publicized trial about a highly emotional issue. People who were not very stable took the matter personally and pronounced themselves willing to mete out justice. Frequently outside court, picket sign in hand, was a young female student who was angry at Weisberg. She said he was not accepting enough of child abuse claims. She said victims don't make up stories like the ones coming out of the Menendez trial.

The carnival outside continued to roll along. Mary Jane Stevenson of the *Daily Journal* wrote a story about a man going on the radio claiming, apparently tongue in cheek, to be the Menendez brothers' acting coach. She also mentioned a line overheard in the courthouse from a prominent defense attorney: "If Leslie wins this one, we're going to bronze her."

The entertainment industry was also continuing to have a good laugh at the expense of the Menendezes. *Saturday Night Live* did a lengthy skit the night that John Malkovich was the host, featuring him as Lyle Menendez and one of the show's regulars as Erik. Malkovich was said to be a Court TV junkie who was fascinated with the Menendez trial, and his characterization showed some familiarity with the character.

In the skit, the fake Lyle and Erik, dressed in sweaters, testified together that the murders were done by two previously unknown brothers, Danny and Jose Jr. These two brothers had never been let out of the house, and nobody had ever seen them.

Asked why there was no official record of their existence, Malkovich, wearing a scraggly black wig, said, "My father said Danny and Jose Jr. didn't deserve to have any official records of their existence because they were weak and not good tennis players."

Then both brothers broke down into stagy sobs.

On October 21, Jill Lansing's first expert took the stand, Stuart N. Hart, an Indiana University professor who had chaired an international task force on the rights of children.

Hart, a silver-haired man with glasses who finished each of his answers with a quick nod of his head, had never testified as an expert witness before, but in straightforward, easy-to-understand language he effectively laid out his case that Lyle had been severely psychologically mistreated. By not trying to expound grandiose theories, he seemed more believable.

This was a trademark of Lansing's defense strategy. There were few fireworks with the prosecution and judge, but she consistently scored points for her client and won respect for her understated, yet meticulously prepared courtroom style.

Lansing's next witness, Jon R. Conte, a professor of social work at the University of Washington, had the results of an MMPI test on Kitty. The MMPI is a standard diagnostic tool; Kitty had taken the test twice in therapy, and Conte had taken the answers and had them rescored to reach what he called a "tentative diagnosis" of the dead woman's mental state.

It seemed bizarre to give a mental diagnosis of a dead woman. Reading from the results, Conte said, "This is a woman who tries to present herself in a favorable light, [who had a] degree of defensiveness, depression, anxiety, and tension." The report said she tended to place blame "on outside situations" and was "impulsive, having shallow and superficial relationships." She was insecure in relationships, with a low frustration level, "very suicidal, disturbed." The profile was of a "possible borderline schizoid personality disorder."

After the defense began its case, Bozanich filed papers asking for complete access to all of Oziel's therapy records. She said that despite the state Supreme Court ruling releasing only one of Oziel's tapes, the defense had put the mental state of the brothers at issue by calling experts to testify about the psychological effects of their upbringing. As a result, she said, tapes of the other therapy sessions should be handed over. As always, the tape she wanted was the December 11 session, which contains the voices of the brothers.

Bozanich said the defense should not be allowed to put on only its selected psychological evidence. "The Menendez brothers bring into the trial their mental condition as evidence from the time they were small children up to the present," the prosecution said in a brief filed with the court. "Therefore, the records of all mental history throughout the pertinent period should be revealed."

Now the attorneys got down to arguing the matter before Weisberg. Michael Burt said the law requires turning over mental-state evidence in cases where there has been a mental diagnosis, such as insanity. But Burt said there had been no such diagnosis in this case.

Weisberg was skeptical. "I'd be hard pressed to find that you don't have that testimony," he said, recalling the array of evidence about beatings and other abuse from age zero onward.

But the defense had a fallback position. The December 11 taping session had apparently been arranged through Jerry Chaleff, Lyle's first attorney. He apparently intended to use the tape if Lyle and Erik were ever arrested and tried for their lives. Then the tape could be played during the penalty phase to show the young men in a sympathetic light. The fact that an attorney was connected with the session gave the defense the opportunity to claim not only a patient-therapist privilege but also an attorney-client privilege.

"Our position is there was a dual purpose at work here," said Burt.

Bozanich complained that the defense was raising a new issue that should have been brought up earlier.

Weisberg stared over the tops of his glasses and asked occasional questions. He frequently pursed his lips as he listened to the answers, but wanted to think things over before ruling.

The next day, a tattered backgammon box filled with Kitty's letters appeared in court. There had been occasional references to the box of letters during the trial, but now Jill Lansing asked Conte for his opinion of them.

Conte said he had read the letters, written in desperation after discovering Jose's affair, and they were consistent with his opinion that Kitty was "self-absorbed, histrionic." As for the letter to Summerfield, in which Kitty wrote about helping Erik with his essay, Conte said this was not a loving mother trying to be there for her son but a woman for whom "socially appropriate behavior is important."

Bozanich had read the letters and was so touched by them she cried. Hearing the psychologist pick them apart in clean, clinical language as evidence of a disordered mind infuriated her.

She began by asking Conte if he felt any compassion for this tortured woman. "Yeah," Conte said.

Bozanich pointed out that Kitty expressed love for her children in the letters. "I don't believe she loved her children," the white-haired, bearded man said firmly.

If Lyle was in such a state of fear, how could he think of picking up the shotgun shells for fear police might be able to lift his fingerprints from them?

"I don't know that's what he was thinking," Conte replied. "People do strange things in traumatic situations." For example, he talked about Jackie Kennedy trying to retrieve parts of her husband's skull after he was shot.

Did he think, the prosecutor asked sarcastically, that Lyle grabbing the shells was "analogous" to Jackie Kennedy's futile attempt to save her husband's life? Was Lyle afraid when he shot Jose in the back of the head?

"Confusion, fear, yes," Conte agreed.

At lunch, Bozanich was feeling confident enough that she had undermined the defense experts to decide not to call her psychological expert, who had sat in on much of the early portion of the trial.

She was even feeling gracious toward the defense. "Given

what they had to work with," Bozanich said, biting into a sandwich. "the defense has done as good a job as possible."

When Conte came back on the stand after lunch, Lansing took over the questioning. She asked if someone was going to make up charges of child abuse, what symptoms might they present? Conte said fakers often come up with flashbacks, which Lyle did not do.

Also, Lansing noted that neither Lyle nor Erik testified that there was a direct threat against their lives when the brothers ran to get their shotguns.

"If you're going to lie, that seems to be the time to come up with a really good, clear threat," Conte agreed.

This was an effective point. Many observers had been waiting eagerly for the revelation of what had preceded the slayings. The story the brothers had told verged on the incredible. Now Jill Lansing was making a positive out of it by arguing that it is so hard to believe that it must be true.

Kitty's older sister, Joan, appeared on the stand. She had gone through her sister's effects after her death and had been shocked to find in her nightstand a paperback novel she said was "sexually explicit." She also found a pornographic tape in the closet.

"I never told anybody" about it, Vander Molen said, sobbing. "All that was left of my sister was her image, and I was trying to protect her."

The appearance of Carlos Baralt, Jose's brother-in-law, on Wednesday, October 27, was like the arrival of a favorite relative. He was so genuinely well liked by both sides that the sense of lingering doubt and suspicion that hung in the halls outside Courtroom N evaporated. Before testifying, he stood in the hallway greeting, in his unassuming way, all the court watchers, writers, and television reporters. In a case where so much was hidden and where reality itself was in dispute, Baralt seemed like a minor wise man who had come to lead everyone closer to truth.

When Pam Bozanich got her turn with him, she asked if the family ever acted normal. She was trying to pierce the image painted by the defense of a twisted and sick family that, in another time, might have inhabited some stony castle on a windswept English moor, drunkenly pillaging the countryside and giving birth to idiot children.

"I would say most of the time," Baralt replied. They had visitors and there was laughter in the house, Baralt agreed. Then Bozanich asked if he was familiar with the way champion athletes are created.

"I have a daughter who excelled quite a bit in sports," Baralt said. "She had to practice every day for a number of hours after school."

This was the Menendez family Bozanich believed in, a family headed by a tough, demanding father, maybe, but one who loved his sons and devoted himself to their success.

Bozanich then asked if Erik's grandmother, Maria, used lemons in her cooking. "She put it on the meat," Baralt said.

Erik had testified that he ate lemon on his food to blunt the taste of his dad's semen, but the prosecution was suggesting that the fondness for lemon might have been a matter of family taste.

The defense may have wondered how the prosecution was getting inside information on the family, but there was no mystery. Maria Menendez apparently liked Bozanich. A friend of hers called the prosecution almost daily with tips, some of which were valuable. Others were less so.

Bozanich asked about the time Carlos and Terry were told during a jail visit that Erik and Lyle had been molested. "Erik was crying," Carlos Baralt said, and Lyle's voice broke as he explained. Erik said he had been molested by his father. Lyle said he had been molested by his mother.

30

Hard Evidence

Dr. Kerry English, a forthright man with iron gray hair who worked at Martin Luther King Hospital in South-Central Los Angeles, was on the stand only a brief time, but he supplied some of the most potentially important testimony for the defense.

English, the medical director of the suspected child abuse team, said he found no evidence that Erik had been sodomized. Physical evidence of molestation is rare. "The mucous membranes heal very quickly in the inner part of the anus," he explained.

But English had reviewed Erik's medical records from the time he was a child and found a reference in 1977 that got everyone's attention. "Hurt posterior pharynx, uvula and soft palate . . . healing well," it read.

Asked if such an injury to the back of the throat could be caused by child abuse, he said yes, "oral copulation."

Of course, there were other things that could have caused the injury—a Popsicle stick, for instance, during a fall. But it was a curious injury, and the first physical evidence on the abuse issue. Everything else had come from the brothers or from friends and relatives who had said they were given the information by the boys.

Terry Moran, the Court TV reporter, said all this was building up, and the sexual abuse issue was now like a big mound in the road. You can get around the mound, but eventually you have to acknowledge the mound is there. He had been convinced the sexual abuse charge was real.

Arrayed against this, of course, was the Jamie Pisarcik statement that Lyle had tried to bribe her to say Jose molested her. If the abuse was real, why would Lyle try to bribe his girlfriend to make up a story about Jose?

Michael Burt asked if there was anything else in the medical records that caught his attention. One thing he noticed was the sheer number of doctor visits. There also were references to headaches, teeth grinding, a speech articulation disorder, and stomach pains. Burt asked if a doctor looking at the range of symptoms would suspect child abuse.

"I'm not aware of any physician in the seventies [who] would ever have thought of the diagnosis of sex abuse," he said. "Today, a small percentage might make the connection."

Bozanich tried to salvage what she could of this witness, asking if there were other things besides oral copulation that could injure the back of the throat. "There are plenty of other accidents that could have caused the injury," he said.

Bozanich then asked if it appeared from the records that Lyle was taken to the doctor a lot. "It did," English said. This was a point for the prosecution on one of the most critical issues, the character of Kitty. The defense was portraying Kitty as an uncaring mother who left her children's wounds unstitched.

As English left the stand, however, the throat injury hovered in the air.

In a hearing outside the presence of the jury, Bozanich pressed her attempt to get her hands on the crucial December 11 Oziel tape, where the brothers are heard speaking about the murders. Weisberg said he would like to listen to the tape before ruling, but the defense had so far not handed it over.

Burt said the defense would consider Weisberg's request overnight. He said privately that the tape was not the smoking gun—or in the words of one of the writers, "smoking tennis racket"—that some people thought.

Outside court that afternoon, fall was in the air, and a cool breeze was blowing across the courtyard. The Court TV correspondent stood shifting from one foot to the other, microphone in hand, getting ready for his daily wrap-up. Just then a woman with long dark dark hair and a lush British accent, who had become a kind of go-between for the brothers and their growing cadre of fans, walked up.

Erik, she said, was upset about all the talk that he was gay. He's not gay, she said, and she hoped that Moran could get that

message out. Moran smiled, but did not commit to broadcasting
Erik's message to the world. This was not public-access TV.

Ed Fenno, a slender, good-looking young man who had been
a onetime house guest of the Menendezes, was an important
witness because he could shed new light on the matter of Erik's
college education. A tennis-playing friend of the brothers, he
had nonetheless told the prosecution that Jose was disappointed
when Erik turned down an opportunity to attend UC Berkeley
in favor of UCLA. This would undermine the defense contention
that Jose wanted Erik nearby so he could molest him.

On the stand, Fenno said he stayed several months at the
mansion, beginning in the fall of 1988, and lived down the hall
from Erik. When Jose wanted to have a talk with Erik, he would
ask Fenno to leave and then he shut the door. He also said
that when he was there, Jose and Kitty locked their bedroom
door regularly.

These things supported the defense case.

Asked about a dinner table discussion of Erik's acceptance at
college, Fenno said Kitty and Jose "were very excited" when he
was accepted at the University of California, Berkeley, which
Jose thought was better academically than UCLA.

But Erik told Fenno he preferred UCLA, which had a better
tennis program. "One of the reasons I stayed after Christmas
was so Erik could train and get a national ranking" so UCLA
would recruit him and he would not have to be a walk-on,
Fenno said.

He was asked whether he had told Zoeller in an interview that
Jose was upset when Erik turned down Berkeley. Fenno couldn't
remember. "I may have," he said. But now, he said, he didn't
know exactly if Erik turned Berkeley down.

When Bozanich took over, she asked if he ever saw Erik lie
to his parents. It was "somewhat common," he said for both
brothers to lie. He mentioned a time when Lyle was driving his
father's Cadillac and sideswiped something, knocking the side
mirror off. "He told some other story," Fenno said. It was
reasonably detailed, he said.

Kitty's therapists were set to take the stand, beginning with
Dr. Edwin Cox, who had seen her just after the family moved to
California. Kitty had been referred to him by her East Coast
therapist, who feared she might commit suicide.

Cox considered her talk of suicide to be serious, not just a

bluff. She had thought of ways to do it. Kitty was so obsessed
with Louise, Cox noted, that she went to New York, stood
outside Louise's residence, and, when Louise came out, walked
by her to get a good look at the woman.

Cox agreed that she had a dependence on alcohol and was
proud it was a classy alcohol, cognac.

Bozanich asked if it was unusual for a woman to be depressed
after discovering her husband had been involved in a long-
term affair.

"No," Cox said.

Cox's appearance gave her the opportunity to go through
portions of his therapeutic notes that could undermine the
defense contention that Kitty hated Lyle.

One portion read "excited about Lyle arriving tonight."

The next defense witness was Jose's number two man at
LIVE, Roger Smith, a plump man with a gray beard who parted
his hair down the middle.

Smith had no affection for Jose, even four years dead. Jose,
he said, leaning slightly forward as he talked, was "totally
controlling, belittling" and used fear to keep people in their
places.

Jose often had a way of entrapping people, leading them down
a path that began with a reasonable statement and ending with a
conclusion that made them look foolish.

"The worst thing you could ever do," in Jose's opinion, "was
to show vulnerability, concern for the other person's point
of view."

Asked about Jose's attitude toward his sons, Smith said Jose
talked frequently about instilling character in his son. "It was a
subject of great importance to him," Smith said. "It struck me
as hypocritical."

He was asked about a comment Jose supposedly made one
time about Lyle: "You are my son, you must be me."

"Yes," Smith agreed. "They had to be winners. He thought
of himself as a winner."

But that remark went beyond the concept of winning and
losing. In combination with all the other things Jose had said and
done, the remark seemed to indicate that Jose wanted to live
not only in his own time, but also in Lyle's, and in Lyle's body.
This sounded like a spiritual body snatch on his own son.

* * *

As court ended one Friday, the British woman stopped by Terry Moran's spot to deliver another missive from the brothers. She said they were being deluged by letters and wanted to thank everyone, and they would reply to them as their "stamp situation" allowed. It sounded like the kind of thing a publicist for a Hollywood star often says when a performer is in the hospital, recovering from an injury.

The sideshow elements of the trial continued proliferating. One reporter said she saw a car with a banner in the window that said, "I believe Erik and Lyle." The car also had a bumper sticker reading, "I Love Hannibal Lechter."

A woman, rumored to be the disturbed daughter of wealthy parents, had come to the courthouse looking for information on the way Lyle and Erik dressed, not just the sweaters but detailed things, so that she could costume herself properly for Halloween, which was Sunday. She was going to trick-or-treat along Elm Drive.

Sure enough, Halloween night—the fourth anniversary of the day that Erik had confessed to Oziel—produced a raft of Erik and Lyle lookalikes. None of them was seen on Elm Drive. Most of the trick-or-treaters there were poor minority kids bused in from other parts of the city in the expectation that Beverly Hills candy would be the best of all. Like whistling past the graveyard, some of them walked up to the locked iron gates, peeked inside the courtyard lighted by several small lamps, and then ran off in search of goodies. Tour buses stop there now, one mother said.

More colorful and bizarre was the Halloween Carnival in West Hollywood. Along with the transvestite Disney characters—the evil queen in *Sleeping Beauty* and Cruella Deville out of *101 Dalmations*—walked a pair of upright young men with blue and gold sweaters tied around their necks. Their hair was close-cropped and they looked as wholesome as any kid out of a sixties sitcom. The only elements of their costume that looked like a costume were the little plastic guns under their arms. Each wore a tag on his sleeve identifying himself as Erik and Lyle Menendez.

Brent Sverdloff and Craig St. John were skilled in Menendez trivia. Brent, who came as Erik, knew the younger brother's correct age and even the address of the Elm Drive mansion.

St. John said the case fascinated him because "their story is so outrageous and it gets more outrageous as time goes on."

"The defense experts sound so ad hoc," said Sverdloff. "It's like a man who's having an affair and making up lies."

Both said they felt the abuse allegations in the case were so excessive and grotesque and hard to believe that the case seemed to have come untethered from reality. The proceedings had more in common with the theater than a search for truth.

"There's something so offensive about it," Sverdloff said.

Back in court, Weisberg turned to the matter that had been hanging over the trial for weeks, the question of whether the prosecution would get its hands on the December 11 tape.

Beginning with a careful recitation of the history of the thorny issue, Weisberg described the rulings by the Superior Court, the Court of Appeal, and finally the state Supreme Court. He said that he had kept in mind the Supreme Court ruling and enforced it throughout the trial, even when it appeared the defense was using the fact that those sessions were privileged as a weapon to somehow portray Oziel's testimony in a different light. It was only after the psychologists and the defendants had testified that the court felt it could rule on the issue of whether the defense had put the defendants' mental condition at issue.

"The court found that what had been tendered here was the mental and emotional condition of the defendants. And I'm quite satisfied that that is what occurred, and I'm quite satisfied that that ruling is a correct ruling."

Turning to the attorney-client privilege. "I think all counsel would agree this is a unique situation, one that factually has not been addressed by any other case in any other context."

Then he said firmly that he believed the December 11 session was "not a confidential communication between a client and a lawyer" and was not protected by the attorney-client privilege.

Wearing her disappointment on her dress, Abramson appeared outside the court that day wearing a blue ribbon with a broken chain, the symbol of a campaign against inter-generational child abuse.

31

Courage Beyond Belief

The next day, a cool Thursday in Los Angeles, Leslie Abramson was not in court. She was adopting a baby, which was being born that morning. She was in the delivery room, it was said, when the court called to find out why she was not at the courthouse.

The baby was a boy, seven pounds five ounces.

The day after that, Erik Menendez was not in court. He had suffered a kidney injury in jail and was bleeding into his urine. "It's not life-threatening," Abramson said, but the doctors wanted him to rest. He was taken to the Los Angeles County Medical Center for treatment in the jail ward.

Abramson said he bruised his kidney in a fall. The trial, now in its fourth month, had ground to a halt. Bozanich compared it to purgatory. "We're never going to get out of here," she sighed.

The length and complexity of the trial, and preparation for it, was reflected in the billings by the co-counsels for the defense, Burt and Marcia Morrissey. While Abramson and Lansing were paid by the estate, Burt and Morrissey drew their checks from the county. This is because the law allows two defense counsel in death penalty cases. Through September 10, Burt had been paid $22,505, while Morrissey had received $88,586.

A court official said that every attempt would be made after the case was over to recover from the estate the money paid to Burt and Morrissey. But it was beginning to seem less and less likely that there would be anything to divide.

Money was also on the minds of the prosecution as the trial sank into a hiatus. Southern California's sluggish economy had pinched the county's budget. "The D.A.'s office has had budget-ary constraints as long as I've had the case," Bozanich said.

Unlike the defense attorneys, funded by the Menendez es-tate, the prosecution was unable to fly around the country interviewing witnesses. "We basically relied on Detective Zoell-er's interviews," Bozanich said.

She liked to refer to the case as the K-Mart prosecution, something that bothered Kuriyama, who wanted a more upscale title. "A cafeteria then," Bozanich suggested. "We're self-serve."

Lyle's attorneys were finally ready to play the December 11 tape. Jill Lansing called Jon Conte back to the stand to try to explain to the jury that what they were about to hear was not what it sounded like, but a script arranged by Jerry Oziel. The defense theory of the earlier sessions had been that Lyle and Erik didn't want to tell their therapist the real cause of the murders, so they went along with Oziel's theory that Kitty's was a mercy killing and Jose was killed because he was controlling.

The tape, said Conte, "raises more questions about Dr. Oziel's technique." He said there were boundary violations of the therapeutic relationship. Many of the things on the tape did not comport with his understanding of the relationships in the family.

"The essential idea that Mom was killed out of mercy I consider to be psychologically naive and not consistent with anything else that was said," Conte charged.

Finally he said the tape "doesn't alter my understanding of what happened."

Then the tape itself was played through a boom box on the witness stand. The sound was bad and the voices were fuzzy, but the jurors were given transcripts to read. As the muffled words tumbled out of the tinny speakers, the jurors bent over the forty-seven-page document. Most showed no reaction, but one woman, an alternate who looked like a businesswoman in glasses and a well-cut blazer, allowed a small smirk to show on her face. As the sixty-one-minute-long tape proceeded, the smirk took root and flowered into a full smile of derogation.

The tape began with a statement by Oziel that his feeling was that there was no real Menendez family, and that the only members with a real bond were Lyle and Erik. Lyle agreed, saying that when Erik found a suicide note from Kitty in a drawer, that "created a huge bond" because Erik called Lyle for help in dealing with their mother.

"What it said is 'I'm sorry I had to do this. I love you both, Lyle and Erik. I love your father. I just can't seem to deal with my own problems anymore,' " Erik said.

But she couldn't go through with it. According to Erik, he listened to Kitty for months after she discovered Jose's affair. "I would come home, my mother would be crying upstairs, and I would be watching TV downstairs, and I would just hear the sobbing and I couldn't go up and see what was wrong."

Oziel asked if they felt like they were sparing Kitty by killing her. Erik said they believed there was no way Kitty could go on living without Jose.

Kitty was "a big thing holding us back" from killing Jose, Lyle said. At first they thought they would just kill Jose and "eliminate the problem," apparently referring to Jose's controlling his children and wife. But there was Kitty to think about.

After finding the suicide note, Lyle went to Kitty to say he would support her if she moved out. But Kitty cut him off. "Lyle, you're fabricating this," she said. Then she brought up the issue of Lyle's girlfriends and the conversation ended, and Lyle said she lost his support.

"I was, you know, gradually being separated from her." And her depression got worse and worse, he said.

Lyle said that he felt, in the end, that he was an instrument of his mother's suicide. "That's where we sort of feel like, you mentioned before, that we were doing her and us a favor. In putting her out of her misery really."

On some level, he felt bad about killing her. "It's a serious sore spot," he said.

But then he launched into a recitation of Kitty's failed life. She worked "like a dog" taking care of the house and children, and Jose refused to take her out places and had affairs. He said his mother could have had a career, but Jose did not allow it. "Dad gave me an ultimatum," she told Lyle. "Take care of the kids and stay home and forget the acting."

Jose, said Lyle, never accommodated himself to Kitty's needs. He tried to tell his father to compromise and go out to some of the dinner parties Kitty enjoyed in Pennington, but his feeling was, "One person controls the show. If I have to do things I don't want to do, even the smallest things, then I don't wanna be a part of the relationship."

Oziel wanted to know how much of the reason for killing Jose was linked to what he was doing to him and Erik and how much was over the way he treated Kitty.

Lyle said the decision to kill Jose had nothing to do with him and Erik. He had already splintered off from the family. "I decided at one point I don't want another cent," he said.

But Kitty was deteriorating, he said. This was even though it appeared to many people outside the family that Kitty had gotten over the affairs. Friends said Kitty and Jose had never been closer at the end.

"We didn't want to get to a point where my mother would kill herself," Lyle said. He didn't want Jose to get away with what he thought would amount to murdering Kitty.

"And so, for my mother's sake, I thought that we did it, we had to come like I was saying before, we had to make a decision. It was one of the harder ones."

Oziel wanted to know what Jose had been doing that caused them to decide to kill him. He suggested Jose's controlling nature, as well as his threats to disinherit them.

Lyle said the threats didn't have much to do with the decision, because Lyle felt he and Erik were strong. Jose, he said, "had raised us to handle doing this thing that was necessary, and that he could deal with it better than any other eighteen- or twenty-one-year-old in the country. 'Cause he had trained us like basic training."

Oziel suggested Jose and Lyle never had a loving bond, but Lyle wasn't completely sold on that idea. He said he felt close to his father at times—they even watched the Super Bowl together—and Jose had cried after the burglaries. "That was the first time he ever cried in front of me," Lyle said.

This was no doubt a shock to the jurors, who had until then heard Jose portrayed as a cold, unemotional machine of a man. But it could have shown just how desperate Jose was growing as he watched the boy he worshiped turn into a deadbeat. Oziel pressed further to understand why Jose had to die. Was it because the boys could never satisfy him?

Lyle agreed, noting that Jose had even criticized Erik for mucking up the burglaries. "If he were in charge of it, he could have handled it way better than Erik."

But even that, Lyle said, was not the reason for killing him. "I still don't think it had anything to do with—killing him had nothing to do with us. It had to do with me realizing a number of things that all culminated, which was, and could have culminated at any point. And it was just a question of Erik and I getting together, and somebody bringing it up, and us realizing the value in it."

Then he returned to Jose's treatment of Kitty, which apparently was a central reason for killing him. He mentioned Jose's plan to go into politics, which would have hurt her worse than the affairs, and the move from New Jersey, which also had saddened her. He also said Jose had Kitty convinced the family had no money. She felt she could not afford tennis lessons and buy clothes. "And I remember a day when I said, 'Come on, Mom.' 'Cause I had bought something. 'How can you say I can't afford this when Dad just got a stock bonus of, worth $6 million?' "

Lyle assumed Jose kept Kitty in the dark in case they divorced. The truth was, though, the family was in financial straits, with two big mortgages to pay. "They were up to their ears in debt," said one person familiar with the details of the Menendez household.

Jose was even delinquent on his taxes. After he died, the estate had to pay $1 million in back taxes to the IRS. But Lyle couldn't believe the money stream could run dry.

Oziel turned to Erik, who had been silent during much of his brother's lengthy remarks. Erik said he didn't like hearing the bad things about his father. "I may not have had a choice at the time" about killing them, "but I regret it now."

He said he liked the feeling he had that his mother and father loved each other and loved him.

"And it's more difficult because of my mother, because I realize what an amazing tragedy of her life was compared to what it could have been. Because of my father. And I hate him for that. And I love him. And it was something that was beyond control."

"What was beyond control? That you had to kill him?"

"Eventually it had to happen," Erik replied.

Erik said he was having bad dreams. "I had a dream where I was trying to convince two of my friends to shoot me. And they wouldn't do it. No matter how hard I tried to convince them, so I took the gun that was in my hand, and shot myself several times in the heart, and then I died, and there was a moment where there is just immense pleasure. . . . And everything was calm and everything was great. And then I woke up in the morning, and I was upset that I was alive."

Erik said he was worried at one point that Lyle might kill himself after the murders. Trying to do some therapy, Oziel asked Erik to tell Lyle he was worried about him. Erik began crying, and Lyle said, "I know."

Lyle said the whole family worked "behind closed doors," but he would like to be closer with Erik. He cited examples where they were not close, but then he began talking about the way their relationship worked that made them sound far closer than mumbling some simple phrases of trust would make them.

"We've sort of worked out some strange relationship where we can convey that, like you said, without having to say it face to face."

Oziel wanted to get them to confront each other, but Lyle said they "hate that hugging shit."

Lyle said he felt that his mother's death was really a suicide.

"Because I, you know, I feel that in her letters to Erik and I, she gave me the permission . . . to sort of, she had given me permission to, to, to please carry out her suicide, and that it was obvious that she had decided in her own mind, she wants to die."

But she couldn't do it, and other family members didn't help. "I had a lot of anger toward my relatives. And my uncles and my aunts. My Uncle Carlos and Aunt Terry, he knew about what was happening to my mother, and did nothing. I just think they were cowards. That what Erik and I did took courage beyond belief."

Lyle said he didn't want to influence Erik unduly in the decision to kill, so he let him sleep on it a couple of days. He said that, in the end, he did what he thought Kitty would have wanted him to do. He said it was only after Kitty refused to leave Jose and return to Princeton and remarry that the situation became dangerous.

"Where Erik and I realized that at any point, sort of subconsciously, the go-ahead was given to 'kill us, to kill me, before you leave.' "

Lyle said it was done quickly and "sort of callously almost" because if they had thought about it too much and considered what it would be like not to have their parents around, that would get in the way of "what was more important. Which was helping your mother really."

This sounded an awful lot like Oziel's statement on the earlier tape that when they had got involved in planning a crime, nothing could stop them. Throughout the playing of the tape, Lyle leaned close to Jill Lansing and read the transcript coolly, betraying no emotion.

The final decision to do the killings sounded almost casual. "It was a little word here, a little word there," he said, noting that it was "almost as if a third party was discussing. And it was just a meeting of the minds. The time is now."

After it was over, Erik was sad. But Lyle's pain was different. He said "you miss just having these people around. I miss not having my dog around. If I can make such a gross analogy."

Gasps were heard as that remark echoed around the courtroom.

The defense theory had been that Oziel, Svengali-like, had influenced the brothers to create a fictional version of events. But on the tape, while Oziel had tried at times to guide the discussion, Lyle in particular hadn't seemed to need much prompting. Oziel hadn't put the words in his mouth when Lyle bragged that he and Erik showed great courage by killing their mother. Nor could he be heard prompting Lyle to compare the deaths of his parents to losing his dog.

Furthermore, there was a chilling, monotonal quality to Lyle's voice as he spoke. There was an emptiness and hollowness to it that seemed to imply that nothing lived inside that voice.

The description of the thought process leading up to the murders was perhaps most frightening in its simplicity. There was a little word here, a little word there, and the two boys reached a meeting of the minds to kill both their parents. Before the twisted majesty of such a concept, Oziel seemed naïve suggesting that Erik tell Lyle he loved him so they could be closer. If Lyle's description was accurate, they were already locked in a macabre spiritual embrace. And Erik once more was in Lyle's thrall. He said he wanted to believe he had a good family, but there was Lyle telling him this problem had to be taken care of.

There was no reference to sexual abuse. Jose had to die, according to the tape, because he was controlling the lives of his family and, even more, because he was a bad husband.

Jill Lansing brought Conte back to reinterpret the tape. He called the therapeutic relationship "inappropriate" and said he didn't "put much faith" in the session.

Bozanich grilled Conte relentlessly, pointing out inconsistencies between the tape and the defense characterization of the family, such as Lyle's remark about Jose crying.

Bozanich noted at one point that Lyle said he would not make the decision to kill Kitty without letting Erik think about it. Isn't that premeditation? Bozanich demanded.

Conte said, "That's not consistent with anything I've learned in this case."

Then she asked about Lyle's reference to missing his parents like his dog.

"I thought it was, as he says, a gross analogy," Conte replied.

Bozanich asked if he was being paid, and Conte briefly appeared to lose his temper. "I got paid for seventy hours in 1992," he said. He said that with all the time he had donated, he probably earned about $7 an hour. He said he would not "stake my reputation" if he didn't believe Lyle was telling the truth.

Shifting gears, the prosecutor asked if his opinion would change if he found that Erik had found Lyle had a hairpiece before the night of the alleged confrontation in which Kitty supposedly ripped it off his head. Bozanich had a witness who remembered Erik talking about the hairpiece months before the killings.

"It might," Conte said.

Outside the courthouse, Conte, a genuinely kind man who looked a little like Edmund Gwenn in *Miracle on 34th Street*, said he thought the tape had "sunk them. But then, they were probably already sunk."

He also said he considered Bozanich the best prosecutor he had ever come up against, though he thought she could be nasty.

As for Lyle Menendez, he said he had found him to be a sincere, gentle person.

Lansing left court that evening in the face of a chill north wind, hurrying along the sidewalk with her head down. The tape, she said simply, "is what it is." But, she said, it didn't make sense. The whole idea of a mercy killing was crazy, she said.

Throughout the trial there had been references to threats of suicide and suicide attempts by Kitty, but little hard evidence that Kitty had ever acted on her threats, at least until Dr. Warden Hamlin Emory took the stand.

Emory was a tall man with a cheerful disposition who showed up one afternoon in tennis shoes and a suit. His house had burned to the ground in the fires that had recently ravaged some of Southern California's most beautiful canyons, and what he had on was about all he had left, other than a cheery smile that belied the trouble he had just been through.

Lightly, standing out in the hallway before being called to the stand, Emory described the tsunami of flame that came roaring up the canyon toward his house above Malibu. "I flew in Vietnam, and I never saw anything like that," he said.

A true West Coast survivor, he said he would rebuild, in the same place. In another canyon, Maria Menendez, Jose's mother, had refused to leave the Calabasas house that was about all that remained of the estate. Courageous as ever, she stood out front with a garden hose while flames swept by her gate.

Emory had been on duty November 8, 1987, when Kitty Menendez was brought into the Westlake Community Hospital suffering from acute Xanax and alcohol ingestion. When Emory saw her, she was in the intensive care ward. Jose was there part of the time. After an examination, Emory wrote in her chart that Kitty was suffering from panic attacks—a feeling of terror that can leave the victim convinced she is about to die of a heart attack—for which she was treated with an antidepressant and the mild tranquilizer, Xanax.

She had taken "an excessive amount" of Xanax but was not suicidal, according to the chart. Emory had written that he suspected a personality disorder, by which he meant someone who was excessively cold, angry, or fear-ridden. "So we have the odd, the angry, and the fearful," he said.

In Kitty's case, he said, she trivialized her problems. She also upset the staff by trying to sneak some pills, according to a nurse's note. Despite this, Kitty and Jose decided that they didn't want her to stay in the hospital.

"If there is a form to sign, give it to me," one of them demanded. "We're leaving."

After that, Emory had seen Kitty from time to time to adjust her medication. Over the next few months, what struck him most about his patient was that she seemed "inordinately more distressed" than most people with her symptoms. Emory never understood why she was so troubled, a cue for the defense theory of inter-generational child abuse.

Implanted Memories

Next into the breach was Judalon Smyth, Oziel's old paramour. Even though she had been the one who, as she put it in a fax to the court one day, handed the prosecution the "guilty parties on a silver platter," she was now a defense witness brought in to further attack the trial's Great Satan—Jerry Oziel.

In the topsy-turvy world of the Menendez trial, it was fitting. Oziel, who had refused to go to the police and only reluctantly turned over his tape recordings, had become a prosecution witness.

Judalon Smyth, an attractive woman with dark hair and a prim, little-girl way of speaking and standing very straight when she talked that gave the impression she wanted to please, gave two days of testimony that disavowed many things attributed to her in the past. Back then, she said, she was brainwashed, and so the things she said weren't really coming from her but from Jerry Oziel.

Smyth, dressed in an aqua suit and clutching a small round purse, was asked by Michael Burt to describe how she met Oziel. She said she called Oziel's office. When he called her back, a relationship began that "flip-flopped" back and forth between therapy and "his idea that he was my ideal person romantically."

In contrast to Oziel's testimony that she was obsessed with him, Smyth claimed that Oziel pressured her so severely that he sometimes kept her on the phone all night, "badgering and haranguing, and manipulating."

Their relationship had become sexual when she and Oziel

returned from a trip to Arizona in late October and discovered that Erik Menendez wanted to talk with him. From Judalon's house, Oziel called Erik and set up an appointment.

Her version of the Halloween night confession was somewhat different now. Smyth said she heard Lyle yelling at his brother but, significantly, now claimed she did not hear him directly threaten Oziel.

The comment Lyle made at the elevator—"Good luck, Dr. Oziel"—was not a threat either. Now Lyle was simply trying to get away from the doctor. Oziel had called Lyle "menacing," but Smyth said he didn't seem that way to her.

Further, Smyth said, the $14 million estate was on Oziel's mind. He felt Lyle and Erik would need his guidance in deciding how to invest their money. He also told her that if she and Oziel needed any money to start a business, he would persuade the brothers to put some up.

On November 2, Smyth said, Oziel was so eager to have her at his office that he drove her there. Arriving an hour early, they did some shopping on Wilshire Boulevard first.

"Did he seem fearful during the period of time that you two were shopping?" Burt asked.

"He didn't seem any different than normal."

Judalon Smyth was systematically tearing down piece after piece of the prosecution case, a case that she had helped to make.

Next, Smyth said Oziel kept talking to her about wanting to get control of the brothers, even suggesting that she bug his office so he could tape-record them without their knowledge. This idea fit well with the defense theory that Oziel had ulterior motives for keeping the brothers in therapy.

As for the crucial December 11 tape, she said Oziel told the brothers it would be made in case they were arrested, so it could be played before the jury to show they were remorseful. But his real motive, she enunciated in a breathy voice, was to get them to say incriminating things so he would have the tape as protection.

He also said it was "a blessing" that Lyle and Erik killed their parents because he could use it to convince his wife that they should divorce for safety's sake.

Then Burt led Smyth through a brief history of her relationship with Oziel to try to show him as a manipulator. Asked by Burt if there was a time in the relationship where she was feeling love for Oziel, she replied that she had been "slipping nto something called a Stockholm syndrome," referring to kidnap victims who identify with their captives.

Then one of the comedic low points was reached when Burt played a tape of one of Oziel's phone calls, in which he burst into song when she said her father, Jim, was coming to visit.

"Just tell her Jim said hello," he sings in a husky Elvis imitation. "She's sitting right over there. I'd know that face anywhere. Just tell her Jim said hello. Just tell her Jim and she'll know."

After several minutes of this, Weisberg irritatedly ordered Burt to turn it off, complaining this was just wasting time. Burt said the prosecution had no objection, but Weisberg snapped, "Well, the court does."

Burt convinced the judge that there was just a little more he wanted to play. The two voices chat about how well their bodies fit together, and Oziel growls. Then Smyth asks how soon he would divorce his wife. Oziel says his wife doesn't want the divorce, then suggests that Smyth call her up and pretend to be Erik, threatening, "I'm going to kill you."

This was the conversation Oziel denied earlier, calling it "absurd." But playing it wasn't necessarily a victory for the defense, because it sounded like he was joking, not seriously planning to put his patients on his wife's trail.

As the hours dragged by in court, more tapes were played and listeners became familiar with Oziel's low voice, sometimes chiding, other times urgent, and Smyth's girlish, coquettish whispers.

"We're going to be stars, not exactly for the right reasons," he says on a tape not long after the police searched his house. "You better get on your makeup and put your dark glasses on. . . There have been hundreds of photographers following me everywhere. It's awful, it's just awful."

On another tape, he urges that they go into a "survival" mode to avoid becoming another Donald and Ivana Trump, referring to the media sensation attending the breakup of the Trumps' marriage.

As the relationship spiraled downward, Oziel is heard complaining that "you've done a lot of horrible things. Anybody else probably would have killed you by now."

The twin themes emerging from her testimony were that Oziel had manipulated and bullied Smyth into a relationship and that many of her earlier statements about what she knew about Lyle and Erik were mistaken.

Judalon Smyth brought a lot of baggage into court. She had signed a lengthy affidavit for the police, had testified in a closed hearing before Judge Albracht on the admissibility of the tapes, and was heard on seven hours of tape-recorded conversations with Zoeller shortly after she went to the police in early March. Besides those things, she had appeared on television. Burt took time to address each issue.

Of the taped interview, Smyth said the police did not ask her to differentiate between what she heard herself while eavesdropping and what Oziel told her, though a look at the transcript shows them specifically asking what she heard. Of the affidavit, which quoted her as saying she "heard a detailed description of the killings," she said the statement contained "inaccuracies."

But the biggest problem was the court hearing, when Smyth testified under oath and gave a very intimate description of what she heard. "When I was in that courtroom I was very frightened and I did something which I later learned was disassociating."

Further, there was the statement to Diane Sawyer of *Prime-Time Live*, who asked if the brothers were proud of what they did. She replied, "Absolutely. They felt they had committed the perfect crime."

This was a dangerous statement because it bolstered Oziel. "Actually, the word absolutely is an Oziel word, and so my answer is really a programmed Oziel answer that I gave," she said to Burt.

At the time she said those things she believed them. But after being in therapy "we have worked on sorting out what I was brainwashed with and what was real."

To be fair to Smyth, whether you believed it or not, this was not exactly a new assertion on her behalf. She had accused Oziel of similar behavior when the police first taped her.

Burt asked if Oziel ever told her he was trying to advise the brothers on how to get rid of the guns. Smyth said yes, a strikingly damning statement on Oziel's ethics if true. It did not comport with the defendants' own statements, however. They said they got rid of the guns the night of the killings. Like so many other things about the case, this detail, never followed up, was a wild card. Once put in play, it was impossible to guess whose hand it strengthened.

Bozanich was fuming over Smyth recanting her earlier statements, and she thought she knew why it was happening. Smyth, she believed, was angry at the D.A.'s office for not filing rape charges against Oziel. Smyth had accused him of attacking her on several occasions and wanted him prosecuted. Bozanich had referred the case to the D.A.'s sex-crimes division, which ultimately had rejected the case for insufficient evidence. It would have been her word against his, Bozanich said. But Smyth apparently came to feel that she was less important to the prosecution than Oziel, who became a chief prosecution witness.

When Bozanich began her cross-examination, she pulled no punches, dragging out a note entitled "The Most Official Sex I.O.U."

"Did you execute this particular document?" Bozanich asked, straight-faced. Smyth said she had.

"And it seems to be witnessed by two people—two people with paw prints; is that correct?"

"Two cats," Smyth corrected. She had simulated the prints of her pets, Shantih and Ishi. The note read, "This I.O.U. is to certify that Judalon Rose Smyth owes Jerry Oziel 500 sex acts to be paid in full over the period of 105 years or life, whichever comes first. Until this I.O.U. is paid in full the giving and the acceptance of this I.O.U. grants exclusive rights to any and all sexual activity on both parties' side until the debt is satisfied."

Smyth said she had been playing a game with Oziel, and he demanded the I.O.U. as payment for losing. "This is what he wanted," she replied primly.

Bozanich asked her if Oziel twisted her arm to write the note. She said no.

Then Bozanich showed her a Valentine's Day card that seemed to contradict Smyth's claim that she became a virtual prisoner of the therapist. "It's hard for me to imagine life before you or without you," she wrote. He was "always in my heart . . . even in the crazy, neurotic episodes I impose on you."

Bozanich asked if she was forced to write that note, which was sent to Oziel's office, and she said she was frightened into writing it because Oziel was displeased with the first card she sent. "I was just trying to cover myself. Because when I displeased him, he said there was no reason for me to be alive."

Bozanich, showing a trace of irritation, said another reason for sending a second card was that she didn't want her lover to open a mushy card in front of his wife.

Smyth dismissed that. "Oh," she smirked, "Laurel and I talked about sex with Oziel quite often. So there wouldn't have been a problem with a mushy card in front of Laurel."

Bozanich asked about the extensive testimony Smyth gave before Judge Albracht in July 1990. Smyth said she testified truthfully, as she knew it then. Bozanich asked if her memory was better three years later.

"In some aspects, yes, because I now have my own memory, not the memory Oziel planted in me."

Over and over Bozanich read aloud portions of Smyth's various public and private statements about the killings and about Lyle's threats. She was not doing it merely to impeach Smyth, but to bring in damning statements the jury had never heard. Even though Smyth was now saying they were not true, their cumulative impact could weigh on the jurors.

One particularly gory section included a description of the bodies after the shooting. "Parts of the body were severed. The arm was shot off. The mother's head was blown off or badly shot up. The defendant spoke of the eyeball coming out of the eye socket, the parts of brains on the wall. . . . After they were sure they dead, they took off their clothes and placed them in plastic bags they had taken to the room for this purpose, knowing the event would be bloody. . . . I believe the defendants stated that they showered before changing clean clothes."

Smyth once again said this was told to her by Oziel, not something she knew on her own. "I was not myself for quite some time," she explained. She said she was suffering from post-traumatic stress disorder when she made many of the statements.

"Are you yourself now?"

Bozanich asked about Smyth's phony suicide attempt. Smyth had opened up her oven and lain on the floor for Oziel to find her.

"Well, first you have to understand that for Jerry Oziel love equals suicide."

Bozanich asked if she testified privately before Albracht that Oziel had patients who were "hit men and he never tells their secrets."

Smyth said Oziel told her about the hit men. "He also made a point that he had said it to Lyle and Erik."

Bozanich asked about Smyth's *PrimeTime* interview. Smyth said after she went to the authorities, she was promised that they would take care of her, but she ended up feeling "abandoned and left to fend for myself against Oziel." Fearful, she decided to go public.

The prosecutor wanted to know if Smyth's primary motivation in going to the public was to have Oziel arrested—not to reveal the crimes of the Menendez brothers. "He was the one who committed crimes against me," she said, "not Lyle or Erik Menendez."

A hush fell over the court. Bozanich went on, "And you were disappointed when the district attorney's office failed to" prosecute Oziel.

"I am very upset that the law seems to decide who they will prosecute and who they won't prosecute," Smyth responded.

Bozanich noted that Smyth had sued Oziel. In fact, she had sued him a second time just days before her testimony, accusing him of assaulting her during a meeting at the offices of a Los Angeles law firm. According to the suit, he pushed against her and whispered, "You slut. You know you still want me." Oziel denied it.

She had no interest in the money, Smyth said. She just wanted to bring attention to her charges against Oziel. But the prosecution, who wanted Oziel as a witness, "wanted to whitewash him and make him look like a good person, when he was not."

Bozanich asked if she wasn't told the accusation would be hard to prove. "Were you told that it would be your word against his?"

Smyth said she was told that if Oziel had to be given immunity, that would be done. She was sick of the "behind-the-scenes" things going on between Oziel and the prosecution.

Bozanich was losing her temper. "You understand Dr. Oziel was not given immunity in this case."

"And we both know why," Smyth said.

The comment hung in the air like smoke. The jury must have been wondering what this meant, and Burt followed up on it when his turn came to question Smyth again.

He asked her why she distrusted the prosecution. "Because I know that Ms. Bozanich would lie . . . that she would deny something she said to me, and that she would make me out to be a liar if I repeated it."

That was enough. Bozanich marched up to see the judge. "Now I'm going to have to testify," Bozanich fumed. "Considering the perjury going on promulgated by the defense, I really find it offensive."

Abramson said Smyth was talking about a conversation with Bozanich in which the prosecutor supposedly told her that if the case against Oziel were filed, the D.A.'s office would have to grant him immunity because of his importance to the Menendez case. Further, Smyth reportedly claimed that Bozanich prevented the state attorney general's office from pursuing a criminal investigation of Oziel. In her three-page fax to the court, Smyth accused the prosecution of trying to stop the medical board from revoking Oziel's license until the trial ended and participating in character assassination against her.

"Without my action there would be no trial," she said in the fax. Then she added, "I prefer not to be involved, but I do have some evidence that suggests Oziel could have influenced the boys to believe that their parents were a threat to them, when in fact they were not."

Bozanich told the judge she had done the opposite of what Smyth was alleging. Further, the medical board had pursued the licensure charges against Oziel. This debate never reached the jurors' ears. The judge decided to strike Smyth's answer about Bozanich and the trial rumbled on, one more flat tire patched up.

"Isn't it true that the reason you're saying these things about Dr. Oziel is because you were in love with him and he was married and he wouldn't divorce his wife and marry you?" Bozanich demanded, wrapping up.

"No, that is not true at all," Smyth replied tartly, drawing up a little. He wanted to marry her, she said, not the reverse.

"Ms. Smyth, you finally succeeded in doing what you wanted to do all along—"

"I'm going to object," Abramson interrupted.

"Which was to have a national forum—"

"I'm going to object," Abramson shouted.

"In which to slander Dr. Oziel—"

"As argumentative," Abramson continued.

"Isn't it true that you are now on national television being able to slander Dr. Oziel the way you always wanted?"

"That's not what I've always wanted," Smyth fought back. "I've wanted justice. I've wanted the police and the district attorney to do their job for everyone, not just for selected people."

When Smyth was done, it was unclear who she had helped or hurt. She had said many damning things about Oziel, but some people had rolled their eyes when they heard Oziel characterized as a sorcerer capable of reaching inside people's minds and twisting the dials like a television set.

Some people left court that day shaking their heads at the way the trial continued to veer off in unlikely directions, but Smyth had a defender in an unlikely place. Al Goldstein, the *Screw* publisher, who was an avid Court TV watcher, said he knew Judalon and didn't think she was "capable of lying. She's sort of an innocent."

Goldstein said he had dated her several years ago, after placing a personal ad in *Los Angeles Magazine*. "Can you handle a paradox?" it asked. He said he didn't want someone like Susan Brownmiller to show up, so he described himself as a "controversial publisher" who was "bi-coastal, intelligent, looking to share good restaurants, good times."

Their first date had been a trip to the Playboy Mansion, but Judalon wanted a platonic relationship.

He talked to her about her testimony. "She's really not sure what she actually knew. I said the worst thing that would come out is you would look like a bimbo or confused. I think she's confused."

Goldstein said the Menendez trial had turned into "a great story. I hope somebody will play me in the movie." He mentioned Richard Dreyfuss.

Tensions were continuing to simmer between the judge and the defense, or at least between the judge and Abramson. At one point during a sidebar conference, Abramson called him a "third prosecutor," according to two attorneys.

Weisberg, they said, ordered the court reporter not to put the remark in the daily transcript.

What was striking, however, is that while the defense complained about Weisberg, as time went on it became apparent that the defense was succeeding in getting most of its evidence in, even the more remote evidence about the dead couple's character. Defense attorneys admitted this privately. "He's a bully," said one. If you hit back, she said, he retreats.

The prosecutors were noticing the same thing and were growing angry about it. They suspected he thought the prosecution had everything they needed to make their case—especially after giving them the December 11 tape—and now he was going to bend over backward to let the defense have its way.

The next day, Leslie Abramson was ready to play the December 11 tape, which she called, with what seemed uncharacteristic understatement, "a difficult piece of evidence." But first she brought on her expert, Ann Burgess.

Looking out from behind squarish glasses, she pooh-poohed

Oziel's technique, ridiculed his conclusions, and contended the brothers were merely satisfying Oziel's script by their answers.

Then the sixty-one-minute tape was played once more. As before, the jurors followed along, turning the pages synchronously as the conversation rattled out of the speakers in the courtroom. Erik, who was heard crying on the tape, wiped his nose and cried again in court. As before, when Lyle compared his parents to his dead dog, there was an audible gasp in the room.

Back on the stand, Burgess had an unusual way of explaining the frequent references on the tape that it was Kitty who was the victim of their father's abuse, not the brothers.

"My father should be killed. There's no question," Lyle was heard saying. Because "he's impossible to live with for myself . . . based on what he's doing to my mother."

"That's a metaphor for brother," Burgess said.

As she left court that day, Bozanich made up a new version of the old Shirley Ellis song "The Name Game."

"Mother, mother, bo brother . . ."

When Bozanich started her cross-examination, she directed Burgess to a place on the tape where Lyle mentions Jose's refusal to go to dinner parties with Kitty. "It wasn't his brother who was missing out on the dinner parties, right?"

"Right," said Burgess, unruffled.

What did she make of Erik's comment that he wished he could have told his mother about "all my relationships with different people?"

"You are aware of the fact," Bozanich suggested, that Erik was ordered to "get a girlfriend" by his mother.

The defense asked for a private conference. Weisberg slid out of his chair and stood over the attorneys like a friendly bald eagle, with a curious, verging-on-amused look to him.

"I'm not going to use the word," Bozanich began.

"The word. No, just the innuendo," said Abramson. "The mind's in the gutter here. Unbelievable. I think it's outrageous. She's trying to go after homosexuality once more."

"I don't infer that," Weisberg said. If so, he was almost the only person in court who didn't.

Ask her, Abramson told the judge. "Don't be Oziel. Ask."

"Well, don't be Judalon Smyth and we'll be fine."

"I think none of us should be either one of them," Abramson joked.

Bozanich said that was her last question on the subject. As

he trial progressed and more and more information came in,
some of it remote in time and context, the homosexuality
question began to loom larger because of the continual skirmish-
ng over it. The defense clearly thought the prosecution was just
doing some block-headed gay baiting, but the defense was
reading a sensitive line too. They seemed to be taking the
position that being gay was a terrible thing.

Back in session, Bozanich drew Burgess's attention to the
last page of the transcript, where Lyle seems to be talking about
his dead dog. "That, you know, whether I hated the thing when
it was around, and I've given it away, now that it's gone, I miss
all the things that . . ."

Was that a metaphor for his parents?

"No," said Burgess. Missing the dog speaks to isolation.

"You reject the idea that if he hated the dog, he hated
his parents?"

"I don't make that giant leap, no."

The last defense witness was Cynthia Erdelyi, a tousle-
headed ex-cop who had driven the route the brothers supposedly took after the killings. It had been the prosecution's belief
that Erik and Lyle could not have purchased the movie tickets,
gotten rid of the guns, disposed of their clothes in a dumpster,
and still made the all-important call to Perry Berman at 11:07,
57 minutes after neighbors on Elm Drive heard the muffled
explosions of gunfire.

But Erdelyi accomplished the drive with minutes to spare.
She drove up Mulholland, then back to the theater complex in
Century City, then out to Santa Monica.

On cross-examination, Bozanich asked if she saw any parking
meters in Century City. "No, I did not," Erdelyi said.

The brothers had said they parked at a parking meter, but
Bozanich had learned through a caller that there were no parking
meters there. In fact, the role of the general public—Court TV
viewers and newspaper readers—was a little talked-about but
important part of the case. Five different callers had supplied
information that Bozanich intended to show the jury later on.

After introducing the drive times, a bit of arcane evidence,
the defense rested. Their case had lasted nearly three months
and they had called fifty-six witnesses. At the end of the day,
cameras were set up in the small plaza outside on the expectation Abramson would stride up with her hair bouncing and give
them some good talking head. But whether from weariness or

dislike of the press coverage or something else, she trudged off down the street to her car, head down, wheeling her cart full of files behind her. She resembled a stout little general who had waged a bloody battle against large odds, with heavy losses, who knew it was foolish to predict the outcome with the troops still engaged.

Reporters ran after her. "Three months and fifty-six witnesses later I'm going home to my son," she said.

Asked how it had gone, she barely raised her head. "I don't know what kind of job we did. I don't have a clue."

She said the most important part of her case had been the defendants' testimony. She couldn't resist a final shot at the psychologist, saying therapy "in the hands of an Oziel" is a "weapon of destruction."

Bozanich, once uncomfortable on camera, came out to the plaza willingly, if not eagerly. Looking up at the reporters gathered around her, her hands clasped behind her back, she looked like a school child called upon to recite.

"Make it quick," she said.

Expressing her deep, and deepening, bitterness over what she was convinced was a defense case made up out of whole cloth, she said there was "a great deal of distance between our case about the murders and their case, which is everything else. Sometimes I kept having to remind myself there were two dead bodies."

Back in her office, Bozanich kicked off her heels, sank into a brown leather chair, and listened to the tape of the phone calls that had come in that day. One after another, angry people used her phone to complain about the rich punks and to urge her on.

Looking thin and worn, Bozanich listened to the calls with a blank expression. She had heard all these things before. She wanted to convict these defendants, who she believed were remorseless, but she wanted justice, not vengeance. Still, she never knew when a caller might have something she could use. Then she put on her comfortable flats and went out the back way to drive home. She was already deep into preparation for her rebuttal case, when the prosecution got one more chance to present witnesses. She had been having trouble convincing some witnesses to help present the parents as something more than the misshapen monsters the defense had paraded before the jury. But now Kitty's brother Brian would take the stand. He was the only person on earth closer to her than Jose—that is, if you don't count her children.

33

Dead Man's Shoes

The rebuttal case was designed to poke holes in the defense version of history on two counts. First, the prosecutors wanted to present evidence contradicting stories told by the defendants of the last week before the killings, and they wanted to rehabilitate Jose and Kitty, who had been savaged on the witness stand.

The first witness on Friday, November 19, was Andy Valentine, a burly ex-New York City detective with a squinty right eye who had guarded Erik Menendez when he went to the U.S. Open tennis matches on August 30, 1989.

He rode with Erik to La Guardia Airport, where he caught a noon flight, he said. On the way to the airport, Valentine remembered that Erik kept hopping out of the limo to dash into computer stores. Each time Valentine dived out and waited outside the store, watching the street vigilantly for the hit men who would never come.

The purpose of this testimony was to shore up Craig Cignarelli, who said he stayed the night at the mansion on September 1 and that Erik confessed to him the next day. But the structure didn't hold.

On cross, Leslie Abramson wasted no time tearing into him. She showed him notes obtained from the agency that employed him, which contained no reference to the U.S. Open. She tested his memory on the route they drove and the time they spent at the tennis stadium at Flushing Meadows. Repeatedly he said he didn't recall or couldn't remember. A onetime resident of the Queens, she seemed to know the city better than he did.

Abramson shredded him so effectively that it was no surprise to anyone that the prosecution did not bother to try to rescue him on redirect. After a short break, Valentine simply disappeared to take a flight back to New York.

More witnesses came up and one by one Abramson knocked them down. She at least raised doubts about their memories, and at worst made them look like liars.

But she was about to face a man who might have walked out of a Frank Capra movie. And who, in his own quiet, unintentional way, would make the defense attorney look like the bad guy.

Grant Walker had a dour, almost puppetlike face with lines around the mouth and a shock of dark hair that fell partway over his forehead. He wrote a nondescript sports jacket and a tie that looked to have been in style in the Kennedy administration.

Like the best Capra characters, he was an everyman. He cleaned pools for a living, earning about $30 per job. He said he was at the Menendez mansion, fixing the switch on the automatic spa control on Saturday, August 19—the day before the killings.

While he was working, he saw Lyle Menendez playing tennis with another man. Erik stood near Jose and Kitty, who were seated at a patio table drawn up next to the tennis court.

Mrs. Menendez, he said, was speaking to Lyle about his tennis. Lyle responded "in anger," using a vulgarity.

Erik, he said, "seemed to be angry with his parents also." This exchange happened about two o'clock.

This was powerful evidence, given in the most low-key, understated way. This was the afternoon, according to the stories of Erik and Lyle, that the brothers had purposely stayed away from the house out of fear of their parents. There was a fishing trip scheduled and they wanted to miss it. But a middle-aged pool man, just the kind of invisible cypher that the brothers would not have noticed, had seen them playing tennis and hurling profanities at their parents.

Michael Burt began the cross-examination of this square-bodied witness who had the potential of unraveling the entire defense case. Burt asked if Walker had ever tried to give his information to the Beverly Hills police.

Yes, he said, he called them on Wednesday, three days after the killings. "I spoke with the officer of the watch," he said. "He said he wasn't interested."

What the cop on duty had actually said when Walker volunteered that he had been at the house Saturday was "So?"

In 1993, he said, his wife called the police again. Now they were very interested.

Burt wanted to know how he could be so certain it was the Saturday before the killings that he was there. "When I heard on the radio a professional murder was committed the day after I was there, you don't forget that," Walker replied in his faintly scratchy voice. "Like the Kennedy assassination, I know exactly where I was."

Leslie Abramson's turn came next. She asked what other jobs he had done that day and he recited his regular route in Hancock Park. Did he have a datebook showing his appointments? He said he had done the route so often he was "like a trained rat."

There were chuckles in the room. Abramson's voice rose a bit as she began moving in on Walker. She asked him to repeat the vulgarities Lyle used, but this backfired. Walker sat there stonelike, then said softly, "I don't choose to say them."

Abramson pressed him again, louder, more insistent. "I feel uncomfortable."

Only when the judge ordered him to say them did he finally volunteer the words "fuck" and "shit and things like that." Then he stared at the ground with a tortured look on his face. The defense attorney looked like a bully who had forgotten that there were still people who were embarrassed by swearing in front of millions of people.

Abramson moved on, asking if he had come forward to testify to get himself on television. No, his wife had pushed him to do it. "She said it was my civic duty."

Flor Suria, a short, heavy woman in a pink sweater who arrived in court with a translator, knew as much about the daily activities in the Menendez mansion as anyone. Monday through Friday she had slept in the house.

Suria cleaned everything. Kitty did the cooking. Kitty and Jose spoke to her in Spanish, she said, but Erik and Lyle did not know how, despite Spanish lessons.

She said she never saw Kitty nor Jose yelling at the boys. She also never heard Lyle crying about having his wig pulled off on Tuesday, or any noise from the fight with Jose in Erik's room on Thursday.

To Burt, she admitted that after the family went upstairs, she went into her room and went to sleep. "But if they would fight, I could hear," she added helpfully.

Asked about magazines in the house, she agreed the Menendezes had some, but "not the kind they said."

Did Kitty get angry about Jamie sleeping in the guest house? Suria said she "wasn't so agreeable. She would say, 'That's my son's girlfriend, and I can't do anything about it.' "

Suria never saw Kitty cry or drink to excess. Of course, her succession of no answers to all the strange behavior attributed to the family might only show, as one reporter noted, that she was a model employee. "See no evil, hear no evil," the writer joked, guessing that Suria would be deluged with job offers on the basis of her testimony.

In the kind of irony that pervaded the trial, the prosecution was about to bring in a woman who once had been so solidly in Lyle's corner that she had worn his engagement ring after he was arrested. This was Jamie Pisarcik, a gangly-looking thirty-year-old woman with a small face and a mass of blond hair that fell down over her forehead. She had, it seemed, changed her mind about Lyle after he admitted to her that he killed his parents.

Still, Jamie hadn't come easily; when Bozanich had shown up at her door one day unannounced, she was not receptive. Then she said she would cooperate only if she was given immunity from prosecution as an accessory after the fact. Bozanich was mystified about why Jamie wanted that protection. She never had any intention of prosecuting Jamie for anything; she had no knowledge that Jamie had ever done anything. But she gave the immunity to her, and now the young woman was on the witness stand, wearing a cream-colored suit.

Jamie had been Lyle's girlfriend, off and on, for about three years. The romance had continued even after the cell door was slammed, until one afternoon in December 1990 when Jamie, who was growing suspicious, asked Lyle to tell her the truth.

They were separated by a glass partition in the jail visiting area, and Lyle did not want to tell her anything over the phone, so he held up a lengthy letter. "He was very sorry that he had had to lie to me so long," it read. "But the truth was, he had killed his parents."

The reason, he explained in the letter, was that his father had molested Erik and Kitty had molested Lyle.

"I don't believe you," Jamie replied. Then they both burst into tears. Shortly afterward, they broke up.

But this was all just scenery for the crucial part of Jamie's estimony. In 1987, Jamie had gone with Lyle to purchase a wig n Birmingham, Alabama. He was losing his hair and wanted to ook his best when he began school at Princeton in the fall. Jamie aid she was visiting Lyle in Beverly Hills two years later when he stopped by Erik's room and had a conversation about he wig.

Erik was laughing about the false hair. "All this time Lyle had his hairpiece and he was amazed. He did not know when Lyle got the hairpiece."

Jamie didn't remember how Erik found out, but that was irrelevant. This was one more hole torn in the fabric of the defense. Erik had testified that seeing Lyle without his wig shocked him into confessing his molestation, which in turn led o the killings.

Before finding out Lyle had killed his parents, Jamie had kept him supplied with reading materials. Among the books she took him, she said, was the story of the Billionaire Boys Club and a book about sign language.

The mention of sign language was curious. At least one reporter said he had seen Paul Mones, the so-called behind-the-scenes coach at the Menendez trial, gesturing from the audience when Erik and Lyle were testifying. Mones denied it.

Pisarcik also said Lyle asked her to go to the law library in Santa Monica and pick up some cases for him. He gave her the citations. She looked at the cases, she said, which were about child molestation, "situations where children had gotten off after killing their parents."

In a soft but firm voice, Pisarcik said these things began to make her suspicious and led her to ask Lyle to tell the truth about the killings. Why didn't he run away? she asked after he told her.

"He said he would have liked to run away, but Erik did not want to."

The only reference to the attempt to bribe Jamie into saying Jose tried to molest her was a single question by Bozanich. Did she have a conversation with Lyle about a movie called *At Close Range*. This was the movie Lyle had asked her to watch in order o fashion a statement about Jose. In that film a young woman is attacked by her boyfriend's father.

"Yes," Pisarcik said.

This was strange. Lyle's admission that he had tried to bribe his girlfriend to say Jose tried to molest her was arguably the most damaging single piece of evidence to the defense—far more dangerous than the Big 5 snafu. Yet the evidence was glossed over so quickly it might have been missed by the jury altogether.

The reason behind it, according to people close to the case, was that Jill Lansing had been Lyle's co-counsel at the time the offer of money was made to Jamie. There were extensive private hearings early in the case about the issue, and Lansing was never accused of doing anything wrong. But when the Pisarcik statement came up several weeks into trial, Lansing allegedly said she would have to withdraw from the case if the matter was vigorously pursued before the jury.

Weisberg supposedly said the attorneys should work out some kind of agreement that would allow the evidence to be introduced without implicating Lansing, or he would declare a mistrial as to Lyle Menendez. This had occurred shortly before Lyle was to take the stand.

Asked about this, Bozanich said she did not want to retry the case. "I thought things were going so well" that she could manage without it.

The final arrangement was that the defense and prosecution worked out a short stipulation that the bribe attempt occurred but Pisarcik would not be allowed to embellish it. "All she could do was say this happened," said one attorney. Lansing declined to discuss the issue.

Bozanich did not regret the decision. One benefit of the agreement was that Lyle admitted the bribe attempt on the stand. Without the agreement, the defense would no doubt have subjected Jamie to a withering cross-examination on the statement, and who knows whether the jury would have believed her. The cross-examination, as it was, was stiff enough, because the defense's thorough investigation had turned up some apparent inconsistencies in Jamie's story.

Jill Lansing launched an all-out assault to discredit Lyle's former girlfriend. Laying her trap, she asked when the wig conversation occurred. Jamie thought it was the spring or summer of 1989, when she flew to California with Lyle for a holiday. She said they went out a lot and played tennis.

Then Lansing produced Jamie's work records at Casa Lupita, where Jamie waitressed, for March and April. Pulling thick mounds of paper from folders, she asked the young woman to tick off a day-by-day accounting of whether she was on duty or not. It turned out she was never off work for more than two days—excepting March 22–27. Was Pisarcik aware that Erik had played in a tennis tournament that lasted from March 17 to 25?

"I have not stated I had the conversation in March or April," Pisarcik replied softly but firmly.

"Do you think of February as spring or summer?"

"Early spring."

"In New Jersey?"

"If I showed you you were working every weekend in February, would you go back to January?" Lansing asked in a rare moment of unveiled sarcasm.

Next, Lansing pulled out phone records for a credit card that Jamie said Lyle had given her permission to use. She admitted she used it even after they broke up for a while before the killings, when Lyle was seeing Christy.

Lansing showed her a list of calls all over the East Coast. Lyle also gave her sisters permission to use the card, the witness said.

"Are you telling us your family had the right to make as many as eleven long-distance phone calls a day?"

Having attacked her memory and her ethics, Lansing now tried to show that Lyle had been a tender lover who treated her well, yet she turned on him. She asked if Lyle had given her presents. Jewelry, watches, teddy bears, she said.

Lansing asked about a letter she had written Lyle in jail about their future wedding. "Do you want to hear what my dream wedding includes?" she asked. "I'd love to get married in the Princeton Chapel." From there it went on in a description of a lavish fantasy wedding that Lansing read in detail, apparently to show the woman's materialism.

Did Lyle buy her a car? "A Christmas present," Pisarcik replied. "A used Saab."

"It cost $11,000, right?" Lansing shot back.

"He drove up with it, with a red ribbon around it," Jamie replied. This was Lyle as Jose again. Jose had delivered a Mercedes to his wife with a ribbon around it. Jamie said she traded the Saab in for a Miata.

What did Jamie do with Lyle's engagement ring? She said she tried twice to return it, then sold it after several stones fell out and were lost.

Lansing also noted that Jamie had involved herself in the running of the restaurant Lyle purchased. One of Jamie's letters to Lyle in jail, where she chided him about letting friends freeload, was read in court. "Do you realize that you have to come up with $100,000 by January" or lose the restaurant? "Be a real businessman, Menendez, not someone who gets taken advantage of. Find out what real friends are, Lyle. I won't let you go throwing money away again. I don't care. You are mine. I'm sick of having people, friends or not, take advantage of you."

This letter was a double-edged sword. While it showed Jamie was assertive in Lyle's business affairs, it also seemed to clearly demonstrate that she loved him, which could bolster her credibility. But there was a hidden benefit for the defense. The letter portrayed Lyle as a soft-hearted dupe who friends walked over. This didn't sound like a criminal mastermind.

Last, Lansing noted, Jamie now had a new boyfriend.

"It was after Lyle told me the truth," Pisarcik said.

The first close family member to testify against Lyle and Erik was Brian Andersen, Kitty's brother, a tall, bulky, white-haired man who leaned forward slightly when he walked and looked owlish behind his wire-rimmed glasses. It had been difficult for Bozanich to get Andersen to the stand. He was a private man. More than this, his own son had testified for the defense, and Brian himself had dealt frequently with defense attorneys early on in the case. But seeing the way Kitty was savaged in the defense case had to have worn on the man. He had finally agreed to get up on the stand and face his nephews, whom he once loved deeply.

But now that Bozanich had succeeded in getting Andersen to court in defense of his dead sister, the opposition was determined to do everything it could to make sure his testimony was limited.

He had seen a different Menendez family than the one described by defense witnesses, including his sister Joan. Far from being crushed, Erik, he thought, had a "puffed-up ego." Both boys were not reluctant to "use some language" on their parents, including words like "goddamn" and "bullshit."

But what Bozanich especially wanted Andersen to talk about were conversations he had had with both parents about the boys' spending habits. Only weeks before the murders, Andersen had overheard an angry conversation between Erik and Kitty over a $900 camcorder Lyle had bought.

"You kids have got to stop" spending, Kitty fumed.

Then during the Kalamazoo tennis competition shortly before

the killings, Andersen had turned to Jose and asked, "What happened with the camcorder?"

"I'm going to have a major discussion with Lyle," Jose said. "This reckless spending has got to stop."

This incident, Andersen said, was "the straw that broke the camel's back," as far as the parents were concerned. Jose told his brother-in-law that Lyle had to learn to support himself; he and Kitty were not going to pay his way forever.

Leslie Abramson objected to Andersen's proposed testimony, claiming she was prepared to show how much money Kitty spent while claiming financial problems. "We have every single item of furniture she bought, including a $40,000 dining table."

Weisberg decided to allow Andersen to mention the camcorder incident, but not the fact that the context of it was family financial problems. So all the jury heard was Kitty fuming that "you kids have got to stop doing these things."

Andersen did get to talk about Kitty as a mother. He said she was affectionate with her sons. Further, undermining the contention that she had kept secrets, a key part of the trial, Andersen said she confided to him that she was having "an infidelity problem" with Jose.

To Andersen, Erik did not seem intimidated by his father. At the matches in Kalamazoo, Andersen saw Erik tell Jose to "shut up" when he was trying to talk to him about the match he had just lost. Jose, Andersen said, gave up in frustration. "I can't communicate with you."

On cross, Leslie Abramson asked Andersen if he saw Erik being taught to ride a bicycle by being pushed downhill without training wheels. "Not that I recall."

Then she asked if Andersen, who gulped down glasses of water while answering questions and seemed to avoid looking at his nephews, had ever seen his sister clench her fists and grit her teeth in anger. Abramson demonstrated, shaking her fists at her side.

"I may have," he replied mildly.

Andersen had said Kitty hugged Erik and was excited for him when he won, but what about when he lost? she asked. Did she say she was sorry he had lost and comfort him?

"Something to that effect."

"No, she didn't, Mr. Andersen," Abramson sternly corrected.

Trying to restore Kitty's image as a secret keeper, Abramson asked if she ever told him she was in therapy.

"She said she was seeing a therapist," he replied.

Abramson looked briefly stunned. She had not been prepared for that answer. Bozanich had not mentioned it in the notes of her interview with Andersen, which she had dutifully turned over to the defense. The reason why is simple: She had not asked Andersen the question, and the answer was as much a surprise to her as Abramson. The defense attorney asked why Kitty was in therapy.

"We discussed that as being something pretty common in California," he said, to general laughter.

There was a serious underlying message there, however. Many of Kitty's East Coast friends, and some family, when stretching their minds to grasp some reason to explain the carnage at 722 N. Elm Drive would say things had been fine until the family moved to California. Kitty, they said, really hadn't wanted to go. Even her sons had referred to that in the December 11 tape. In these people's opinion, the California dream was toxic for this family.

Of course, some might argue that the freewheeling lifestyle did not create the demons; they had been there for years, chained in the dark. California just loosed them.

Once again showing the thoroughness of the defense preparation, Abramson later suggested Andersen was testifying against his nephews to get a share of what was left of the estate. She disclosed that he had filed a document in probate court claiming that his side of the family might stand to inherit if it was proved that Kitty died a few seconds after Jose, as it appeared.

The defense attorney suggested Andersen grew angry after a probate judge said he would not listen to the assertion unless the Menendez brothers were convicted, which would mean they would lose all rights to the estate.

"And after it was taken off calendar, you volunteered to testify?" Abramson asked.

"If that's how the chronology works out," he replied.

It was an effective tactic, though Andersen got a shot in at the attorney when he blurted out that Abramson had threatened to quit when she wasn't paid on time.

It turned out, Abramson said, there wasn't much left of the estate to fight over. She said the value was between $700,000 and $800,000, almost all of that wrapped up in the Calabasas house, which was on the market for $2 million.

Kitty's close friend Karen Wiere, now remarried and taking the oath as Karen Farrell, recalled the bridge date she had planned with Kitty on the night of August 20. That afternoon, she said, she called from Santa Barbara, where she was spending the weekend, to say she would not make it back in time. Kitty was disappointed and said, "Even if you get in late, call," she said.

Marlene Eisenberg, Jose's former secretary for fourteen years, had never talked to any media, but now Bozanich brought her to the stand to reveal a side of Lyle Menendez the jury had never seen.

He and Erik both had testified they grieved after the murders, but Eisenberg, riding in a limousine with Lyle after the memorial service in Hollywood, saw a relaxed, confident older son.

He crossed his legs and asked, "Hey, Marzi, who said I couldn't fill my father's shoes?"

"Make your own tracks in life," Eisenberg replied. "Don't try to fill his shoes."

Lyle extended a tassled loafer. "You don't understand. These are my father's shoes," he joked.

Other people had heard Lyle's macabre jokes at his father's expense, but this was within days of the killings.

Eisenberg, a middle-aged woman who wore her brown hair tied in a bun, had more to say about her boss's son. She said that a day or two after the killings, Lyle told her he didn't hear the shotgun fire because he was bathing at the time.

"I don't know," he told her. "I was in the shower. I didn't hear anything."

The impact of this was hard to measure, since Lyle had already admitted he lied about the night of the killings. It mostly showed Lyle had an apparently endless capacity for telling stories, and difficulty keeping them straight. But the prosecution wanted the jury to fit this piece of evidence into their theory of the case. Lyle had been in the shower, but not during the killings. They believed he took a shower afterward to wash off the blood.

As the trial drew to a close, Terry Baralt, the brothers' beloved aunt, sat in her home in New Jersey and tried to work through all the things she had seen and heard at the trial. What was true and what was false?

The Kitty and Jose she had heard people describing were strangers, not the people she had known. And she had known them better than anyone. Take the talk on the witness stand about the ferret filling the house with droppings. Terry had been there. Kitty was no domestic goddess, but the hard little balls of ferret feces were picked up and they didn't fill rooms. Everything had been exaggerated and twisted.

"I have a tremendous problem believing it," she said after watching the defense case.

But then, the two young men who could shred their parents were strangers too. The Lyle and Erik she had known were loving, caring people. She was, she said, "caught in between the brothers I loved and the Jose I loved."

As the case wound down, Lyle and Erik still called her frequently from jail. "They're scared," she said.

As much as she hated what they did, Terry was still their aunt and would not forsake them. "What they've done is absolutely horrendous," she sighed. "But I can't turn my back on them."

34

Lost Dreams

Finally. On Friday, December 3, the juries heard the last of 101 witnesses. It was tennis coach Mark Heffernan, called by the defense to neutralize the testimony of the pool man, who claimed to have seen the brothers playing tennis with a coach on the day before the murders. Heffernan said he was the brothers' only tennis coach in the summer of 1989. He denied being at the mansion that day.

On that confusing and contradictory note, both sides rested. The marathon legal exhibition had generated 25,539 pages of courtroom transcripts, but it was not quite over.

Going into closing arguments, both sides could feel satisfied. The prosecution appeared to be in a strong position because Bozanich and Kuriyama had gotten much of their evidence in, even the critical December 11 tape, which was so damaging to Lyle. On that tape he was heard saying he let his brother sleep on the question of killing his parents. If that wasn't premeditation, what was? The prosecutors had even scored points during the defense case, punching holes in the brothers' version of the last days before the killings.

It was true there were pieces of evidence the prosecution failed to get in. The screenplay was never admitted; nor was there testimony about a pillow case full of cameras and a statuette that had been found in a credenza behind Jose's desk after the killings. Police were unable to link it to the Calabasas burglaries, or anything else. This was one more unexplained little mystery in a case full of them.

The juries also never got to hear about a conversation Lyle

had had with one of his best friends shortly before his arrest, which showed that Erik was not the only talkative killer. According to Zoeller, who said he heard the story later on from the friend, Lyle and his pal were driving along Coldwater Canyon Boulevard in the foothills above Beverly Hills one day when they crossed Mullholland Drive. Gesturing to his left, Lyle said, "That's where the shotguns are."

The friend's reaction was not recorded. But these things aside, the prosecution's case got to the jury mostly intact. Then Judge Weisberg gave the prosecution another victory when he declined to give the juries an instruction that could lead to an acquittal. He said there was "simply no evidence" that an average person would have been in fear of his life, as the brothers said they were, given the events that occurred the night of August 20.

He did allow the jury to consider a manslaughter verdict.

But the defense had plenty of reason for hope as well. Despite his obvious skepticism and discomfort with this kind of evidence, Weisberg had allowed Abramson and Lansing to bring up all kinds of remote anecdotes about the parents, putting them on trial for their own deaths. Even to the extent of allowing one witness to complain that Kitty needed a bleach job. In the hands of less skillful attorneys, the whole thing almost certainly would have looked like a bad imitation of a fraternity blackballing session. But this defense team had proved its worth by weaving it all together into a seamless whole, convincingly showing Kitty and Jose to be something less than parents of the year, even if you didn't buy the contention that they were monsters.

And closing arguments gave the defense attorneys a fresh opportunity. This is the point when many a canny lawyer has turned things around, artfully framing the case for the jury in such a way that they set aside everything they had heard until then. Over three days of dramatic oratory, Leslie Abramson would use every bit of her considerable skill to try to convince twelve people to take one more look at the facts. As she moved through the evidence, explaining away problems, accusing prosecution witnesses of being bald-faced liars and fame seekers, it was as if she was taking the jury on a stroll in the park and reasoning out loud with them. Come, she seemed to be saying, let's figure this out together.

But first it was Lyle's turn. Bozanich was sarcastic and belittling, allowing her disgust to show through when she called

Erik and Lyle "spoiled, vicious brats" who got the "best defense Daddy's money could buy."

Directing the jury's attention to the bulletin board, where a photo of Kitty in a strapless pink formal gown was pinned, she said, "This is the woman who gave birth to them." Then she turned to a gruesome autopsy photo. "This is what they did to their mother."

And she had a trick up her sleeve that showed defense attorneys aren't the only ones with a flair for high drama.

She revealed that her own father, a courtly man who was frequently in the audience during the trial, had been beaten and abused as a child. But, she noted significantly, he had not killed his parents. Instead he had run away and joined the Navy, ultimately becoming an officer aboard the first nuclear submarine, the *Nautilus*.

"For all those children who were severely abused and who became useful members of society, this defense is an offense," she sniffed derisively.

Abramson, in her turn, was mesmerizing, stalking the courtroom, doing snide impressions of prosecution witnesses.

As she had done over and over again, she devoted special energy to attacking Oziel. She talked of a "tense . . . nerve-wracking" trial. "And, it was like that for virtually every witness. . . . People on the witness stand in this case were frightened to death.

"But there was one cool cucumber, one unflappable person, so sure of his own rectitude, and that was Dr. Oziel," she said bitterly.

Mocking the therapist, she recalled the way he coolly deflected her questions. " 'Well, Mrs. Abramson, you know full well . . . ' "

The words peeled off her tongue in total contempt.

"Arrogant. Arrogant. Conscienceless man."

She didn't even spare Judalon Smyth, a defense witness.

"Which one would you rather have a cup of coffee with?" she asked, provoking some of the trial's loudest courtroom laughs.

Turning to the sexual-abuse issue, Abramson posted black-and-white pictures of Erik and Lyle as small children, naked, with only their lower bodies showing.

She stuck pins repeatedly into the picture of Erik, grinding them sadistically into the bulletin board, even digging into the penis with one, recalling graphically Erik's testimony that his father had stuck tacks into him while abusing him.

She noted that the prosecution believed the abuse was fabricated. "Prove it!" she snapped.

And Abramson finally did something that the prosecution had hoped Erik would do years before—she broke ranks with Lyle. She spoke of a "bond that can never be broken in this family—the bond between the two brothers." But at the same time she pointed out that it had been Lyle who squeezed off the final shotgun blasts.

"Now, with respect to analyzing the shooting in this case, I don't want Erik to be taking the rap for Lyle," she told jurors. "The evidence in this case does not prove that Erik killed anybody."

Of course, by this time Lyle's jury had already retired to deliberate, so the schism was of no use to the state. But if Erik's jury had to have a fall guy, Abramson implied, let it be, this time, big brother.

Concluding her remarks, Abramson told the jurors that she had a "fantasy" about Erik.

"I want to see him walk down a street, not in chains and not in shackles and not with a deputy sheriff standing next to him."

There was no way the low-key Kuriyama could match the pyrotechnics of Abramson, and he decided that he wouldn't try. "I'm not going to try to be somebody that I'm not," he said outside the courtroom.

Dressed in his usual conservative dark suit, he made his points in under three hours. He told the jurors that the defense had attempted "to dazzle you" to obtain a manslaughter verdict. "I'm going to ask you to base your decision in this case on common sense."

Kuriyama also took one of the biggest risks in the trial when he flatly told the jury that Erik was homosexual. The reason for raising the sensitive issue, Kuriyama told jurors, was that "if the defendant were engaging in consensual sex . . . with other men, that would account for him being able to describe what he described for you, his sexual encounters with his father."

But there was a danger that raising the issue at the end of the trial could look like a cheap, homophobic shot.

In the privacy of the D.A.'s law library after he concluded his remarks, Kuriyama admitted he had been taking a chance on offending the jurors. Still, he felt it was a risk worth taking.

Christmas was just days off and the trees in the courthouse plaza were stripped of their leaves, an entire season having passed during the life of this trial, when Erik's jury retired to deliberate on a separate floor of the courthouse from where Lyle's jury was already hard at work.

As the days passed, Terry Moran, the *Court TV* correspondent who had delivered some of the most impartial and incisive commentary on the trial, kept a vigil with his camera crew outside. Every day, as the juries asked for testimony to be read back, he and other observers debated what it meant.

Finally, on January 13, the Erik Menendez jury announced it was hopelessly deadlocked. The foreman, a professor at California State University, Northridge, told Judge Weisberg that their positions had not changed appreciably since deliberations had begun, and Weisberg declared a mistrial.

Leslie Abramson said she did not consider the coutcome a victory, but to get a hung jury with the facts she had going in was a stunning conclusion to the six-month legal exhibition. Cynics said this was one more proof that only the rich could afford real justice. Others, however, said the outcome was hardly justice but an example of how a jury's emotions can be inflamed by a hot-button defense like child abuse.

District Attorney Gil Garcetti, who had replaced Ira Reiner, said he would retry the defendants. "It's not over," Garcetti said. "I'd rather have a hung jury than a manslaughter verdict because this is a murder case."

Reporters swarmed over the courthouse plaza. Asked whether she would represent Erik in a second trial, Abramson said she would if she could, but she could not go bankrupt to do it. The estate was drained and she openly suggested someone ought to start a defense fund.

As for Erik, she said he was "exhausted" and disappointed to be facing another year behind bars during a second trial.

Some legal experts suggested the prosecution would be in a far stronger position the second time around because they would know the defense strategy going in. Others speculated that the heart-tugging defense mounted on behalf of the brothers would probably always sway at least one juror. One juror who believes the tale of fear. One juror who felt mistreated by his or her parents. One juror who feels that abused people have the right to kill their abusers.

Some horrified legal experts suggested that the jury had sanctioned revenge as a legal defense, despite the fact that society had established laws precisely to prevent citizens from taking things into their own hands. Others, reflecting on this and some other high-profile cases that had produced baffling outcomes, said it was becoming apparent that too many jurors were taking personal or political agendas into the courtroom, instead of objectively considering the facts presented to them. That is, child abuse is such a terrible thing that we jurors must send a message with our verdict that it must stop, no matter what the facts are in this particular case.

Some wondered whether one consequence of the much talked-about fracturing of society into smaller and smaller components, each with its own point of view and aggrieved constituency, would be more and more deadlocked juries, especially when presented with a case with social or political overtones. In any group of twelve people, there are likely to be people with a grudge against society for one thing or another that a smart defense attorney can exploit.

Frustrated and disappointed, Bozanich was ready to try the case a second time. She had revised her opinion of Abramson. She still considered her "a lousy human being," but admitted her skills as a defense attorney. Indeed, Leslie Abramson had done a terrific job for her client.

Lyle's jury appeared to be heading for a deadlock as well when the 6.6 Los Angeles earthquake hit on January 17. Not only were the homes of several jurors damaged, since all lived in the area where the quake hit hardest, the San Fernando and Santa Clarita valleys, but Weisberg's courtroom was knocked out of commission. Deliberations were put off for a week while alternate arrangements were made.

Then, on Tuesday, January 25th, the Lyle Menendez jury also told Judge Weisberg that it was deadlocked. "The gap is too wide," one of the jurors told the judge.

Among those watching the strange outcome from far away was a longtime female friend of Jose's. She recalled the way he had bragged ceaselessly about his two model sons, and the way he spoiled them, giving in to their demands, denying them nothing. If they were reckless, he would say to her, "That's the way boys are."

But not long before he was killed, Jose had called her in an uncharacteristically somber mood. It was as if his eyes had been opened to some unwelcome reality. Referring to Erik and Lyle, Jose said, "Sometimes your hopes and dreams don't come true."